THE AMERICAN HERITAGE SERIES

American Catholic Thought on Social Questions

THE AMERICAN HERITAGE SERIES

Under the general editorship of

Leonard W. Levy and Alfred F. Young

American Catholic Thought on Social Questions

Edited by

AARON I. ABELL

Late Professor of History,
University of Notre Dame

THE BOBBS-MERRILL COMPANY, INC.

A Subsidiary of Howard W. Sams & Co., Inc.

INDIANAPOLIS • NEW YORK

Printed in the United States of America
Library of Congress Catalog Card Number: 66-30548

First Printing

CONTENTS

PART FOUR The New Pluralism

FOREWORD

The documents of this anthology richly illustrate two interrelated themes. They demonstrate the diversity of reactions among American Roman Catholics over the past century to the problems common to an industrialized, urban, and often heartless society. As such, they are indispensable to the understanding of such central themes of recent American history as the conflict between liberalism and conservatism, the pattern of the labor movement and the flowering of social service and the welfare state. At the same time they illustrate the conflicts within the Catholic church as it adjusted to American life; conflicts ranging from the battles over "Americanization" in the nineteenth century to the debates of the 1960's between the advocates and opponents of the "new pluralism." Students of American history should be no less interested in this second theme, one in which they will find numerous parallels to other groups in American history.

All the writings assembled for this anthology are by Catholics. Beyond this, the other guiding canon of selection has been to assure representation for diverse points of view, both official and unofficial. Here one may find such famous spokesmen of the hierarchy as Archbishop John Hughes, Bishop John Lancaster Spalding and James Cardinal Gibbons, as well as representatives of the well known National Conference of Catholic Welfare and the National Conference of Catholic Charities. Here too are the trenchant writings of priests who have made a mark on their time: Edward McGlynn, Henry George's supporter; John Ryan, the pioneer Progressive; Charles Coughlin, the "radio priest"; and John Courtney Murray, Jesuit theologian. And lastly there are the lay voices, from that of businessman Michael O'Shaughnessy, who espouses corporatism, to the voice of Dorothy Day, whose Catholic Worker movement endorses Christian poverty. Catholics and non-Catholics who seek a historic perspective on the present dilemmas within the Catholic church are bound to be amazed at the many-sidedness of the American Catholic heritage.

On the basis of his monograph, *American Catholicism and Social Action: A Search for Social Justice, 1865-1950,* Aaron Abell was recognized as the outstanding authority on the subject of this anthology. It was typical of the breadth of his interests and training, however, that his first book was *The Urban Impact on American Protestantism, 1865-1900,* originally his doctoral dissertation at Harvard University.

A past president of the American Catholic Historical Association, he was active in many other circles of the historical profession. Readers will find in this anthology—which Professor Abell was working on at the time of his death in 1965—the same command of history and painstaking craftsmanship that established his reputation in his field.

This book is one of a series of which the aim is to provide the essential primary sources of the American experience, especially of American thought. The series, when completed, will constitute a documentary library of American history, filling a need long felt among scholars, students, librarians and general readers for authoritative collections of original materials. Some volumes illuminate the thought of significant individuals, such as James Madison or Louis Brandeis; some deal with movements, such as that of the Antifederalists or the Populists; others are organized around special themes, such as Puritan political thought, or American Catholic thought on social questions. Many volumes take up the large number of subjects traditionally studied in American history for which, surprisingly, there are no documentary anthologies; others will pioneer in introducing new subjects of increasing importance to scholars as to the contemporary world. The series aspires to maintain the high standards demanded of contemporary editing, providing authentic texts, intelligently and unobtrusively edited. It will also have the distinction of presenting pieces of substantial length which give the full character and flavor of the original. The series will be the most comprehensive and authoritative of its kind.

Alfred F. Young
Leonard W. Levy

INTRODUCTION

Social questions have figured prominently and well-nigh continuously in the thought and action of the Roman Catholic Church during its near century as a sizable minority in the United States. Catholic thought has been concerned with all the major involvements of the Church in American society. These have been chiefly in the multiplying personal and collective disorders of an urban and industrial civilization that have found expression in demoralizing poverty and class conflict. These evils encouraged many Catholics, lay and clerical, to study social maladies and to elaborate remedies ranging from the rehabilitation of dependents and defectives to social reconstruction through radical economic planning.

I. CONDITIONS OF CATHOLIC GROWTH

American Catholic thought on social questions is inextricably bound up with the growth of the Catholic Church in the United States. Catholic social influence in America was necessarily negligible until well into the nineteenth century. Catholics were too few to command much attention from the country's religious, social, and political leadership. Inasmuch as they numbered only twenty-five thousand at the end of the Revolution, their growth from natural increase and conversions in the next generation or two did not appreciably improve their relative position in the general population. Opportunity for impressive gains came with the resumption of mass immigration after 1825. A good part of the Germans, nearly all the Irish, and most of the "new immigrants" of non-Hebrew persuasion—French Canadians, Poles, Czechs, Slovaks, Magyars and Italians—were Catholic in background and preference.

The central question was, would Catholic immigrants and their children keep their religious faith as they adjusted their lives to the American environment? A conclusive answer could not be given because religious statistics were unreliable, and research resembling present-day studies in the sociology of religion was rarely attempted. A sizable part of the Catholic body feared (as most Protestants gleefully assumed) that Catholicism and American civilization were incompatible. These apprehensive Catholics subscribed to the notorious "leakage" theory which measured Catholic "losses" in millions of souls. The great majority of ecclesiastics and publicists, on the other hand, insisted not only that Catholic teachings and America's free institutions were compatible but that the two should positively reinforce each other. Among the first to present adequately the factual and theoretical basis of this viewpoint were, respectively, the Most Reverend John Hughes, Archbishop of New York, and Orestes A. Brownson, philosopher and publicist, both great Catholic leaders during the middle third of the nineteenth century.

At the height of the Know-Nothing agitation, Archbishop Hughes contended that the substantial increase (by slightly over two million) of the Catholic population in the United States since the Declaration of Independence served to undermine the widespread assumption that the Catholic Church could flourish only in lands where it enjoyed state support or suffered official persecution. While he admitted that hundreds of thousands of Catholic immigrants had abandoned their religion, he maintained that their alienation stemmed from social disorders such as toilsome poverty, broken homes, and epidemic disease, and the lack of adequate pastoral care, and not from the impact of American liberty. He denied that the Catholic immigrant population had consciously experienced any incompatibility between its religious faith and the country's free institutions. Native American converts to Catholicism, although numbering less than a third of the apostate immigrants, were numerous enough to provide a "true test," of this conviction, the Archbishop believed, for these "freemen who love freedom" would not enter the Church at the sacrifice of legitimate liberty. Foreign-born Catholics were fewer than native-born Catholics: proof, Hughes argued, that the members of the Church drawn from the three main sources of Catholic strength—the immigrant masses, the Catholic colony in Maryland, and the native American converts to the faith—had measurably succeeded in transmitting their faith to their descendants (see Document 1).

Brownson, a convert and an editor, also aimed at inspiring his fellow Catholics with confidence in the future (see Document 2). While Hughes concentrated on history and statistics, Brownson discussed the philosophical and sociological aspects of the religious situation in lectures, books, and magazines, notably his own, *Brownson's Quarterly Review,* with a thoroughness and brilliance that seldom has been equalled and never surpassed. He pointed out that as Catholics gained in numbers and influence they could expect to encounter periodic waves of bitter anti-Catholic sentiment. But they should not feel discouragement to the point of turning against their country and their non-Catholic neighbors. On the contrary, they should love their fellow countrymen and seek their conversion to Catholicism. By so doing they would underpin the constitutional system with a stronger and more effective religious faith. For American institutions, as evidenced in the political and social order, were based on the natural law of justice and equity, and were therefore in harmony with Catholic teachings, and, indirectly, the outcome and fruit of these teachings. The manifest destiny of America, according to Brownson, was to realize the Christian Ideal of Society in both the Old World and the New. A prime factor in the success of this truly providential mission would be the speedy acceptance of Anglo-American nationality by all Catholic ethnic groups.

This, many were reluctant to do. They did not deny that the American constitutional system was deserving of all praise, but they rejected American nationality on the ground that it was culturally, morally, and religiously debasing. They rightly held that the two—the political order and the nationality—were not inseparable; that it was possible to accept the one and reject the other. By the same token they should have readily discerned that the monstrous evils they encountered in America were only incidents, not inherent aspects of Anglo-American nationality. Yet the opinion widely prevailed in immigrant circles throughout the nineteenth century that the Catholic immigrant who lost his old-world nationality was likely to lose his faith and character. "Denationalization is demoralization"—this was the summary conclusion of the Reverend Anton H. Walburg, the urbane and perspicacious pastor of St. Augustine's Church in Cincinnati, who professed to represent all Catholic immigrants, the "new" as well as the "old," the English-speaking no less than the non-English-speaking (see Document 3).

Two-thirds of all Catholic immigrants had left the Church, he wrote in 1890, and the defections would continue to mount unless the inroads of Americanization could be checked. Walburg acknowledged that there was a true Americanism which aimed at the promotion of morality and virtue and therefore desired the growth and spread of the Catholic Church. But true Americanism was a minor influence compared to false and spurious Americanism, the earmark of the powerful and dominant Anglo-American nationality. Although it won the country's independence and established the constitutional system, the American nationality reveled in mammon worship and spawned fanaticism, intolerance, and radical, ultra views on matters of politics and religion. It was contemptuous of Catholicity and had alienated from the Church a major portion of the Catholic population. Catholic growth depended on the preservation of foreign nationalities in America. To this end he was active in the Deutsch-Amerikaner Priester-Verein (German American Priests' Society), a group devoted to strengthening German Catholic nationalism.

He expected only temporary and partial success. The foreign enclaves could not be retained indefinitely; in due course the American nationality would encompass the entire population. The most that could be hoped for was to delay or prolong the Americanizing process. This would enable the foreign-born Catholics to keep their faith intact and to launch a campaign for the conversion of all America—a task which only immigrant-oriented, not Anglo-American, Catholics could accomplish.

To the extent that they were real, the Catholic differences on Americanization served to reinforce, indirectly at least, divergent views on social action. The many who were dubious of Americanization were inclined to social passivity, to shun the public arena and to isolate themselves as far as possible against the impact of moral and social evils. But not all opponents of Americanization exhibited this ghetto mentality. Zealots for Americanization, on the other hand, were often ready, in conjunction with non-Catholic moralists, to wage war on crime, immorality and social injustice. It was the ardent friends of Americanization who during the 1880's and 1890's advanced and defended a comprehensive program of economic and social reform which steered a middle course between the extremes of individualism and socialism. The Americanists hoped that their efforts in this direction would win favor among progressive Protestants and lessen anti-Catholic sentiment. Not all Catholics, to be sure, required motivation of this sort to support reform. Nor did all Americanists display interest in social reform.

As immigration showed no sign of abating, the two parties by the turn of the century were in a mood for accommodation. They now realized that Americanization was not a policy to be arbitrarily imposed or stubbornly resisted but rather a process of acculturation. The immigrant deserved sympathy and understanding. This could be shown by providing immigrants with American-born priests able to speak in the appropriate foreign tongue and by extending them ample and varied social service.

Irrespective of their views on Americanization and social reform, the more discerning Catholics devoted thought to the effects of urban industrial development on the Church's growth. For the two were by no means co-extensive. As all could see, the enlarging urban work force, made up in substantial degree of Catholic immigrants, swelled the Church's membership. These gains were imperiled, however, by the inequities and falsehoods associated with the new industrial system. Not the least of these was the widespread belief, born of both greed and sincere conviction, that ethics must be kept out of the factory and the market place, that competition under the rule of supply and demand afforded all the regulation that industry needed—an automatic control with which law and ethics must not interfere. Employers were encouraged by this laissez-faire philosophy to pay workers as little as possible and in periods of depression to cut their wages to the starvation point in order to maintain the customary level of dividends and profits. If employers deemed their course of action to be normal and morally permissible, employees damned it as criminally unjust. Now antiquated and no longer relevant was the Christian expectation that out of fear of God's displeasure and wrath the poor should be contented with their worldly lot and the rich should "consider the poor" and treat them with generosity and fairness.

Many Catholic thinkers did not approve the laissez-faire philosophy. But they were powerless to counteract it in the early phase of American industrialism. For one thing, the Catholic Church lacked influence over employers of labor: the vast majority were non-Catholics and consequently under no obligation to heed the injunction to deal fairly and justly with their employees. Catholic thinkers, for a time, especially the more conservative ones, could see no morally permissible alternative to laissez-faire policy. In their opinion any serious attempt to change or reform the social order must terminate in revolution and anarchy. They could see no halting point between the stability of the status quo and the chaos of radical overturn. In some degree Catholic thought in this country mirrored the impasse in Europe between the Catholic Church and the liberal movement. But chiefly, American Catholic thinkers were apprehensive of reform in its American setting. Rightly or wrongly, they believed that the reforming impulse stemmed from the humanitarian and antislavery crusades of pre-Civil War days and that it was inherently and inexorably socialistic and anti-Christian.

Obliged to shun general reform, Catholics might well have assumed an attitude of massive passivity. Instead they were urged to seek and apply remedies which were unmistakably religious. These must come, some thought, from the counsels of Christian perfection, an exalted and uncompromising type of Christian charity which aimed to apply to modern situations the Christian communism of the early church. Its most widely known advocate in the middle third of the nineteenth century was T. Wharton Collens of New Orleans, jurist, and lifelong student and critic of social movements. He had only contempt and scorn for infidel socialism which inspired so many plans and associations for the care of the poor. In some respects a liberal, Collens acknowledged that many reform proposals—they ranged from almsgiving to state socialism—were not vitiated by irreligion. But he considered these secular remedies utterly inadequate. They were too self-centered and restrictive in the bestowal of their benefits to be truly effective. The only satisfactory solution lay in associations of Christian families, vowed to poverty and obedience, seeking perfection and devoting their material energies and surplus productivity to the poor. As these associations multiplied and influenced society, they would in due time usher in an earthly utopia of faith and charity. In terms of economic theory and practice this meant, he thought, that "labor cost" was the "just limit of price" and that the cost or value of an article was determined by the average amount of labor time expended upon it (see Document 5).

Collens' views exerted little influence during his lifetime, and this was the case for many years thereafter. Not until the Great Depression of 1929 did perfectionist views deeply penetrate the social consciousness of the Catholic laity. Since the early 1930's the Catholic Worker movement, led by Dorothy Day and dedicated associates, has demonstrated that reformers who accept voluntary poverty are most likely to attain their ends (see Document 31). But in Collens' day this attitude did not figure conspicuously in Catholic social effort. Catholics did share, however, his intense fear of socialism and distrust of extensive government function. They believed that education and charity prospered best under private and religious auspices. Thus, in their earlier history, they opposed state support of secondary and higher education. They did not oppose a public system of common schools, provided private and denominational schools were permitted to share the revenues. They favored—and secured to a limited extent—state subsidy of their more important and expensive charities.

It is also true that the Catholic hierarchy favored the enforcement of existing laws safeguarding the Sunday and regulating the liquor traffic, and the enactment of more stringent ones. For the most part, however, the Church relied on moral suasion and its own efforts in the religio-social field. Only the Church itself, through the associated endeavors of its members, could minimize the hazards to the faith and morals of a poor immigrant working people living in an urban environment. In the pastoral letters of the Plenary Councils of Baltimore, notably the Third (1884), official Catholic thought on the protective role of charities and Catholic societies is set forth (see Document 8).

Throughout American Catholic history many thoughtful Catholic leaders have deplored the concentration of Catholic immigrants in cities. In the earlier period, despite the abundance of frontier land, the Irish preferred the cities and largely ignored agriculture. Many of them were demoralized by the saloon and by corrupt politics, and their numbers were kept down by a low marriage rate, a fantastically high infant mortality rate and by broken home life. It was noted also, as time passed, that under conditions of urban materialism city populations failed to reproduce themselves, and that such vigor as the Catholic Church in America displayed seemed to come from members reared in rural surroundings, either in this country or abroad. In the hope of arresting the cityward drift, champions of rural virtue established numerous Catholic colonies on the frontier in the course of the nineteenth century, but no mass exodus from the cities followed in the wake of these efforts (see Document 9). Nor did the innumerable rural life conferences of later years appreciably enhance the attractions of the farm for either the urban or the rural population.

II. THE EMERGENCE OF CATHOLIC SOCIAL LIBERALISM

In its formative period of growth and influence the Catholic Church lived largely to itself and did not encourage its members, either clerical or lay, to enter into cooperative relations with the non-Catholic community. But this attitude rapidly changed after 1880; Catholics then, with the permission and sanction of the ecclesiastical authorities, increasingly joined with other Americans in trade unions and countless reform and charitable organizations. Cooperative participation was necessary chiefly to combat injustice in the industrial realm. "For some years the Church stood at the crossroads," recalled Cardinal Gibbons in his autobiography.[1] "It had to choose between

[1] James Cardinal Gibbons, *A Retrospect of Fifty Years,* I (Baltimore: John Murphy Company, 1916), Introduction, x.

allying itself with what looked like elements of disaster and revolution, or consenting to a theory of economics which could not be justified upon Christian principles. The duty had been laid upon it of preserving society, the rights of property and at the same time protecting the rights of individuals to the fruits of their labors; also protecting the poor from the encroachment of uncontrolled capital" (see Document 10).

In their desire to usher in a more just and humane type of private property and capitalism, reform-minded Catholics supported labor unionism of the conservative or non-revolutionary kind, protective social legislation, the arbitration, both voluntary and compulsory, of labor disputes, and moral and charitable movements of a largely non-economic character. These were not exclusively Catholic ends; they could be achieved only as Catholics cooperated with social liberals of all faiths and persuasions—the orthodox, the heterodox and those with no religious views. This was brought out in the lively controversies involving the Knights of Labor (see Document 10), the Single Tax movement (see Document 11), the anti-laissez-faire philosophy of Pope Leo XIII and his American precursors and followers, and the Charity Organization Societies (see Document 12).

If satisfactory progress were to be made, Catholics would obviously have to lend wide support. This could occur only if Catholics continued to Americanize rapidly on a vast scale. Only Americans could appreciate and participate in the social movement. Moreover, Protestants and other non-Catholic Americans would not welcome association with a medley of immigrant Catholic ghettos. The social movement, from the Catholic side, included, therefore, a crusade for social justice, cooperation with non-Catholics, and rapid Americanization of immigrants. These three factors together constituted American Catholic social liberalism, which enjoyed great vogue during the last two decades of the nineteenth century. Its best expression was in the two Catholic Congresses (Baltimore, 1889, and Chicago, 1893) in which laymen, with clerical advice, discussed the social question in all its range and implications (see Documents 13 and 14).

Some Catholics—not many—opposed the social movement because they considered it both unnecessary and undesirable. Perhaps best representative of this view was the St. Louis journalist and scholar, Condé B. Pallen, who over a period of four decades after 1890 repeatedly equated all but the mildest forms of state intervention in industry with the tyranny of socialism and contended that no more was necessary in the social field than almsgiving and charitable endeavor under exclusively Catholic auspices (see Document 15). If few Catholics shared his narrow, doctrinaire views, many wished to minimize social reform and to seek instead a stronger defense of "Catholic interests" under the law and at the bar of public opinion. In the wake of the American Protective Association movement, Catholics in growing numbers felt the need to stress their constitutional rights. They smarted under the whip of discriminatory treatment: double taxation in education, inadequate representation on administrative boards, and denial of a voice in the control of our new colonial possessions. This sense of grievance chiefly motivated the formation in 1901 of the American Federation of Catholic Societies which, until World War I, served as a non-partisan pressure group (see Document 16).

The redress of grievance did not monopolize the attention of the federated societies, not even during their first years. From the beginning, they lashed out at socialism, liberalism, industrial violence, divorce, etc., notwithstanding their inability or unwillingness for a time to suggest feasible remedies. Meanwhile, younger men in the Church continued the probe of social problems for solutions along positive lines. Among these was the Reverend John A. Ryan whose name was to be synonymous with Christian social ethics for nearly five decades. Early in the century he clarified the concept of the living wage, the right to which derived from the worker's personal dignity and essential needs irrespective of such utilitarian considerations as custom, bargaining power, or equivalence between work and pay (see Document 17). Ryan's contemporary, the Reverend Peter E. Dietz, worked to give Catholic social principles organizational and programmatic support. Through the Militia of Christ, which he formed in 1910 among Catholic trade union leaders, he brought the Catholic social message before both the American Federation of Labor and the American Federation of Catholic Societies (see Document 18).

III. SOCIAL EDUCATION AND ORGANIZATION

The thought and activity of Ryan and Dietz were in line with the growing conviction among Catholics that they must educate and organize for social purposes. Only through knowledge and concerted effort, it was felt, could the Catholic leadership keep in sympathetic touch with the increasingly powerful labor and humanitarian movements and counteract their strong tendency to become secular, if not positively anti-Christian, in method and aspiration. The primary need was for a sociologically educated priesthood. While it was necessary for relatively few clergymen to become scholarly experts in social science, all seminarians should be given a sound orientation in the subject as an integral part of their theological formation (see Document 19). Less urgent but still important was the need for lay men and women in significant numbers to seek professional training in the charity and social service field. There was a widely felt need for new methods of charity and a trained personnel to use them (see Document 20).

Lay amateurs and sisterhoods of charity were in charge of the Church's remedial charity—poor relief and the vast array of institutions for the orphaned, the erring, the sick, the aged, and the dying. But charity of this type all but ignored the crying need of the Catholic masses for popular education, recreation, and social adjustment. To the "end houses" of remedial charity must be added, as a leading Catholic journalist insisted at the turn of the century, the "half-way houses" of prevention and rehabilitation, such as temperance and fraternal societies, young men's clubs, homes for working girls and women, employment bureaus, and social settlements in the tenement districts. Catholics were drawn to the new charity through the realization that some immigrants, notably Italians and Mexicans, were beyond the reach of church and school and could be influenced only by the "well considered methods" of the social settlement and its adjuncts. Moreover, the poor in all the immigrant ghettos, not just the non-churchgoers, could profit from social work which served to arouse desire for self-improvement, to stimulate initiative, and to create a sense of civic responsibility.

The new social service, with its case-work techniques and trained personnel, affected every area of Catholic welfare, including family relief, dependent child care, and juvenile delinquency. Catholics were not of one mind on the merits of the new charity. As was to be expected, the rationale of the new approach was explained by the enlarging corps of social scientists in the Catholic colleges and universities, and widely acted upon, notably by Catholic lay women who, after the turn of the century, took a prominent part in social movements. Others were less favorably disposed, among them many a veteran almoner of the St. Vincent de Paul Society. The "conservatives" as against the "progressives" feared that the new methods, particularly the use of salaried workers, introduced a worldly, if not a mercenary, motive into Christian charity (see Document 21). The tension between the two groups was considerably lessened, however, when the sisterhoods, after World War I, incorporated many modern techniques into their working forces (see Document 22).

Catholic interest in social education and organization involved rural as well as urban America. The conviction grew that the missionary and social zeal present in cities should be carried to the countryside. The effort was all the more worth the making because the birthrate was higher, and the Christian virtues, as it was assumed, were more easily developed in rural areas than in cities. Moreover, a numerically significant rural Catholicism would furnish recruits for urban Catholicism—recruits sorely needed after 1914 when immigration ceased to be a major source of Catholic growth. Real success was contingent, no doubt, on the ability of Catholic leadership to make rural life economically and socially attractive and religiously effective. This is what the Reverend (later Bishop and Archbishop) Edwin V. O'Hara, sponsor of the Oregon minimum wage law for women, and a few associates set out to do, chiefly through the agency of the National Catholic Rural Life Conference which they formed in the early 1920's (see Document 25). The Catholic rural life movement threw its weight behind vacation religious schools, private and public welfare aids, cooperatives, the family-sized farm, and other measures in behalf of embattled farmers, including the recent collective bargaining efforts of the militant National Farmers Organization.

Catholic rural life, as well as the broader concerns of social service and economic reconstruction, profited from the hierarchy's decision at the end of World War I to make social action an integral and positive part of the Church's mission—a full, if somewhat belated, recognition that Catholics needed education and direction no less than liberty in the social field. The bishops set up the National Catholic Welfare Council, in 1919 (National Catholic Welfare Conference after 1922), which operated through an administrative committee of bishops, and through five departments, each headed by a bishop from the administrative committee and conducted by clerical and lay experts. The social action department, with the Reverend John A. Ryan as director, had for its guidance an incisive statement on industrial problems and remedies, namely, the so-called Bishops' Program of Social Reconstruction, which had been written by Ryan and promulgated on Lincoln's birthday, 1919, by the administrative committee of bishops of the National Catholic War Council. The Bishops' Program was destined to become more widely known than any of about sixty other proposals for postwar social reconstruction (see Document 24).

The Program looked to both the near and the more distant future. The bishops believed that the States should, and in fact would, pass the necessary minimum wage and social insurance laws to guarantee all workers a living wage. These measures were essentially remedial in character: they implied no radical change in the existing economic order and they were attainable within a reasonable time. The "more distant developments" should bring "ultimate and fundamental reforms" which would permit and encourage the majority of workers to "become owners, at least in part, of the instruments of production." This diffusion in the ownership and control of property was to be effected through consumers' and producers' cooperatives and co-partnership arrangements between employers and employees. This would mean the sharing by labor in the profits, ownership, and management, and therefore would bring about a substantial modification of the wage system.

As the formulators anticipated, this phase of the Bishops' Program met with widespread opposition. The average middle-class American suspected that the least interference with the wage system was a step toward socialism; he did not understand that producers' cooperatives and partnership arrangements were designed to reestablish private enterprise through the cooperation of like-minded individuals working independently of government. Employers did not wish to share ownership, profits, or management with their employees. Not many wage earners were anxious to assume managerial responsibilities. Nor were they strongly impressed by the argument, so well developed by the Reverend Raymond A. McGowan, assistant director of the social action department, that the labor movement put less stress on wages and hours and more on industrial reorganization. As industrial productivity increased, counseled McGowan, the workers should seek to register their gains not in a fatter pay envelope, but in ownership and control of industry through cooperatives and the various forms of co-partnership.

The backers of the Bishops' Program expected its criticism of the wage system to be poorly received. They had anticipated no serious objection to labor legislation on the state level, including "the legal minimum wage," or to a federal child labor law. They were amazed, then, when the general public displayed indifference to these measures and acquiesced in the invalidation of many of them by the United States Supreme Court. Even more distressing was the fact that their fellow Catholics, by the tens of thousands, joined in the hue and cry against social legislation. Thus Catholic obstructionists probably exerted a decisive influence against ratification of the child labor amendment to the federal Constitution.

The authors and champions of the Bishops' Program were highly conscious of constitutional limitations on legislative action in the social field. The Program was designed to operate chiefly on the state, only incidentally on the federal, level. The Program called for several federal measures in behalf of consumers and the general public, only the barest minimum of federal intervention in industry. Thus the bishops wished the War Labor Board to continue as a peacetime agency "with all the power for effective action that it can possess under the Federal Constitution." This would mean, they thought, authority to investigate and mediate industrial disputes but not to enforce collective bargaining rights in the manner of the later Wagner Act and other New Deal labor business leaders, the NIRA sought to check overproduction and ruinously low prices—the result, it was widely held, of excessive and unfair competition, low wages, long hours, and child labor. The codes, therefore, provided for a minimum wage of from twelve to fifteen dollars a week, reduced the work week to forty hours, and abolished child labor. These features were designed to stimulate re-employment, increase purchasing power, and improve working conditions. In Section 7 (a) the NIRA recognized the right of workers to organize for their self-protection. This and other provisions prompted O'Shaughnessy to write that the NIRA ended "industrial slavery" in the United States and aimed to establish a nation-wide partnership status "between employers and employees for the orderly conduct of industry."

He soon experienced disillusionment. He found that all major groups—corporation managers, labor leaders, workers, farmers, and consumers—"were considering this program from a standpoint of personal self-interest." Most at fault were the business leaders whose high-price policies exploited the consuming public and restricted the purchasing and productive power of workers and farmers. He was pained to discover that the leaders of both capital and labor sought domination, not partnership. By herding workers into company unions employers aimed to impair the effectiveness of the collective bargaining principle on which the NIRA was based. Equally wrong was the attempt of an "over-lordship of labor organizers" (craft leaders of the American Federation of Labor) to represent all workers rather than to encourage their organization, as the law intended, on a nation-wide scale, industry by industry. All Catholic advocates of co-partnership deplored the weakness of organized labor, and many agreed with the Reverend (later Monsignor and Bishop) Francis J. Haas that the vocational group system could not be instituted until all, or nearly all, workers were unionized.

Some Catholic social actionists showed little enthusiasm for integrated occupations, that is, partnerships of labor and management under government supervision. These were the Catholics who did not believe that the economic malady issued primarily from conflicts between employers and employees. Thus "radio priest" Charles E. Coughlin and his large following were sure that the country's ills were the result primarily of financial and monetary disorders. Coughlin's remedy was public ownership or the nationalizing not only of banking, credit, and currency, but also of power, light, oil, and natural gas, and of God-given natural resources—"public necessities which by their very nature are too important to be held in the control of private individuals" (see Document 29).

At the other end of the economic spectrum were the antimonopolists who, on behalf of farmers, craftsmen, and small tradesmen, hoped to reverse the trend toward concentration in business. Their ablest spokesman was Frederick P. Kenkel of the Central Verein who wished government to be divorced from corporate enterprise rather than used, as the economic planners desired, to incorporate labor and agriculture into the monopoly structure. In his view, low wages, even low farm prices, would be in the public interest, provided relief was afforded the people from high tariffs, unfair taxes, intolerable debts, and the excessive prices exacted, often for inferior wares, by trustified industries.

It is not too much to say that Catholic social theories were taken up and made truly operational by the Catholic Worker movement launched in the early 1930's by Dorothy Day, journalist, social worker, and erstwhile Communist, at the suggestion apparently of Peter Maurin, a French-born itinerant social philosopher. Miss Day and her co-workers lived in the slums in "houses of hospitality" which combined the functions of soup kitchens, discussion clubs, and reform centers. By their willingness to remain poor and to perform manual as well as intellectual labor, these dedicated Christians were able to aid and influence the homeless and unemployed worker, to bring the so-called Catholic program "down to the level of the people," to show the discontented masses that there was indeed a Christian alternative to the Communist solution. They personified the teachings of the Social Encyclicals by widely circulating their monthly paper, *The Catholic Worker,* by joining picket lines and otherwise participating in strikes and union organizational activities. In close touch with the workers and their leaders, the Catholic Workers took the initiative in forming the Association of Catholic Trade Unionists and in starting labor schools in order to counteract Communism while presenting positive Christian social solutions (see Document 31).

The Catholic Worker movement supported social security legislation, the vocational-group system, and other reform efforts such as subsistence farming and the consumer cooperative movement. While supporters of the movement recognized that governmental action was necessary and helpful, they always stressed "personal responsibility before state responsibility," and favored a massive, though personalized, charity to lessen cold, hunger, and sickness. The shelter afforded by city and state to the unattached unemployed, they thought, "is liable to make them leprous in soul and utterly incapable of working for sustenance or salvation," but through houses of hospitality "in the shadow of the Church" men would be recalled to Christ "and to the job of rebuilding the social order."

IV. THE NEW PLURALISM

The Catholic Worker movement has exerted a continuous influence since the Depression Thirties. While Miss Day and some of her followers urged Christian pacifism as the only sure road to world security in an atomic age, others nurtured in or associated with her movement have brilliantly expounded the philosophy of religious and social pluralism, a central viewpoint in religio-social matters since World War II. The basic concerns of pluralism revolve around the problem of promoting tolerance and the necessary moral and spiritual unities amid conditions of diversity and incipient conflict. Obviously, contemporary pluralism is only a new version of an old story in a land synonymous since colonial days with multiplicity of sects and religious freedom by constitutional fiat.

No doubt, the problem of pluralism has assumed new shape and form. Until recently Protestantism furnished the motivating ideals of American civilization and shared the prestige of its achievements and triumphs. So long as this interpenetration endured—until far into the twentieth century—the major competing faiths, Catholicism and Judaism, were tolerated minorities with minimal influence on society. By the end of World War II this situation, it was apparent, had ceased to prevail and reputable Protestant historians were speaking of Protestantism in Post-Protestant America. Not only had Catholic and Jewish adherents increased greatly in number, but they were unmistakably making great strides in wealth, education, cultural standing, and general well-being. No longer was Protestantism in a position to give religious direction to the nation on any moral or social issue. More damaging to the ideological dominance of Protestantism than the competition of its rivals was the thrust of secularist ideals which the unprecedented postwar gains in church membership obscured but did not repel. Inasmuch as in secularism the three faiths faced a common enemy, it behooved them, as they slowly realized, to put an end to their cold war and to plan strategies, singly and in cooperation, calculated in due time to make spiritual motivation regnant in personal and social striving.

In a pluralist society each group faced the problem of reconciling its special interest with the general or common interest. In theory, the Catholic Church with its claim to be all-inclusive was bound to be ill at ease in a society which seemingly thrived on the principle of sectarian exclusiveness. In practice, however, friction was confined to education and certain items of natural-law morality: government refused to subsidize Catholic schools, and public opinion did not accept Catholic views on divorce, birth control, censorship, and the like. However cogently Catholic controversialists might argue that the Church's position on these issues was right and just, non-Catholics were unimpressed. They were sure that the Catholic Church was a self-centered institution so intent on advancing its ecclesiastical interests that it lost sight of the general interest and of the rights of opposing persons and groups. As Catholic thinkers seriously examined this criticism, they were obliged to acknowledge that it contained a measure of merit. The outcome has been that in recent years some of the ablest philosophers and theologians have explored the whole question of religious pluralism. Their assumption has been that the continuous reconsideration of points in dispute will in the end establish harmony between the Catholic group interest and the general religious and social interest.

The attainment of harmony would entail, it was generally agreed, a more positive, less compromising Catholic commitment to democracy and freedom. In Catholic tradition, the conviction held that forms of government were of minor significance, that it mattered little whether one, few, or many ruled so long as the power in authority avoided tyranny and oppression and respected natural rights and the rights of the Church. All but unchallenged in Catholic thought before World War II was the Aristotelian-Thomistic conclusion that ideally the best form of government was a mixed construction of monarchical, aristocratic, and democratic elements. This theory, for all its plausibility, had little or no relevance to the new realities in the political and social order. It afforded the people but the frailest of weapons against the assaults of totalitarianism from right and left. This realization inspired two neo-Thomists, non-Catholic Mortimer J. Adler and Dominican Walter Farrell, to collaborate in a most exhaustive demonstration that democracy was not only a permissible but the best and the only truly just form of government (see Document 32). They claimed that the Catholics who were influenced by the democratic emphasis in political thought were presumably better prepared to combat Fascist and Communist propaganda and to thwart minority rule by Communists or racketeers in labor unions. They also advanced the cause of pluralism for, by adding their weight to the American consensus in support of democracy, they made Americans generally less fearful of Catholicism and more disposed to grant a sympathetic hearing to its special demands and requirements.

There was considerably less need for Catholics to theorize on democracy than to clarify their position on church-state relations. For so long as it could be plausibly argued that American Catholics were not wholly committed to the principle of religious freedom, no satisfactory pluralism was possible. A few highly influential Catholics, notably the Reverend John A. Ryan, had publicly defended the so-called thesis-hypothesis concept of church-state relations, that is, that in lands where Catholics predominated, non-Catholic worship should be suppressed—the thesis—while in countries like the United States where they were a minority, they should insist on religious freedom—the hypothesis. If all Protestants looked upon the theory as a prime example of pragmatic cynicism, some feared it imperiled their future existence. Realizing that no amount of reassurance that the theory would in all probability never be applicable to America could allay alarm, a group of Catholic thinkers, with John Courtney Murray, S.J., at their head, worked out an elaborate refutation (see Document 33). What really mattered was not "the religion of the state," said Murray, but "the freedom of the Church." Truth was not compromised if the state failed to make Catholicism the established or preferred religion—the question of state support or non-support of religion was one of expediency and policy, not moral truth. The only requirement in the realm of truth was that the Church's freedom be respected by political authority. This could be best assured, not by concordats or formal arrangements, but by the active and intelligent participation of Catholic citizens in the democratic processes of the body politic. Progressive Catholics in growing numbers now believe that all persons may claim liberty of conscience as a Christian right, concerning which belief a dogmatic formulation was made by Vatican Council II.

Theories of democracy and of church-state relations did not monopolize or exhaust the pluralist impulse. It impelled Catholic thinkers to consider with an open mind questions on which only one opinion and no debate were permissible before World War II or even before the election of John XXIII to the Papacy in 1958. Much more than was the case in former days, sympathy and understanding permeated discussions of the secular public school, of domestic relations, including the problem of family limitation, and of the merits and achievements of Protestantism and other non-Catholic religions. By and large, Catholic thinkers hoped that the injunctions of the natural law would be brought into closer touch with the moral realities of life in the contemporary world. If this were done, Catholics would be encouraged to exercise an ever-increasing amount of responsible freedom in all fields of moral and spiritual endeavor.

Catholic thinkers, in the face of the totalitarian threat, also insisted that the social emphasis must be on the freedom of the person to achieve self-fulfillment—the intrinsic purpose of the social good. Inasmuch as the social good included many and diverse kinds of self-fulfillment, it should operate through pluralistic structure. Inasmuch, also, as the state or ultimate society could not, certainly in its collectivist forms, elicit the economic self-interest and creative participation of individuals, it should have only a subsidiary function, that is, it should aid or help but not seek to control or direct the creative participation of individuals in family life, local communities, and free associations such as political parties, trade unions, cooperatives, and cultural and religious societies. While not all Catholic social thinkers defined social pluralism in exactly these terms, they all professed belief in pluralism in the economic and social as well as in the religious sphere.

Catholic social thinking since World War II has indeed revealed pluralist attitudes. While the old issues continue to be discussed, with attention still centering on unionism and the vocational group system, the focus of interest has noticeably shifted. More emphasis is placed now on individual freedom than on mass or group freedoms. This was conspicuously evident in the opposition to compulsory unionism. Chiefly out of fear that legally enforced union membership placed independently-minded workers at the mercy of union leaders, some Catholics urged the country to return to the voluntarism of Gompers' day (see Document 37). The "labor priests," it is true, called for the extension of unionism and its compulsory maintenance. But they also insisted that union members develop a sense of personal responsibility and, through the use of democratic processes, free their organizations of Communist and criminal influences.

The perennial Catholic interest in a guild social order also took a pluralist form after World War II. At the suggestion of labor leader Philip Murray the vocational group system came to be known as the Industry Council Plan. The more thoroughly the Plan was studied the more evident it appeared that Catholic thinkers were less willing than they formerly had been to place the whole of American economic life under guild control. They would exclude wages, prices, and profits from the jurisdiction of the proposed councils and authorize them to deal only with lesser matters: personnel and social security issues such as pensions, sick benefits, unemployment compensation, and vacations. Nor did Catholic thinkers favor the creation of formal guild structure apart from and above existing managerial organizations and labor unions—even if this was a requirement in strict theory. They believed, on the contrary, that the cooperative tendencies in American industry were stronger than the combative and conflicting ones, and that, therefore, an economy essentially guild in character would in due time emerge through the processes of evolutionary growth (see Documents 35 and 38).

The impact of pluralism on American Catholic thought is most plainly evident in the conviction that the Church should multiply and diversify its social efforts. Emphasis should shift from economics to sociology, from unionism and industrial relations to the revitalization of community life. The realization has dawned in the last decade that the social problem is more than a question of wages, hours, employment levels, and industrial peace. It is also a question of wretched slum housing, health neglect, physical and cultural impoverishment, racial discrimination, and a host of other chronic maladies and maladjustments (see Document 36). Paradoxically, the two, economic prosperity and blighted communities, may and in fact often do co-exist. By way of remedy, Catholic social actionists are coming to see the need for a new kind of community and regional planning in which major attention is placed on broadly educational and cultural rather than on strictly economic factors. The growing enthusiasm in Catholic circles for the study of the sociology of religion (see Document 34) will, no doubt, suggest areas of worthwhile endeavor.

SELECTED BIBLIOGRAPHY

Bibliographical information on American Catholic social thought is scattered, sketchy, and inadequately evaluated. There is no guide to this area of Catholic thought and activity —an indication, no doubt, of a merely peripheral interest in this branch of historical scholarship. Helpful, however, are recently published general guides to American religious history: John Tracy Ellis. *A Guide to American Catholic History*. Milwaukee: The Bruce Publishing Company, 1959, especially pp. 64–65, 67, 68, 71, 107–109; Edward R. Vollmar, S.J. *The Catholic Church in America: An Historical Bibliography*. New York: The Scarecrow Press, 1963; and Nelson R. Burr. *A Critical Bibliography of Religion in America*. (*Religion in American Life*, Vol. IV, edited by James Ward Smith and A. Leland Jamison. Princeton, New Jersey: Princeton University Press, 1961). The Ellis work is a select, classified, and annotated bibliography. Also select, Vollmar's author guide is especially valuable for its inclusion of many unpublished master's essays and doctoral dissertations on Catholic history at degree-granting Catholic institutions of higher learning. Burr's study, a piece of monumental scholarship, presents a classified narrative estimate of significantly relevant materials, pages 453–486, 588–590, 720–723, 732–734, and 741–743 being devoted to the social aspects of American Catholicism.

For books and pamphlets, many of which are concerned with social questions, the student should consult Wilfred Parsons, S.J. *Early Catholic Americana*. New York: Macmillan Co., 1939, covering the period through 1830; and Walter Romig. *The Guide to Catholic Literature*. Detroit: Walter Romig and Co., 1940ff, in several volumes, the first on the years 1888–1940, and an additional volume on each four-year period since 1940. Historians of American Catholic social thought have not attempted to amplify and correct Paul J. Fitzpatrick and Cletus F. Dirksen, C.PP.S. *Bibliography of Economic Books and Pamphlets by Catholic Authors, 1891–*

1941. Washington, D.C.: Catholic University of America Press, 1941, a useful work, although restricted in time and scope and woefully select and incomplete even for the years covered.

Manuscript and other archival collections are located and briefly described in Thomas F. O'Connor. "Catholic Archives of the United States," *Catholic Historical Review*, XXXI (January 1946), 414–430; Henry J. Browne. "The American Catholic Archival Tradition," *American Archivist*, XIV (April 1951), 127–139; and Thomas T. McAvoy, C.S.C. "Manuscript Collections Among American Catholics," *Catholic Historical Review*, XXXVII (October 1951), 281–295, and "Catholic Archives and Manuscript Collections," *American Archivist*, XXIV (October 1961), 409–414. Philip M. Hamer, ed. *A Guide to Archives and Manuscripts in the United States*. New Haven: Yale University Press, 1961, all but itemizes the contents of Catholic archival collections. Pending further study, no judgment is possible concerning the importance of Catholic newspapers in the formulation and diffusion of social thought. Appolinaris W. Baumgartner. *Catholic Journalism, A Study of its Development in the United States, 1789–1930*. New York: Columbia University Press, 1931, lists, dates, and locates the 118 Catholic newspapers in existence in 1930, many of which had long histories. By far the best collection (two hundred or more) is owned by the American Catholic Historical Society of Philadelphia and housed at St. Charles Borromeo Seminary at Overbrook, Pennsylvania. Only in recent decades has Catholic periodical literature been systematically indexed: the *Catholic Magazine Index*, I–III (July 1937–December 1938), and the *Catholic Periodical Index*, 1930–1933, 1939–, initiated by Paul J. Foik, C.S.C., who wrote *Pioneer Catholic Journalism*. New York: United States Catholic Historical Society, 1930, excellent for Catholic newspapers and magazines published before 1840.

Many pronouncements of the hierarchy have expounded social doctrine. The more important ones are available in two collections: Peter Guilday, ed. *National Pastorals of the Ameri-*

can Hierarchy, 1792–1919. Washington, D.C.: National Catholic Welfare Conference, 1923, and Raphael Huber, O.F.M. Conv., ed. *Our Bishops Speak.* Milwaukee: Bruce Publishing Company, 1951. Wilfred Parsons, S.J., analyzed at some length the material presented in the latter volume: "Social Thought of the American Hierarchy," *Social Order,* II (1952), 259–278. Some of the material in the Guilday and Huber volumes is contained in John Tracy Ellis. *Documents of American Catholic History.* 2nd ed., Milwaukee: Bruce Publishing Company, 1962. This collection is supplemented by H. Shelton Smith, Robert T. Handy, and Lefferts A. Loetscher, eds. *American Christianity: An Historical Interpretation with Representative Documents, 1607–1960.* 2 vols., New York: Charles Scribners' Sons, 1960, 1963. Besides significant articles, the bi-monthly *Catholic Mind* (New York: The America Press, from 1903) reprints the more important official Catholic documents from all over the world. For a warm appraisal of this publication, see B. L. Masse, S.J., ed. *The Catholic Mind Through Fifty Years.* New York: The America Press, 1952.

The social views of American Catholic Bishops since 1919 have been voiced in statements issued at the conclusion of their annual meetings and through the National Catholic Welfare Council ("Conference" since 1922) and its Social Action Department. The ideas and techniques of the Conference were reported in its monthly journal, *The Bulletin* (1919–1929), the *N.C.W.C. Review* (1930–1931), and finally, *Catholic Action* (1933–1953). For a half century or more the opinions of individual bishops have been submerged, so to speak, in the collective body. If today nearly every bishop issues social pronouncements from time to time as a matter of course, rare are the contemporary prelates who can match the range and vigor in the discussion of social questions that characterized their distinguished predecessors in the late nineteenth and early twentieth centuries. Preeminent among these were James Cardinal Gibbons, Archbishop of Baltimore, 1878–1921; John

Ireland, Bishop and Archbishop of St. Paul, 1875–1918; and John Lancaster Spalding, Bishop of Peoria, 1877–1916. Besides his brilliant chapter on the Knights of Labor (see Document 10 in this anthology), Cardinal Gibbons included significant statements on citizenship and church-state relations in *A Retrospect of Fifty Years.* 2 vols., Baltimore: John Murphy Company, 1916. In *The Church and Modern Society. Lectures and Addresses.* 2 vols., St. Paul: Pioneer Press, 1905, Archbishop Ireland claimed a social mission for the Church in no uncertain terms and presented a wealth of fact and opinion on the temperance, education, and labor questions. Bishop Spalding voiced his social views in his *Religious Mission of the Irish People and Catholic Colonization.* New York: Catholic Publication Society Company, 1880, excerpts from which constitute Document 9 in this anthology; and in *Socialism and Labor and Other Arguments, Social, Political and Patriotic.* Chicago: A. C. McClurg and Company, 1902. Agnes Claire Schroll, O.S.B., has written *The Social Thought of John Lancaster Spalding.* Washington, D.C.: Catholic University of America Press, 1944. The scholarly Bishop of Fall River, Massachusetts, William Stang, wrote an excellent commentary on the history of the Catholic social movement and on Pope Leo XIII's labor encyclical in *Socialism and Christianity.* New York: Benziger Brothers, 1905, in which he pleaded for labor legislation and trade unionism as checks on the inroads of socialism.

More than the bishops, the clergy elaborated social thought. The "Paulist" Fathers (priests in the Congregation of St. Paul the Apostle) were unsurpassed in the dissemination of social thought, especially during the last third of the nineteenth century. Their influence was exerted partly through their sermons and lectures, notably those of their founder, Isaac T. Hecker, but mainly through their monthly magazine, *Catholic World* (New York: from 1865), in which a host of competent writers, generally of progressive outlook, discussed social questions in all their fascinating variety. The magazine was especially good on problems of urban charity and on the theory of state intervention in the industrial sphere. The early articles were unsigned. Vincent F. Holden, C.S.P., who is about to finish his biography of Father Hecker, has identified the authors and listed for my use the ones who explored Catholic thought on the charity situation. They were men and women well qualified to write on their respective topics.

The priest who most ably brought out the economic implications of Christian social ethics was John A. Ryan, whose ideas on human welfare were formulated and expounded in more than a dozen books and nearly a hundred articles and pamphlets. Of special importance were *A Living Wage: Its Ethical and Economic Aspects.* New York: Macmillan Co., 1906; *Distributive Justice: The Right and Wrong of Our Present Distribution of Wealth.* New York: Macmillan Co., 1916; *Social Reconstruction.* New York: Macmillan Co., 1920; and *A Better Economic Order.* New York: Harper and Brothers, 1935. His autobiography, *Social Doctrine in Action: A Personal History.* New York: Harper and Brothers, 1941; Patrick W. Gearty, *The Economic Thought of Monsignor John A. Ryan.* Washington, D. C.: The Catholic University of America Press, 1953; and Francis L. Broderick, *Right Reverend New Dealer John A. Ryan.* New York: Macmillan Co., 1963, illuminate his life and thought. Preoccupied with the teachings of the Social Encyclicals, Ryan believed that a new relationship between capital and labor was the key to social justice. This was the view of his contemporary, Peter E. Dietz, whose journalism, fugitive pamphlets, and voluminous correspondence were used by Mary Harrita Fox in her biography, *Peter E. Dietz, Labor Priest.* Notre Dame, Indiana: University of Notre Dame Press, 1953. A few priests minimized the importance of industrial relations and called instead for drastic changes in the existing social order. Thus Dr. Edward McGlynn wanted the state to confiscate economic rent while Charles E. Coughlin, a half-century later, campaigned for federal ownership and control of money and banking (see Document 29). An enlargement of these views may be found in Sylvester L. Malone. *Dr. Edward McGlynn.* New York: Dr. McGlynn Monument Association, 1918; Stephen Bell. *Rebel Priest. A Biography of Dr. Edward McGlynn.* New York: Devin-Adair Company, 1937; James Jeremiah Green. "The Impact of Henry George's Theories on American Catholics," a doctoral dissertation, 1956, at the University of Notre Dame; and Charles Joseph Tull. *Father Coughlin and the New Deal.* Syracuse: University of Syracuse Press, 1965. On the other hand, Edward A. Keller, C.S.C. *Christianity and American Capitalism.* Chicago: Heritage Foundation, 1953, does not think that substantial interference with capitalistic enterprise by labor or government is morally permissible.

Some attention is given to social thought in the general historical surveys of the Catholic Church in the United States, the best of which is John Tracy Ellis. *American Catholicism.* Chicago: University of Chicago Press, 1956, a volume in the *Chicago History of American Civilization,* edited by Daniel J. Boorstin. Social thought and practice will no doubt be an integral part of forthcoming Catholic histories by Ellis, McAvoy, and possibly others. To be commended, for their stress on recent lay social movements and immigrant acculturation, are Leo Richard Ward, C.S.C., ed. *The American Apostolate. American Catholics in the Twentieth Century.* Westminster, Maryland: The Newman Press, 1952, and Thomas T. McAvoy, C.S.C., ed. *Roman Catholicism and the American Way of Life.* Notre Dame, Indiana: University of Notre Dame Press, 1960.

The first historical study of American Catholic social thought over a broad span of years was made by a candidate for the doctorate in sociology at the Catholic University of America, now a leading sociologist of religion, C. J. Nuesse. *The Social Thought of American Catholics, 1634–1829.* Westminster, Maryland: Newman Book Shop, 1945. He showed that Catholics in early America, the better to safeguard their unique status as a religious minority, developed a conformist social outlook, accepting basic items in the pre-Civil War zeitgeist, notably the cosmopolitan spirit of the eighteenth century and the nationalist and bourgeois points of view. If in the years since 1830 the stamp of originality has been impressed on significant segments of Catholic social thought, the conformist tendency has been tenacious and shows signs in our day of regaining its early dominance. Father McAvoy, University of Notre Dame archivist and historian, is the scholar who has most thoroughly explored the uniqueness-conformity dichotomy in American Catholic history. His views on this subject may be found in numerous articles, notably the ones on the Catholic minority in the United States, 1789–1917, in *Historical Records and Studies,* XXXIX-XL (1952), 33–50, published by the United States Catholic Historical Society of New York, and in the University of Notre Dame journal, *The Review of Politics,* X (January 1948), 13–34; XII (January 1950), 3–19; XV (July 1953), 275–302; XXI (January 1959), 53–82; and in his book, *The Great Crisis in American Catholic History, 1895–1900.* Chicago: Henry Regnery Company, 1957; paperback edition, slightly abbreviated and retitled, *The Americanist Heresy in Roman Catholicism, 1895–1900.* Notre Dame, Indiana: University of Notre Dame Press, 1963. The last is a study of "Americanism" as a theological and social movement of worldwide influence. McAvoy explains and defends the cultural approach to American Catholic history in "A New Technique of Writing Religious History," *The University of Portland Review* Portland, Oregon: The University of Portland Press, 1955, VIII, No. 1, 9–17; and in "American Catholics: Tradition and Controversy," *Thought,* XXXV (Winter, 1960), 583–600.

Other scholars interested in the cultural approach include Robert D. Cross. *The Emergence of Liberal Catholicism in America.* Cambridge: Harvard University Press, 1958; Colman J. Barry, O.S.B. *The Catholic Church and German Americans.* Milwaukee: The Bruce Publishing Company, 1953; and several biographers of prominent "Americanist" leaders: Vincent F. Holden, C.S.P. *The Yankee Paul: Isaac Thomas Hecker*. Vol. I, Milwaukee: The Bruce Publishing Company, 1958; John Tracy Ellis. *The Life of Cardinal Gibbons, Archbishop of Baltimore*. 2 vols., Milwaukee: The Bruce Publishing Company, 1952; James H. Moynihan. *The Life of Archbishop John Ireland*. New York: Harper and Brothers, 1953; and Patrick Henry Ahern. *The Life of John J. Keane, Educator and Archbishop*. Milwaukee: The Bruce Publishing Company, 1955. These writers have given due attention to the impact of American nationalist ideologies on ethnic groups. The editor of this anthology has insisted that eagerness to placate anti-Catholic public opinion almost as much as the desire to advance the cause of charity and justice motivated Catholics to launch a social reform program. See A. I. Abell, "Origins of Catholic Social Reform in the United States: Ideological Aspects," *Review of Politics,* XI (July 1949), 294–309; reprinted in M. A. Fitzsimons, Thomas T. McAvoy, C.S.C., and Frank O'Malley, eds. *The Image of Man. A Review of Politics Reader*. Notre Dame, Indiana: University of Notre Dame Press, 1959, pp. 381–391; and his *American Catholicism and Social Action: A Search for Social Justice, 1865–1950*. Garden City, New York: Hanover House, 1960, paperback edition, Notre Dame, Indiana: University of Notre Dame Press, 1964.

Catholic thought on the more important phases of Catholic action—labor, charity, and social service—is analyzed in: Henry J. Browne. *The Catholic Church and the Knights of Labor*. Washington, D.C.: The Catholic University of America Press, 1949; Marc Karson. "The Catholic Church and the Political Development of American Trade Unionism, 1900–1918," *Industrial and Labor Relations Review,* IV (July 1951), 527–542, and at greater length in his book, *American Labor Unions and Politics, 1900–1918*. Carbondale, Illinois: Southern Illinois University Press, 1958, pp. 212–284; Vincent A. McQuade. *The American Catholic Attitude on Child Labor Since 1891*.

Washington, D.C.: The Catholic University of America Press, 1938; John O'Grady. *Catholic Charities in the United States. History and Problems.* Washington, D.C.: National Conference of Catholic Charities, 1930; Donald P. Gavin. *The National Conference of Catholic Charities, 1910–1960.* Milwaukee: The Bruce Press, 1962; Marguerite T. Boylan. *Social Welfare in the Catholic Church. Organization and Planning Through Diocesan Bureaus.* New York: Columbia University Press, 1941; Marguerite T. Boylan, ed. *The Catholic Church and Social Welfare: A Symposium.* New York: Greenwich Book Publishers, 1961.

Laymen—one can only guess as to their number—have participated, and a few have assumed leadership, in the Catholic social movement. The same applies to lay women. If historians have not entirely ignored, they certainly have failed to focus attention on the work and thought of lay folk in social Catholicism. Biographies are few and of minimal importance: John O'Grady. *Levi Silliman Ives. Pioneer Leader in Catholic Charities.* New York: P. J. Kenedy and Sons, 1933; Thomas F. Meehan. *Thomas Maurice Mulry.* New York: The Encyclopedia Press. 1917; Sister M. Sevina Pahorezki. *The Social and Political Activities of William James Onahan.* Washington, D.C.: The Catholic University of America Press, 1942; Mary Augustine Kwitchin, O.S.F. *James Alphonsus McMaster. A Study in American Thought.* Washington, D.C.: The Catholic University of America Press, 1949; Eric F. Goldman. *Charles J. Bonaparte, Patrician Reformer.* Baltimore: Johns Hopkins Press, 1943; and Walter Romig. *Josephine Van Dyke Brownson.* Detroit: Gabriel Richard Press, 1955.

As a collective group, lay Catholics have received more attention. Laymen furnished nearly all the membership and much of the leadership in the myriad of Catholic societies of which most were interested in some aspect of the social question. The social thought of lay Catholics in several of the major special-purpose organizations is discussed and evaluated in

Daniel T. McColgan. *A Century of Charity. The First One Hundred Years of the Society of St. Vincent de Paul in the United States.* 2 vols. Milwaukee, Wis.: Bruce Publishing Company, 1951; M. Liguori Brophy, B.V.M. *The Social Thought of the German Roman Catholic Central Verein.* Washington, D.C.: The Catholic University of America Press, 1941; Joan Marie Donohoe, S.N.D. *The Irish Catholic Benevolent Union.* Washington, D.C.: The Catholic University of America Press, 1951. These organizations published journals which were concerned with theory and trends as well as with facts: *St. Vincent de Paul Quarterly* (New York, 1895–1916); *Central-Blatt and Social Justice* (St. Louis, 1908 to 1940), published now under the title *Social Justice Review; Irish Catholic Benevolent Union Journal* (Philadelphia, 1873–1900); *Bulletin* (Philadelphia, 1880–1909, irregular) and the *News* (Philadelphia, 1886–1897), total abstinence journals. Although a satisfactory history of the Knights of Columbus is yet to be written, the social attitudes of that important fraternal organization are displayed in its monthly journal, *Columbia* (New York, from 1921).

The social thought of the Catholic Lay Congresses of 1889 and 1893 is analyzed at some length in Abell, *American Catholicism and Social Action,* pages 98–117, which makes use of the William J. Onahan Papers and Correspondence at the University of Notre Dame. The papers and resolutions of the two Congresses were published: William H. Hughes, publisher, *Souvenir Volume Illustrated. Three Great Events in the History of the Catholic Church in the United States.* Detroit, 1889; and J. S. Hyland and Co., compilers, *Progress of the Catholic Church in America and the Great Columbian Catholic Congress of 1893.* 4th edition; Chicago, 1897. Sister Mary Adele Francis Gorman's doctoral dissertation (1962) at the University of Notre Dame, "Federation of Catholic Societies in the United States, 1870–1920," is excellent on the lay social movement and its influence on the genesis of the National Catholic Welfare Conference. The most important lay social group, the Catholic Workers, is discussed by its co-founder and steadfast leader, Dorothy Day, in her semi-autobiographical works, based on her diaries and newspaper, *The Catholic Worker* (New York, from 1933): *House of Hospitality.* New York: Sheed and Ward, 1939; *The Long Loneliness.* New York: Harper, 1952; and *Loaves and Fishes.* New York: Harper and Row, 1963. Miss Day's crusade was reinforced by Richard Deverall and Norman McKenna, young graduates of Villanova College, who launched *The Christian Front,* I-IV (January 1936–June 1939), "a monthly magazine of social reconstruction published and edited by Catholic laymen," and when Fascists and Jew-baiters appropriated its title, continued the journal as *Christian Social Reconstruction,* IV–VII (September 1939–June 1942). Deverall, in his memoirs, "This Way It Was," *Social Order,* XI (1961), 195–200, 259–264, 303–308, 351–355, 403–408, 451–456; XII (1962), 35–41, 59–64, 125–130, 179–183, 286–290, writes interestingly of his editorial labors and of his work as executive secretary of the Michigan Association of Catholic Trade Unionists in the faction-torn and Communist-infiltrated Detroit labor movement.

Catholic social thought in latter-day America has been deepened, amplified, and fascinatingly enriched by several Catholic learned societies. Their contributions may be found in *Report of the Proceedings and Addresses* and the quarterly *Bulletin* of the National Catholic Educational Association (Columbus, Ohio, from 1904); the *Proceedings of the Annual Meeting* of the American Catholic Philosophical Association (Baltimore, from 1926); the American Catholic Sociological Society (Chicago, from 1938) and its quarterly *The American Catholic Sociological Review* (from 1940); the Catholic Economic Association (Milwaukee, from 1941) and its semi-annual *Review of Social Economy* (from 1942); the *Proceedings of the Annual Convention* of the Catholic Theological Society of America (Washington, D.C., from 1946); the *Papers* of the Catholic Commission on Intellectual and Cultural Affairs

(Washington, D.C., from 1946); and the monthly *Social Order,* 1947–1963, of the Institute of Social Order, in association with St. Louis University (from 1947). The research and writing encouraged and published by these societies have brought to bear a vast amount of critical commentary over the whole range of American Catholic social thought and practice. A good part of this material is historically orientated, examples being John LaFarge, S.J. "The Catholic Intellectual and Social Movements," a paper read at a meeting of the Catholic Committee on Intellectual and Cultural Affairs, St. Louis, May 15, 1955, and printed in *The Catholic Mind,* LIII (September 1955), 551–559; Richard J. Ward. "The Role of the Association of Catholic Trade Unionists in the Labor Movement," *Review of Social Economy,* XIV (September 1956), 79–100; Rupert J. Ederer, "The Industry Council Arrives in America," *ibid.,* XIX (September 1961), 155–165; Martin E. Schirber, O.S.B. "American Catholics and Life on the Land," *Social Order,* XII (May 1962), 193–208; and Edward Duff, S.J. "Catholic Social Action in the American Environment," *ibid.* (September 1962), 300–314.

Present-day Catholic social theorists, for the most part, are not unduly disturbed by the inroads of secularization. In their view only the "fellow travelers" in the different churches have been secularized; the majority still believe in "salvation" and hope to secure it through the faithful performance of religious duties. The educational task is to persuade these true believers to make meaningful applications of the new social and intellectual insights. For argument along these lines, see the Boston *Pilot's* editor, Francis J. Lally. *The Catholic Church in a Changing America.* Boston: Little, Brown and Co., 1962, and sociologist John L. Thomas, S.J. *Religion and the American People.* Westminster, Md.: The Newman Press, 1963.

ACKNOWLEDGMENTS

The manuscript for this volume was substantially complete when Aaron Abell died suddenly in October, 1965. In the previous two years it had been my privilege, as one of the General Editors of the American Heritage Series, to have worked with Professor Abell in planning the volume. I have tried to prepare the manuscript for publication in the spirit of his scholarship.

The documents, with one exception, were selected by Professor Abell. To conform to the canon of selection that he had agreed to, namely that all documents be from Catholic sources, a statement by the Association of Catholic Trade Unions (Document 30) was substituted for a short description of the ACTU by a non-Catholic source. With two exceptions the documents are reprinted as Professor Abell edited them. In Documents 4 and 32 I have added the conclusion of the article, allowing the author to complete his argument. The arrangement of documents is also as Professor Abell left it, save that the documents in Part IV have been placed in chronological order. Only minor stylistic changes have been made in the introduction, headnotes and captions, to assure clarity of expression.

I wish to express appreciation to Mrs. Aaron Abell who allowed me to assume responsibility for the manuscript, to Vincent P. De Santis, Chairman of the Department of History at University of Notre Dame, who helped to make the necessary arrangements, and to the Reverend Thomas T. McAvoy, C.S.C., University Archivist at Notre Dame. Father McAvoy, with whom Aaron Abell frequently discussed this volume, is himself a well known scholar of American Catholic history. He gave generously of his time to assemble the manuscript, select and write the headnote for the ACTU document, photocopy several missing documents, check Aaron Abell's own copy and go over the entire proof.

Alfred F. Young

PART ONE

Conditions of Catholic Growth

1 Archbishop John Hughes

LIBERTY AND ENLIGHTENMENT NOT OBSTACLES TO CATHOLIC GROWTH

In a lecture delivered before the Young Catholics' Friend Society in Baltimore in 1856, Archbishop John Hughes discussed at some length the three sources of Catholic population in the United States: the Catholic colony of Maryland, the immigrants, who prior to 1856 were mostly of Irish and German extraction, and the converts—chiefly native American Protestants. Inasmuch as native-born Catholics in America substantially outnumbered those of foreign birth, even in a period of massive immigration, Hughes concluded that all these groups were largely successful in transmitting their faith to their descendants. He candidly acknowledged, nevertheless, that descendants of immigrants by the hundreds of thousands had lost their religion—a "leakage" he felt was the result of the physical disability, abject poverty, and lack of pastoral care from which so many of them suffered. The losses had not stemmed, he insisted, from any felt conflict between the Catholic Church and the American system of church-state relations. American Catholic history since the Declaration of Independence had amply shown that the unique position of the Catholic Church in this country, where it was neither the favorite nor the foe of the civil government, was no obstacle to its growth and influence. He made much of what he called the "true test" of Catholicism's compatibility with enlightenment and liberty, namely, the numerous freedom-loving, native American converts of high character and social standing.

Hughes' argument went far to set the Catholic Church in its true light before the American public—to disabuse anti-Catholics of the complacent assumption that "Catholicity wastes away under the full light and liberty of the United States," and to reassure Catholics on this issue. While his views were not new, they were strongly put and carried the weight of his enormous prestige. An Irish immigrant himself, he held the positions of co-adjutor bishop, bishop, and archbishop of New York successively for nearly three decades (1837–1864). Hughes was widely recognized as the leading organizer in urban Catholicism, destroying "trusteeism" and otherwise disciplining his flock; encouraging the immigrant masses in his jurisdiction, chiefly the Irish, to improve their economic and social position; and ministering to their spiritual welfare through a phenomenal expansion of churches, schools, and charitable institutions. A successful fund raiser and builder, Hughes has inspired many bishops since his day to follow in his footsteps. The controversial skill, with which, by artfully combining pugnacity and conciliation, he so demonstrably improved the image of the Catholic Church in the public mind impressed these men, and encouraged them to adopt his view that the Catholic leakage, while extensive, had been grossly exaggerated and stemmed from bad social conditions and not from the impact of American liberty.

There is no subject which has elicited such varied and contradictory speculations as an attempt to understand the present condition of the Catholic Church in the United States. Members of that Church, and members of other denominations, have indulged in speculations with regard to its members, the sources from which they are derived, and its powerful endurance amid the novel circumstances in which it finds itself in a free country. And the circumstances are indeed novel; because from the beginning of Christianity until the declaration of American independence that Church has never found

---

"Lecture on the Present Condition and Prospects of the Catholic Church in the United States," delivered before the Young Catholics' Friend Society, at Baltimore, January 17, 1856, in *Complete Works of the Most Reverend John Hughes,* Lawrence Kehoe, ed. (New York, 1865), II, 122–132.

herself face to face with the civil government of any country except as its favorite or as its foe.

The pagan emperors of Rome, as you know, opposed it with persecution unto death. When Constantine became a Christian he favored it, and his successors pretended to favor it with their earthly patronage, until his descendants degenerated into petty disputants of theological questions, and prepared the way for the incoming of those who became the masters of the fallen empire. They, in their turn, necessarily, because they were ignorant, though brave, fell under the instruction of Christianity; and, in forming the germ of the present governments and nations of Europe, in their social capacity, the Church herself was brought in as part and portion of the governments thus interested, and they as civil rulers from the beginning professed to protect her. In later times, when changes of religion came, whilst she was petted in Catholic countries she was persecuted in Protestant countries; and thus up to the present time, or the period to which I have referred, she has never found herself face to face with the country, and in rivalship with creeds, in which no favor was to be shown on one side or the other. And hence it is that this new problem has furnished a theme for the inquiry of philosophers, of every religion, on both sides of the Atlantic ocean. And when I had the honor of being invited to deliver a lecture for the benefit of young men who devote their energies to protect their still younger brethren who may be exposed to forfeit both their faith and morals unless protected, surrounded as they are by so many dangers and temptations, I thought that no subject, though a most difficult one it is, would be more in keeping with the spirit of their purpose than an endeavor to elucidate the question to which I have referred—namely, *The condition and prospects of the Catholic Religion in the United States.* By some it has been supposed that the Catholic Church was making almost incredible progress in the absence of all restraints and discouragements placed upon her by the Legislatures of the States, and that her course was onward and prosperous. By others it has been assumed that the action of the institutions of this country was so powerful upon the Catholic mind that the Church not only made no progress, but she was actually retrograding, and in this confusion of ideas I could see but one way in attempting—and it will only be an attempt, for the matter is surrounded with difficulties—to elucidate what I may think now to be the actual condition of the Catholic religion here, and what are its prospects. In the first place, the Catholics who are here now are derived from three sources. One is, the primitive stock of the Maryland colony; the second is, immigration; and the third, is an element which has hardly yet been brought into the account, but which I think deserves to be considered an element in elucidating this matter—that of the conversion of persons of other religions.

These are the three and only sources, and in endeavoring to follow out my ideas, it will be necessary for me, in order to use the shortest words, to repeat frequently the terms Catholic and Protestant. I beg you to understand, that in this reference, I waive all theological and polemical questions, and I consider for the present, and for my purpose, these two religions as simply rival demonstrations in a noble competition, as to which shall render to God the most glory, and to man the greatest benefits. If, therefore, any syllable escapes me calculated to offend any one of this audience, I beg it to be understood, that I retract such an expression by anticipation, even before it is uttered. It would be unbecoming in me to avail myself of an occasion like the present, when I am honored by the presence of many who are not of the Catholic religion, to say one word which could give offence to any one in the least. For my purpose, it is necessary for me to take within my view a period of seventy years;—that is to say, from a period between the declaration of Independence and the formation of the Constitution. The beginning for that period will be the year 1785, in which the Very Rev. Father John Carroll, the representative of Maryland, a Jesuit priest, was appointed by the Holy See, and invested with spiritual authority as the Superior of the clergy in this country. Until that time, such authority came through the Vicar Apostolic of London, and at that period he was appointed, and here is a proper starting point for us to determine this question, because, although there remained for long years enactments upon many of the statute-books of different States, discouraging Catholics, I shall not take them into account, but shall consider that from 1785 to 1856, the Catholics of the United States have stood upon a perfect equality as to the law with their Protestant fellow-citizens.

Now we must begin by asking who and where were the Catholics in 1785. Archbishop Carroll speaks of them, and finds that in Maryland there were between sixteen and twenty thousand. In Pennsylvania there were about eight thousand, according to the best accounts. A priest was appointed for New York in that year by Father Carroll, and he reports that he found a congregation of two hundred there. Except the Catholics of Maryland, those of Pennsylvania and other States, with rare exceptions, were all foreigners. Nevertheless, in those trying days, when Carroll himself had taken such a patriotic part in vindicating the rights of his country, and when the Catholics of Maryland were redeemed from all former prejudices, not only by their own candor, but by the great and illustrious name of Carroll, and his connection with the work, it so happened at the same time, that in Pennsylvania, of the eight thousand Catholics there, there were three conspicuous, trusted and honored in the great work of preparing the country for the result which has been so gloriously attained. One of these was Moylan, the first Quartermaster-general of the American army; the second of these was Fitzsimmons, a member of Congress; and the third was Commodore John Barry, the founder of the American navy.

All these were Catholics, and considering the paucity in numbers of the general body, were at least quite conspicuous, and well qualified to confer honor upon it, and remove any prejudices existing against it. Now, to the Catholics of Maryland there have been accessions made ever since that period, and you will find, that although the colony of Maryland had been founded by Catholics, and although the first declaration of religious liberty, or the strongest approach to it, was there enunciated, nevertheless, from the revolution of 1688, they were disfranchised, and for the period of seventy years made no progress. Immigration was not permitted, and severe laws were enacted against them, and Governor Sharp, in 1758, himself a Protestant, computed them at that time as one in thirteen, in the population of the colony. Immediately after the American revolution, however, and perhaps before, some of these had gone to Kentucky, and there they introduced Catholicity. But except the three sources to which I have referred, you may look over the expanse of the whole United States, and no history mentions the existence at that period of any community of Catholics in any part thereof. Individuals, and perhaps solitary families of the Catholic faith, might have been found here and there, but these are the three sources from which, as I will call them, the native, hereditary, and American Catholics are to be derived.

How was it in respect to other things? There were at that time few Catholic churches in the whole of the United States. One was at Philadelphia, one was at Goshen-hoppen, one was at Conewaga, and I believe one at Baltimore was about finished, and that was St. Peter's church. Besides this, there was no public Catholic church in the State of Maryland. There were no Catholic schools or colleges to prepare young men for the ministry, or, in fact, Catholic schools or colleges of any kind. There were no Catholic hospitals or orphan asylums, nor any institutions of this character. There were only Father Carroll and twenty-four priests; three of whom were incapacitated by age from doing duty. The glorious missions of the French Jesuits among the Indians in the Eastern States, at the North, and along the rivers of the West, though limited to a certain extent, had passed away, and form nothing in the account we are now considering. The accessions of territory which have since taken place, are not to be counted in this original, hereditary Catholic population. Louisiana came in by purchase eighteen years after the period I speak of, and her population, though born on the soil, was small. Florida, which was brought into the Union, or at least acquired as territory afterwards, though it had belonged to a Catholic government, had a population scarcely worth mentioning. Since that time, the acquisition of Texas from another Catholic government has been made, but its population also was sparse; and yet still further, the acquisition of California, which had gold, but few inhabitants, has been made. And lastly, New Mexico has been acquired; but all these acquisitions have been of countries with immense territory, but comprising within their limits, in point of numbers, an insignificant original Catholic population. So far, therefore, we give an account of the condition of the Catholic Church at the beginning of the period of seventy years, which, in our circumstances, has been the first and most distinguishing period of light, civil liberty, and universal equality before the law.

Whence now, it may be asked, has been the increase in the present numbers of the Catholic people? The increase has been from immigration, and I think upon that subject very erroneous ideas prevail, both among Catholics and Protestants. I think that immigration has been vastly overrated, and from an examination of the best authorities within my reach, both official and scientific, on the English and American side, I have every reason to believe that immigration into this country has been much smaller than has been generally supposed, though necessarily large. It has not been possible for me to procure correct and accurate accounts of the immigration into this country, except from the British empire, but we can easily understand and conjecture what it would be from the continent of Europe.

In the first place, we know, in regard to this immigration, that there is no distinction made, in the authorities upon this subject, excepting in one or two instances, between the inhabitants of one country and those of another, so that the immigration from the British empire has been described and considered in general terms; and we know further, that so far as Catholicity is concerned, neither Wales nor England, nor Scotland, which contributed much in the earlier stages of immigration to the population of the United States, furnished any addition to the Catholic body. It remained, therefore, for Ireland, as a part of the British empire, to furnish Catholic immigrants, and you will, perhaps, be surprised, when I mention that up to the year 1825 the immigration from the British empire counts but little over 300,000. The statistics from which I derive my information appear to be exceedingly accurate, much more so than those which have been presented by the later authorities in this country.

In the first place, after the establishment of peace, there was very little good-will between the two countries; but, on the other hand, there was a remnant of rancor still remaining upon the one side, and self-congratulation upon the other. The immigration which began, or at least which was first noted, was in 1794, when it was 10,000. It goes on diminishing until the close of the war, but for four or five years previous to that time, the immigration was so slight that it is scarcely to be taken into the account. From the close of the war it increased, but still in moderate degree, up to the year 1825, when it was found to have been a little more than 300,000.

I may mention further, that during this period the greater portion of immigrants from Ireland were not Catholics but Protestants; that is to say, they were Presbyterians from the north of Ireland, who settled, some in New Jersey, and in great numbers in Western Pennsylvania. Many of their descendants are now found in Western Virginia, in Tennessee, and in Ohio. From that class of people, therefore, the great majority of immigrants came at that period, nor does the tide of Catholic immigration appear to have set in towards this country with any great force until after the close of the Revolutionary war.

It would be tedious and tiresome to go through the dry details of statistics, and repeat how many came in this or that year. However, it is enough for me to say that the immigration from Great Britain and Ireland, which, up to 1825, was a little over 300,000, reached in the following twenty-five years 1,453,325, and since that period, from 1850 to 1856, there have arrived at the city of New York alone, 1,319,236 immigrants. During this period nine-tenths of the immigrants to this country landed in New York, and there is no account of those landing elsewhere. The statistics we have upon this subject would authorize this conclusion, that the immigration from Great Britain and Ireland, since 1790 until the present year, has amounted to about 3,250,000.

Now, if we were called upon to determine to which religious party these immigrants belonged—this matter enters not into the account of the statistics of immigration—although for the last fifteen years perhaps four-fifths of the Irish immigrants were Catholics, still, taking the whole period of time the proportion would be much greater upon the other side, the Protestant side. From the continent of Europe, from Sweden, Norway, and most of the German principalities and States, nearly all the immigrants were Protestants. There were very few Spanish and French immigrants.

The object of these remarks is first to impress upon you a just conception of the amount of immigration, and how far it has contributed to the actual results of the Catholic religion, as it now exists in this country; and secondly, to meet the objection which has been urged on both the Catholic and Protestant side, to the effect that Catholicity wastes away under the full light and liberty of the United States. It is not long since a nobleman in the House of Parliament proclaimed on the authority of a letter written by a priest of Ireland, who was opposed to immigration, that the only way to convert the Irish would be to remove from them the pretence that they were persecuted by the State, and to make them equal before the law by sending them to America, and then indeed, in a short time, they would renounce their religion and become like other sensible men.

The result of the immigration here I think will satisfy you, that though this has been the case to a lamentable degree, it does not in the least prove that the Catholic religion is not fit and competent to hold her own, no matter how great the light and liberty may be. It is true that hundreds of thousands of the descendants of the Catholic immigrants have fallen away from their religion. It is equally true that they have hardly added any thing to any other denomination of Christians. It is true that they have fallen simply into a state of indifference, and, alas! sometimes into a state of infidelity.

This is not because they have examined their religion in the light of the age, or in the presence of equality. Not at all. Calamities of one kind and another, the death or ignorance of their parents it may be, or their remote situation from the opportunities of practising and learning their religion, account sufficiently for the falling away of those who are acknowledged to have been lost to the Catholic Church. Again, though the number of immigrants into this country alone might equal the whole number of the present population, still the slightest inspection will satisfy you as to the fallacy of the reasoning of those who misjudge this question, and will convince you that the immigration pouring into the country is like water cast into a vessel that is leaky, and that will not retain any quantity it receives. According to the laws recognized in statistics, the very common laws of mortality, immigrants to this country are dying at the rate of one in three; and this is because they are especially exposed to the accidents of life, to sickness, hardship of every kind, and toilsome poverty. They are especially exposed to epidemics, whether in the form of cholera, yellow fever, or any thing else which decimates them, and therefore the common allowance of mortality is not sufficient to express the proportion of the deaths in their case.

Now, therefore, if it be true that the action of this age of light and of freedom is detrimental to the progress or the existence of the Catholic religion, in the presence of other free denominations, how are we to account for the progress of the Catholic religion actually made, according to the statistics published in this city, in the Catholic Almanac? It must be that the original Catholic population of Maryland and their descendants have kept the faith and propagated it to a great extent, or, besides the living immigrants, a vast number have been preserved, and have not fallen away, but inherited the faith of their foreign-born ancestors, and are perpetuating it.

But the other element to which I have referred is conversion; and although I am quite satisfied that the number of converts does not equal the one-third of the descendants of Catholics who have passed away from the faith, nevertheless I consider it a great element, essential for explanation of the condition of the Catholic Church at this time.

We find, by the census of 1850, that there were then in the United States nineteen million five hundred and fifty-three thousand and sixty-five white inhabitants, of whom two millions two hundred and forty thousand five hundred and thirty-five were of foreign birth. Now, those of foreign birth were made up of all the nations I have mentioned; and the only two nations which contributed in any considerable degree to the augmentation of Catholics were Ireland and Germany; and in that year (1850) the Irish, according to the census, numbered nine hundred and fifty thousand in the whole United States. Of this a very considerable portion were Protestants; and of the remainder, according to the laws of mortality, there would be a reduction of one-sixth, up to the present time; so that by the closest examination, and arranging the results according to the best ascertained authority within reach, it follows as an approximate calculation that at the present day there are in the United States, say eleven hundred thousand Catholics born in foreign lands, over eight hundred thousand Irish and three hundred thousand Germans, because of the German immigration there are two Protestants for one Catholic. Though the number is not great, I wish it to be understood that I consider this a high estimate of the foreign-born Catholics of the United States. And yet we find in the Catholic Almanac for the year 1856, that the Catholic population, by the enumeration, as reported by the different dioceses of the United States, is two millions three hundred and ninety-seven thousand five hundred; thus leaving eleven hundred thousand foreign-born Catholics, and the balance twelve hundred and ninety-seven thousand five hundred. We should take into the account, too, a great loss, owing to the majority of parents leaving their children unprotected—not receiving an education, and owing to their poverty, being compelled to select habitations distant from religion and its ministers. Although this loss is so great, it is impossible to explain these statistics without supposing that many fell in with the doctrines of their ancestry, who propagated their faith and hope to those born in this country.

A third element is that of conversion; and so far as it is a test-question, here is a true test whether or not Catholicity can compare with any other denomination of Christians, where there is neither popularity on the one side nor prejudice on the other. It is the number of conversions; for while many speculate, and admit, with expressions of gratitude, that the Catholic religion is useful and beneficial to mankind, in her regions of despair and darkness, they say that it never can bear the test of light in the presence of equal education. And here is the test: when I say conversions, not in boastful terms, but which we ascribe to the Almighty, I mean those of American birth, freemen who love freedom, who would not sacrifice legitimate freedom while embracing Catholicism—and who, understanding both sides of the question, have not hesitated to make sacrifices of worldly interests and advantages—for what purpose? To bear testimony to the truth which they had examined and which came under their notice, and by an act of simple faith embraced. Not for worldly motives. And here is the field and theatre, the sphere on which, it was said, it could not stand!

We all know that, from the time of Archbishop Carroll to the present day, there have been numerous converts. In New England, East, West, South, everywhere, there is scarcely any congregation that does not number its converts; and those converts take better care to instil their faith into the minds of their children than those who receive their faith from Catholic parents.

What, then, is the condition of the Catholic Church as compared with the time of Archbishop Carroll? Seventy years ago, not going out of this period, in the history of the United States of America, was the first occasion on which the Catholic Church was tried by such circumstances.

What is the condition to-day of the Catholic Church, its population made up of three elements? Two millions three hundred and ninety-seven thousand five hundred souls. Then there were twenty-two or twenty-three priests; now there are seventeen hundred and sixty-one priests. Then there was no bishop to ordain priests, if there were candidates; now there are seven archbishops and thirty-five bishops. There were but the four churches I have mentioned, and now there are nineteen hundred and ten churches, besides other stations where divine worship is held, to the number of eight hundred and ninety-five. Then in the Catholic Church there was not a Catholic seminary for the training of Levites for the sanctuary; now there are thirty-seven seminaries appropriated exclusively to the training of youth to serve both God and man. Then there were no colleges; now there are twenty-four, incorporated by the States in which they are placed. Then we had but one female academy; now we have one hundred and thirty. But it is unnecessary to go on, and give other evidences of progress; these are sufficient.

Here, then, are circumstances which I adduce to refute the calumny expressed abroad as well as at home—a calumny against light and liberty, as if the Catholic Church were necessarily inimical to Protestant or any other liberty—a charge against the Catholic Church, which, it is said, may thrive when protected and surrounded by the patronage of civil government, as in Catholic countries, and which, persecuted, flourishes like certain weeds, growing and producing the most vegetation when trampled on. They say we increase when persecuted on one side, and receiving the patronage of civil government on the other. They say that the Church cannot win its own battles, and cannot meet the steady gaze of a free people and an enlightened age. This is the calumny refuted in making the exhibit of statistics regarding the condition of the Catholic Church in the United States.

Now as to our prospects. Notwithstanding the poverty of Catholics, they have succeeded in producing the results to which I have referred—I will not say in spite of light and knowledge, but in harmony with them, during the period of seventy years under this great and extensive republic. What, then, is the prospect with regard to the Catholic religion? The prospect is, that it is going on increasing by the medium of native-born Catholics in this country. The prospect, with superior advantages, and the benefit of instruction in almost every part of the country, and the presence of priests where it is necessary, looking to spiritual interest, for them to reside, that Catholics will instil into their descendants the knowledge of their religion and the lessons of virtue which they have received, and which they prize more than life. And this religion will extend, not by miraculous means, but will hold its own from the moment that immigration diminishes. It will not lapse and fall away into indifference and infidelity, of which writers have so much reason to complain.

My impression is, however, that immigration will diminish. That it will cease, is not at all probable; for the relations of kindred are too numerous to suppose that there will not constantly be persons passing from one side of the Atlantic to the other, even should they not expect any temporal advantages by the change.

Immigration, as I have said, will diminish. The country has had enough of it. The welcome is not so cordial as it was; the hand of kindness of other days is not stretched out any more, and the immigrants feel that they are not now so ardently welcomed. This will restrain them to some extent. On the other hand, the population of Ireland has been much thinned, so many having been driven from her soil by famine, or interred in her bosom by pestilence; and this will influence the immigration from that country not a little, while they will be restrained by motives of religion and philanthropy from coming hither, in consequence of the reception which awaits them. The third reason is, that the governments of Europe will, as far as may be in their power, employ their influence for the same purpose. Although in the darkened minds of political economists, who arrange things according to profit and loss, it may have been the doctrine of the British that the extensive grazing farms were adapted to the purpose of improving the breed of cattle, much more profitably to the proprietor than the crowded neighborhood of peasants, yet there was famine [on] one side and pestilence in the rear of famine. They who could escape had every inducement to leave the land for broad sheepwalks, for which they were occupied.

But there are such things as wars. Wars do occur. Nations find it more profitable, if not in a pecuniary sense, in a spirit of national pride, to have a numerous hardy and brave peasantry, to meet the enemy against whom they will not be strong enough to contend. It is not at all probable that if Great Britain could have recourse to its favorite recruiting ground in 1855, with the same results of success as under Wellington in 1815 and preceding years, in that contingency it is not at all probable that the British army would not have been able to take the Redan at Sebastopol. The failure was not for the want of bravery, but a want of force; and this exhibits that nation, so reckless of the lives of her own people, descending, and almost consigned, to the second rank, whereas she was formerly in the first. I think these considerations will operate on both sides of the Atlantic to diminish immigration; and the burden of sustaining the Catholic religion in this country, in the same scale of progress, will devolve on the immigrants now in this country, and those who are born therein.

Within the period to which I have referred, the adherents of the Catholic religion have evinced no special love for that state of society in which their enemies pretend they prosper best. If any one says you love darkness, point to your colleges. Was it the love of darkness that stimulated a poor population to establish those institutions of learning? If any say you are disloyal to the country, point to every battle from the commencement of the country, and see if Catholics were not equal in the struggle, and as zealous to maintain the dignity and triumph of the country as those with whom they fought! Nor was it in the contest with Great Britain alone, against whom it is supposed we have an hereditary spite, but against Catholic Mexico they fought with an equal courage. Although they aimed the point of the sword at the breast of their brother Catholics, they aimed it not the less, and in every contest they endeavored to maintain liberty as well as right. Courage is one side, and engaging in the contest is another. And when allusion is made to their social qualities, may you not point as an answer to the fact that when pestilence and plague had spread their dark pall over your cities, they were ready to go with others into the glorious work of charity and humanity; and, if necessary, sacrifice their lives to mitigate pestilence and disease.

On that score, what justification can there be to say that they love despotism because they are accustomed to it, and not liberty, because they never realized what it is? Before Columbus discovered the Western Continent there was a people in Europe acquainted with the rights and privileges of republican government. In Italy there was a republic of great prosperity before the discovery of America. If no other instance could be alluded to, there was one little republic (San Marino) installed in the Papal States. How long? For fourteen hundred years she has continued to preserve her liberty. Though Catholic, she is against the one-man power. Her supreme authority is not given into the hands of one man, but two, because her people love equality, and one man might deceive them in matters of control. The whole republic is not much larger than the District of Columbia, yet she has maintained her government and freedom for fourteen hundred years. She is too just and wise to be disturbed, and too insignificant to excite the jealousy of her more powerful neighbors. Yet these people have had their periods of filibustering, and troubles growing out of feuds with some neighboring barons. Notwithstanding, they have kept on, and are not afraid.

And now speaking of this republic, which is an enlargement of such a model, what should be the desire of every man who loves her? It should be what the Catholic religion desires—no more light than she possesses, no more liberty than the laws by which this country has made such astonishing progress; leaving religion to take care of its own concerns, every denomination managing its affairs in its own way. Prospering as no country has ever prospered, what ought to be the wish of every man who loves his country? That she may remain, preserving her liberty and the laws of justice and equality as long as the Republic of San Marino, and as great a century hence as she designs to aspire.

2 Orestes A. Brownson

CATHOLICS AND AMERICA'S PROVIDENTIAL MISSION

No believer in the Manifest Destiny of America to extend its territorial boundaries and to secure therein the blessings of republican institutions pleaded his cause more ardently than Orestes A. Brownson, who exulted in the "Providential Mission of America" to realize the "Christian Ideal of Society in both the New and the Old World." He argued that American institutions, or, in other words, the political and social order, the "civility," of America embodied the Christian ideal because they were based on the natural law of justice and equity. He believed, however, that the loss of confidence in Protestantism by the original Anglo-American population had undermined the moral foundations of the great social structure. It was Brownson's view that the American people could again be motivated to accept moral restraints and thus preserve their institutions only if they embraced Catholicism which, with its free-will theology and natural-law theory of politics, had all the strength of the now-waning Calvinism and few of its weaknesses and repulsive features.

Although the majority of Americans were hostile or indifferent to Catholicism, he said, they would become interested and receptive if Catholics, especially immigrant Catholics, evidenced in thought and action that they not only approved American institutions but recognized that they were the outcome of Catholic teachings. American Catholics must, above all, repudiate the theory of religious persecution and subscribe wholeheartedly to the American principle of church-state relations. Catholics should not be unduly depressed by recurring anti-Catholic movements of the Know-Nothing variety or vent their rage during these anguished periods against the whole of the non-Catholic population. They should understand, on the contrary, that these movements were directed quite as much against the culture and shortcomings of the immigrants as against their Catholic faith. Catholics should love their non-Catholic fellow countrymen and seek their conversion.

Brownson, a philosopher-journalist and unquestionably the greatest American Catholic intellectual of the nineteenth century, spoke for his fellow converts and indeed for all Catholics fervently interested in the defense or extension of Catholicism along liberal lines. This did not imply that the men and women under his influence subscribed to any one social theory.

Brownson himself was highly critical of many dominant tendencies in American life, notably, industrial capitalism and equalitarian or unlimited democracy, the sources, in his opinion, of "wage serfdom" and plutocracy. But his slightly younger friend, the Reverend Isaac T. Hecker, founder of the Paulist community, was a confirmed optimist, with a lyric faith in democracy and humanitarian reform, the origins of and sanction for which he found in the basic dogmas of Catholic theology. Irrespective of specific social beliefs, persons in the Brownson tradition were friendly to American civilization, unusually sensitive to attacks upon it, and ever ready to support measures which seemed likely to improve or maintain it.

Any one who reads Dr. Spalding's book[1] must find the objection, now growing somewhat stale, that Catholicity is hostile to our political and social order, for ever silenced, if not by his arguments, at least by his tone and spirit. No American can read it without feeling that the Catholic religion is at home in the American breast, if we may so speak, more American than the greater part of Americans themselves, and that it is just what is needed to complete and consecrate the American character. The author is not one of those Americans who have no sympathy with the institutions of their own country, and are really foreigners in their sentiments and affections. He sees, what some Catholics even, though of American birth and lineage, do not see, that the natural relation between our religion and the government is that of concord, and not of an-

---

Orestes A. Brownson, "Mission of America," *Brownson's Quarterly Review,* New York Series, I (October 1856), 409–444 (excerpts).

[1] [Martin John Spalding, *Miscellanea: Comprising Reviews, Lectures, and Essays on Historical, Theological, and Miscellaneous Subjects.* Ed.]

tagonism. The dominant sentiment of the country is non-Catholic, but the political and civil order is in accordance with Catholicity, and the duty of all Catholics is to place a generous confidence in the government, to love and cherish it as their own. Dr. Spalding never thinks of asking whether he is American in thought and feeling, for he lives Americanism, which is his natural, as Catholicity is his supernatural life. He tells us by his spirit and example that Catholics are an integral portion of the American people, and that we are to let the warm current of American life flow through our veins, to assume as a matter of course our position as free American citizens, and to study, understand, and loyally perform our duties as free-born Americans.

The lesson conveyed by the illustrious Bishop of Louisville, is opportune and important. Owing to the fact that the active Catholic population of the country is in great part made up of recent emigrants from various foreign nations, with habits, manners, usages, sentiments, affections, and traditions, different from those of the great body of the American people, an impression has been produced that Catholicity is here a foreign religion, or, in the main, only the religion of certain classes of foreigners, and that to be Catholic is to be un-American. Hence a war is excited against us in the name of American patriotism. On the other hand, a considerable number of Catholics confound the sentiments of a portion of the American people with the American political order itself. Finding a majority of the people hostile, or at best indifferent to Catholicity, they look upon the American civil and political order as at war with their religion, separate themselves in their feelings from it, and forget that the government is as much our government as it is that of non-Catholics, and that we are as responsible for its doings as any other class of citizens. They obey the laws, but do not love the American institutions, and look upon the government as an enemy to be distrusted, and whose actions are always to be construed in a hostile sense. They have no confidence in the American state, and believe neither in its will, nor in its ability to serve our holy religion. They do not admit that as Catholics they are under any obligations to it, and they regard themselves as at liberty to express their distrust of it, or to declaim against it as loudly and as fiercely as they please. Certainly these are not the majority, they are in fact only a feeble minority of the Catholic body; but they are numerous and clamorous enough to give the Know-Nothings a pretext for opposing us in the name of American patriotism. They do more harm than is commonly imagined. They check the free expression of the deep loyalty so natural to the Catholic heart, and obstruct by their coldness, their suspicions, and their lack of American sympathy, those efforts which Catholic charity and Catholic zeal, in obedience to the earnest exhortation of our Holy Father, Pius IX., would prompt for the conversion of those of our countrymen who are still in spiritual darkness, and sitting in the region and shadow of death. They exert an unhappy influence within and without, and are, if they did but know it, as uncatholic as unpatriotic in their spirit and tendency. . . .

It is but simple truth to assert that ours, at present, is the country towards which Catholics throughout the world should especially turn their hopes, and that it is the last country in the world which they should set down as hostile to the Church and her interests. The American people, in their national capacity, have never rejected the Catholic faith; as a government they have never made war on the Pope, have never cast off the authority of the Church. They have never, since their birth as a nation, performed one act of hostility to the Catholic religion, martyred or persecuted a single Catholic, and their first act on winning their independence, establishing their Federal government, and remodelling their State constitutions, was to repair the injustice of the mother country towards the Church, and to place Catholics, in their religion, on a footing of equality with Protestants. We as a nation are not guilty of the sin of persecution or apostasy. We have never dishonored or blasphemed the Spouse of the Lamb. We have done no injustice to Catholicity, and have repaired the injustice of the country from which we sprang. We have opened here an asylum for the oppressed Catholics of all lands, and given them the equal rights of American citizens. We are not under the curse pronounced against persecutors, apostates, and blasphemers. We are as a nation entitled to the gratitude and love of the Catholic heart throughout the world; and Catholics, especially American Catholics, should be prompt to acknowledge the generous and noble conduct thus far pursued by the American state. For noble and generous it was in a non-Catholic people in the last century, when all Europe was rising in rebellion against the Church, when fashion and literature had discarded Catholicity, when the Holy Father was soon to be dragged a prisoner from his throne by his apostate sons, and to die in exile, and when even Catholics themselves were willing to accept restrictions on their liberty, to proclaim the equality of Catholics, then too few to have any weight in the councils of the nation, and to open to them here an asylum alike from religious and civil tyranny. No nation on earth has ever, the circumstances considered, done a nobler act, one of greater service to the Church of God. And think you that that act is not registered in heaven? Think you that it will be suffered to go unrewarded? Think you ingratitude towards the American state, the denunciation of the American people, or alliance with their enemies on the part of Catholics, will be suffered to go unpunished? What is or can be baser on the part of Catholics than to curse the hand that has knocked off their fetters, and to place themselves in an attitude of hostility to their liberal benefactor? Are we not, indeed, to ascribe the late Know-Nothing movement as much to the forgetfulness, by some amongst us, of the generosity of the American people, or their refusal to recognize it, as to the hatred of Catholicity entertained by the more violent of the sects? And should we not regard that movement as an admonition from Heaven to be on our guard against disloyalty, and the encouragement of foreign or unpatriotic tendencies in any portion of our body? Every Catholic should love America, rejoice in her prosperity, labor for her true interests, and pray for her conversion. . . .

As a people we have very generally the conviction that Divine Providence has given us an important mission, and has chosen us to work out for the world a higher order of civilization than has hitherto obtained. We look upon ourselves as a providential people, as a people with a great destiny, and a destiny glorious to ourselves and beneficent to the world. This fact indicates generous instincts and a noble nature, and it will not be without its influence in kindling lofty aspirations in our bosoms, and urging us on in the path of a true and legitimate ambition. We believe ourselves the people of the future, and that belief itself will do much to make us so. There is more than meets the eye in the popular expression, "Manifest Destiny." We have a manifest destiny, and the world sees and confesses it, some with fear and some with hope; but it is not precisely that supposed by our journalists, or pretended by our filibusters,—although these filibusters may be unconsciously and unintentionally preparing the way for its fulfilment. It may be our manifest destiny to extend our government over the whole American continent, but that is in itself alone a small affair, and no worthy object of true American ambition. It is desirable only inasmuch as it benefits the new territories annexed to the Union, and secures our frontiers, and protects us in the peaceful elaboration and extension of the new social order of the world. The manifest destiny of this country is something far higher, nobler, and more spiritual,—the realization, we should say, of the Christian Ideal of Society for both the Old World and the New. Many things below this, and in themselves far enough from being in harmony with it, Divine Providence may permit, and compel to serve it, but these should never be the term of our ambition; they should never be encouraged by us,—should be carefully eschewed, or at best tolerated only as unavoidable evils for the time being.

This manifest destiny of our country, showing that Providence has great designs in our regard, that he has given us the most glorious mission ever given to any people, should attach us to our country, kindle in our hearts the fire of a true and holy patriotism, and make us proud to be Americans. Especially should it endear the country to every Catholic heart, and make every Catholic, whatever his race or native land, a genuine American patriot; for it is the realization of the Christian Ideal of Society, and the diffusion through all quarters of the globe, for all men, whatever their varieties of race and language, of that free, pure, lofty, and virile civilization which the Church loves, always favors, and has from the first labored to introduce, establish, and extend, but which, owing to the ignorance, barbarism, and superstitions retained, in spite of her most strenuous exertions, from pagan Rome and the barbarian invaders of the empire, she has never been able fully to realize in the Old World.

Let no one, because we thus speak, hastily conclude that we overlook the discrepancy which exists between the actual character of a large portion of our countrymen and the principles of our American order. We do no such thing. We do not blind or deceive ourselves as to the actual manners and morals of a large portion of the population of the country, nor as to the errors, the vices, the corruptions, which abound in both public and private life. Our readers know that we have for years dwelt on these, even to satiety, and that we have spared our countrymen none of their faults. We concede that our faults are numerous and grave, and that, if they are not corrected, they will compromise our mission. But without seeking in the least to disguise or to extenuate them, we still retain our hope in our country's future, for they spring from no inherent vice in our constitution. We see in them a ground for encouragement, rather than of discouragement; for they are either foreign to our real character, or are such as indicate a rich and generous nature, not yet grown effete. They grow out of the abuse of sound principles and grand qualities. They result, for the most part, from the fact that the bulk of our old American population have lost their confidence in Protestantism, without having acquired faith in Catholicity, and are therefore thrown back on nature alone, without the restraints or the aids of Christianity. But this need not surprise or alarm us. It was to be expected, and might have been foreseen. There is an inherent antagonism between our American order and Protestantism claiming to be a divinely revealed and an authoritative religion, and as Protestantism has not been able to retain life and vigor enough to suppress our American civilization, it has been forced to give way before it.

This inherent antagonism between our American political and social order and Protestantism claiming to be a supernatural religion, has not been sufficiently noted either by Protestants or Catholics. Protestant authors overlook it altogether, claim our American system as the creature of Protestantism, and contend that its natural enemy is Catholicity. Catholic writers have usually contented themselves with denying that the Church is incompatible with Republicanism or hostile to true liberty. That at the epoch of American colonization, absolute monarchy very generally obtained in Catholic Europe, and that it would have been very difficult to have found in a single Catholic state colonists that could or would have founded institutions like ours, I am willing to concede. That the early Anglo-American colonists were, with few exceptions, Protestants, and Protestants of the most rigid stamp, is a well-known fact, and cannot be denied. But in founding the American state they did not follow their Protestantism. They were bravely inconsequent, and "builded better than they knew." The liberty they loved, the political and social order they introduced and sustained, were only accidentally connected with their Protestant religion, as the absolutism of the sixteenth and seventeenth centuries was only accidentally connected with Catholicity. In both cases the connection was unnatural, and could subsist only for a time. Monarchy in Catholic countries for a period became absolute, through the weakness, servility, or cupidity of Catholics. It suppressed the popular franchises and very nearly enslaved the Church herself; but the hour of trial came, and monarchs found the altar, deprived of its freedom, could not sustain the throne. The people believing the Church, because she was the victim, was the ally of despotism, turned against her, and God permitted the horrors of the French Revolution to teach those who had tried to make religion subservient to arbitrary and oppressive government, that liberty is an instinct and a necessity of human nature, and that whoever tamely surrenders it to the monarch is faithless to his duty as a Catholic and as a man. The Catholics who identified their religion with the political *régime* so eloquently defended by the great Bossuet and impersonated in Louis the Fourteenth, were as much out in their reckoning as the Jacobins, who identified liberty with the rejection of the Gospel, the persecution of the Church, and the worship of the goddess of Reason. Protestant authors who identify our American order with Protestantism commit a like mistake, and wander equally far from the truth.

Our Protestant ancestors founded the American order, not on their Protestantism, but on the natural law, natural justice and equity as explained by the Church, long prior to the Protestant movement of Luther and his associates, and they only followed out those great principles of natural right, justice, and equality, which Catholic councils, doctors, and jurisconsults during fifteen hundred years had labored to render popular. The merit of our ancestors was, that in an age when Caesarism almost every where triumphed, and substituted the maxims of pagan Rome for those of natural justice, they remained faithful, and dared attempt to found a new world on an equitable basis. But in doing so they adopted a basis incompatible with the preservation of Protestantism as a religion. The basis they adopted was that of the natural law, natural reason, and justice; but this natural reason, this natural law, natural justice, Protestantism denies, and must deny; for it asserts the total depravity of human nature, declares all acts done in a state of nature to be sin, and denies nature to make way for grace, and reason to make way for faith. At least this is the character of all Evangelical Protestantism, especially of the form of Protestantism embraced by our ancestors, and indeed of all Protestantism that is not pure rationalism. Here, then, is a fundamental antagonism between Protestantism and American civilization, and it is clear to the dullest understanding that the one can exist and develop itself only at the expense of the other. Either Protestantism must get the upper hand and eliminate the American system, or the American system must get the upper hand and eliminate Protestantism. The latter is what has happened.

Moreover, Protestantism, basing itself on a subjective fact, private judgment or private illumination,—very good, and never to be spoken lightly of in its sphere,—has no bond of union, and necessarily, where not restrained by outward civil force, splits into innumerable sects and parties. If the civil order has, as with us, for its fundamental principle, its incompetency in spirituals, and is bound to recognize all these sects and parties as standing on a footing of perfect equality before the law, the people in all their political action are obliged to treat them all as alike sacred, and seeing no objective ground of preference among them, very naturally come to regard one sect as good as another, and then to treat them all with indifference, perhaps, with a superb indifference, to fall back on the reason and nature on which their political and social order is founded, and practically to place their politics above their religion. This is what has been the result. There are very few, comparatively speaking, of our non-Catholic countrymen, who really believe in any positive religion, and even the fiercest

Evangelicals have abandoned or are abandoning all dogmatic theology. The forms of religion, no doubt, are observed after a fashion, for the majority of our people, though without faith in any particular religion, have still a belief that there is a religion of some sort, and that it is essential to the health of the soul, and the preservation of the state,—a belief of great value as the foundation on which the Catholic is hereafter to build, but comparatively of little value in the practical conduct of life. The effect thus far of our institutions has been, as might have been foreseen, to bring the majority of our people back to simple nature, and to leave them without any positive religion. Their institutions have proved too strong for their Protestantism, and hence we see in the Know-Nothing movement, the politicians carrying it over the ministers.

Now it is not surprising that in this state, thrown back on nature alone, there should be the vice, crime, corruption, profligacy, which threaten so seriously our institutions; for nature alone is not sufficient, even under the best government and laws, to sustain the virtue and integrity of a people. But this need not discourage us, for this sad state of things is only temporary, and will last only during the period of transition from a religion incompatible with our order of civilization, to another which accepts, consecrates, and sustains it. Many of our non-Catholics feel this, and hence they demand with some earnestness the Church of the Future, and not without a good degree of confidence as well as hope, that it will come. They are right. Protestantism is outgrown, and has fallen into the past. One needs not to be a prophet, or the son of a prophet, to foretell that it is not to rule the future. But the Church of the Future exists, and already exists in our country. Between it and our institutions there is no incompatibility, for Catholicity accepts, nay, asserts the natural law on which our American order is founded. The Church does not recognize the Protestant doctrine of total depravity. She does not deny nature in favor of grace, nor reason in favor of faith. She presupposes nature, asserts natural justice and equity, and maintains the rights of reason. She comes not to destroy the natural, but to fulfil—to purify, elevate, direct, and invigorate it. That is, she comes to give us precisely the help we need, and as our country is the future hope of the world, so is Catholicity the future hope of our country; and it is through Catholicity bringing the supernatural to the aid of the natural, that the present evils which afflict us are to be removed, and the country is to be enabled to perform its civilizing mission for the world.

In speaking of a new order of civilization we do not suppose a new development of Christian doctrine, or any modification of the Church herself. Christian doctrine and the Church were perfect in the beginning, and as they are divine, or represent the Divinity in human affairs, they are unalterable. We are not arguing either for something in advance of Christianity as it has been professed in every age from the Apostles downward, or for a modification or adaptation of the Church to a new order of things. We believe in progress *by* Christianity, not in it; by the Catholic Church, not in it; and the new order of civilization we speak of is not a new Christianity, but a new progress in society, which places it as civilized society in more perfect harmony with Christianity, with Catholicity or the Church. The foundations of this civilized society have been cast broad and deep in America by our Protestant ancestors, following not their Protestantism, but natural reason and justice as explained by Catholic doctors. The sentiments, the manners, the morals of the people, are very far from being in perfect harmony with Catholicity; but the *civility,* the political and social order, what we call the institutions of the country, being founded on natural right and equity, are in perfect accordance with it; for Catholicity republishes the law of nature, —natural right and equity,—and gives it new and higher sanctions. All that is needed to realize in practice the Ideal of Christian society is to bring the sentiments, manners, and morals of the people into harmony with American institutions, or the American political and social order. This Protestantism could not do, and therefore has been obliged to give way; this reason and nature alone,—on which our non-Catholics are thrown back,—cannot do, for reason and nature alone, without the assistance of the supernatural providence of God, are, as the history of the world proves, practically as impotent to sustain true and genuine civilization as they are to save the soul or secure the bliss of eternal life; but this Catholicity, which has the promise of the life that now is and of that which is to come, can do, and will do, if permitted; and in doing it, will effect, without undergoing any change or modification in herself, a new and higher civilization than the world has hitherto known.

We know there are persons who pretend that Christianity culminated in the thirteenth century, and imagine that the reign of antichrist is commencing and the end of the world is not far off. But we are not of their number. Even in the days of the Apostles some thought the end of the world was near at hand; when the Barbarians overturned the Roman Empire of the West, some thought the end of the world had come; again, in the year 1000, there was a prevalent persuasion in many countries of Europe that the world would end with that year; and indeed, in every age since the founding of the Christian Church, individuals have been persuaded that that day and hour of which no man knoweth, not even the Son, but the Father only, was about to strike; but we do not think that Christianity has yet more than fairly begun her mission. Only a small portion of mankind has become Christian, and in no nation has society as yet been thoroughly Christianized. As yet Christ has nowhere made his religion as universal and all-pervading as was false religion in the old Pagan world. His victory over Satan is not yet, save in principle, completely won. Why should not his religion become as general in society, pervade as thoroughly all departments of public and private life, as Gentilism did in the old Roman world? Have we not the promise that the end should not come till the Gospel of the kingdom had been preached to all nations? And can it be said to have been preached to those nations in which it has been at best barely announced to a few individuals, and which it has never converted or annexed to the kingdom of Christ? What right have we to say, as some of us do, that a nation which has once thrown off the faith has never been reconverted? Instances are not wanting in which the same people has been converted several times over. If no nation can be recovered to the faith that has once thrown it off, why does the Church sanction prayers for the conversion of England? Why does she authorize missions and prayers for the conversion of heretics? What right have we to limit the mercy of God? While there is life there is hope, and there is no nation or individual on earth that we have the right to assert cannot be converted to God. Let us beware of fatalism, and especially beware of seeking to find in God's providence an excuse for our indolence, our absence of missionary zeal, and our neglect of duty. The nation of the Goths was originally converted from paganism to Christianity by Catholic Missionaries; it fell into the Arian heresy to please the Emperor Valens, and to gain his assistance against its enemies; but the Goths were subsequently reconverted to Catholicity. The world lapsed into heresy or infidelity may be recovered, and will be so, when Catholics learn to live in accordance with the religion they profess.

We dismiss all the counsels to indolence or despair drawn from the supposed impossibility of regaining nations once lost, or from the supposed approaching end of the world. We know not when the world will end, but our business is to live as if it might end to-morrow, and as if it were not to end for a thousand ages to come. We are to look at the work God gives us to do to-day, and to do it with all our might. Catholicity is here to perfect our civilization, and to make ours the land of the future. But Catholicity does not work irrespective of human agents. She works as a help, as an assistance, a power, an influence, but not as an irresistible force. She works on free-will and conscience, gives the power to do, but does not do the work without the co-operation of free agents. She does not take a people, will they, nill they, and by main force raise them to virtue or civilization. The Church deals with the world as she finds it. She takes things as they are, and seeks to remedy what is amiss, not by violence, not by revolutionary measures, but by Christian charity. She finds Cæsarism established; she makes no direct war on it; but seeks to infuse into the heart of the monarch the sense of justice and humanity, to impress on his mind and conscience that he is himself under law, and must one day render an account of his conduct, that he holds his power as a trust, and that the king is not "in reigning, but in reigning justly." She finds the broad distinction of rich and poor, the few gorged with superfluous wealth, and the many suffering for the want of the necessaries of life. She does not excite the latter against the former, nor demand an agrarian law or an equal division of property; but consoles the poor with the assurance, that if they bear their poverty with resignation, for Christ's sake, theirs is the kingdom of heaven, and admonishes the rich that they are but stewards, and that what they have more than they need for themselves belongs to the poor, and that if they withhold it, they must answer for their lack of charity and their abuse of their stewardship. She finds masters and slaves; she does not command the relation to cease; but she teaches the slave to render cheerful service to his master for Christ's sake, and the master that the slave is his brother, a man like himself, for whom Christ has died, a soul with all the rights and dignity of a human soul, and therefore that he must treat him with justice and humanity, respecting in him the image of God and the rights of conscience. Her mission is not to revolutionize states and empires, and by force to introduce and sustain even the political and social order that best harmonizes with her own principles. The political and social changes needed she leaves the people, inspired by her teaching, and following the dictates of justice and prudence, to introduce for themselves, as they see proper, or as circumstances permit.

. . . . The American mission is not restricted in its intent or in its results to a narrow and exclusive nationality. The legitimacy of American nationality is in the fact that it is not exclusive, that it is founded on the principles of natural justice and equity, and is as broad as the human race. It embraces and absorbs all distinctive nationalities, and moulds all into one family in the natural order, as Catholicity does in the supernatural. We must recognize no cliques at home or abroad, and neither divide nor suffer ourselves to be divided by the accidents of birth or race. Are we not all men and Catholics? Is not the American mission in the interest of all Catholics and of all men? Then why should not foreign-born as well as native-born Catholics labor for its realization? We appeal alike to all Catholics, wherever born, whencesoever they come, or whatever their national peculiarities. All who have American hearts, love the American mission, and are willing to devote themselves to the cause of religion and the advancement of civilization, are in our sense of the word Americans. They are our countrymen, our fellow-citizens, and we will have no other rivalry with them than that of seeing who will best adorn our religion and serve American civilization.

If there is division between native-born and foreign-born Catholic citizens, we wash our hands of it. It is not we who have made it, and it shall never be we who make it. If we have complained of some foreign-born Catholics, it has not been because they were foreign-born, but because they held themselves aloof from the natural-born citizens, regarded themselves as pertaining to a separate nationality, and felt that they must conduct themselves as foreigners rather than as men who are to "the manner born." It has been because they have attempted to force their narrow and insular nationality upon our continental hearts, and seemed unable to feel themselves our equals unless they were recognized as our masters, and permitted to lord it over us. But these of whom we have complained, though making much noise, are only a small part, and that neither the more intelligent nor the more virtuous part of our foreign-born population. The more numerous, intelligent, and respectable portion of foreign-born Catholics, those who have some stamina, and are not afraid of being lost in the crowd unless distinguished by a foreign badge, or labelled with some un-American nationality, are as American in their convictions, intentions, and affections, as those born on the soil, and not seldom even more so. No native-born American would for one moment dream of excluding these from the American army, or of realizing the American mission without their coöperation.

We insist, indeed, on the duty of all Catholic citizens, whether natural born or naturalized, to be, or to make themselves, thorough-going Americans; but to be Americans is to understand and love American institutions, to understand and love the American mission, to understand and love American liberty, to understand and love American principles and interests, and to use with a free and manly spirit the advantages of American citizenship to advance the cause of religion and civilization. Those who will not be Americans in this sense, we disown, we hold to be "outside barbarians," and not within the pale of the American order. They have no business here, and the sooner they leave us the better. They have no lot or part in our work, no part or lot in the American mission. But whoever does his best to be in this sense an American, whoever is devoted to true American interests, and is fired with a noble ambition to promote the glory of America, we embrace as a countryman, wherever he was born or reared; we hold him to be our fellow-laborer, and to him we make our appeal. To all such we say, here is a glorious work to be done, in which you may perform a glorious part,—a work which you will be doing, whenever preparing yourselves for your part as Catholics, as citizens, or as men,—to which every noble sentiment you cherish, every generous sacrifice you make, every disinterested act you perform, every prayer you breathe even in secret, every living word you drop from your lips, will contribute. The field is as broad as your activity, the work as high as your ambition, as great as your thought. You may, if you will, add a nation, a nation destined to rule the future, to your Church, and to the world a new civilization. You may bring faith to the doubting, hope to the desponding, and peace to the troubled,—send freedom to the down-trodden millions of the Old World, redeem long-oppressed continents, and fill with joy the broken-hearted friends of the human race. Let each one work in his own sphere, according to his ability and opportunity, but always with a view to the greater glory of God, and with a firm reliance on Him for support and ultimate success.

3 Anton H. Walburg

THE THREAT OF AMERICANIZATION OF THE IMMIGRANT

Many Catholics denied that the ready absorption of Catholic immigrants into the Anglo-American population would facilitate its conversion to Catholicism. On the contrary, they alleged that Americanization corrupted the immigrant's morals and destroyed his faith. Although there were countless variations on this theme, no writer stated it more strongly and urbanely than Anton H. Walburg, the scholarly pastor of St. Augustine's Church in Cincinnati. The influence of the Anglo-Americans on the immigrants, in Father Walburg's view, was only a little less demoralizing than that of the white man on the Indian. The Anglo-American nationality, he claimed, was boastful and arrogant, intolerant and fanatical, and above all, preoccupied with material wealth, in the pursuit of which it trampled on every cardinal virtue and practiced every form of refined wickedness. Moreover, the American nationality was so puffed up with spiritual pride, so steeped in materialism, that it was impervious to the spirit and doctrines of the Catholic religion. The eagerness with which so many Catholic immigrants had sought entrance into the American nationality had deprived the Catholic Church of two-thirds of its rightful membership.

Walburg admitted that the Catholic Church had scored a remarkable record, but in his opinion, the progress achieved was not due to Americanization, but to the effort made to keep alive the languages and nationalities of the foreign elements. Although, for example, in New York, where the Americanization policy was followed, the German Catholic losses were frightfully heavy, in Cincinnati, where foreign nationalities were encouraged, amazing progress had occurred. Walburg urged all foreign groups, through annual conventions and other means, to cultivate as fully and as long as possible the language and customs of their respective homelands. In the end, all foreign-born Catholics would enter the irresistible American nationality, but wisdom dictated that the entry be delayed until the immigrants gained more numerical strength and more experience in maintaining Catholicism under New World conditions. Then, the fond hope of converting all America to Catholicism might possibly be realized.

In the decade after Walburg's writings appeared, the battle between the Americanizers and their opponents was fought to a standstill. Each side veered from its original position, finally agreeing that slow, steady Americanization was as desirable as it was inevitable. The policy was to be effected through the employment of American-born priests able to speak in the appropriate foreign tongue, and the provision, when necessary, of an ample and varied social service.

CHAPTER IV

THE AMERICAN NATIONALITY

"Now the broad shield complete, the artist crowned
With his last hand, and poured the ocean round;
In living silver seemed the waves to roll,
And beat the buckler's verge and bound the whole."

"Westward the course of empire takes its way,
The four first acts already past;
A fifth shall close the drama of the day,—
Time's noblest offspring is the last."

With regard to Americanism we make a distinction. There is a true and a false Americanism. True Americanism consists in the promotion of the peace, the happiness, and the prosperity of the people, and in the advancement of the public good and the general welfare of the country. As virtue is the principle, and the chief support of a Republic, true Americanism aids and encourages whatever promotes the growth of virtue and morality. It makes no distinction between natives and foreigners, considering all born free and equal, all entitled to the enjoyment of life, liberty, and happiness, and extends the hand of welcome to all nations. There is an analogy between true Americanism and the Catholic Church. She, too, invites all to enter her fold, is established for all nations and all times,

---

Anton H. Walburg, *The Question of Nationality in its Relation to the Catholic Church in the United States* (Cincinnati, 1889), pp. 39–46, 48–51, 55–57, 60–62.

and makes no distinction of color, rank, condition, or nationality. And, since the Catholic religion promotes virtue, piety, and morality, true Americanism must desire the growth and spread of the Catholic Church.

False Americanism is a spirit of pride and self-conceit, and looks with contempt upon other nationalities. It is a boasting, arrogant spirit. It glories in the biggest rivers, the tallest trees, the grandest scenery, and considers this country superior to every other country on the face of the globe. It is a pharisaical, hypocritical spirit, putting on the garb of virtue when all is hollowness and rottenness within. It is a spirit of infidelity and materialism. False Americanism is mammon worship. It adores the golden calf and is directed to the accumulation of wealth with an ardor which is unquenchable and with an energy which never tires. The eagerness for wealth is paramount and controls every other feeling. The ideal set before every American youth is money. Money is not only needful, but is the one thing needful. Money is a power everywhere, but here it is the supreme power. Abroad, there is the nobility, the pride of ancestry. This is vanity artificial and empty, yet it is not so degrading as money. Abroad, eminent worth counts for something. But here, we acknowledge only one god, and his name is Mammon. Who is the distinguished man in any village, town, city, or metropolis? Is it the learned man, the skilled mechanic, the creative artist, the great lawyer? No! the preference is given to the richest man. No matter how he acquired his wealth, no matter how miserly he is, he is the observed, the pointed out, the envied one. All render him homage. The eminent lawyer, the wise physician, the man of learning, show him deference and attention even to the point of servility. This is the great evil of false Americanism, the curse of our society. It is demoralizing us. The hunger and the thirst after money consume like a raging fire all warmer sympathies, all better feelings of our nature. It dwarfs all higher aspirations. What are moral excellence, culture, character, manhood, when money-bags outweigh them all? How can better sentiments be impressed upon the children, when all about them teach them that these are of no value without money? Hence the startling dishonesty in the race for riches. Hence the bribery of officers, the purchase of office, the corruption and jobbery, the general demoralization, that threaten our institutions.

And with its vaunted independence, this spurious Americanism, in its ostentatious display of wealth, stoops to Foreignism, copies European fashions, imports a Parisian cook, and considers itself fortunate to exchange its wealth for the musty title of some needy descendant of the nobility.

In Europe, a man enjoys his competence; but here, no one has enough. No laborer is satisfied with his wages; no millionaire, however colossal his fortune, ceases in his greed for more. From the first dawn of manhood to the evening of old age, the gold fever continues to increase in strength and violence, till death puts an end to the raging malady.

The American nationality, properly so-called, is the Anglo-Saxon or the Anglo-American nationality, the descendants of early settlers who came from England. These can justly claim the honorable distinction of being called the American nationality. We were, in the beginning, substantially an English people. The first settlers in this country, the Pilgrim Fathers, were English. They had a long and bloody struggle to maintain against the Indians and suffered untold privations and hardships in effecting a firm and permanent foothold in this country. Notwithstanding all obstacles, the first colonies improved, and by dint of perseverance, courage, and industry, became very prosperous. They resisted British tyranny and oppression. They severed their allegiance to the British crown, declared the United Colonies to be free, independent, and sovereign states, at the same time mutually pledging to each other for the support of this declaration, their lives, their fortunes, and their sacred honor, and thus created the American nation. They founded the government of the United States, framed the Federal Constitution, and the Anglo-American nationality and have been the directing and ruling power in this country till the present time. All real American history centers in and clusters around them. Although the Irish, the German, and other nationalities, proved to be valuable accessions to our population, yet our forefathers were English, and the rank and position we hold among nations is due to the Anglo-American nationality, which is therefore entitled to the honor and glory of being called the American nationality.

Notwithstanding this pre-eminence, and the fact that whatever is honorable in our history and worthy of esteem in our institutions, is owing chiefly to our forefathers, who, it is often said, builded better than they knew, nevertheless the American nationality, when tried by the test of true Americanism will in many respects be found wanting. It is often the hotbed of fanaticism, intolerance, and radical, ultra views on matters of politics and religion. All the vagaries of spiritualism, Mormonism, free-loveism, prohibition, infidelity, and materialism, generally breed in the American nationality. Here, also, we find dissimulation and hypocrisy. While the Irishman will get drunk and engage in an open street fight, and the German drink his beer in a public beer-garden, the American, pretending to be a total abstainer, takes his strong drink secretly and sleeps it off on a sofa or in a club-room. Who are the trusted employes, the public officers, that enjoyed the unlimited confidence of the people, and turned out to be hypocrites, impostors, and betrayers of trusts? As a rule they are not Irish or Germans, but Americans. Who are the devotees at the shrine of mammon? Who compose the syndicates, trusts, corporations, pools, and those huge monopolies that reach their tentacles over the nation, grinding down the poor and fattening in immense wealth? They are not Germans or Irish, but Americans. Who are the wild and reckless bank speculators, the forgers, the gamblers, and the defaulting officials? They are not Irish or

German, but Americans. Read the list of the refugees to Canada and you will find it made up of American names. We meet here also all species of refined wickedness. The educated villain, the expert burglar, the cool, calculating, deliberate criminal, generally belongs to the American nationality. Where the foreigners are corrupt they have in a great measure been corrupted by the example of Americans. A republic that is not based upon morality and religion, where virtue is depressed, is ripe for an ignoble grave.

The Anglo-Saxon nationality has always been in England and in this country the bulwark of Protestantism and the mainstay of the enemies of the faith. It is so puffed up with spiritual pride, so steeped in materialism, that it is callous, and impervious to the spirit and the doctrines of the Catholic religion. It is true there are eminent converts in England and a few in this country; but they have no followers; the bulk of the people are as remote as ever from entering the Church.

Where are the doctors, the lawyers, the statesmen, the politicians, the bankers, the capitalists, the mechanics, the laborers, the farmers, the manufacturers, of the Anglo-Saxon nationality who have embraced the faith? Probably not as many of these can be found in the whole body of the Catholic Church as there are Catholics in the smallest diocese. Religion seems to make no impression upon them; they are as hostile as ever to the Church, and, though they perhaps wish it well as doing its share to keep the turbulent foreign element in check, they have not the remotest idea of becoming Catholics themselves. And now we are asked to assimilate with this element, to adopt its usages, customs, feelings, and manners. That can not but prove detrimental to the Church. Are we going to lead our simple, straight-forward, honest Germans and Irish into this whirlpool of American life, this element wedded to this world, bent upon riches, upon political distinction, where their consciences will be stifled, their better sentiments trampled under foot?

But, it will be said, religion will keep them from rushing to this end, will sustain them in the path of virtue and rectitude. Nonsense! Denationalization is demoralization. It degrades and debases human nature. A foreigner who loses his nationality is in danger of losing his faith and character. When the German immigrant, on arriving in this country, seeks to throw aside his nationality and to become "quite English you know", the first word he learns is generally a curse, and the rowdy element is his preference to the sterling qualities of the Puritans. A German aping American customs and manners is, in his walk, talk, and appearance, in most cases, an object of ridicule and contempt. Like as the Indians in coming into contact with the whites adopted the vices rather than the virtues of the latter, so the effort to Americanize the foreigner will prove deteriorating. It has been observed, that the most noisy, disorderly, unruly class are the native, would-be American, Germans, and often, for that matter, too, the young Catholic Germans.

A man, in giving up his nationality, shows a lack of character. No educated German of any standing will deny his nationality, and such men as Carl Schurz and J. B. Stallo, who have gained national reputation, also remain intensely German. But it may be said, the Irish lost their language without losing their faith. The Irish, however, did not lose their nationality, and they were simply robbed of their language, they did not willingly abandon it. There are men here in Cincinnati who make the Irish language a special study, and an Irish sermon was preached here lately with marked success. Let but an effort be made to revive the Irish language, and it will be hailed with satisfaction by a large number of Irish in the United States. . . .

The Church has made marvelous progress in this country. This has, however, not been brought about by Americanizing the heterogeneous elements of our incoming population, but by sustaining and keeping alive the languages and the nationalities of the foreign elements. Though not so flattering to our vanity it might prove more profitable to us to examine the losses we have sustained instead of rejoicing over the gains we have seemingly made. Gen. Von Steinwehr, an excellent statistician, gives the following estimates of the various nationalities for the year 1870:

Anglo Saxons, 8,340,000; Irish, 10,255,000; Germans, 8,-930,000; Italian and French, 1,016,000; Dutch and Scandinavians, 728,000; other nationalities, 4,236,000. Total population in 1870, 33,595,000. The present population of the United States is estimated to be 60,000,000.

In the same proportion, as given above for 1870, we would have at present about 20,000,000 Irish-born and 16,000,000 German-born population.

Now there ought to be about 18,000,000 Irish Catholics, about one-third of the Germans, say nearly, 5,000,000, Americans, Poles, Italians, etc, 2,000,000,—total, 25,000,000.

According to Hoffmann's Directory the number of Catholics for the present year, 1889, is 8,157,676.

This shows a loss of two-thirds of the Catholic population to the faith. The loss of this immense number can, in a great measure, be attributed to the fact that they have been Americanized, that they have lost their nationality, and with their nationality their religion. According to a census gathered by Father Enzleberger, we have 1,500,000 German Catholics, and our loss from the above estimate is therefore 3,500,000.

The comparative census for Cincinnati in the years 1846, 1850, and 1880, is as follows:

	CHURCHES		POPULATION	
	Irish	*German*	*Irish*	*German*
1846	4	3	12,117	25,912
1850	5	7	13,616	30,628
1880	9	21	15,077	46,157

This shows an astonishing increase in the number of German churches and the German Catholic population, which is owing to the fact that the Germans have retained their language and nationality, even though many of them have joined the English-speaking congregations.

A similar result is observed in the German Protestant churches. In the year 1842, a certain Frederick Rammelsberg maintained that the German language would soon die out in this country and that everyone should speak English. He established an English-speaking congregation among the German Lutherans. And what was the result? While his church scarcely survives, the German-speaking Lutheran churches have increased from five at that time to twenty-five at the present time.

From the flourishing condition of the German Catholics in Cincinnati, let us look to New York, which has the third largest German population of any city in the world, ranking next to Hamburg and Berlin. Of the population of New York, which is 1,206,299, about one-third, or 400,000, are Germans, and of these, about 125,000 ought to be Catholics. Now there are eleven German churches in New York with a probable membership of 30,000, which shows the frightful loss of three-fourths of the German Catholic population.

Dr. William H. Egle, Historian of Central Pennsylvania, in his "Notes and Queries," gives numerous instances where Irish Catholic families,—even whole Catholic settlements,—forsook their faith, and became Methodists, Baptists, Presbyterians, etc. Further investigation would show that they Americanized, that they were no longer Irish, and therefore no longer Catholics.

The annual immigration of German Catholics is about 50,000, of Irish Catholics about the same. 100,000 Italians arrived here in the last 18 months, 100,000 French Canadians are expected in the Eastern States this season, and a large number of Poles, Hungarians, and Catholics of other nationalities come every year. These all have still the embers of faith smoldering in their hearts which might be fanned into active life by nursing their nationality. A nucleus of the more wealthy and educated classes in each nationality could be formed, and annual conventions held in different cities where they would hear addresses in their native language, sing their native songs, keep up their old associations, and in other ways keep alive their nationality. The interest that the Church would thus take in them would not be without reward. While the American nationality is said to be deteriorating, we would, by retaining a hold upon the foreign nationalities who are multiplying, as with the blessing that rested upon the children of Israel in Egypt, in the course of time possess the land. These conventions or gatherings would certainly be productive of good results. Nor is there any danger of interference in diocesan regulations, for no king or potentate is so sure of the respect and obedience of his subjects, as is a Catholic bishop, provided they are good Catholics. . . .

The condition of the French Catholics in the United States, as compared with the gratifying results of the Canadian policy, is not very encouraging. Except in New Orleans, where French sermons are still preached in the Cathedral, they are mostly infidels or merely nominal Catholics. That overflowing French population which is inundating our Eastern States from Canada, is in danger of losing its faith when it becomes Americanized. The religious question in Canada, however, is of easy solution. It was a fortunate thing that the Catholics were all French, and belonged to one and the same nationality, and could therefore be easily held together and maintain themselves. They were thus kept from marriages and associations with heretics and unbelievers. If they had been divided, if, for instance, the Irish, German, and Polish nationalities had been represented among them, each nationality might and probably would have struggled for the mastery, and hence rivalry and bitter feeling would have been generated. The result probably would have been that each faction in turn would have yielded to English influence, agreed to drop their own distinctive nationality and to enter the English camp.

The School Committee of Haverhill, Massachusetts, some time ago discovered a school taught by the Franciscan Fathers and attended almost exclusively by children of the French Canadians, who are now swarming in the manufacturing towns of New England. The Committee discovered that the general grade of instruction was far below the general average of the State schools; that some of the teachers did not understand English; that the teaching was largely in French; and, finally, that the history of Canada, not that of the United States, was being taught. On the strength of these defects, and, fortified by a statute to do so, the Committee closed the school for general worthlessness.

Thus far they had not exceeded their powers. A little later they found that some of the late pupils were attending no school and were thus violating the truant law. Their parents were arraigned for the offense of neglecting the schooling of their children, and the whole subject was passed upon by the Police Court of the city. The trial resulted in the acquittal of the parents, solely through the vagueness of one of the provisions of law, intended to be very definite and peremptory.

Now these Franciscan Fathers must have come to the conclusion, after their experience, that Americanism is a delicate tender plant, since it could not endure the teaching of a few children in the French language and in Canadian history, especially as, in view of the prospective annexation of Canada, the history of that country would also be part of United States history, they were really anticipating and ahead of the times. And when they reflected that millions of immigrants, ignorant of United States history and of the English language, were naturalized, that the elective franchise and full-fledged citizenship was given to 4,000,000 negroes—this mass of ignorance—they must have suspected that other motives were at the bottom than the pretended danger to our institutions, and that the School Committee, profiting by the experience of Great Britain in Canada, had determined to nip French education in the bud.

The French Canadians in the Eastern States met with little encouragement and assistance from their brethren in the faith, who agree with the School Committee that United States history and the English language must be taught. It cannot but lessen their attachment to the Church and the country, to be deprived, in this boasted land of freedom, of the liberty they enjoy in Canada, and thus to be prevented by legal process, from following their own plans in educating their children and preserving them in the faith.

From the foregoing we can conclude that religion and nationality go hand in hand, that religion sustains nationality, and nationality is an aid to religion. We have seen, that where the Irish, German, and French were isolated, their language and nationality encouraged and fostered, they were kept true to the faith, and that they generally lost their faith in proportion as they Americanized. . . .

It is doubtful whether the object of the originators and supporters of the movement to strengthen and perpetuate the German nationality in the Church in this country can be attained. This nationality has deserved well of the Church, dotted the land with churches, schools, and institutions, and is therefore justified in making lawful efforts to prolong its life and maintain its existence. The Germans stand second to none as loyal, faithful children of the Church, and it seems unjust to reprove them for showing signs of vitality and arousing their energies in the great cause for which they have so successfully labored. When, in the course of time, the German nationality should come to an end, and when its days are numbered by the years that are past, may the children of the German pioneers, who follow them in another, the American nationality, cherish and preserve as the richest legacy, the spiritual title-deed of their holy religion.

No foreign nationality can permanently maintain itself in this country. It is, of course, natural that immigrants should wish to find again their fatherland in this land of their adoption, but they will Americanize in spite of themselves! The

American nationality will finally prevail. It assimilates the children of foreigners, and is strengthened by contributions from foreign sources. Foreign nationalities will be absorbed by it and flow in the current of American life.

However, the transition from one nationality to another, is always a dangerous process, and it will not do to hasten it and to force foreigners to Americanize. For the present we should remember that the American nationality counts for little or nothing in the American Church, and if it is ever to be converted, it must be done by the clergy and population already Catholics. The most efficient portion of our Catholic body are of foreign birth and training, and will be for some time to come. However we may work for non-Catholics, we must carry with us the sympathies and affections of the Catholic body. This body is composed of various nationalities with peculiarities of languages, habits, and prejudices. If these are opposed, and the national sensitiveness wounded, they may become irritated and indifferent, and lose their affection for the Church. We cannot move much in advance of the public sentiment of our own body. We must hold a tight rein, check the impatience to Americanize, and, though there may be some wrangling among conflicting nationalities, if we move slowly we will finally land in the American nationality with the Catholic body under full control and faithful to the Church.

The Church is not trammeled by nationalities and is adapted to all nations. She does not take part in the idiosyncracies, in the antagonism and war, of races. All are placed on a footing of equality, and a Hindoo or a Hottentot can be as good a Catholic as a Frenchman or an Italian. The various nationalities, with their differences of race, color, manners, habits, and usages, form a beautiful mosaic in her glorious temple.

The American nation is yet to be added as another rich gem in her crown. It is true we are one hundred years old. But what is one hundred years in the life of a nation, or the life of the Church? We are still laying the foundation of national greatness and prosperity; the Church is still sowing the seed that is to penetrate the living mass of American society, and subject it to the truth and sanctity of the Gospel. Let us then continue to sow, it may be in tribulation and sorrow, that future generations may reap in joy a rich and abundant harvest.

> "And all the clouds that lowered upon our house
> In the deep bosom of the ocean buried."

4 George Dering Wolff

THE DANGER OF "SOCIALISTIC COMMUNISM"

Inasmuch as most Catholics were wage-earners, urban industrial growth brought about a ratio of increase in Catholic population greater than that of any other religious denomination. But many, virtually all, Catholic thinkers feared that irreligious socialist thought and propaganda would likely alienate a large part of its working-class membership. This danger was early and thoroughly explored by journalist George Dering Wolff, who had entered the Catholic Church from the German Reformed ministry through the influence of the "Mercersburg Theology," a High Church movement among German-American Calvinists. In the pages of the erudite journal, the American Catholic Quarterly Review, *of which he was a founder, Wolff analyzed the industrial situation in Pennsylvania coal mining and railroading in the wake of the Panic of 1873–1878.*

The workers took violent exception to a policy of the great corporations—wage-cutting during depression periods in order to maintain the accustomed level of profits. Only the influence of the Catholic Church over many of the workers kept socialistic communism in check. Industrial strife, Wolff argued, was the inevitable outcome of the socialistic outlook which had come to dominate American thought in the years since the intellectual and humanitarian revival of the 1830's and 1840's. On public school education with its endless emphasis on the equality and perfectibility of all men, Wolff placed chief responsibility for the spread of socialistic communism in the United States.

Only as men regained faith in Providential circumstance, he thought, could they hope to check the socialist menace. Change in the outward arrangements of society would avail little.

When thirty years ago the storm of revolution swept through Europe, overturning thrones and shaking to their foundations the most firmly established governments, its movements were watched in this country in a like spirit to that in which meteorologists note the course of intertropical cyclones, and study the atmospheric and the glacial phenomena reported by explorers of polar regions. It was not supposed that the time should ever come when the people of the United States would have to confront socialistic movements as portentous facts actually existing in their own midst.

True, there had been previous to 1848, and there have been since that year memorable in European history, sporadic efforts to exemplify practically the Arcadian paradise which socialistic philosophers confidently predict will follow universal acquiescence in their notions. Attempts were made at Brook Farm and some other points to actualize the ideas of socialism under their most refined form. . . .

George Dering Wolff, "Socialistic Communism in the United States," *American Catholic Quarterly Review,* III (July 1878), 522–562 (excerpt).

The experiment was made under conditions the most favorable to success, if it had been possible for it to succeed under any conditions. It was made by men of the highest moral character and honesty of purpose, possessed of, or able to command, ample pecuniary means for procuring whatever they deemed necessary to success, men of the highest order of intelligence and intellectual and social culture. Yet it quickly "came to grief." The amiable philanthropists who committed themselves to this sublimated socialistic scheme soon tired of the realities that confronted them in their attempts to carry their ideas into practical effect. The poet, who sang in mellifluous verse the delights of strolling at early dawn over dewy meads, found it quite another thing to wade at break of day through dank grass to his farm work. The metaphysician soon became disgusted with his task of feeding pigs, and the chemist of sweating over a churn in vain efforts to make "the butter come."

Then another disappointment, they soon found, was in store for them. The few Hodges and Pollies whom they induced to unite with them in forming their socialistic Arcadia, could not be persuaded to join with any hearty appreciation in the intellectual exercises with which toil on the farm and work in the house were intermingled. They could not listen, or, if they did, it was with unmistakable signs of weariness, to the philosophic discourses and the poetic rhapsodies with which it was sought to furnish relaxation and refined pleasure after the day's labors had ended. Their thoughts remained obstinately wedded to their horses and ploughs, their milk-pans, their brushes and brooms; or, if they went beyond, they were fixed upon subjects entirely too utilitarian and commonplace to form any bond of union or sympathy with their more intellectual associates.

Personal piques, too, personal likes and dislikes, jealousy, and wrangling invaded this philosopher's paradise. Every one had some fault to find either with the underlying ideas of the scheme or with the manner in which those ideas were attempted to be practically carried out. The enterprise could not be made self-supporting—a patent, practical condemnation of the whole experiment—and it was soon abandoned in disgust.

. . . .The members of the Brook Farm Association "had individually," as Mr. Hawthorne says, "found one thing or another to quarrel with in their past lives." Yet, strange to say, or rather not at all strange, for this seems to be a common method with humanitarian philosophers and reformers, they never thought that the right thing for them to do would be first to set themselves right; they at once conceived the idea of "improving the world." Human nature, according to their theory, was in itself all that it needed to be; all that was required was to remove certain obstacles external to itself, obstacles that stood in the way of its peaceful, harmonious culture and development. That done, "a higher life" could at once be realized than that which is "governed by the false and cruel principles on which human society has all along been based."

At bottom, therefore, notwithstanding all the æsthetic features of the scheme, and the amiable spirit which seemingly animated it, it aimed at the destruction of society as it has always existed, and at its total reconstruction or, rather, recreation. The Brook Farm experiment was therefore in perfect harmony with the fundamental idea of socialism, which is that human society is, and ever and always has been, based on principles that are "false and cruel;" that the evil which is in the world, and the cause of its misery, has its seat not in the heart of man, but is generated by the structure of society; that society, therefore, must be overturned from its lowest foundation, that it is the mission of socialism to do this, and then to re-create society, and so to organize it that the existence of evil and its invariable consequence and concomitant, misery, shall be impossible.

It was not our purpose at the outset to examine in detail the Brook Farm undertaking. We intended simply referring to it as one among many socialistic attempts in the United States to realize, under one form or another, "a higher mode of life" than is supposed to be possible under the existing structure of society. Contrary to this intention we have dwelt upon it at greater length, because it was one of the best in form and intention, if not the best, that has been made; it was conceived in the most amiable and philanthropic spirit, and it was most free from the ideas of wild revolution and positive hatred of Christianity, that characterize the general socialistic movement.

Many other attempts to realize socialistic principles have been made in the United States. . . .

The various attempts to exemplify socialism in the United States, to which we have referred, were seemingly without effect upon the public mind. They, at most, numbered but a few thousand persons, separated into little communities, not counting in any instance more than two or three hundred members, and in many instances not more than twenty or thirty. They involved most divergent and contradictory ideas, and in no case commended themselves by their practical working to the better sense of the American people. Yet it would be a mistake to suppose that the ideas which their founders and supporters put forth did not take hold upon the American mind. Their leading notion, that society was all wrong, and that if it could be set right and reconstructed, the antagonisms which afflict mankind, and the miseries growing out of those antagonisms, would all disappear, made numerous converts. Protestantism, protesting against what had been one of its dominating errors, the total depravity and corruption of human nature, and the cold, stern, rigid Calvinism which is the logical result of this error, swung over to the opposite extreme, denying the positive existence of sin as an inherent element in fallen humanity, and the need of divine grace to regenerate it. The Protestants of the United States fell speedily into this error, even where they professedly held to their Calvinistic creeds. In New England this was especially the case, and New England was the centre of intellectual light to the whole United States. Humanitarianism became the prevalent religion. The development of humanity by means of its own powers and capacities was the grand idea. The causes of evil were all external to our nature. "Excelsior" was the cry. With more perfect social arrangements man would improve, advance, develop, mount upwards, and soar into the empyream. . . .

The practical efforts to actualize these ideas, however, made no progress. The associations that were formed to carry them out would not work smoothly. The sweet, perfect harmony which it was predicted they would bring about was never realized within the experimental associations. On the contrary they became the very embodiment of *dis*harmony; and, in some instances, ended in a regular *row* among the members. The *Tribune* itself, the great exponent of the new gospel, could not be conducted on the principles it advocated. The Tribune Association, organized as a step towards the practical realization of those principles, became in fact simply a joint stock company. Fanny Wright's intended demonstration of the feasibility of socialistic ideas on a cotton plantation cultivated by negroes who were to work out their own emancipation by earning the amounts paid to their previous masters, ended in an utter failure. And in every form and shape in which it was attempted to exemplify practically socialistic communism, the attempt proved entirely unsuccessful.

Then the cry was raised, "Our ideas are all right, but our efforts to realize them practically are premature. Men are not yet prepared to adopt them; they have been too long accustomed to the old ways and habits of society to abandon them in a day; those habits have become a second nature to them. We must prepare mankind for the radical change in their traditionary ideas, in their habits and modes of life, in their entire character, which the adoption of our system requires. Men must be educated out of their old life, and into the new life of communism. The present generation is intractable. We must look to the next generation, take hold of the young, enlighten and educate them, before socialism can obtain universal acceptance among mankind. We must have one common system of education for the children of all classes, the rich and the poor, the high and the low."

The common-school system was thus to be made the grand instrumentality for the propagation of socialistic ideas,[1] and it has been energetically and effectively employed in that way. Socialism has not been professedly taught in our public schools, yet its fundamental ideas have been inculcated in them, and their practical influence has told powerfully in the diffusion of those ideas.

It needs but a glance through the favorite text-books for exercises in reading and declamation in our common schools, particularly those in use some fifteen and twenty years ago, for we are glad to say that they have improved somewhat in late years, to convince any one of the entire truth of the charge we here bring against the common school system. Those text-books were filled with extracts, beautiful in style, subtle and eloquent in argument, from the writings of New England rationalists and transcendentalists, in which man himself was set forth as the supreme object of worship, the ideal of human life. The highest acme of human aspiration was the development of human nature, not in the Christian sense, but in one that entirely ignored Christianity. The future life, if not denied, was referred to only in so vague and shadowy a way as to suggest the thought that it was nothing more after all than a beautiful dream, the creation of imagination, projecting into the future mere fancies suggested by the realities of the present life.

The true purpose of our existence was itself, and that purpose was to be attained by the perfect unfolding of our natural ca-

[1] [Long footnote quotation from Orestes A. Brownson omitted. Ed.]

pacities and powers. For that, humanity was self-sufficient. Thus all need of divine grace, of divine assistance, was put out of view. No limits to human capability were recognized. The capacities and powers of our nature were susceptible of infinite development. The circumstances that surrounded the individual, growing out of his social position and surroundings, often interposed obstacles to that development. Therefore they must be persistently fought with and surmounted.

The idea that there was anything providential in the individual's circumstances and position was ignored, and the profound Christian philosophy of St. Paul: "I have learned in whatsoever state I am therewith to be content," had no place in this common-school literature. Had any one advocated it as a rule of life he would have very quickly acquired the reputation of being behind the age, a reactionist. In fact, our common-school literature and the whole traditionary influence that surrounds the pupils while attending those schools, inculcate the principle not of content but of constant discontent. There is no recognition of providential circumstances as pointing out or directing our course in life; the idea inculcated is that the individual must keep up a constant fight with his surroundings and circumstances. Unlimited aspiration, inordinate ambition to rise above his condition, unrestrained longings for what he does not possess, is the practical lesson constantly taught in our public schools. Social status, social surroundings and circumstances are the great obstacle to the realization of these longings and ambitious desires; therefore society comes to be looked upon not as the state in which by the laws of his own being as well as the teachings of divine revelation the individual is intended to exist, but as the great obstacle to his progress in realizing his destiny.

Then, too, the natural equality of all men is another doctrine that enters largely into our common-school literature. Inequality, it is often more than hinted, is the result of social maladjustments and partiality, society lavishing its favors on some, imposing burdens on others. These causes of inequality should not exist; they must be removed. In other words, society must be destroyed and then reconstructed, re-created.

Thus our common-school system has been sowing the seeds of socialistic communism in the minds of the young. The leading ideas of its literature are in perfect harmony, though expressed in polished phrase and with subtle circumlocution, with those of Mr. Justus Schwab and other outspoken revolutionists of the reddest hue, who employ plainer and ruder words. That these ideas have taken root and borne fruit after their own kind, any one may easily convince himself by glancing over the essays and addresses delivered by graduates of the public-school system at their exhibitions and commencements; and not unfrequently too in the addresses which the principals of our public normal and high schools from time to time deliver.

But though the seeds of socialism were thus, in years not long past, scattered broadcast upon a soil prepared to receive them, and though in the form of speculative ideas they found ready entrance into the minds of a great portion of the people of the United States, yet they lay seemingly dormant. The conditions favorable to their vigorous germination and appearance above the surface were not present. Most persons who held them as parts of their philosophy, felt that, however desirable it might be in the distant future, when the United States should have become overcrowded with a population struggling in fierce competition for the bare necessaries of life, to "organize labor," and re-create society after the fashion proposed, yet that that time had not quite arrived. The greater portion of our country was still unoccupied. Even in our longest-settled States forests were to be felled and farms opened out. The exhaustless soil of prairies had scarcely felt the plough. Our coal and iron ore had scarcely been touched by the miner's pick. Cities were springing up as if by magic, each requiring thousands of mechanics and laborers to build it. Our manufactories were scant of operatives. There was work for every one who wanted work, and at good wages. As for capital, the universal feeling was that we had not enough; that more capital in this country meant more work, and higher pay, and better times for workingmen. Thus, the general feeling was, with those who had unconsciously become converts to one or another of the ideas of the socialistic philosophy, that however true socialism might be in theory, the time had not as yet come to carry it out in practice in these United States.

The anti-slavery excitement then took almost exclusive possession of the public mind, and that was followed by the war to which it gave rise, between our Northern and Southern States. After the war followed a short period of abnormal industrial activity to replace the waste of property which it caused, whilst the destruction of human life which it involved had lessened the number of workmen, and kept up the prices that had been paid for labor during the continuance of hostilities. The high wages received by workingmen and laborers led them into a more expensive, and in some instances an extravagent mode of life; it created artificial wants, and accustomed many to regard the gratification of those wants as an actual necessity. The disbanding of our immense armies threw upon the country vast numbers of persons who had become demoralized, who had lost the habit of regular industry, and could not brook a life of humble toil and economy.

Meanwhile French and German infidels have been flocking into the United States, deeply imbued with revolutionary socialism.

It is the fashion among our newspapers to attribute the sudden exhibition of socialistic communism to these foreigners. It is unquestionably true that to them is due its open expression in its wildest, rudest form; but they have simply enunciated the logical practical consequences of the socialistic theory. The seeds of socialism have long been germinating and taking root in our soil; and now that pinching poverty, actual destitution, and want of the barest necessities of life have come upon so many thousands of workingmen, the fierce fire of passion engendered by this deplorable condition, has only hastened the growth of what was heretofore beneath the surface, and caused it to spring more rapidly into visible open existence.

The people of the United States may well look at home for the most potent causes of the prevalence of socialist notions among themselves. Our whole popular political philosophy is permeated with these ideas. Our common-school literature, our non-Catholic pulpit discourses not unfrequently, and our Fourth of July harrangues, almost without exception, set forth in unqualified terms the equality of all men, not their equality before God, but their unconditioned, absolute, natural equality as regards this world, and the self-sufficiency of human nature in the exercise of its natural capacities, unassisted by divine grace, and independent of any divinely established relations, to determine and work out its destiny. Our legislatures and courts are actively and most effectively engaged in the same bad work. The easy dissolution of the marriage tie, the constant effort to rule out of legislatures and courts all recognition of religion and of divine authority as the basis of human government, and other acts and features which characterize the whole movement of society in the United States, may be pointed to as furnishing ample ground for the charge we here make. It must be remembered that ideas which seem harmless when put forth in merely philosophic form and as speculative theories, and which, as held by persons in comfortable circumstances entirely satisfied with their present social status, are entertained only as dreams which they never expect will be realized, nevertheless gravitate downwards. They gradually reach others less speculative and more practical than themselves, less contented with their social position and condition. They at last find lodgment in the minds of the idle, the lazy, the rude, the dishonest, the reckless, the scheming adventurer and demagogue, of those who are suffering for want of the bare necessities of existence, who have nothing to lose, and hope they may possibly gain, from whatever changes or convulsions society may undergo; and in their minds these ideas take their logical, practical form in the cry, "Bread or blood," "Down with capitalists, down with the laws that protect them;" in the form of open defiance of government and indiscriminate destruction of property.

Our leading newspapers are energetically engaged in belittling the socialistic movement, and endeavoring to check its manifestations by ridicule and intimidation. They are telling the men who are its ostensible leaders, who, after all, are nothing more than adventurers less shrewd and more reckless than others who keep themselves in the background, that the people are prepared to put down by force attacks upon property and attempts to institute a reign of license in the United States. Yet the very ideas these newspapers constantly enunciate, hostile to religion, recognizing no divine basis of human society, no source of authority in law and government other than the mutual consent of men, no divine sanctions for individual property, for the marriage relation, for parental authority and for filial obedience—these ideas which form the staple of our newspaper and periodical literature, of our most popular political essay writers and orators, lie at the very root of socialism, and foster the growth of socialistic notions. Thus almost the entire influence and power of American literature is, consciously or unconsciously, on the side of the socialistic movement.

The movement has become an actually existing fact, and a fact, too, of more dire portent than is commonly believed. We had evidences of this last summer in the reluctance of our State troops to put down the lawless men that took possession of our railroads, and the still more lawless persons that stood at their backs and supported them. The difficulty in promptly bringing the law to bear, did not arise merely, or mainly, as our newspapers would have us suppose, from want of discipline, or habits of military obedience on the part of our citizen soldiers, or from inability to quickly concentrate troops at points where their presence was required. It was caused chiefly, we are well convinced, by a feeling of sympathy with the rioters, though not with the destructive means and way in which the rioters sought to accomplish their purposes. . . .

[Wolff next summarizes fifteen "propositions" of "socialistic communism". In his refutation he emphasizes the impracticable historic examples of the failures of Communism. He dwells at greater length on the contemporary strife between labor and capital, leading to a conclusion that "the abuse of power by capitalists consequently is chronic; that by workingmen is occasional and temporary." Ed.]

This brings us to the concluding question of our protracted discussion: Is there no remedy for this perpetual abuse of power? no remedy for the antagonisms that exist among men, and which here in the United States, as well as in other countries, are showing themselves more plainly and more portentously every day in the existing strife between those who have money and those who have it not?

If there is not, the strife will continue, and with every day's continuance will become fiercer. The subjection of the laboring classes by the moneyed men will become more confirmed and more galling. They will be pressed down into even deeper depths than as yet they have been. A chronic condition of dependency, a serfdom, a real slavery ten times worse in its moral effects than ever negro slavery was, will be their lot. For money is powerful, and nowhere more so than in the United States. This is attempted to be denied, or rather concealed, for denial of so patent a fact is preposterously silly. Capitalists in this country more than anywhere else on the earth hold the reins of power; and our supreme and all-absorbing idolatry of material prosperity strengthens their hands.

If the process going on in our midst continues, it will soon bring us to a condition of things like that of Greece and Rome in ancient heathen times, or far worse, culminating in fierce intestine social insurrections, in which the scenes of the French Revolution of '93 will be re-enacted, until society in self-defence will turn against the struggling masses, and pitilessly bring them again into subjection. May this danger plainly impending over us be averted. That it may be, we must apply an effectual remedy to the state of things now existing in our midst.

We have seen that the schemes of socialists are impracticable, and that even if they were practicable, they could only be realized by the destruction of individual liberty, of the established institutions of government, of all that is comprehended in the term civilization, and, last and above all, of religion.

The ultimate objects which socialists desire to reach are many of them good: the limiting of human selfishness; the wresting of power from hands who misuse and abuse it; the alleviating of misery. These purposes no one can object to. The misfortune is that socialists adopt the very means which will defeat the objects they professedly have in view; their sin is that they oppose the only means by which men can be regenerated and delivered from their miseries.

So, again, human government, conducted merely with a view to temporal ends, recognizing no other basis or source of authority than the mere will of the governed, furnishes no remedy. For, whether the government acts through an absolute monarch, a king holding his crown under a constitution, or a president and congress elected by the votes of a whole people, it expresses, after all, unless it acknowledges higher sanctions than man can give it, nothing else than the wishes, and carries into effect nothing else than the purposes, of those who happen to possess and exercise the greatest amount of power in the nation, whatever be the shape that power assumes, and by whatever means it be exercised, be it in the form of an army holding down the people with bayonets and Krupp guns, or in the form of capitalists controlling legislators and executive offices, or of both combined. A republican form of government is plainly no guarantee against this; for in no form of government can legislators and executive officers be so easily manipulated by those who possess influence and power, as under a republic.

Where, then, is the remedy to be found? Or have mankind been left to a condition of constant enmity, culminating from time to time in intestine strife and fierce bloody conflicts between those whose interests, gauged only by regard for temporal ends, continually antagonize?

The remedy, if there is one, cannot possibly consist in any alterations or changes in the industrial, social, or political relations of men, leaving their natures unchanged. The cause of the trouble is not external to human nature; consequently an external remedy will be powerless. The cause and source of the trouble is in the nature of man; it is sin which produces selfishness. That is the cause of the difficulty, and to that the remedy must be applied. Is there a remedy for this, one that can limit and restrain it, and finally expel it?

There is a remedy, though men too often forget it, and when urged upon their attention, too generally ignore it, despise it, deny it. It is the Christian religion. Not the vague, formless, unreal thing popularly called Christianity, to which men have given the name, but which is utterly destitute of the power which Christianity does possess and does exercise; not the so-called Christianity whose vaunted merit is that it is creedless, that it has no positive fixed dogmas; in other words, that it holds forth no defined truths to challenge the acceptance of men. Such a Christianity, if such were Christianity, could have no power or influence. It would itself be dependent, as is in fact the form of religion that thus boasts itself, entirely on the mere pleasure of the individual, whether he will be ruled by it or not. It is more unsubstantial than a shadow, and has no real power to restrain men from following out the selfish bent of their sinful nature to any extent. Before the fire of passion, in the heat of desire to effect a purpose, it disappears as flax in the flame.

The Christianity to which we refer is the religion which Christ established in His Church, which is carried to the ends of the earth, and perpetuated by His Church, which has the guarantee of His promise, and is the fulfilment of that promise, to be with His Church "all days unto the consummation of the world," which has creeds and dogmas embodying and proclaiming fixed, unchangeable, positive, definite truths, and which urges upon men the acceptance of those truths, and the carrying out of those truths into actual practice in their lives, under the sanctions of divine authority, and under the alternative of their salvation or damnation throughout eternity.

Is it demanded that we point out the manner in which the Christian religion provides a remedy for the antagonisms to which we have adverted, the answer is plain and simple, though to bring forward all the proofs and illustrations of its effectual power that might be adduced, would require volumes.

1. Christianity in the Church takes hold of the poor. To them the Gospel is especially preached. It limits and regulates their desire for temporal comfort. It teaches them resignation, submission to Providence, not as a vague powerless sentiment, but as a positive duty. It keeps constantly in their minds the thought that Providence determines their lot on earth, and that though it be an humble and a hard one, under a temporal point of view, yet it is ordered in divine wisdom, and if they accept it in the spirit of filial faith and submission, it will prove to have been ordered in infinite mercy. Christianity diverts their attention from their weary life in this world, its privations, its suffering; teaches them that if they offer up those privations, that suffering in union with the sacrifice upon the cross, they will be recompensed a hundred fold hereafter; that life on earth is short, but the future life is eternal; that existence here has higher objects than what one shall eat and wear; that its real

end is to prepare us for enjoying the Beatific Vision in the kingdom of heaven; that hatred, envy, jealousy, are mortal sins; that we must love even those who are severe and unjust to us; that vengeance belongs not to us but to God. The Church ever holds up the truth that those who accept poverty and bear it in the right spirit, from love for God, will be blessed more abundantly than all others; that our divine Lord, though possessor of the glories of heaven, and Creator and Ruler of the Universe, yet for our sakes became poor, was found in the form of a servant and had nowhere to lay His head.

These truths the Church enforces by precept and example. They are not empty words with her; and the poor know and feel it. She exemplifies her teachings in the daily life of her Religious, and of saintly men and women, who in every country on earth, strip themselves of worldly honors, of high station in society of wealth and all its temporal advantages, and adopt instead a life of self-abnegation, of utter poverty, humility, constant labor.

Thus these truths are brought home to the poor, not in the manner in which persons outside the Church sentimentalize and philosophize about them, but in their living reality and power; and thus the fire of wicked passions which toil, suffering, and privation engender is quenched, useless longings and ambitious desires for a condition beyond reach are repressed, and vain strugglings after what cannot be attained are suppressed. Contentment and cheerfulness, acquiescence in what is recognized as providential circumstances drive out discontent, jealousy, hatred, and the other wicked passions to which discontent and inordinate ambition give rise.

2. The Church lays hold of the wealthy in like manner. It enforces upon them the truth that power under every form is accompanied with temptations to misuse and abuse it. That this is the case with riches; so peculiarly the case that our divine Lord expressly declared that it was difficult for the rich to enter the kingdom of heaven; that while the acquiring and possession

of money is not wrong, yet the *"love"* of it is *"the root of all evil;"* that the wealth of the rich is not their own, but is given to them in trust, and in order that they may employ it as stewards employ the possessions of their master.

These lessons, too, the Church enforces, not with words destitute of significance, but accompanied with countless examples. She holds up before the wealthy the roll of canonized saints, of those who are honored by the Church in heaven and on earth as the most faithful followers of Christ and the greatest benefactors of men, because they stripped themselves of wealth, and when rich became poor; because they loved the poor, denied themselves for the poor, toiled for the poor, devoted their whole lives to the poor. Thus the Church continually teaches the wealthy to "consider the poor," to employ the power which wealth gives, not to grind them down into deeper poverty, but to be just and generous and charitable to them; to regard them not with contempt or indifference, but to look to their interests, to sympathize with them, help them, love them.

3. The Church, where allowed to exert her proper influence, in like manner takes hold of government. She teaches rulers that the power lodged in their hands is from above, and is not to be exercised arbitrarily, or in the spirit of partiality, for the elevation of some and the depression of others, but for all without respect of persons; that though the object of government is immediately for the protection of men in their temporal pursuits, yet that mediately and ultimately it is for the advancement of the glory of God, through the elevation and moral and religious improvement of men. The Church reminds rulers that human society and all its institutions rest upon divine principles and sanctions, which dare not be disregarded; and that in the observance of them is to be found the only safeguard of society, the only surety for its peaceful existence, for the stability of government, and for its fulfilling its proper purpose.

The questions may be asked, Why the Church has not done all this? If the Church has this power, how comes it that universal concord and peace do not reign among men? that injustice and oppression have any existence? The answer is plain and simple. It is because men oppose, hate, and resist the Church: because men pervert relations designed to help and elevate them into means for depraving themselves, for promoting selfishness, abusing power, engendering wicked passions; because they pervert government, which has been clothed with authority in order that it might suppress evil and be a protection and defence to the Church, into a most potent engine of resistance to her action. Men are free agents, and as God will not, cannot, against their own free-will, lift them out of the "bondage of corruption," the sinfulness of their own nature, which is the source and cause of all their misery, neither can the Church, unless they co-operate with her by consenting to the truth, and corresponding with the grace which she continually holds out to them.

Wherever the Church's influence reaches, and to the full extent to which men allow that influence to operate upon them, she does the beneficent work which we have cursorily described. Look at what she achieved during the Middle Ages, the manner in which she broke down barriers that divided mankind, and instituted cordial relations between those whose hands had been at each other's throats. Peoples who were fierce savages were transformed into civilized nations, their rude and cruel customs one after another abolished; the bondman, the badge of whose condition was an iron ring around his neck, whom his master might slay at will as he would a dog, emancipated and elevated to the condition of a free man and to the relation of a Christian brother; the harshness and severity of feudalism, that system of "blood and iron," first ameliorated and then utterly abolished; the fetters of the captive broken off, and the chains of the slave gradually worn away by the gentle attrition of charity, until they dropped off unknown almost by himself and his master. The wealthy and the powerful, the noble and the king, were made to feel that Christ was the LORD of lords and the KING of kings; that the highest object to which their power and their wealth could be and should be devoted, was the greater glory of God through the amelioration of society, the suppression of wickedness, the relief of the suffering. The poor were made to feel that poverty and a lowly condition of life were not absolute evils, that they might readily be turned to such good account that they would become blessings; that they should not envy the rich, nor hate those of higher station than themselves, nor resist those who exercised lawful authority, but love them, honor them, obey them.

What the Church has done for society, for men of all ranks and conditions of life in past time, she may and can do now if men will allow her free course of action. She will do it, provided men in the exercise of that free-will with which God has endowed them, do not wickedly oppose her. She *is* doing it, and to an extent that many even of her friends do not perceive nor understand, while her enemies deny it. When the latter do acknowledge it, they acknowledge it with a view to misrepresenting it, and that they may turn it into a justification of their hatred and opposition.

5 T. Wharton Collens

A CHRISTIAN COMMUNIST'S QUEST FOR THE "EDEN OF LABOR"

Having in such large numbers experienced the hardships and miseries of poverty, Catholics as a group had no desire to make this condition a religious way of life. But the few who did found an able theorist in the Louisiana lawyer and judge, T. Wharton Collens, who urged Catholics to embrace voluntary poverty as an aid to Christian perfection and the only sound basis for the solution of the labor problem. He proposed that, after the example of the early Christians and the "reductions" of the Jesuit Paraguay Missions, Catholic married couples, vowed to poverty and obedience, live together in community not only for their mutual improvement but also—and mainly —for the production of surplus wealth for the poor in general, irrespective of race or creed. Collens directed a tirade of wrath against communistic ("communitarian" is the current term) communities of the worldly type, be they infidel or secular, on the alleged ground that they were self-centered and selfish, interested only in the welfare of their own members. He thought, too, that many less radical remedies, such as trade unionism and labor legislation, lacked range and strong motivation. Only Christian communism could wipe out destitution and secure satisfactory Catholic growth.

Collens' social thought mirrored his life experience (1812–1879). From early manhood interested in reform, he had devoted much attention to the defense and criticism of social movements. In his earlier life he had subscribed to the communitarian views of Robert Dale Owen and Charles Fourier. On losing confidence in secular remedies and becoming a devout Roman Catholic in later life, he expressed his associational perfectionism in terms of Christian communism. He also put his thought into the phraseology of political economy. The ideal economic system, as he explained in Equity *and* Labor Balance, *journals of the Christian Labor Union of Boston, which he helped to found and support, and in his imaginative book,* The Eden of Labor, or the Christian Utopia *(1876), would be one in which labor cost or the average labor time expended on commodities and services determined their exchangeable value.*

Collens pioneered in the rise of the post-Civil War social gospel. More recently, his central idea—voluntary poverty—has occupied a similar position in the Catholic Worker movement and its affiliates. This is not to suggest that these groups were influenced by or even acquainted with Collens and his ideology.

It would be vain obduracy on the part of a Catholic to close his eyes to the deep and wide-spread clamor of the voices, great and small, that are now discussing "social science," and proposing solutions of the "labor question." These matters, in every imaginable manner, are obtruding themselves upon the attention of the manufacturer, politician, and legislator; and must soon command that of the farmer and merchant; and by and by, even the solicitude of the church. Indeed, we should not say "by and by;" for already, while the world is agitated by the strikes and the labor congresses, while the parliament of Great Britain, through its committees, is carrying on the minutest investigations of the eight-hour and higher wages movements, our holy father at Rome has pronounced public allocutions against *socialism.*

. . . The contest is now raging in every direction, not only on the question of *Who* shall take care of the poor, but *How* they shall be cared for, and *What* are the rights and remedies they are entitled to?

The origin and object of the controversy is agreed on by every one. The dissent is upon what shall be the principle and the method according to which the desired relief shall be gained. Infidelity, under the name of socialism, would have it done without God, on grounds of naked natural equity or rational justice. It would act independently of religion, Chris-

---

T. Wharton Collens, "Views of the Labor Movement," *Catholic World,* X (March 1870), 784–798 (excerpts).

tian faith and Christian charity. It would push the church aside, and presume to finish in another name the work our Lord Jesus Christ commenced more than eighteen centuries ago.

Hence, unless one prefers to hide his head in the sand, with the vain notion that the immense flood roaring and rising round us does not exist, because he does not see or hear it, it is time for him, if he is a Catholic, to consider from the point of view of his faith what stand he should take, and what is his duty toward the poor and toward society in the crisis the struggles of laborers for power in the state will soon bring on in this country of universal suffrage. It is not merely a question of giving and distributing alms and assistance that is to be solved, but great problems of social organization and rights are put before us. We must decide, (1) what there is in the labor movement that religion approves and encourages; (2) what there is in it religion condemns; and (3) what it contains that is merely temporal or indifferent to the church.

It certainly has something of each of these three elements.

In any way the matter is approached it presents a religious as well as a political question to be solved, a religious as well as a political duty to be performed; for it involves the rights of the poor on us, and our duty to them *as Christians.* What if the demands of the laborers were just, and that, notwithstanding this, we should oppose them? While socialism, as a whole, should be opposed, it is admitted that the present poor-laws and charitable institutions are insufficient, and some more thorough system of relief must be adopted. The working-men insist that this shall be done, and for this purpose claim to elect those who are to govern the state, and make the laws. Religion cannot neglect to interfere without leaving multitudes of souls of the poor to be seduced into the naturalism, sensualism, and infidelity the socialists purpose as the consummation of the movement. Nor does the question of our religious duty toward the poor in this crisis cease to demand an answer upon a mere refutation of socialistic theories. It does not suffice to show that the Utopias of Babœuf, Owen, Cabet, St. Simon, Fourier, and Noyes are abominable, but the just principle of economic distribution must be found and applied under penalty of eternal anarchy. The negation of one medicine as unfit does not dispense from finding another that will cure, when, indeed, a disease exists; and we take it for granted that no Christian who has heard or read of the successive burdens and hardships of the poor operatives and peasants of Europe will say that there is no disease to be cured, or who is heartless enough to abandon the case on the ground that it is incurable. Certain it is that the hard-working poor will not concede that they suffer no injustice—will not cease to demand permanent relief; and if religion ignores, denies, or abandons the sick, they will resort to philosophical quacks, who will lead them to their moral and religious ruin. Worse; are foreseen by his holiness Pius IX., they will repeat the apostasy of the French revolution, and with the same sacrilegious and despotic spirit, but with more cunning and method, prohibit religion itself.

Their main lever in accomplishing this will be the labor movement, if they succeed in controlling it. Hence, what *we* shall do with it, is a question of vital importance.

At the outset the Catholic must give a negative answer to all propositions and plans for disturbing *vested rights* or violently resisting the laws, or lawful authority, under pretence of establishing justice. This proposition needs no argument to show its wisdom and conformity with divine law.

Next, the Catholic will oppose agrarianism, which is the *forcible* taking of all property to distribute it in *equal* portions among the people. This is forced equality; a very different thing from associated labor.

Finally, the Catholic will also even oppose association when she would organize corruption and irreligion under the guise of philanthropy and fraternity.

No doubt these are the features of the labor movement his holiness Pius IX. designated under the general title of socialism when, on the 17th of June last, in his allocution to the cardinals, he said:

> "Thus, to-day we see on one side revolution, bringing in her train THAT *socialism* which repudiates morals and religion and denies God himself; while on the other side we behold the faithful and true, who calmly and firmly expect that good principles will resume their salutary empire, and that the merciful designs of Deity will be realized."

The plain duty of lopping off socialism, and of casting it aside, being performed, there remains, (1) reform through just legislation; (2) legal contracts for mutual relief; (3) co-operation or association of work-fellows; and (4) the realization of perfect Christian charity.

We think we could prove that all the purely secular remedies—such as cooperation, mutuality, and the like—are delusive, and in themselves inadequate; but it is not our present purpose to examine this branch of the subject. A volume would not suffice. It is only necessary to remark, *en passant,* that there is nothing in the organizations included under the general name of coöperation contrary to religion; but at the same time there is nothing in coöperation that springs from religion; it is a mere economic contrivance. It is not a *religious* solution of the problem of social distress; and since we have argued that religion must be able to give a temporal as well as a spiritual answer to the complaints of the poor, we will pass by all minor and transitional questions, and consider only what the earthly Utopia of faith and charity would be; and inquire what method might now be adopted to inaugurate the practical reign of Christian fellowship, in which the laborer would necessarily reap the reward he is justly entitled to.

Yes, religion has also its earthly new Eden, that will give full satisfaction to the over-burdened and underpaid workman. Let us try to picture it in our imagination, in order to judge from a study of the ideal whether it would be possible to make it a reality. To do this, we should begin by stating the principles on which this ideal should be founded; and we should also mention such historical facts as may serve to enlighten us on the practical application of those principles.

The Scriptures and the church teach that there are degrees of merit, beginning with that minimum of righteousness sufficient to save us from damnation. From that point the degrees rise one above the other till they ascend beyond the regions of *prohibition* and *precept* to the realms of *counsel* and *perfection.* There is the man who is willing to obey God so far only as to refrain from violating the ten commandments. Then there are those who, besides this, give alms and do other works of mercy for Christ's sake; and finally, there are those who, seeking for the Holy Spirit, labor for and do works necessary to attain *perfection.*

Excuse this positing of doctrines familiar to us all. They are stated as parts of our argument.

Among the immediate disciples of Christ there were not only shepherds, mechanics, fishermen, physicians, and farmers; but also tradesmen, and even lawyers and soldiers. Some were rich, and nevertheless were regarded as having merited heaven. Zaccheus is an instance of this class; to please God, he gave as much as half of his goods to the poor. He went only halfway in perfection. It is clear that if people generally refrained from committing any of the offences mentioned in the ten commandments, justice would reign, and therefore many social grievances of the worst kind would disappear. True, this would not suffice to give affirmative happiness, but it would be the negation of positive moral woe. Works of mercy are necessary to dry all tears; and charity has the genial warmth that makes the smile bloom again on the countenances of those who have wept. Now, charity is first pity and sympathy; and then it is sacrifice. It has beautiful demonstrations of love in words and demeanor, but it fully realizes itself in sacrifices; and these sacrifices are of every extent. Some are small but cheerfully offered, as the widow's mite. Some are proportionately large, as the apportionment Zaccheus made; but some are unlimited, as the triple vow of poverty, chastity, and obedience of the regular clergy.

Jesus said to him, *If* thou wilt be PERFECT, go, sell what thou hast, and give to the poor; and thou shalt have treasure in heaven: and come, and follow me. (Matt. xix. 21.) Blessed are ye (willingly) poor, for yours is the kingdom of God. (Luke vi. 20; Matt. v. 3). Where thy treasure is, there is thy heart also. (Matt. vi. 21.) You cannot serve God and Mammon. (Matt. vi. 24.) He who hath left house, etc., . . for my sake and for the gospel, . . shall . . receive a hundred times as much, *now in this time;* . . and in the world to come life everlasting. (Mark x. 29. 30.)

From these and numerous similar speeches of our Lord, and from a spirit of gratitude, his disciples were inspired with the desire of attaining perfection. Those who remained steadfast notwithstanding the crucifixion, or rather because of the crucifixion, gathered around the apostles and pronounced the vow of poverty. "All they that believed were together, and had all things in common." (Acts ii. 44.)

This is the first instance of *real* communism that ever occurred in the world, and it was the logical product of the teachings of our Lord and his apostles. That it was the logical product, could be easily shown by argument on the language of Scripture; but it suffices that it was approved by Peter and the other apostles. They knew best; and, indeed, gave example by becoming members of the community. That it was the first instance of real communism, we assert without forgetting the Essenes, the Lacedemonians, and the like, from whose systems it is easy to distinguish the apostolic community of goods.

And here we ask particular attention to the grand and glorious trait which distinguishes Christian *reductionism** from so-

* We make the word from the name the Jesuit fathers gave to their establishments in Paraguay. They called them *Reductions*.

cialism, agrarianism, coöperation, and all other worldly plans of association.

The object of worldly association is merely to benefit its own members in secular welfare. It has no outflowing. It is a partnership for distribution of products, profits, pleasure, or knowledge among the members, contributors, or coöperators only. Thus it was with the Essenes. The principle and purpose of their community of goods was *not* the extension of its benefits to the neighbor. They had and enjoyed their wealth among themselves exclusively. Their associations were just as selfish as any individual; the only difference being that in one case it is a single person and in the other a company that is selfish, and clannishly withholds its own from the rest of the world. They did not practise true charity, that charity which goes beyond home. The communication of the Essenes began and *ended* at home. It did not, therefore, resemble the Christian charity described by St. Paul; they had no idea of it. Modern society has many examples of participation like that of the Essenes. The free-masons and other mutual aid societies are of this kind.

Of course, reciprocity or coöperation existed in the apostolic community; but this was only incidental and secondary. One of the main elements of charity is its universality, and therefore it extends far beyond mere mutuality. It gives—it is not a contract of exchange or insurance. Associations of the Christian kind do not limit themselves to themselves. Besides mutual help, they give help to any and all men. Indeed, most frequently Christian charitable institutions entirely lose sight of any mutuality. The members, as it were, forget themselves individually, think of no restitution, and have their whole attention and sentiments, with those of the company, fixed beyond their own wants and upon the alleviation of the burdens and pains of the poor in general. Every reader knows of many illustrations of this difference. We need not mention particular cases.

Indeed, the very nature of Christian charity precludes the limiting of benefits to the members of a society. Therefore, the moment any company resolves to contribute or work for the purpose of a division among its own members exclusively, it can have no claim to be acting on the principle of charity. Charity ignores any such distinction; she tends toward all men indiscriminately; she feels for them all alike, as brethren and neighbors; she sympathizes with all; she is spontaneous, she is expansive, she radiates. She loves; and her love overflows: then runs in diverging rills to every door.

Association recommends itself to the Christian from other considerations than those of economy, security against want, multiplication of productions, and increase of wealth. He enters into association to increase his power with God, to attract grace, to set up a common defence against sin, to have the strength of union against Satan, to have more time and opportunity to do good, and to do it more efficiently. The fundamental motive of the Christian throughout is love of God and man, piety and mercy. It is the spirit of sacrifice; it is actuated by no prospect of self-advantage; or, at worst, it expects personal advantage only through and under the universal good. This was the absolute self-abnegation and exuberance of love out of which the apostolic community spontaneously sprang.

It is an error to suppose that the primitive Christians abandoned their community of things upon their first dispersion or flight from persecution. (Acts viii. 1.) It continued long afterward, as we learn from the fathers of the church. Justin Martyr, (*Apol.* c. 2,) describing Christian society as it was in his time, (A.D. 150,) says,

"We who formerly delighted in adultery, now observe the strictest chastity; we who used the charms of magic, have devoted ourselves to the true God; and we who valued money and gain above all things, now *cast what we have in common, and distribute to every man according to his necessities.*"

The writings of other primitive fathers contain similar passages.

It needs no argument to make a Catholic see how the *solemn* vows of poverty, chastity, and obedience must be a development or consequence of the manners and customs of the primitive Christians. Even in Justin's time, community of goods was the prevailing practice among Christians; but as the faith spread itself widely, and as whole nations were converted, the great majority were incapable of that intense zeal and of those aspiring sentiments that may achieve perfection. Those who aimed so high were in a small minority when counted apart from the total population; and they found it necessary to seek freedom and escape persecution by resorting to solitude, or to fortify themselves against the general lukewarmness by solemn vows, or to resist the influence of the world by separate association. Hence, at first, those who sought to attain perfection fled to the desert, imitating the ancient prophets. They were the Theban hermits or anchorites. Then appeared companionship in mortification in the unital homes of the cenobites and monks. Then, long afterward, came the companies of militant charity: the Jesuits, Sisters of Charity, Lazarists, and many others.

Persons who wish to rise above the ordinary degree of piety, above the common level of Catholic practice, generally attempt full perfection. Animated by the spirit of self-sacrifice and an ardent desire to imitate our Lord, they not only devote themselves to poverty and obedience, but also to chastity. They are not content with less than the three vows, the fulness of perfection.

Just here, we wish the reader's attention to an important point, through which we expect to arrive at a solution of the questions propounded in the beginning of this article. It is that, though generally we see the "three vows" practised together, we would be in error if we supposed that they are inseparable, and that Catholicity admits only of the two extremes—the common level or triple perfection. On the contrary, among the wonders and beauties of Catholicity there is the wonder and the beauty of her myri-multiform adaptability to the holy wants of all dispositions, tastes, and nationalities. The plasticity with which Catholicity suits herself (without deterioration and with always an upward tendency) to every degree and variety, of practical virtue, is marvellous. She is, indeed, all things to all men without ceasing to be the spouse of Christ. Hence, within her fold there are, besides the common law of faith and discipline, multitudes of approved forms of devotion, giving egress and exteriority to every peculiarity of good impulse the soul may experience. There are saints of every trade, occupation, habitude, and condition to be imitated. There are many kinds of confraternities, sodalities, societies, and orders—both lay and clerical—formed to accomplish every good work. The number of these ways, rules, methods, forms, and associations is so great, a description of them all fills volumes.

Sometimes a number of laymen combine to do a charitable work without forming any vow. Often they make only *simple* vows; but many engage themselves by *solemn* vows. In some cases the counsel of chastity is followed without that of poverty; the secular priesthood is an example of this kind. Sometimes the vow of poverty has been made without that of celibacy, as in the case of Ananias and Saphira.

St. Barnabas, in the first century; Saints Justin, Julian, and Lucian, in the second century; Saint Clement of Alexandria, Tertullian, Origen, and St. Cyprien, in the third century; and Arnobius and Lactantius, in the fourth century, say (Bergier, vol. i. p. 380) that between Christians all things were in common; but we easily gather from other statements and allusions in their works that they did not mean a community by *virtue of any positive* RIGHT or precept. They meant the generous liberality, the voluntary self-sacrifice, that characterized the manners and customs of the Christians. None asserted conjoint ownership or other *title* to their neighbor's property, nor did any pretend to demand authoritatively, as the obligation of a contract, a participation or use exigible by virtue of the membership of Christ; but all, actuated by Christian fellow-feeling, gave spontaneously and freely, so that none were allowed to suffer from want of subsistence. The effect was the same, or better, than if all things were in common by virtue of a legal obligation or contract. It was the same as if all Christians had made a solemn vow to deprive themselves, in order to be able to relieve all cases of suffering poverty they knew of. The vow of poverty has no other temporal object. Its theory is the doctrine of charity, not that of any natural social right.

Gradually this unmeasured charity appeared to diminish; for the whole empire being theoretically though not practically converted to Christianity, the Christians at heart were lost in the immense crowd of merely nominal believers, and were but partially able to know each other and communicate. At the same time, so widely and deeply corrupt were the people, even the poor, that *charity herself was forced to be cautious.* In fact, the number of sincere Christians, and therefore of charitable persons, had not diminished; but was so small *in proportion* to the number of the distressed, that even by bestowing their all they could produce no sensible diminution of the general misery.

The situation was almost identical with that of the present time; and the plainest remedy would have been then, *as it would be now,* a great augmentation of the number of Christians imbued with the spirit of charity and disposed to self-sacrifice.

The Catholic Church made many glorious efforts to effect this cure by increasing the number of the faithful and true, and by organizing her charitable agencies. She gave birth to those missions and institutions by which the spiritual nature and intention of Christianity was preserved, perpetuated, and disseminated, even through barbarian conquest and feudal oppression. To be able to devote themselves to promoting their own and their neighbor's salvation, and to help the sick, the oppressed, and the poor, the members of the monastic and chivalric orders generally bound themselves by "three vows;" and if they ever omitted any one of the three, it was the vow of poverty. The holy knights, for instance, frequently vowed themselves to chastity and obedience; but not always to poverty. Chastity and obedience are not considerably thwarted by the possession of worldly riches; and they may without very serious detriment dispense with the restraints of poverty: but poverty is very difficult without chastity; for the hardships of poverty are grievously multiplied by the necessity of providing for a family. Hence, even in the remotest times, the orders have added the vow of chastity to that of poverty.

Doubtless there have been, since apostolic times, many isolated instances of the vow of poverty being made by *an entire* FAMILY. Among the tertiary or lay brethren of the regular orders, cases of such a combination might easily have happened. We take it for granted that if a husband *and* wife make the vow of poverty, they would (if otherwise correct) be accepted as a tertiary or lay brother and sister of any regular order bound by the three vows, such as the Franciscans, Jesuits, etc. We know, however, of only one recorded instance of there having existed, since apostolic times, a distinctly and duly organized congregation, sodality, company, or community of *married* Catholics living under the obligations of a solemn or even simple vow of poverty. The schismatics or heretics cannot even adduce a single instance; for, as already noted, their societies are not willingly poor, but the object of their association is comfort and wealth.

The one instance I refer to is that of the Jesuit REDUCTIONS in Paraguay.

Yet, long before the beautiful results obtained by the Jesuit fathers in Paraguay, the good such establishments might do had been clearly foreseen by excellent and learned Catholics. That confessor of the faith, Sir Thomas More, who was beheaded by Henry VIII. for refusing the oath of supremacy, wrote the first *Utopia,* founded on the idea of a community of goods among a whole people. Since that day the idea has fermented, and will not allow the world to rest until it is practically fulfilled by a *Christian* people; for it is a Christian idea, based only on Christian motives, and wholly impracticable outside of the Christian religion. It was to emulate the example set by the Jesuits that several Christian, though schismatic or heretical, societies have been partially successful in realizing this idea. These are the Moravians, Rappists, Shakers, and Ballouists; but we are satisfied the work of realization must be resumed by Catholic hands, and with Catholic motives, and on Catholic grounds, before it can be permanently and beautifully successful.

Here several questions present themselves together:

1. What are the distinctive motives and grounds of an apostolic reduction to the rule of community?
2. What essential Catholic conditions should the organic rule of such an establishment embody?
3. Would such establishments tend to disseminate the faith and strengthen the church?
4. Are the times propitious, and do surrounding circumstances demand missionary attention to this matter?
5. Is there place in the economy of the church militant for the operation of communities of families having property in common?

We fear that the editor would not allow the space necessary for an elaborate answer to these questions. We will therefore endeavor to be very brief.

1. A socialist would say that the only motive for association is a desire to better our worldly condition; that, therefore, association is recommendable only so far as it facilitates in-

creased production, thorough economy, equitable distribution, and greater security; and that it is only by convincing men of these tangible advantages that they will be induced to give up individualism for combinism. So their phalansteries and familisteries are nothing but contrivances to save and gain time, labor, and money for the benefit of the company, and in rivalry with, and exclusive of, every other company and the remainder of mankind. It is only the old principle of self-interest, covetousness, greed of gain, love of money, exercised by partnerships or corporations instead of single persons. Thus, some of these companies will get very rich, while others, though burning with covetousness and discontent, will fall into great poverty. But besides selfish motives moving men, there are others more powerful and certainly more Christian. For instance, a *catholic* community of goods would rest on directly the opposite of self-interest, and be induced by charity counteracting the excess of egoism. True, as in the other case, association would be only a means, and also a guarantee of safety, economy, and increase; but how different the ulterior object! The final causes of a catholic "reduction" to community of goods would be: (1) to live apart from the evil example of the world; (2) to sustain and encourage one another in the faith and its practices; (3) to secure the rearing of children in the practice of religion; (4) to be able to hear mass oftener, and indulge more frequently and expansively in prayer and other sweet and consoling devotions; (5) to save and increase wealth indeed, though *not for self*, not for the company and its members beyond the absolute necessities of life, but *for external charity*—distribution among the poor neighbors, or the establishment of similar companies; (6) the "reductionists" (We venture to generalize the name they had in Paraguay) would work in a spirit of self-sacrifice to please God; (7) they would offer up their voluntary privations as acts of love, penance, and prayer; (8) they would be actuated by aspirations to merit grace and attain perfection; (9) be moved by a desire to display faith before the world, and to concentrate its light so that it might radiate far and wide; and finally, (10) they would cherish the thought that their zeal might be efficient in strengthening the influence, facilitating the operations, and increasing the glory of the church. What an immense difference between reductionism and socialism!

2. The essential conditions of such an association would be the vows of poverty and obedience, under such sanctions and guarantees and inspired by such hopes as only the Catholic Church can give; and, since the society would admit persons living in marriage, and since the church teaches the indissolubility of the marriage-tie, the *unity of the consent* of husband *and* wife to the acceptance of these vows previous to admission. The vow of poverty would be a *sine qua non,* since without it the society would be liable to the precariousness of all secular enterprises; and since, also, without this vow the society would not have the mark, the trait, the essential quality that distinguishes disinterested reductionism from riches-and-comfort-seeking socialism. The vow of obedience to a superior authority, such as a clerical director or a bishop, is also indispensable. Those who have had opportunity of observing the interior operation of a socialist or Protestant association must be fully sensible of the importance of this condition. They are distracted by divided counsels, inconsistencies of purpose, obstinacy and pride of opinions, rival ambitions, and the like. The end is generally ruin. They only succeed in proportion to such *modicum* of humility and obedience as they have contrived to incorporate in their rules and intention. Sometimes it is only the acknowledged superiority and energy of character of a founder or leader that preserves the organization. As soon as this personage dies, his creature goes also into dissolution. Hence, we say the vital conditions of a "reduction" are, (1) Christian fervor; (2) Christian humility; (3) Christian marriage; (4) Christian poverty, and (5) Catholic obedience.

3. We have before us an account of the Paraguay missions, from which we copy the following passage, (p. 52),

> "It sometimes happened that the number thus collected was far too great to admit of their being received as permanent dwellers in the 'reduction;' and in this case their instructors would furnish all that was needed for *the founding of a new one,* not only supplying corn, cattle, and clothing from their own stores, but giving what, to an Indian, was most difficult to bestow, their active and personal cooperation in *building a new 'reduction.'*"

This extract answers the question whether such a company would tend to disseminate the faith and strengthen the church. The process of increase would be in geometrical proportion. Each reduction would have several offspring, and these, in turn, would also each evolve several others. This was the case in Paraguay. There, in a few years, the reductions became so numerous that they lined the banks of the Parana and Uruguay, extended far into the interior, and, in the words of an historian, formed "a Christian republic, where, far from the dwellings and evil designs of the colonists, the spirit of the primitive church revived." Alas! that this caused the envy and jealousy of the world of avarice and ambition. In one more generation, if the Jesuit fathers had not been banished, the Christian republic would have been permanently established. The glorious example they set should not remain fruitless. There is a possibility of similar work and similar results in the midst of the moral desert of civilization. It is time that the shepherds should gather their lambs into visible and safer folds. The lambs should not be left to straggle among the wolves of this moral wilderness. Surely the fact of these straggling members of the flock being married should be no objection to their being provided with a refuge when the couple seek it with unity of will, and would fain find in it the opportunity of serving God. Surely, the fructification of such a work would be wonderful; for its beneficence and Christian spirit would be so apparent that thousands of poor Catholics would eagerly join it, and tens of thousands of lost sheep would be reconverted so as to follow the religious and beautiful life thus made practically possible. This power of multiplying themselves, this productiveness by thirty, seventy, and a hundred fold, is a peculiarity of this kind of association; for, while socialistic and coöperative societies are concentric, a Christian association or reduction, by virtue of its voluntary self-privation and consequent making of a disposable surplus, and by virtue of its desire to bestow in charity this surplus, is evolutive and prolific.

4. Surrounding circumstances in these times not only demand the attention of the church to the subject of association, but the world now offers facilities which, though very different from those that existed in Paraguay, are far more favorable and congenial. In Paraguay, the reverend fathers found people capable of discipline, but barbarous, ignorant, and suspicious. In civilization to-day, instead of savage ignorance, we see foolish infidelity and moral corruption; but, at the same time, a belief in the benefits of association is spreading itself continually. This belief evinces itself in every direction. It resolves and attempts a great many forms of combination. The conviction that good will flow from the industrial association of those who labor is becoming more and more intense. Several secular efforts, based on mere worldly advantage or mutuality, have proved seriously successful. The tendency of work and business is toward the organization of corporations. The capitalists have set the example by their monster companies and monopolies. The plain deduction is, that this tendency affords a favorable opportunity for forming reductions. To neglect it would be to neglect making all things work together unto good to such as, according to God's purpose, are called to be saints. (Rom. viii. 28.)

5. To say that there is no place for communities of families in the economy of the church, would be to deny her beautiful adaptability to all grades and varieties of virtue and good

works. That she should reject and oppose socialism, with its *cortége* of free love, heresy, blasphemy, covetousness, naturalism, and woman's dispersion, let us loudly declare; but to say that there should be in the system of the church a place only for such apostolic communities as are composed of celibates, would be to condemn her history, which tells us of the community at Jerusalem, and of the reductions of Paraguay. We cannot suppose there is a grade or kind of real perfection that the church would reject, if, indeed, that grade or kind be in conformity with evangelical counsel. It is said that keeping the vow of poverty would be too hard for married people, who are naturally impelled to seek riches for the sake of their children. It is said that parental bias, solicitude, and duty would create great obstacles, hard to be overcome. Supposing this, still we say, all things are possible *with God.* The merit of those who, with God, could conciliate these two obligations, and accomplish both, would only be greater in the eyes of the church. Certainly, no Catholic will say that the counsels in regard to voluntary poverty are meant only for celibates, and that only celibates are entitled to gain the consequent blessings. "Blessed are the" willingly "poor, for theirs is the kingdom of heaven." Certainly, a man and wife are entitled to earn the benefits of this willing poverty as well as any monk or nun. The married poor are entitled to make the same sacrifice and take part in the same work to enhance the glory of the church, and to merit the same reward. Association makes the sacrifice and the work possible to the celibate. It creates a similar possibility for married people. The wondrous powers of combined labor and economy are well known. The fields in that direction are wide and free, and ready for *good* seed. Instead of thinking that associations of married people are in any wise incompatible with Catholic doctrine and discipline, a little reflection will convince us that it is, on the contrary, the long-neglected link that completes the circle of good works. Infidels would fain seize the position, and try to adapt it to naturalism and cupidity; but their attempts have been simply ridiculous. The reason is obvious: the vow of poverty and all its consequences is possible only in and through the motives inspired by the Christian religion. They cannot exist and cannot be imitated outside. True association, that which is productive of moral good and social happiness, that which springs from charity, *belongs* to Christianity, and it is impossible to separate it from her. It was practised by the primitive disciples, it was praised and taught by the fathers of the church, it was and still is fulfilled by the celibates in the monasteries, it was successfully applied in the reductions to a whole people; and we conclude that the place once occupied by saintly tribes and families under the wing of the church is still vacant and open to their return and reëstablishment.

6 Levi Silliman Ives

AGAINST SECTARIAN PARTIZANSHIP IN PUBLIC INSTITUTIONS

In the early winter of 1857 Levi Silliman Ives, son-in-law of the High Church Protestant Episcopal bishop J.H. Hobart and himself a bishop in that church for some twenty years before embracing Roman Catholicism, delivered two lectures in behalf of the Society of St. Vincent de Paul of New York City. In them he advanced the view that elementary education should receive as much attention from the charities as did relief agencies and other eleemosynary institutions. His lectures were an impassioned argument—indeed a diatribe—against the New York public school system, which, by excluding "distinctive" religious teaching, undermined religion and morals (after the

Prussian school example) and, by permitting "non-sectarian" Protestant instruction, did violence to the Catholic conscience. Ives poured righteous wrath on the public asylums and protectories into which the courts herded indigent and wayward Catholic children without making any provision for their religious welfare, permitting the managers of these institutions to exclude priests and Catholic teachers.

Ives acknowledged that possibly the state could exercise benevolent functions fairly, but, in his opinion, the various levels of non-federal government were disposed to discriminate in that they supported a system of public schools only, while, at the same time, they subsidized some classifications of private welfare agencies. He therefore suggested that the state subsidize Catholic schools and charitable organizations (he made no distinction between asylum and school). He obviously preferred, however, that education and charity be left almost entirely in private hands.

LECTURE II

In my lecture the other day, I endeavored to show you from the nature of man, and the purposes of his being, that his *mental* faculties could not be safely cultivated, independently of the training of his *moral* faculties; and hence that his education, in order to be a blessing to himself and to society, must be intrusted to those authorities who rightly have charge of his spiritual and immortal concerns.

Beyond this it was my object to point out, in several particulars, the utter incompetency of the State to conduct the education of the poor;—and then to apply the general principle

---

Levi Silliman Ives, *Church and State Charities Compared with Special Reference to the System of New York State Charities* (New York, 1857), pp. 33–34, 44–53.

to *the Public School System of the State of New York.* In doing this I proved the danger of that feature of this system which shuts out religious teaching, and showed from its results the urgent necessity of an immediate change. I now proceed to protest against this system of State policy for the poor, as highly objectionable in another *essential particular.* It operates *unequally,* and hence *unfairly.* It favors certain denominations of Christians, while it violates the rights of conscience in the case of others.

"How can this be so?" demands one, "since this system imposes precisely the same restrictions upon all—allowing none to inculcate within its precincts *sectarian* views." We know its restrictions—we know its professions—we know too that our objection is valid, even on the supposition that its restrictions were observed, its professions fulfilled to the very letter. *The plea is, that the State puts us all on the same footing.* This might be fair, if we all really or religiously stood on the same level. But is this the fact? Suppose the State should pass a law requiring every one of its citizens to take an oath to serve in the army, thus putting them all "on the same footing," would this be fair to *Quakers* and *Moravians,* who are religiously and conscientiously bound not to do either? The State prohibits everything *sectarian.* But what does the State call sectarian? Does it give this title to an *extemporaneous form of worship?* Certainly not, for this it permits and practises in its institutions; and still this is sectarian worship, and offensive to a large class of Christians. Again we demand, what does the State call sectarian? Would it bestow that name upon instructions about *the Church and the sacraments?* Aye, *certainly!* For these, as viewed by Catholics and high-church Protestants, are absolutely prohibited; and hence Catholics and high-church Protestants are the only people affected by this prohibition, as they conscientiously hold that it is only through the *Church and sacraments* that truth and grace can be imparted, while the surrounding sects ascribe to them little or no efficacy, and therefore think it no hardship to have them shut out. *This is the way that the State puts us all on the same footing!* . . . .

We have, however, another page in this strange history which we are bound to unfold. The State has adopted two Reformatory Asylums belonging to Protestants, for the vagrant and delinquent children and youth of this city. One, "the House of Refuge," on Randall's Island, the other, "the Juvenile Asylum," on 175th Street. We are concerned with them mainly as the institutions where the State, or Common Council of the City of New York, keep all those young offenders which they do not lock up in their prisons. The most desperate of these are sent to "the House of Refuge," while the youngest and least hardened are intrusted to "the Juvenile Asylum." In the first of these institutions the inmates are supported by grants from the State funds, (raised by taxation,) as the case may require. In the other, they are provided for by a gift from the State funds of 70,000 dollars in the outset, and by a direct tax of forty dollars annually for each pupil—imposed on Catholics and others, as all State taxes are—except as the children shall be placed there by the Commissioners of Emigration; in which case they are to receive yearly forty dollars each from funds intrusted to these Commissioners. In addition, the schools of the Asylum are made, by an act of the legislature, to participate in the distribution of the school fund in the same manner as do other schools.

Beyond this, it is necessary to know that a majority of the children and youth committed by the city authorities to these private Protestant Asylums, are admitted to be Catholics, and in many cases to be guilty of no other offence than idleness in the streets. That owing to the great influx of poor foreigners from Catholic countries, large numbers of helpless children are continually found floating on the surface of Society, and, falling into the hands of the police, are, under the "truant law," committed for vagrancy, or something else, to these houses of Reform. Catholics, therefore, as a body, have little or no opportunity of knowing even the existence of these young sufferers till their names are inserted on the records of the police, and their bodies are enclosed within the confines of the Asylum. And yet, as a large proportion of them are, by baptism, members of the Catholic Church, that Church has the deepest interest and responsibility in their religious training. But the moment they enter within the walls of these houses of correction, that moment they are placed under Protestant discipline, and the Catholic parent, and the Catholic priest, and all members of the Catholic Church are, as instructors, absolutely shut out. Alas! how forlorn the condition of such poor sufferer as a member of Christ! His catechism taken away—his intercourse with those whom God hath made his natural and responsible guardians cut off, and every memento of his relation to God's family by baptism removed, the poor child finds himself associated with criminals, and subjected to Protestant guides, to Protestant worship, to a Protestant Sunday-school, a Protestant Bible, a Protestant training.

His very presence in this house of correction marks him as a special offender against God. The first thing, then, is to lead him to repentance. But how is the Catholic child to be led by a Protestant hand to repentance, without a violation of the pretended rule, that no sectarianism is to be taught? In what is he told that repentance consists? Is he told that which his parents or his Church hold to be true? That which by the obligations of his baptism, he is bound to learn? Is he told that he must examine in his conscience for each and every deadly sin of his life, and, bewailing it in the bitterness of a contrite heart, seek absolution from it through the sacrament of penance in his Church? Alas! no. But in the place of it, he is taught that which his Church pronounces to be false. Yes, and should the heart of the young penitent, in spite of his Protestant teaching, still cling to the faith of his baptism, is he allowed to act upon it? Should that heart, under the recollection of former lessons, yearn for his Catholic teachers, would they be permitted to come to him? Should the grace of baptism kindle within him a desire to be prepared for his first communion, would the Catholic pastor be admitted as his instructor? Should an awakened conscience impel him to cry out for absolution of sin, and an humble spirit seek it according to the appointment of God at the confessional, would the Catholic priest be allowed to enter and administer peace to his troubled soul? Alas! awful, yea cruel, as the fact may seem, none of these privileges would be granted. We have the assurance from the authorities over these institutions themselves. And why are they not granted? Simply because these things are thought to be contrary to the gospel by the sectarian teachers in authority—while every sect in fellowship with them are allowed unchecked license in the inculcation of Protestant views. Strange as the fact may appear, in such a land as this, and, in State institutions, Catholic children, for whose support Catholic parents are taxed, are not allowed to receive Catholic instruction! Indeed the evil stops not here. These same Protestant authorities have been empowered by the State, to hold the rein upon these children after their release from the House of Correction—to apprentice them at their pleasure, and hence to fasten, if so disposed, this Protestant influence upon their future lives. Yea, country Protestant societies, where these children are placed, have actually been gotten up, to act in conjunction with the Asylums here, to keep these children up to the mark of their Protestant training.

But do not misunderstand me. We are not complaining of the benevolent efforts of Protestants—not complaining of the active solicitude of the State. As mere private efforts, they are most exemplary; and especially so, because of their openly sectarian character. As merely active solicitude, that of the State cannot be too earnest and efficient. But what we do complain of, and complain of as a sore grievance, is, that the State, in showing her solicitude, should consent to become a sectarian;—should link her influence with partisan schemes to proselyte Catholic children, and then force money from Catholics to sustain these schemes. We do complain, not that Protestants should act on Protestant grounds, but that they should call in the power of the State to make Catholics act on these grounds; and that the State, under whose protection we live—that is pledged by her constitutional law to ensure to all equally "the sacred rights of conscience,"—should yield her power to such an end—should decree a statute by which every truant Catholic boy or girl is placed at the mercy of a Protestant policeman, and at the will of a Protestant magistrate, to be committed, without witnesses or jury, with the brand of infamy upon him, to a purely Protestant private institution, from which all Catholic teaching is positively and by order excluded, and which Catholics, by a direct tax, are compelled to support. We do complain of it, as a great hardship—a crying abomination—that our children should be wrested from us, by the strong hand of the State, subjected to a system of sectarian proselytism, and we made to help in sustaining the outrage against ourselves. Suppose the State had ventured to take an opposite course—had committed her young Protestant offenders to Catholic asylums—what would have been the result? What but a Protestant outcry and assault that ere this would have broken down the government? The injustice to us, then, is only the penalty of our political weakness.

But, says the State sectarian, "Catholic neglect of these children, has made Protestant charity and State interference necessary." Protestant charity in aid of the distressed is one thing; State interference to convert Catholic children to Protestantism, and make Catholics pay for it, is quite another thing.

Admit, if you will, that Catholics are behind [in] their duty—are indisposed or unable to do all which the necessities of their poor demand, has the State, on that account, a right to complain of them? The burden of charity imposed upon Catholics, in this city, from the large immigration of their needy brethren, is, in proportion to their means, fourfold that of any other Christian communion. What has the State done to show her sympathy for them, and to help them in the hour of their necessity? What, but take advantage of this necessity to entice their children from their faith? In all reason and justice, Catholics might have looked for some pecuniary favor from the State; but what have they received, but a heavy yearly tax of some 250,000 dollars upon their small means, to enable Protestants to operate successfully against them? History does not record a more shameful act of injustice. I doubt whether England, with all her oppression of Catholics, exhibits any thing more unjust than this. What! the State complain of the neglect of Catholics! It is the complaint of Pharaoh! The old demand: "Deliver the accustomed number of bricks—but no straw shall be given you."

But we have not done with this point. During the last month or two, a certain organ has widely spread through this city, a complaint against Catholics, which we are bound to notice. We have nothing to do with the respectable individuals who have published this complaint,—except to hold them responsible for the publication, as we find their names attached to it, as its authors. "The Thirteenth Annual Report of the New York Association for Improving the Condition of the Poor," on its 25th page, has the following language:—"The great mass of our paupers and felons are of foreign birth or parentage, and chiefly Roman Catholics. The records of the Association show that more than *seventy-five* per cent. of its beneficiaries are of the same class, and consequently, that a corresponding ratio of its labors and outlays are for their benefit; while *not one* per cent. of its pecuniary means comes from persons of that faith. Such an expenditure of Protestant funds and efforts, for the exclusive advantage of foreigners and Romanists, will scarcely find a parallel elsewhere—certainly not out of the pale of the Protestant Church." Mark, *first,* "the records of the Association show that *seventy-five* per cent. of the paupers and felons are foreigners and Roman Catholics." As an answer to this statement, as it respects "felons," I offer "the records of the Police

Registry," showing that of late, a fearful preponderance of high crime is found among our *native* youth and Protestant Germans. In regard to paupers, we are prepared to admit that no one class is likely to furnish so large a number as that of Irish Catholics. But we feel bound to add, that, for a considerable proportion of these, our Protestant countrymen have made themselves responsible,—inasmuch as these paupers, or their families, have been reduced to this state, by the hardships and dangers of that kind of labor to which, through Protestant cupidity, they have been subjected; and, in which the health of some, and the lives of others, have been lavishly sacrificed. Observe, in the *second* place, the complaint against Catholics for not aiding the Association; and the boast, in respect to Protestants, for their great, their unparalleled liberality. Another passage in the report will show how utterly groundless are both the *boast* and the complaint. In regard to the latter, let me ask, Why should Catholics aid this Association? On page 41, the report makes the Association mainly responsible for the passage, in 1853, of the famous "Truant Law," under which Catholic children may be forced from their parents, because of their extreme poverty, and made ever after to acknowledge, in the State, a higher relationship and a more absolute authority than the parental. Why, I repeat, should Catholics feel themselves under obligation to help an Association, which, by its own confession, has been instrumental in thus trampling upon their most sacred rights, in thus procuring the enactment of a law, which they cannot otherwise regard, than as identifying itself with the Socialism of France, in entering the *family*—that sacred compact formed by God himself—sundering the family ties, and violating the sanctity of the domestic altar? Why should Catholics feel themselves bound to lend their aid thus to strengthen the instruments of infidelity, and rear a fabric of political despotism in their midst?

But we have on the same page another confession of this Association, which is valuable as showing the *motive* of this unparalleled "expenditure of Protestant funds and efforts for the exclusive advantage of Roman Catholics." The confession is, that soon after the passage of this iniquitous act of 1843, the Association gave notice to all its visitors to apply the act, and not to give any alms without the recipient would become pledged to submit to its oppressive conditions; and, in case the parent was unable to take his children from him, and send them to "the House of Correction," or, what is the same thing, to "the Protestant Juvenile Asylum." That asylum, as we have seen, which shuts out all Catholic instruction. You see, then, we have arrived at the *motive* of this unparalleled "expenditure of Protestant funds and efforts for the exclusive advantage of Catholics!" It is confessedly, that, by this means, the Association may draw Catholic children within its net, and compel them to become Protestants, or victims to its terrible displeasure!

"But," said a Protestant to me the other day, "what shall the State do with those vagrant children, if it does not commit them to Protestant institutions?" My answer was: "If this horrible outrage upon parents must be perpetuated, why not commit the *Catholic* children at least to *Catholic* asylums, with the 40 or 60 dollars annually for each child?" "But," rejoined my friend, "it is news to me that Catholics have any institutions, in which they could receive poor children." "Yes," I answered again, "notwithstanding the discouraging circumstances under which they labor, Catholics in this city have done something in the way of Charity—enough, at least, to show the State their willingness with greater means to do more! That, in the midst of the clamor against them, they have some friends to speak in their behalf;—that, even after being robbed of 250,000 dollars annually, by the State, to keep up the most costly and burdensome school system ever fastened upon a deluded people, Catholics can point to their hospitals, and asylums, and charitable associations and school-houses, with the 15,000 poor children educated in them at their *private cost,* and say to the State,

These are our pledge that we will not misuse the bounties intrusted to us by God for the poor.—Say to the State, 'Consent for once to try us—to give us the same chance that is granted to our Protestent neighbors—to give us back the treasures you have extorted from us—we ask not that others should be taxed for us as we have been for them; we will be content with the return of our own. Yea, more generous still, we will ignore the past, and be thankful to you for permission, to use our own for the future,—to dispense hereafter our means of charity in our own way. Grant us but this—grant us the privilege which nothing but tyranny can withhold—and we pledge to you our sacred honor, that, with one-half the outlay of your all-devouring public school system, and without intrenching upon *family rights,* too, our poor schools and asylums shall exhibit a result which will show, at least, that you have hitherto done us flagrant injustice.' "

7 The Paulist Viewpoint

NEW TASKS IN CATHOLIC CHARITY

In 1865 the recently formed Missionary Priests of St. Paul the Apostle (Paulists) began publication of the Catholic World *which has continued as a monthly periodical to the present day. From the first the magazine stressed Catholic responsibility for social welfare. In early issues the journal examined the whole question of Catholic charity in a series of noteworthy articles, one of which is here reproduced. Although the article is unsigned and its author unknown, it reflects the views of the*

Rev. Isaac T. Hecker, founder of the Paulists and editor of the magazine.

The article made crystal clear what Catholics must do in order to be more effective in charity. It pointed out that although Catholics comprised nearly half the population of New York City and a much larger proportion of the city's pauper population, they were not one-fourth as active as Protestants and Jews in organized charity. Catholics, he insisted, should realize that Protestants were motivated primarily by a desire to conserve and improve society, only incidentally to proselytize dependent Catholics. Although more churches and schools were needed and should be erected, the Catholic body should also, after the Protestant example, give more attention to the physical wants of the poor. Most in need were the forty thousand vagrant children of the city. They should be fed, clothed, and instructed; and their home life improved—this work to be done through the establishment of mission-houses, set up and operated by lay people under the direction of the Sisters of Charity or the Sisters of Mercy.

This article was a brilliant item in the literature of the urban Catholic crusade and was prophetic of the later more mature Christian social settlement movement.

If we recur again to a subject on which we have two or three times already addressed the readers of THE CATHOLIC WORLD, it is because we are so deeply impressed with its importance, and because we are persuaded that in any matter which so highly concerns the Catholic cause all our friends must be heartily interested. The generosity of Catholics toward their church is almost proverbial. They give more to religion than any other denomination; they give more liberally in proportion

---

[Anon] "The Charities of New York," *Catholic World,* VIII (November 1868), 279–285.

to their means; and they give spontaneously. And nowhere is their generosity more strikingly shown than in the great cities of America, where they have built so many scores of costly churches, and raised up convents and orphan asylums, and where they have given almost every parish its free school, though the law has compelled them likewise to pay taxes for the support of common-schools to which they cannot in conscience entrust their children. Here, in New York City, we have had a particularly heavy task to perform. As this is the landing-place of most of the Catholic immigrants, besides being the chief city and business centre of the country, the growth of the Catholic population has been especially rapid, and it has grown in principal measure by the influx of the poorer classes, who, while they stand in greatest need of the help of the Church, are able to do least for its support. It is a notorious fact that, while a large proportion of the more thrifty immigrants move out to the West, and help to build up Catholicism in our new States and territories, the destitute and shiftless almost invariably remain in the large cities. Hence, the growth in the material resources of the Church in New York does not keep pace with the growth in its numbers. The well-to-do immigrants who have settled here, and the American-born Catholics, children of the last generation of settlers, or else converts from Protestantism, have a task of peculiar difficulty, as they must provide not only for the natural increase in their own numbers, but for the spiritual wants of their poorer brethren, who have no means of providing for themselves. And it is a task which seems to grow harder and harder every year. The congregations increase much faster than the churches. Children multiply faster than the schools. With all the unremitting labors of our successive bishops and archbishops, and all the untiring exertions of our zealous priests, there are not yet churches enough in New York City.

We must remember this peculiar condition of our Church when we undertake to compare Catholic with Protestant charities. The noblest work of benevolence is that which assists our neighbor to save his soul; and Catholics understand perfectly well that they can make no better disposition of their alms than in contributing to supply the poor with opportunities of hearing Mass, receiving the sacraments, and learning the principles and precepts of their faith. Hence, their liberality has been directed first toward the building of churches and the education of priests, and next toward the support of Catholic schools. While there was so much to be done in these directions they felt comparatively little disposition to spare either money or attention in feeding the hungry, clothing the naked, or nursing the sick. Of these corporal works of mercy they have, indeed, done much in proportion to their means; but they have, very rightly, thought more of feeding the hungry soul than the hungry stomach, more of curing the sick heart than the wounded body.

While Catholics have thus been so much occupied in looking after the things of God, that they have been unable to devote more than an ordinary amount of care to the physical wants of God's unfortunate children, the case with Protestants has been very different. They are in no want of churches; they have more already than they know how to fill. They need no free-schools, for the State system of education satisfies all their requirements. They have abundant wealth, and are willing to devote a share of it to benevolent purposes. In the majority of cases we believe that they give to such enterprises out of the best religious motives; for we have no patience with the narrowness of mind which suspects the disinterestedness of all Protestant charity, and seems to imagine that no man who is so unfortunate as to be a heretic can possibly do a good deed from a good impulse. Many Protestant benevolent institutions are maintained, no doubt, for the purpose of bribing poor destitute Catholics to abandon their faith; but all are not. Protestants are doing a great deal in the way of genuine beneficence; and it is more becoming, as well as more politic, for us to frankly recognize and imitate whatever praiseworthy actions they perform, than to inquire too closely and suspiciously into their ulterior motives.

A book which has recently been published in New York puts us in a position to compare, with very little trouble, the work accomplished by Protestants and Catholics in the way of organized charity in this city. Its title is, *The Charities of New York, Brooklyn, and Staten Island,* by Henry J. Cammann and Hugh N. Camp. (Octavo, pp. 597. Hurd & Houghton.) The authors have had much to do with various institutions of benevolence—principally, we believe, with those connected with the Protestant Episcopal denomination; and their purpose in preparing this volume was to give a brief history and description of all the organized private charities of New York and its suburbs, partly to show what has been done for the relief of suffering humanity, and partly to guide alms-givers in making an intelligent disposition of their liberality. They seem to have performed their task with care and impartiality, permitting each institution to speak for itself through one of its officers or special friends, or in an official report, and making no attempt to compare the number and efficiency of the establishments of different faiths. A conscientious desire to be just toward Catholic, Protestant, and Jew is apparent throughout. The record is not a complete one; but the deficiency, we have reason to believe, is the consequence, in chief measure, of the neglect or unwillingness of the proper persons to furnish the requisite information. We have supplied these omissions as far as possible, but the story is not yet told in full; though for purposes of comparison the table which we give below is probably sufficient. We have added several important societies and institutions which are not included in the book, namely, the New York Prison Association, St. Stephen's Home, St. Francis' German Hospital, the Society of St. Vincent de Paul, and some others; and we have omitted all which are supported entirely, or almost entirely, by appropriations from the city or State, such as Bellevue Hospital, the New York Blind Asylum, etc., as well as those which do not properly belong to New York City. The figures represent the number of persons who have obtained aid or shelter from these various organizations during the past year. The admirable Mission-House in St. James' parish has gone into operation since last year, and therefore cannot be included in the table.

CATHOLIC

1.	St. Vincent's Hospital	832
2.	St. Francis's German Hospital	592
3.	St. Stephen's Home for Destitute Little Girls	100
4.	St. Patrick's Male Orphan Asylum	550
5.	St. Patrick's Female Orphan Asylum	390
6.	St. Joseph's Orphan Asylum	150
7.	St. Vincent's Orphan Asylum	85
8.	House of the Good Shepherd	500
9.	Institution of Mercy	2845
10.	St. Vincent de Paul Society	——
	Total	6044

PROTESTANT AND JEWISH

1.	St. Luke's Hospital	1027
2.	Society for the Relief of the Ruptured and Crippled	1684
3.	Women's Hospital	189
4.	German Hospital and Dispensary	——
5.	Eye and Ear Infirmary	8038
6.	Mount Sinai Hospital	1028
7.	Infirmary for Women and Children	137
8.	Nursery and Child's Hospital	572
9.	Leake and Watts Orphan House	100
10.	St. Luke's Home for Indigent Christian Females	31
11.	American Female Guardian Society and Home for the Friendless	5033
12.	P. E. House of Mercy	112

PROTESTANT AND JEWISH (Continued)

13. Orphan Asylum	186
14. Colored Orphan Asylum	254
15. Orphan Home and Asylum of the Protestant Episcopal Church	158
16. Society for the Relief of Half-Orphan and Destitute Children	230
17. Hebrew Benevolent and Orphan Asylum Society	150
18. Five Points House of Industry	1000
19. The Sheltering Arms	157
20. Children's Aid Society	8192
21. Five Points Mission	——
22. Association for the Relief of Respectable Aged Indigent Females	79
23. Magdalen Society	37
24. Ladies' Union Aid Society	65
25. Colored Home	800
26. Union Home and School for Children of Volunteer Soldiers and Sailors	350
27. Asylum for Lying-in Women	395
28. Women's Prison Association	350
29. New York Prison Association	——
30. Presbyterian Home for Aged Women	22
31. Society for the Relief of Poor Widows with small Children	——
32. Howard Mission and Home for Little Wanderers	100
33. Working-Women's Protective Union	——
34. Association for Improving the Condition of the Poor	——
35. The Home in West Houston street	112
36. Samaritan Home for the Aged	——
37. Protestant Episcopal City Mission	——
38. Working-Woman's Home	120
39. Ladies' Christian Union	150
40. House and School of Industry	102
Total	31,860

This is not a pleasing comparison. Out of fifty institutions here enumerated, only ten belong to us. Out of 37,904 persons annually relieved by the fifty charities, our share is only 6044. The case is not so bad, however, as it appears on first inspection. Our Sisters of Charity and Mercy perform an immense amount of benevolent work outside of their own houses and asylums, nursing the sick, consoling the afflicted, watching in public hospitals, feeding the hungry, and visiting the prisoner; work which cannot be measured by figures, because there is no record of it except in heaven. Benevolent labor of the kind to which our sisterhoods devote themselves is undertaken by various of the non-Catholic organizations enumerated in the above table, and largely increases their apparent predominance over our own establishments, because they sum up in statistical form what is done, and we do not. Then again, several of the charities set down as Protestant are entirely unsectarian in their character, and we dare say draw a fair proportion of their support from Catholic sources. Not so bad as it seems, we say; yet surely bad enough. Perhaps we ought not even to claim credit for what the sisterhoods do, for theirs are in reality labors of individual benevolence, and the Catholic community at large shares little or nothing of the expense, the trouble, or the merit of them. The Catholics of New York are supposed to number four hundred thousand—nearly half the population of the city—and it is notorious that they comprise a great deal more than half the pauper population. Are we doing a fair proportion of the work of taking care of our poor? Moreover, pauperism increases *ten times as fast* as the whole population. The growth of the entire number of inhabitants in thirty-four years has been ninety per cent; the increase in the number of those receiving charitable relief has been during the same period no less than nine hundred per cent. What provision are we making to meet the terrible responsibility which this state of society entails?

We can hardly question that the time has come when the

physical wants of these unfortunate classes should awaken in us serious consideration. We have done well to look so carefully after the building of churches, and of course we must not relax our efforts or check our generosity in the slightest degree on account of these additional calls upon us. We must work also for our schools as we have never worked before. Systems of education all around us are daily improving, and Catholic schools must not be left behind. Perhaps it may be found possible to make some arrangement by which we can be relieved of the disadvantage under which we now rest. Catholics and Protestants should have but one and the same end in view in the education of the young; and we are not without hope that the love of fair play which belongs to the American people will enable us in time to compose the old school-quarrel, which has been such an injury to the community. How this may be done, it would lead us far from our present subject to consider. We trust it will be done some day, but meanwhile our church schools have a right to the most generous support. Churches and schools must come first; but when we have given them all they need, we are not to stop there. Protestants are fully awake to the danger which threatens the public welfare from this rapid increase of a destitute class, and are working hard to effect a reform. If we do not take care of our own poor, they will not only provide for their physical wants, but will soon acquire charge of their souls. Such institutions as the Five Points Mission, the Howard Mission, the Children's Aid Society, the Association for Improving the Condition of the Poor, however honestly they may be conducted, are powerful engines of proselytism. Their managers may be actuated by the most disinterested benevolence, they may use none but legitimate means of influence; but is it any wonder that they draw many Catholics, especially children, away from the faith, when we let them have the field so completely to themselves? Against the Association for Improving the Condition of the Poor, we can set off, indeed, our noble Society of St. Vincent de Paul, though its resources are far smaller than they should be; but to take the place of the three other important charities mentioned above, we Catholics can show little or nothing.

First, we ought to look after the children. The adult sick and suffering are in less spiritual danger; for in most of the hospitals, except those of a strictly denominational character, they can enjoy the visits of priests and sisters. For the destitute who are strong enough to work we can offer no better resource than that which the Citizens' Association is now striving to afford in the organization of a Labor Bureau, by which the superfluous hands of the city may be distributed among the farming regions, where labor is badly needed. Sectarianism appears to have nothing to do with this enterprise, and it offers relief in the best possible way, by enabling the poor not to eat the bread of idleness, but to earn an honest living. For the aged and friendless, who are past work and have no provision for the sunset of life, we still have no asylums; but their claims must be postponed until those of the children are satisfied. We are told that our city contains no fewer than 40,000 vagrant and destitute children. What a fearful seed of crime and misery this sad multitude constitutes, growing up in every kind of ignorance and vice, and ripening for the prisons! What are we doing for them? We have orphan asylums; but most of these children are not orphans, and even if they were, the asylums have not room for a tithe of them. We have the Protectory, at Westchester; but that is only for young criminals, who must be committed on a magistrate's warrant, and must, moreover, be the children of Catholic parents. Now, thousands of these young vagrants have never yet fallen within the grasp of the law; thousands are the children of no faith whatever, and, if brought before a justice, would have to be sent to the Protestant instead of the Catholic asylum. And, even if all these children could be brought under the control of our Protectory Association, twenty such asylums as the excellent one at Westchester would not hold them. No! there is much for us yet to do; there are thousands of poor little children upon whom Catholic charity has not yet laid a finger.

We spoke, in a former number of The Catholic World, of the noble mission-school which the zeal and perseverance of one good priest has founded in St. James's parish in this city. If almost every church in New York were able to build an institution of a similar kind, we might rest satisfied; but what is one mission-school among 40,000 children? What can one over-worked clergyman do toward performing a task which is the duty of the entire Catholic community? It is a sad and humiliating thing to confess; but Protestants seem to appreciate the claim which these vagrant children have upon the public much better than we do. The Protestants are not idle: they have their Refuges, their Industrial Schools, their "Homes," their missionaries, right in the heart of the vagabond population; they spare neither trouble nor money to catch these souls; and we are ashamed to say they capture a great many who are rightfully our charges. If we let this continue, will not God have a terrible account to exact of us some day?

We are gratified to know that what we have heretofore said on this subject has not been without its effect. There are some good brethren who seem to believe that it is the duty of all Catholic writers to defend those of the faith from every aspersion, to cover up all their defects, to excuse all their wrong-doings, to hold them up as perfect models of the Christian life, and to ignore or decry every good work undertaken by heretics. Such as these were offended at the account we gave of the Howard Mission, and similar Protestant institutions. But others have listened to us in a more sensible frame of mind, have acknowledged the justice of our remarks and have offered to contribute their purses whenever an effort is made to supply the want we have indicated. Made it will be and must be, before long. Now, who will make it?

We had written thus far, when we received an unexpected answer to our question in the following letter from a charitable Catholic lady:

TO THE EDITOR OF THE CATHOLIC WORLD:

Rev. Father: The thought of doing something for the neglected children of New York prompts me to write to you. Since the moment that I read the letter that you published in The Catholic World, they have scarcely been out of my mind. I have offered up all my prayers and communions for them, and I have prayed especially for them every day. I had no thought that I could do anything else, but sometimes I think that, if all should content themselves with praying, there would be nothing done. I am afraid I cannot do much, for I do not know how to begin, and I have so little confidence and I know so few people. But I felt as if I could not pray any more without trying to do something also. Perhaps the work could be begun by an appeal something like the following:

TO CATHOLIC MOTHERS

"Of forty thousand vagrant children in New York we cannot doubt that far more than one half have inherited the Catholic faith." —Catholic World for Aug. 1868.

More than twenty thousand Catholic children in New York, homeless, uncared for, ignorant, and abandoned! Can we Catholic mothers think of this and sit quietly in our homes with our little ones around us? Can we shut from our ears their cries of sorrow, from our eyes their little forms trembling with cold and hunger, or from our hearts the thought of their desolation? No, we cannot, and we would not; for is it not most especially our right, our duty, and our privilege to do for them? Our priests are overworked, they cannot do everything; let us, then, beg their blessing and begin this noble undertaking. We have not much to do, only to prepare the way. The Sisters of Charity or Mercy are ready and longing to care for these little desolate ones. We have only to put the means in their hands. Already a Catholic lady of New York has given one thousand dollars for this end, and we have only to follow her as far as we are able. I think ten others can be found in our city to imitate her example. If we can, let us give largely, for it is but lending to the Lord; if we have but little, let us give of that, not forgetting that the widows mite was more than all else cast into the treasury. Shall we let the snows of another winter find these little ones still unclothed and unsheltered; shall we let their souls perish here in the midst of churches and altars, while our priests and missionaries in distant lands are shedding their blood for the heathen? Let us Christian mothers begin our work earnestly, let us pray and labor for these little ones; they are here in our midst, and before God we are responsible for them.

Respectfully, * * * *

Our correspondent, we believe, has gone to work in the right way, and, unless we greatly misjudge the Catholic ladies of New York, her appeal will be heard. The best plan, we think, would be to establish, in the heart of the poorer quarters of the city, a mission-house under the charge of Sisters of Charity, or Sisters of Mercy, who should make it their whole business to visit the destitute in their homes, teach them how to lead decent lives, see that their children were brought into Sunday and day schools, that the whole family went to mass and confession, and that the children received proper care at home. It is much better to persuade parents to train up their offspring properly than to take the children out of their hands and rear them in mission-houses and asylums. The family relation ought to be rigidly respected; for God's plan of education is a good deal better than anything we can invent in place of it. For homeless and orphan children, the Sisters might see that admission was procured into the Catholic establishments already provided for those classes; for the sick and the starving they would ask relief from the charitable throughout the city, and whatever we placed in their hands we might be sure would be judiciously distributed. There are generous Catholic women enough in New York to the foundation of such a house, and provide for the support of a small community to take charge of it; and there are many who would highly value the privilege of co-operating with the Sisters in their holy work. Let them come forth, effect an organization under the sanction of the ecclesiastical authority of the diocese, begin at once to raise the money required, and a great undertaking, the parent of many others, will be effected. When we once get into the way of practical benevolence, we shall be surprised to see how easily one foundation will follow another, and how the habit of alms-deeds will become so fixed that it will seem easier and more natural to give than to refrain from giving.

8 Pastoral Letter

MORAL GUIDELINES, AND SUPPORT FOR CATHOLIC SOCIETIES

The Pastoral Letter of the Third Plenary Council of Baltimore, 1884, ranks among the most influential documents ever issued by the American hierarchy. It was a remarkably successful popular exposition of Catholic faith and morals for the guidance of the laity and the general priesthood. While it reaffirmed the social teachings in the pastorals of previous Councils, it was particularly concerned with the proper observance of the Lord's Day and the conditions under which Catholics could morally join and form societies and associations.

The letter warned that the sanctity of the Christian Sunday was imperiled by greed and dissipation as shown by an excess of seeking after material gain and pleasure, and it recommended the strengthening and enforcing of the Sunday-closing law and other safeguards. Relying chiefly on moral suasion, however, the bishops pleaded with the faithful to avoid intemperance, preferably through total abstinence; to abandon the liquor traffic, and to seek a more becoming way of earning a living. Although the Council recognized that the proliferation of societies was an outgrowth of democracy and Christian brotherhood, the members felt that avoidance of excess should apply to societies also. It was believed that only a few socie-

ties were deliberately bad, but that many, nevertheless, exerted a dangerous influence because they ignored Christian ideals, monopolized the loyalty of their members and exacted from them oaths of secrecy. The bishops endorsed the existing categories of Catholic societies and urged their extension into all fields of religious and moral endeavor.

The Pastoral Letter of 1884 well mirrored the Catholic social thought and action that had taken shape in the preceding generation and it anticipated and influenced the future as well. It aligned Catholic temperance sentiment behind the rising anti-saloon crusade; it forbade any ecclesiastic to condemn any society without the consent of the archbishops, and this served to encourage Catholic workingmen to affiliate more confidently with the trade union movement. The over-all emphasis of the Pastoral on the relevance of Catholic faith and morals to the perfection of American citizenship put vigor into "Americanism" in all its aspects.

The Lord's Day

There are many sad facts in the experience of nations, which we may well store up as lessons of practical wisdom. Not the least important of these is the fact that one of the surest marks and measures of the decay of religion in a people, is their non-observance of the Lord's Day. In traveling through some European countries, a Christian's heart is pained by the almost unabated rush of toil and traffic on Sunday. First, grasping avarice thought it could not afford to spare the day to God; then unwise governments, yielding to the pressure of mam-

---

The Pastoral Letter of the Third Plenary Council of Baltimore, 1884, on Sunday Desecration, Intemperance and Forbidden Societies, in *The National Pastorals of the American Hierarchy (1792–1919)*, Peter Guilday, ed. (Washington, D. C.: The National Catholic Welfare Council, 1923), pp. 253–262.

mon, relaxed the laws which for many centuries had guarded the day's sacredness—forgetting that there are certain fundamental principles, which ought not to be sacrificed to popular caprice or greed. And when, as usually happens, neglect of religion had passed, by lapse of time, into hostility to religion, this growing neglect of the Lord's Day was easily made use of as a means to bring religion itself into contempt. The Church mourned, protested, struggled, but was almost powerless to resist the combined forces of popular avarice and Cæsar's influence, arrayed on the side of irreligion. The result is the lamentable desecration which all Christians must deplore.

And the consequences of this desecration are as manifest as the desecration itself. The Lord's Day is the poor man's day of rest; it has been taken from him,—and the laboring classes are a seething volcano of social discontent. The Lord's Day is the home day, drawing closer the sweet domestic ties, by giving the toiler a day with wife and children; but it has been turned into a day of labor,—and home ties are fast losing their sweetness and their hold. The Lord's Day is the church-day, strengthening and consecrating the bond of brotherhood among all men, by their kneeling together around the altars of the one Father in heaven; but men are drawn away from this blessed communion of Saints,—and as a natural consequence they are lured into the counterfeit communion of Socialism, and other wild and destructive systems. The Lord's Day is God's Day, rendering ever nearer and more intimate the union between the creature and his Creator, and thus ennobling human life in all its relations; and where this bond is weakened, an effort is made to cut man loose from God entirely, and to leave him, according to the expression of St. Paul, "without God in this world."[22] The profanation of the Lord's Day, whatever be its pretext, is a defrauding both of God and His creatures, and retribution is not slow.

[22] Ephes. ii. 12.

In this country, there are tendencies and influences at work to bring about a similar result; and it behooves all who love God and care for society, to see that they be checked. As usual, greed for gain lies at the bottom of the movement. Even when the pretence put forward is popular convenience or popular amusement, the clamor for larger liberty does not come so much from those who desire the convenience or the amusement, as from those who hope to enrich themselves by supplying it. Now far be it from us to advocate such Sunday-laws as would hinder necessary work, or prohibit such popular enjoyments as are consistent with the sacredness of the day. It is well known, however, that the tendency is to rush far beyond the bounds of necessity and propriety, and to allege these reasons only as an excuse for virtually ignoring the sacredness of the day altogether. But no community can afford to have either gain or amusement at such a cost. To turn the Lord's Day into a day of toil, is a blighting curse to a country; to turn it into a day of dissipation would be worse. We earnestly appeal, therefore, to all Catholics without distinction, not only to take no part in any movement tending toward a relaxation of the observance of Sunday, but to use their influence and power as citizens to resist in the opposite direction.

There is one way of profaning the Lord's Day which is so prolific of evil results, that we consider it our duty to utter against it a special condemnation. This is the practice of selling beer or other liquors on Sunday, or of frequenting places where they are sold. This practice tends more than any other to turn the Day of the Lord into a day of dissipation, to use it as an occasion for breeding intemperance. While we hope that Sunday-laws on this point will not be relaxed, but even more rigidly enforced, we implore all Catholics, for the love of God and of country, never to take part in such Sunday traffic, nor to patronize or countenance it. And we not only direct the attention of all pastors to the repression of this abuse, but we also call upon them to induce all of their flocks that may be engaged in the sale of liquors to abandon as soon as they can the dangerous traffic, and to embrace a more becoming way of making a living.

And here it behooves us to remind our workingmen, the bone and sinew of the people and the specially beloved children of the Church, that if they wish to observe Sundays as they ought, they must keep away from drinking places on Saturday night. Carry your wages home to your families, where they rightfully belong. Turn a deaf ear, therefore, to every temptation; and then Sunday will be a bright day for all the family. How much better this than to make it a day of sin for yourselves, and of gloom and wretchedness for your home, by a Saturday night's folly or debauch. No wonder that the Prelates of the Second Plenary Council declared that "the most shocking scandals which we have to deplore spring from intemperance." No wonder that they gave a special approval to the zeal of those who, the better to avoid excess, or in order to give bright example, pledge themselves to total abstinence. Like them we invoke a blessing on the cause of temperance, and on all who are laboring for its advancement in a true Christian spirit. Let the exertions of our Catholic Temperance Societies meet with the hearty co-operation of pastors and people; and not only will they go far towards strangling the monstrous evil of intemperance, but they will also put a powerful check on the desecration of the Lord's Day, and on the evil influences now striving for its total profanation.

Let all our people "remember to keep holy the Lord's Day." Let them make it not only a day of rest, but also a day of prayer. Let them sanctify it by assisting at the adorable Sacrifice of the Mass. Besides the privilege of the morning Mass, let them also give their souls the sweet enjoyment of the Vesper service and the Benediction of the Blessed Sacrament. See that the children not only hear Mass, but also attend the Sunday-school. It will help them to grow up more practical Catholics. In country places, and especially in those which the priest cannot visit every Sunday, the Sunday-school ought to be the favorite place of reunion for young and old. It will keep them from going astray, and will strengthen them in the faith. How many children have been lost to the Church in country districts, because parents neglected to see that they observed the Sunday properly at home and at Sunday-school, and allowed them to fall under dangerous influences!

Forbidden Societies

One of the most striking characteristics of our times is the universal tendency to band together in societies for the promotion of all sorts of purposes. This tendency is the natural outgrowth of an age of popular rights and representative institutions. It is also in accordance with the spirit of the Church, whose aim, as indicated by her name Catholic, is to unite all mankind in brotherhood. It is consonant also with the spirit of Christ, who came to break down all walls of division, and to gather all in the one family of the one heavenly Father.

But there are few good things which have not their counterfeits, and few tendencies which have not their dangers. It is obvious to any reflecting mind that men form bad and rash as well as good and wise designs; and that they may band together for carrying out evil or dangerous as well as laudable and useful purposes. And this does not necessarily imply deliberate malice, because, while it is unquestionably true that there are powers at work in the world which deliberately antagonize the cause of Christian truth and virtue, still the evil or the danger of purposes and associations need not always spring from so bad a root. Honest but weak and erring human nature is apt to be so taken up with one side of a question as to do injustice to the other; to be so enamored of favorite principles as to carry them to unjustifiable extremes; to be so intent upon securing some laudable end as to ignore the rules of prudence, and bring about ruin instead of restoration. But no intention, no matter how honest, can make lawful what is unlawful. For it is a fundamental rule of Christian morals that "evil must not be done that good may come of it," and "the end can never justify the means," if the means are evil. Hence it is the evident duty of every reasonable man, before allowing himself to be drawn into any society, to make sure that both its ends and its means are consistent with truth, justice and conscience.

In making such a decision, every Catholic ought to be convinced that his surest guide is the Church of Christ. She has in her custody the sacred deposit of Christian truth and morals; she has the experience of all ages and all nations; she has at heart the true welfare of mankind; she has the perpetual guidance of the Holy Ghost in her authoritative decisions. In her teaching and her warnings therefore, we are sure to hear the voice of wisdom, prudence, justice and charity. From the hill-top of her Divine mission and her world-wide experience, she sees events and their consequences far more clearly than they who are down in the tangled plain of daily life. She has seen associations that were once praiseworthy, become pernicious by change of circumstances. She has seen others, which won the admiration of the world by their early achievements, corrupted by power or passion or evil guidance, and she has been forced to condemn them. She has beheld associations which had their origin in the spirit of the Ages of Faith, transformed by lapse of time, and loss of faith, and the manipulation of designing leaders, into the open or hidden enemies of religion and human weal. Thus our Holy Father Leo XIII has lately shown that the Masonic and kindred societies,—although the offspring of the ancient Guilds, which aimed at sanctifying trades and tradesmen with the blessings of religion; and although retaining, perhaps, in their "ritual," much that tells of the religiousness of their origin; and although in some countries still professing entire friendliness toward the Christian religion,—have nevertheless already gone so far, in many countries, as to array themselves in avowed hostility against Christianity, and against the Catholic Church as its embodiment; that they virtually aim at substituting a world-wide fraternity of their own, for the universal brotherhood of Jesus Christ, and at disseminating mere Naturalism for the supernatural revealed religion bestowed upon mankind by the Saviour of the world. He has shown, too, that, even in countries where they are as yet far from acknowledging such purposes, they nevertheless have in them the germs, which under favorable circumstances, would inevitably blossom forth in similar results. The Church, consequently, forbids her children to have any connection with such societies, because they are either an open evil to be shunned or a hidden danger to be avoided. She would fail in her duty if she did not speak the word of warning, and her children would equally fail in theirs, if they did not heed it.

Whenever, therefore, the Church has spoken authoritatively with regard to any society, her decision ought to be final for every Catholic. He ought to know that the Church has not acted hastily or unwisely, or mistakenly; he should be convinced that any worldly advantages which he might derive from his membership of such society, would be a poor substitute for the membership, the sacraments, and the blessings of the Church of Christ; he should have the courage of his religious convictions, and stand firm to faith and conscience. But if he be inclined or asked to join a society on which the Church has passed no sentence, then let him, as a reasonable and Christian man, examine into it carefully, and not join the society until he is satisfied as to its lawful character.

There is one characteristic which is always a strong presumption against a society, and that is secrecy. Our Divine Lord Himself has laid down the rule: "Every one that doth evil, hateth the light and cometh not to the light, that his works may not be reproved. But he that doth truth cometh to the light that his works may be made manifest, because they are done in God." [23] When, therefore associations veil themselves in secrecy and darkness, the presumption is against them, and it rests with them to prove that there is nothing evil in them.

But if any society's obligation be such as to bind its members to secrecy, even when rightly questioned by competent authority, then such a society puts itself outside the limits of approval; and no one can be a member of it and at the same time be admitted to the sacraments of the Catholic Church. The same is true of any organization that binds its members to a promise of blind obedience—to accept in advance and to obey whatsoever orders, lawful or unlawful, that may emanate from its chief authorities; because such a promise is contrary both to reason and conscience. And if a society works or plots, either openly or in secret, against the Church, or against lawful authorities, then to be a member of it is to be excluded from the membership of the Catholic Church.

These authoritative rules, therefore, ought to be the guide of all Catholics in their relations with societies. No Catholic can conscientiously join, or continue in, a body in which he knows that any of these condemned features exist. If he has joined it in good faith and the objectionable features become known to him afterwards, or if any of these evil elements creep into a society which was originally good, it becomes his duty to leave it at once. And even if he were to suffer loss or run the risk by leaving such a society or refusing to join it, he should do his duty and brave the consequences regardless of human consideration.

To these laws of the Church, the justice of which must be manifest to all impartial minds, we deem it necessary to add the following admonition of the Second Plenary Council:[24] "Care must be taken lest workingmen's societies, under the pretext of mutual assistance and protection, should commit any

[23] John iii. 20, 21.

[24] No. 519.

of the evils of condemned societies; and lest the members should be induced by the artifices of designing men to break the laws of justice, by withholding labor to which they are rightfully bound, or by otherwise unlawfully violating the rights of their employers."

But while the Church is thus careful to guard her children against whatever is contrary to Christian duty, she is no less careful that no injustice should be done to any association, however unintentionally. While therefore the Church, before prohibiting any society, will take every precaution to ascertain its true nature, we positively forbid any pastor, or other ecclesiastic, to pass sentence on any association or to impose ecclesiastical penalties or disabilities on its members without the previous explicit authorization of the rightful authorities.

Catholic Societies

It is not enough for Catholics to shun bad or dangerous societies, they ought to take part in good and useful ones. If there ever was a time when merely negative goodness would not suffice, such assuredly is the age in which we live. This is pre-eminently an age of action, and what we need to-day is active virtue and energetic piety. Again and again has the voice of the Vicar of Christ been heard, giving approval and encouragement to many kinds of Catholic associations, not only as a safeguard against the allurements of dangerous societies, but also as a powerful means of accomplishing much of the good that our times stand in need of. Not only should the pastors of the Church be hard at work in building up "the spiritual house,"[25] "the tabernacle of God with men,"[26] but every hand among the people of God should share in the labor.

In the first place, we hope that in every parish in the land there is some sodality or confraternity to foster piety among

[25] Pet. ii. 5.
[26] Apoc. xxi. 3.

the people. We therefore heartily endorse anew all approbations previously given to our many time-honored and cherished confraternities, such as those of the Sacred Heart of Jesus, of the Blessed Sacrament, and of the Blessed Virgin.

Next come the various associations for works of Christian zeal and charity: the Society for the Propagation of the Faith, and the Holy Childhood, than which there are none more deserving; societies for the support of Catholic education; Christian doctrine societies for the work of Sunday-schools; societies for improving the condition of the poor, among which stands pre-eminent the Society of St. Vincent de Paul; church-debt societies; societies for supplying poor churches with vestments and other altar requirements; local sanctuary societies; and other methods of uniting the efforts of the people of the parish for useful and holy purposes. It ought to be the comfort and the honest pride of every Catholic to take an active part in these good works; and if any are hindered from contributing a portion of their time and labor, they should contribute as liberally as they can out of their pecuniary resources.

Then there are associations for the checking of immorality, prominent among which are our Catholic Temperance Societies. These should be encouraged and aided by all who deplore the scandal given and the spiritual ruin wrought by intemperance. It is a mistake to imagine that such societies are made up of the reformed victims of intemperance. They should be, and we trust that they everywhere are largely composed of zealous Catholics who never were tainted by that vice, but who mourn over the great evil and are energetically endeavoring to correct it.

We likewise consider as worthy of particular encouragement associations for the promotion of healthful social union among Catholics,—and especially those, whose aim is to guard our Catholic young men against dangerous influences, and supply them with the means of innocent amusement and mental culture. It is obvious that our young men are exposed to the greatest dangers, and therefore need the most abundant helps. Hence, in the spirit of our Holy Father Leo XIII, we desire to see the number of thoroughly Catholic and well organized associations for their benefit greatly increased, especially in our large cities; we exhort pastors to consider the formation and careful direction of such societies as one of their most important duties; and we appeal to our young men to put to good profit, the best years of their lives, by banding together, under the direction of their pastors, for mutual improvement and encouragement in the paths of faith and virtue.

And in order to acknowledge the great amount of good that the "Catholic Young Men's National Union" has already accomplished, to promote the growth of the Union and to stimulate its members to greater efforts in the future, we cordially bless their aims and endeavors and recommend the Union to all our Catholic young men.

We also esteem as a very important element in practical Catholicity, the various forms of Catholic beneficial societies and kindred associations of Catholic workingmen. It ought to be, and we trust is everywhere their aim to encourage habits of industry, thrift, and sobriety; to guard the members against the dangerous attractions of condemned or suspicious organizations; and to secure the faithful practice of their religious duties, on which their temporal as well as their eternal welfare so largely depends.

With paternal affection we bestow our blessing upon all those various forms of combined Catholic action for useful and holy purposes. We desire to see their number multiplied and their organization perfected. We beseech them to remember that their success and usefulness must rest in a great measure, upon their fidelity to the spirit of the Church, and on their guarding carefully against influences that might make them disloyal. The more closely pastors and people are united in good works, the more abundantly will those associations be blessed and their ends accomplished, the more perfectly will all Christians be united in fraternal charity, and the more widely and firmly will the Kingdom of Christ on the earth be established.

9 Bishop John Lancaster Spalding

FRONTIER COLONIZATION TO SOLVE URBAN EVILS

The Religious Mission of the Irish People and Catholic Colonization *by the Most Rev. John Lancaster Spalding, Bishop of Peoria, Illinois, is one of the finest books in its field. It is an eloquent and thoughtful commentary on the social and religious superiority of rural life as compared to life in the city. In the excerpts given here, Bishop Spalding asserted that the concentration of Irish immigrants in the great cities, the factory towns, and the mining districts had almost halved Catholic growth. He tried to demonstrate that the cities literally destroyed body and soul. By means of the Irish Catholic Colonization Society, which he headed, and other systematic efforts, he hoped that thousands upon thousands of urban Catholics could be relocated in farming communities on the frontier. He believed that colonization should be the chief Catholic interest inasmuch as in a rural environment Catholic concerns —the work of religion, of charity, of education, of temperance, and of lay co-operation—were the more easily promoted.*

Spalding was aware, however, that extensive colonization faced almost insurmountable obstacles. He regretted that the late Archbishop Hughes had thrown the weight of his great influence against the movement at a time when the prospects of success seemed in retrospect to have been bright indeed. In Spalding's opinion, Hughes's outlook was narrow and provincial. Spalding's background and training inclined him to take a hopeful, if not a romanticized, view of rural life. Born into a central Kentucky Catholic family of colonial Maryland ancestry, Spalding, after the example of his uncle, the Most Reverend Martin John Spalding (Archbishop of Baltimore, 1864–1872), prepared for the priesthood. Several years of post-seminary study in European universities not only familiarized him with modern thought, but also permitted him to observe the vigorous Catholic life in many rural regions of Continental Europe. Experience as a missionary in New York City under Paulist auspices focused his attention on the moral wastelands of the country's growing cities.

. . . .The territorial distribution and the occupations of our Irish Catholic population are before our eyes, and their children and descendants are chiefly where they are and engaged in the same pursuits. About eight in every hundred are on the land, though not all as owners of the soil. The remaining ninety-two out of every hundred are chiefly in the tenement-houses of our great commercial cities, in the cottages of the factory towns, in the huts of the mining regions, in the shanties on the railroads and public works of the country, or living as domestic servants in the houses of the wealthy. A worse condition of affairs, so far as the welfare of the Irish people and the future of the Catholic religion in this country are concerned, I can hardly imagine. Apologists have not been and are not wanting who find this agglomeration of the Irish in the great cities and factory towns a providential occurrence. Yes,

---

John Lancaster Spalding, *The Religious Mission of the Irish People and Catholic Colonization* (New York: Catholic Publication Society Company, 1880), pp. 113–122, 138–149 (excerpts).

it is as providential as the penal laws, the confiscations, the massacres, and the famines which have made Ireland for centuries the home of all suffering and of all sorrows.

Lecky has said that if the Irish had been less chaste they would not have died of hunger by hundreds of thousands. But it was better to die of hunger than to be less chaste; and possibly it would have been better to die of hunger than to cross the Atlantic only to sink into the tenement-house and the factory mill. But what good has come of this crowding of the people in the cities, either to themselves or the Church? It has facilitated the creation of episcopal sees, some one has written; but it is safe to say that the number of bishops in the United States would be double what it is had the Irish Catholics settled on the land.

In the early ages, we are told, Christianity was propagated from the cities as from vital centres. There is no parallel whatever in the situations, and the argument is founded upon ignorance of the radical contrast between pagan and Christian civilization in respect to distribution of population. In imperial Rome the cities were the civilized world. In Christian times the basis of power and empire is the country. Of old the peasant was a slave; but now the farmer is Christ's and nature's freeman. "The congregation of foreign-born emigrants," says a writer in the *Catholic World* (July, 1877), "most of whom are Catholics, has had the effect of making the Catholic Church in these cities a noticeable and a respectable fact, of thereby accomplishing one of the preliminaries in the work which it has yet to perform in the republic." This I confess to be unable to find to be even plausible. The Catholic Church, in the first place, is the most noticeable and respectable fact in the wide world, and whoever is unable to see this will most certainly not be impressed with its truth by viewing the crowds of our people in the great cities. On the contrary, the traditional conceit that Protestant nations are superior to the Catholic is kept alive and strengthened by the contrast which exists between

Protestants and Catholics in these commercial centres and manufacturing towns. It is, of course, easy enough to explain that the Church is in no way responsible for this; but "things seen are mightier than things heard," and the prejudiced eye accepts the fact that pleases it, and asks for no explanations. The religious prejudices of Americans are dying out because their faith in Protestantism is day by day growing weaker; but I am profoundly convinced that the condition of our people in the tenement-houses and the factory towns is an obstacle and not a help to their conversion. Who can travel through New England without being forced to recognize the existence of two distinct and separate peoples there? The one has wealth and social position; the other does the drudgery and hard work. If nothing else had been left for our people to do but to make themselves the slaves and servants of others, we might accept the humiliating position in silence; but to congratulate ourselves upon the good there is in it seems to be little less than folly. For myself, I cannot see the jewel in the toad's head. This collecting of large multitudes of poor laborers upon single points has, no doubt, by creating parishes of fifteen and twenty thousand souls, made the erection of fine and showy churches possible. But to what purpose is this outward splendor, if the temple within the conscience falls to ruin? The pyramids of Egypt, it is said, were built by slaves; and I see not how one can look with complacency upon magnificent structures when he knows that the building of them means the absence of home and a future for God's people. Half a dozen churches serve the purpose of an episcopal city as well as a hundred; and, in fact, one of the chief difficulties in the administration of the large dioceses of this country is the necessity of maintaining, at great outlay of money, asylums and orphanages which are always crowded. Institutions of this kind would be hardly needed had the masses of our people settled upon the fertile lands which were to be had for nothing.

The true view of this whole matter, and the only view which

will commend itself to a thoughtful and observant mind, is the one to which John Francis Maguire has given expression in the following words: "I deliberately assert," he writes, "that it is not within the power of language to describe adequately, much less to exaggerate, the evil consequences of this unhappy tendency of the Irish to congregate in the large towns of America. . . . It is easy enough to explain why and how those who should not have remained in the great cities did so, but it is not easy to depict the evils which have flowed, which daily flow, which, unhappily for the race, must continue to flow, from the pernicious tendency of the Irish peasant to adopt a mode of livelihood for which he is not suited by previous knowledge or training, and to place himself in a position dangerous to his morals, if not fatal to his independence."*

New York, which is the great American city, is also the chief centre of the Irish population of the United States. There were in New York in 1870, 202,000 natives of Ireland; and if to these we add the children and descendants of Irishmen the number was probably not far from half a million. There were at that time some sixteen thousand and more tenement-houses in New York, inhabited by a population of over half a million, by far the greater portion of which was Irish and Irish-American. The wretched sanitary condition of these tenement-houses the Commissioners of the Metropolitan Board of Health declared to be the first and at all times the most prolific cause of disease in the city. They were built almost solely with a view to profit and without any regard to the health or comfort of the occupants. They were overcrowded, ill-ventilated, and filled with noxious sewer-gas and the miasma from the stagnant water with which the cellars were often flooded to the depth of several inches.

In portions of the Fourth Ward the population of the tenement-houses was in 1864 "packed at the rate of about 290,000

* *The Irish in America,* pp. 214, 216.

to the square mile," while even in London the density of population has never gone beyond 175,816 to the square mile. The descriptions given by the sanitary inspectors of these habitations and their inmates would soil a page intended for all eyes. People who live in this atmosphere and amid these surroundings must drink. The perfectly sober would die there from mere loathing of life. At every step there is a low dram-shop, and even the children acquire the appetite of their parents for alcoholic stimulants.

The destruction of infant life in this atmosphere is without parallel. "The rate of mortality in children under five years of age in New York," say the Commissioners of the Board of Health, "is greater than in any city with which this board has correspondence; and the cause of this excess will best be sought in the miserable housing and habits of the laboring classes, and in the multiplied sources of foul air in our two cities. . . . From various data now in hand the conclusion is warranted that death has in each of the past two years taken nearly one-third of the total number before the first birthday."

This high death-rate is not confined to the infant population of the tenement-houses. The occupations of the masses of the Irish people in the United States are precisely those which are most fatal to human life, either from the character of the work itself or from the kind of existence which it necessarily involves. Whatever lowers morality diminishes vitality, and the inspired word, Death is the wages of sin, is a truth which is experimentally verifiable. Not only do drunkenness, gluttony, impurity, wrath work unto death, but whatever disturbs peace of conscience or interferes with wholeness of character cooperates to the same end. Peace and tranquillity are the atmosphere of life; trouble and anxiety are the agents of death. Laborers who build railroads, construct levees, and dig canals, or who are employed in mines and foundries, or as engine-drivers or hackmen, are not only more exposed to fatal accidents than others, but they are also less protected from the hurtful influences of climate and change of season. They have bad food and water, are often compelled to live in tents and shanties, frequently fall ill of acute diseases, and in these attacks they have no proper medical aid or nursing. They are paid off at stated times, so that once a week or once a month they are flush with money, and in their surroundings the only indulgence which presents itself is a debauch. The mortality from disease of those who lead such lives will not fall far short of that of an army in the field, where the deaths from exposure and hardship exceed the loss of life in battle.

The work of the factories is, as all admit, specially fatal to women and children. "Woman," says Dr. Weber, "is weaker than man. Like the child, she has a more mobile character, and consequently continuous occupation fatigues her more than man. Her digestion is more rapid; she eats less at a time, and ought, therefore, to interrupt her work to take nourishment oftener than man. She is also more agile, and can in a given time go through a greater number of precise and quick movements than man. Hence there is an increasing demand for woman's work in the shops and factory mills, since this ease and quickness of movement enable her to adapt herself so readily to the motions of machinery; but to do this she expends an excessive amount of vital force. The difference is like that between running and walking. The necessity of remaining for hours in a standing posture is the cause of still greater hurt to her physical constitution. Some relief she might get if, on leaving the shop or the factory, she was permitted to rest, but at home she finds household duties and the care of children awaiting her." There are few sadder sights than the poor women of the cotton and woollen mills of New England, so many of whom are Irish girls, whose cheeks once bloomed with health as fresh and fair as the purity of their hearts. In the manufacturing towns of England and of other parts of Europe there are doubtless scenes more gloomy; but there no escape seemed to exist from this death in life, while in our own land everything ought to be possible rather than this slavery.

These considerations, and others which will readily suggest themselves, give the true solution of the difficulty concerning the smallness of the Catholic population of the United States. It is constantly asserted that the natural increase of the Catholic immigrants would give us to-day a population of not less than twelve millions, whereas our numbers do not exceed seven millions. Therefore, it is argued, five millions, or nearly one-half, have fallen away from the Church. Nothing could be more fallacious. Comparatively few have abandoned the faith, and our losses are chiefly to be sought for in the almost incredible infant mortality among our people, in the high death-rate among the immigrants themselves, and in the fact that large numbers of them have not married at all. It was this exceptional mortality of Catholic parents which threw upon the world thousands of orphans at a time when the Church was not yet prepared to offer them asylum; and very many of them doubtless fell into the hands of Protestants, and were so lost to the Catholic cause. And, as I have shown, there was a remnant who settled on the land; and as there was no organization or guidance in this movement, many took up Government claims or bought farms without any thought of their surroundings, and found themselves in Protestant neighborhoods beyond the reach of priest or church. They, of course, soon became indifferent, and their children grew up without any knowledge of their faith, and frequently joined some one of the sects. The intermarriage of Catholics with Protestants has been, and is still, another cause of loss to the Church in this country; but the fountain-head of the evil, compared with which all other causes of loss are insignificant, was the fatal and never sufficiently to be deplored concentration of the Irish immigrants in the great cities, the factory towns, and the mining districts. . . .

When we turn now to consider what is to be done in order to sink deeper the foundations of the Church in this land, which is half the world, so that they shall uphold a glorious and imperishable temple of God, many thoughts urge themselves upon our attention. In the first place, what our fathers have been doing we must continue to do. New dioceses are to be created, new parishes are to be formed, more priests are to be ordained; the religious orders are to be multiplied and strengthened; works of charity which are founded for the care of the orphan, the reformation of the fallen, the nursing of the sick, and the sheltering of the aged, must continue to receive all encouragement and assistance. Then there is the still greater work of the religious education of the young. A system of education which excludes the teaching of religion is, in our eyes, a radically and essentially false system. We do not object to taxation for the support of schools; we are not opposed to laws which render school attendance obligatory; but we do not accept, we never can accept, for our own children a system of education which ignores what we hold to be the fountain-head of all true knowledge and of all right conduct—the inculcation of the love and fear of God through the teaching of definite religious doctrines and practices. It is not a part of the duty of true and loyal American citizens that they should all think alike on questions of education any more than on questions of religion. We use our privilege not to be on the side of the majority, and we suffer for it, though the loss may be gain. The consequence, however, is that we are compelled to form a system of our own. We have some twenty-three hundred parochial schools, in which there are over four hundred thousand children. This work must be continued until every parish shall have its school. More than this, some system of grades, examinations, and superintendence of diocesan boards must be introduced into our schools. Standards and tests of qualification in the teachers, whether secular or religious, should also be fixed by some central authority, so that it shall no longer depend upon accident whether the school is Catholic except in name.

Something of this kind has already been begun here and

there, and the work of organization will doubtless be continued. And for the higher education, it is impossible to remain content with the present Latin schools and elementary theological seminaries. A system of education which does not receive as its crown a true and real university is not only incomplete, but deprived of its surest defence and the master-light which should shine upon the steps of those who tread the humbler paths of knowledge. But if this centre of Catholic culture is to exist in our age and country it must be created, with deliberate and conscious purpose. To hope that it will come as a natural and spontaneous development is to cherish a delusion.

Then there is the great and holy cause of temperance—the all-earnest and ceaseless warfare upon one of the arch-enemies of our people and our faith in the United States. It is God's work to spend one's self and to be spent in unwearying efforts to assist in creating a public opinion which will more and more hold drunkenness to be one of the foulest and most loathsome of vices—the spirit of the fiend working the ruin of man, of woman, of the child; breaking into the sanctuary of home with murderous hand and polluting its sweet air with pestilent breath; filling with its inhuman victims prisons and asylums, and peopling the abyss of hell.

It is important, too, that more serious efforts should be made to bring the negro population of this country under Catholic influence; and this can never be done until we fully recognize that this is a work which must be taken in hand by the bishops and priests of the United States. To expect any great results from the labors of missionaries sent out by foreign seminaries is to ignore the essential conditions of the problem with which we have to deal.

It is doubtless most desirable also that steps should be taken to organize a Catholic Congress which will meet annually or biennially, the constitution and workings of which will be similar to the *Generalversammlung* of the Catholics of Germany. No other means, it seems to me, will so certainly and effectively bring about the intelligent co-operation of the clergy and laity for the furtherance of Catholic interests. The troubles which arose from trusteeism have tended to make laymen more or less indifferent to our religious wants, because of the concentration of the whole management of the affairs of the Church in the hands of ecclesiastics. Our organization, however, is now so perfect that we can without fear invite the active aid of the laity; and any work which will tend to cause Catholics in general to take a more intelligent interest in the progress and welfare of religion will prove most salutary.

But greater than this, and more urgent than all else, is the cause of Catholic Colonization, which gathers up into itself the work of religion, of charity, of education, of temperance, and of lay co-operation. By Catholic colonization I mean the systematic and deliberate effort to take our people from the great cities and factory towns, from the mines and railroads, from domestic service in hotels and private houses, and to place them upon the cheap and fertile lands of our country. I would co-operate with those who advertise that "no Irish need apply" by striving to make Irishmen and Irishwomen unwilling to ask any man to hire them. I would labor to lift them out of the fluctuating and uncertain state in which they are at the mercy of commercial crises and the mutations of trade, without a permanent home, and therefore without the possibility of historic growth or the opportunity of exerting a lasting influence. I would show to them that the atmosphere in which the life of the family is enfeebled will necessarily prove fatal to the reverent and religious habit of mind which is one of the chief glories of the Irish race. I would proclaim that it is vain to hope that Catholic schools will form a noble and Christian character in children who have no home. I would declare that parents who wilfully and knowingly bring up their children amid surroundings which must be a proximate occasion of ruin have denied the faith and are worse than infidels. I would point out the plain fact that the Irish race, in its present floating and unsettled state, can have little hope of a future in America, and will pass away and leave no monument worthy of itself.

But it is needless to enlarge upon a subject with which I have been dealing all along; and, besides, there is probably no thoughtful or observant person whose sympathies are with the Irish people and the Catholic religion who is not ready to admit that it would be difficult to exaggerate the evil of which I speak. No one, I presume, would think of denying that it would be immeasurably better for the people and the Church if the hundreds of thousands who are working in the factory mills or the mines, or living in the tenement-houses of the great cities, were securely settled on their own land. On this point there are not, I imagine, two opinions among serious persons. But there are large numbers who will take the view that the evil is remediless, and they will probably think it a mistake to bring out in such strong relief, as I have sought to do, the dangers which may justly be apprehended from a state of things which, after all, cannot be greatly changed. And it is possible, I must confess, that a right appreciation of the facts may justify them in this opinion. In the first place, there is a static quality in masses and numbers which it is difficult to overcome. The crowd of men are more passive than active, and will endure an almost incredible degree of misery and oppression rather than seek relief which can be found only in radical changes. They prefer to endure the ills they suffer rather than fly to others they know not of. Then there is the intoxication of city life, which seems to deprive the poor, even more than those who are well to do, of the power of seeing things as they are, so that they often imagine that it is better to be wretched in the company of thousands than to dwell in comfort and independence in the bosom of one's own family. Their prejudices against country life are more unreasonable and therefore more difficult to overcome than those of the educated, who often look forward to the quiet of some rural home as the peaceful refuge of their old age, where, far from the maddening crowd, they may give the thoughts and loves of their closing days to God and the soul. It is a dream only, but filled with images of what is deepest and most heavenly in the human heart.

Again, it must be admitted that the causes which in our day drive multitudes of the laboring classes in Europe and America to swell the population of the industrial centres tend also to keep them there. Their presence has helped to build up interests, both religious and secular, which, it might be held, would be endangered if it were possible, by systematic and persistent agitation, to bring about any considerable redistribution of population. At points where large numbers of Catholics have been gathered costly churches, and occasionally schools also, have been erected, and these structures are frequently still encumbered with debts. It is in accordance with psychological laws that, in such circumstances, the pastors should feel no great enthusiasm for a cause which might have the effect of lessening the revenues with which they are to meet their obligations. As the gas-jet by which we write seems as large as one of the fixed stars, so do our own little projects rise mountain-high before our eyes and shut from view great and universal causes. It is not surprising, then, that instances should be known in which the pastors deliberately set their faces against any attempt to persuade their people that the life of an operative in a factory mill is not as desirable as any other. And it is held that in so acting they are but following the example of one of the ablest and most enlightened prelates of the Church in America. I refer, of course, to Archbishop Hughes, whose views on this subject, as brought out by a project to found an Irish colony in Nebraska in 1857, it is impossible to pass over in silence in a treatise such as this. These views, it is proper to remark, are found in a brief address, which is evidently an impromptu and incidental utterance, inspired by what he considered a disregard of his episcopal authority, and delivered, as its tone indicates, under a feeling of strong disapprobation of the proceedings of a colonization convention which had been recently held in Buffalo. He suspected the good faith of some of the members of that convention, and openly declared that there were landowners among them whose sole aim was to advertise their own property. It is not surprising, under such circumstances, that the general impression made by the archbishop's speech should have been that he was opposed to the settlement of the Catholic people upon the land, though he expressly declared that he "had ever given to the emigrant who came in his way the advice rather to seek a home in the West than remain in our cities." He fully accepted, therefore, the general principle which underlies all honest efforts to induce the poor to make homes for themselves in the country. In the very next breath, however, he openly condemns all colonization schemes, all systematic efforts to accomplish what he nevertheless admits to be desirable. "But," he says, "that was one by one, in the natural order, not by an artificial combination of men who were unfit to govern a township if anybody gave them one; it was by no combination, because emigration from Ireland hither, and from hence westward, was a natural thing." He stated also that in one of his early dreams he had wished to form an association for the purpose of buying ten or twenty thousand acres of land in the present State of Wisconsin, with a view to forming a Catholic settlement; but when he mentioned the project to men of means and intelligence they had condemned it as wholly impracticable. He protested, moreover, against all attempts to build up exclusively Irish towns, and ended by saying that, so far as he himself and the clergymen of his diocese were concerned, he desired that "religion should not be debased by being brought into questions of this kind."

That Archbishop Hughes became the opponent of colonization is, I am persuaded, most unfortunate. No other man has ever had such influence over the Irish Catholics of the United States, and no other could have done so much to make them realize that their interests for time and eternity required that they should make homes for themselves on the land. To imagine that questions of this kind do not concern religion and the ministers of religion is a fatal mistake. This is primarily and essentially a question of morality. The important consideration is: What surroundings will best protect the sanctity of the family, preserve the purity of childhood, and promote the growth of religious character? When we deplore the poverty of our people in the cities we are thinking above all of the sin and degradation of which, in such an atmosphere, poverty is so often the occasion; and so through the whole argument the moral element is decisive. Now, religion rests upon morality; it is not the intellect but sin which undermines faith; and to seek to exclude the priest from active participation in movements which affect the moral welfare of his people is to condemn him to impotence.

To oppose, in the matter of settlement upon the land, what is supposed to be the natural order to artificial combinations—that is, to approve of the individual who buys a farm, but to condemn a number of individuals who enter into an association in order to secure along with the farm advantages of church, school, and society—is, upon the very face of the matter, to take up an untenable position. If it is desirable that the poor should get homes upon the land, organized efforts to assist them in doing so cannot but be praiseworthy; and when there is question of settling in new and distant parts of the country it cannot be said that the natural order is to go one by one. Here certainly the *vœ soli* may be applied with special force. The point raised as to the unwisdom of attempting to establish exclusively Irish towns is of no importance. In the first place, this is not an aim of Irish Catholic colonization. No such national exclusiveness exists. Americans, Germans, Norwegians, and others may, if they so desire, and in fact often do, settle in the Irish colonies of the West. Still there is no reason to fear that evil would result from exclusively Irish settlements. The

Irish citizens of the United States are intensely American, and possession of the soil will but strengthen their spirit of patriotism.

We come back again, then, to our original position, that it would be the greatest of blessings to hundreds of thousands of our poor people who are working in factories and mines, or engaged in other hired service, if they could be settled in their own homes upon the cheap lands of our country. The evil of their present mode of life is great; is it also remediless? I have stated the reasons which make one doubt whether there is hope of bringing about any great change in the territorial distribution and occupations of our people; and I will now say that my own conviction is that there is hope, and that this is, of all others, the work which in our day the Catholic Church in the United States is called upon by God's providence to accomplish.

PART TWO

The Emergence of Catholic Social Liberalism

10 James Cardinal Gibbons

THE STAKE OF THE CATHOLIC CHURCH IN THE LABOR MOVEMENT

The central figure in the decision of the Catholic Church in America to support the cause of organized labor was the Most Reverend James Cardinal Gibbons, Archbishop of Baltimore. Although the Holy See had twice upheld the condemnation of the Knights of Labor by the Archbishop of Quebec, Cardinal Gibbons believed that the condemnation was unjust, imprudent and unnecessary. His memorial to this effect, which he presented to the Church authorities in Rome early in 1887, was so persuasive and convincing that they agreed to lift the ban on the Order. In the chapter on the Knights in his autobiography, published in 1916, Gibbons reprinted the English translation of the memorial (the original was in the French of Bishop John Ireland, of St. Paul) and gave it historical perspective in an illuminating prefatory note.

Gibbons was unreservedly, almost belligerently, friendly to organized labor. Unionism was the only defense of the toiling masses against the "mail-clad" power of "hard and obstinate monopoly." He warned that an alliance, or even apparent alliance, between the Church and the powerful rich would alienate Catholic wage-earners from the Church and drive them into the camp of revolution. He also insisted that in America, a country of "mixed people," Catholics could not live in social isolation. He was at great pains, therefore, to minimize the danger to the faith of Catholics from their association with Protestants, atheists and socialists in labor unions and in civic and philanthropic organizations.

Gibbons' thought and timely action tightened the bonds of sympathy between the Catholic Church and conservative trade unionism in America. This in turn may well have served, as many historians and social scientists think, to prevent the growth of a powerful revolutionary labor movement and the emergence of an independent labor party in American politics.

THE KNIGHTS OF LABOR

Prefatory Note

A few words of explanation will be necessary that the reader may understand the causes which led up to my presenting the following document to the Sacred Congregation of the Propaganda.

Ever since the Reformation the democratic and co-operative institutions of medieval Europe have been upon their deathbed. In the year 1500 most Englishmen, for instance, owned their own homes, but by 1600 between two-thirds and three-fourths only were still in possession of their own lands. By 1700 one-half still had the economic buttress of a home behind them; but by the year 1900 less than one-tenth of the population possessed all the land of the country.

And what is true of real property is true also of the means of production. Trade and business in the middle ages were conducted on the principles of mutual help and assistance, and unlimited competition was never thought of. But with the breaking down of the corporate feeling of united Christendom, methods of business were introduced which would have seemed deeply immoral 100 years before.

The discovery of the new world with its abounding riches and consequent opportunities for exploitation was another factor which greatly increased the evil. But what brought these economic evils to a head was the invention of machinery in the

---

James Cardinal Gibbons, *A Retrospect of Fifty Years* (Baltimore: John Murphy Company, 1916), I, 186–209.

last half of the eighteenth and the first half of the nineteenth century.

Those who live in these days cannot conceive of the state of society in the seventies and the eighties. The money of the country was not only concentrated into the hands of a very few people, but by means of this money this small oligarchy was put in the position of getting complete control of our free institutions. The mass of people dispossessed of land and of the means of production, and retaining only a figment of political power, were by no means satisfied with this arrangement. All the more so as large numbers of the working people, that is to say the dispossessed, were members of the Catholic Church, and among Roman Catholics there is and must always be a memory of a better tradition which preserved to every man as much individual liberty as was compatible with the rights of his fellow men.

Accordingly numerous societies for the protection of the working man rose during the administration of President Cleveland—societies to which working people began to adhere more and more steadfastly as their only protection from economic slavery, but which were vehemently attacked upon the other side as destructive, revolutionary and even anarchic; and indeed the oppression of the wealthy was driving the poor into excesses of which the anarchist riots of Chicago were but one example.

These societies could not long escape the wise oversight of the Church, and it was a foregone conclusion that in a few years the principle of such organizations of working people must either be approved or condemned. On the one hand great numbers of Ecclesiastics were alarmed at the revolutionary principles which undoubtedly disgraced some members of the trade unions; the more so as many of them were at least nominally secret societies. So great was this alarm in Canada that the Canadian Bishops obtained from the Holy See a condemnation of the Knights of Labor for Canada. But if many Bishops were alarmed at what they considered the revolutionary tendencies of these associations, many other Bishops, including Cardinal Manning and myself, were equally alarmed at the prospect of the Church being presented before our age as the friend of the powerful rich and the enemy of the helpless poor; for not only would such an alliance, or even apparent alliance, have done the Church untold harm, but it would have been the bouleversement of our whole history. Moreover, to us it seemed that such a thing could never take place. The one body in the world which had been the protector of the poor and the weak for nearly 1800 years, could not possibly desert these same classes in their hour of need.

It was under such circumstances that I consulted with Mr. Cleveland, President of the United States, and Mr. Pouderly [Powderly], who was President of the Knights of Labor, and at a meeting of the Archbishops of the country I asked Mr Pouderly [*sic*] to tell their Graces exactly what the obligation of secrecy consisted in. This he very kindly consented to do, and he showed us plainly on that occasion, first, that secrecy was only enjoined upon the members by a simple pledge, and not by an oath; secondly, that this secrecy was only approved by the society of the Knights of Labor in so far as it was necessary to protect their business from enemies; thirdly, that there was nothing in the obligation of secrecy which would prevent any individual manifesting his conscience in the tribunal of Penance privately, or which would prevent the heads of the order from giving the necessary assurances and manifesting everything to competent ecclesiastical authority even outside of confession.

Only two out of the twelve Archbishops were for condemnation; the rest agreed with me that we must do all in our power to prevent any such condemnation of the Knights of Labor in our own country, as would drive them into the camp of revolution.

Accordingly when I sailed for Europe in 1887 to receive the Cardinal's Hat it was part of my mission to present the plea of organized labor, which I did by presenting the following document to the Cardinal Prefect of Propaganda. I cannot say that the task which I had imposed upon myself was an easy one, but I am thankful to say that it proved not an impossible one, and that the Knights of Labor in the United States were not condemned.

It was a great consolation to me when a few years afterward the late Pontiff, Leo XIII annunciated the principles which underlie the Church's moral teaching with regard to economics, in his famous Encyclical "*Rerum Novarum.*"*

"To His Eminence Cardinal Simeoni, Prefect of the Sacred Congregation of the Propaganda:

"Your Eminence—In submitting to the Holy See the conclusions which, after several months of attentive observation and reflection, seem to me to sum up the truth concerning the association of the Knights of Labor, I feel profoundly convinced of the vast importance of the consequences attaching to this question, which is but a link in the great chain of the social problems of our day, and especially of our country.

"In treating this question I have been very careful to follow as my constant guide the spirit of the encyclical letters, in which our Holy Father Leo XIII has so admirably set forth the dangers of our times and their remedies, as well as the principles by which we are to recognize associations condemned by the Holy See. Such was also the guide of the Third Plenary Council of Baltimore in its teachings concerning the principles to be followed and the dangers to be shunned by the faithful either in the choice or in the establishment of those various forms of association toward which the spirit of our popular institutions so strongly impels them. And, considering the evil

* In preparing this Memorial, I gratefully acknowledge the valuable aid of the venerable Archbishop Ireland, of St. Paul, and of Rt. Rev. Bishop Keane, who were then in Rome.

consequences that might result from a mistake in the treatment of organizations which often count their members by thousands and hundreds of thousands, the council wisely ordained (n. 225) that, when an association is spread over several dioceses, not even the bishop of one of these dioceses shall condemn it, but shall refer the case to a standing committee consisting of all the archbishops of the United States; and even these are not authorized to condemn, unless their sentence be unanimous; and in case they fail to agree unanimously, then only the supreme tribunal of the Holy See can impose a condemnation: all this in order to avoid error and confusion of discipline.

"This committee of archbishops held a meeting towards the end of last October, at which the association of the Knights of Labor was specially considered. To this we were not impelled by the request of any of our bishops, for none of them had asked it; and I must add that among all the bishops we know of but two or three who desire the condemnation. But our reason was the importance attached to the question by the Holy See itself, and this led us to examine it with all possible care. After our deliberations, the result of which has already been communicated to the Sacred Congregation of the Propaganda, only two out of the twelve archbishops voted for condemnation, and their reasons were powerless to convince the others of either the justice or the prudence of such condemnation.

"In the following considerations I wish to state in detail the reasons which determined the vote of the great majority of the committee—reasons whose truth and force seem to me all the more evident after this lapse of time; nor will I fail to do justice to the arguments advanced on the other side:

"1. In the first place, though there may be found in the constitution, laws and official declarations of the Knights of Labor things that we would not approve, still we have failed to find in them those elements so clearly pointed out by the Holy See which would class them among condemned associations:

"(a) In their form of initiation there is no oath.

"(b) The obligation to secrecy by which they keep the knowledge of their business from enemies or strangers is not such as to hinder Catholics from manifesting everything to competent ecclesiastical authority, even outside of confession. This has been positively declared to us by their chief officers.

"(c) They make no promise of blind obedience. The object and laws of the association are distinctly declared, and the obligation of obedience does not go beyond them.

"(d) They not only profess no hostility against religion or the Church, but their declarations are quite to the contrary. The third Plenary Council commands (n. 254) that condemnation shall not be passed on any association without the previous hearing of its officers or representatives. Now, their president, when sending me a copy of their constitution, declared that he is a devoted Catholic; that he practises his religion faithfully, and receives the sacraments regularly; that he belongs to no Masonic society or other association condemned by the Church; that he knows nothing in the organization of the Knights of Labor contrary to the laws of the Church; that, with filial submission, he begs the pastors of the Church to examine their constitution and laws, and to point out anything they may find objectionable, promising to see to its correction. Assuredly, there is in all this no hostility to the authority of the Church, but, on the contrary, a disposition in every way praiseworthy. After their convention, held last year in Richmond, he and several of the principal members, devout Catholics, made similar declarations concerning the action of that convention, the documents of which we expect to receive shortly.

"(e) Nor do we find in this organization any hostility to the authority and laws of our country. Not only does nothing of the kind appear in their constitution and laws, but the heads of our civil government treat with respect the cause which such associations represent. The President of the United States told me personally, a few weeks ago, that he then had under consideration a proposed law for the amelioration of certain social grievances, and that he had had a long conversation on these topics with Mr. Powderly, the President of the Knights of Labor. The Congress of the United States, in compliance with the views presented by President Cleveland in his annual message, is at present engaged in framing measures for the improvement of the condition of the laboring classes, in whose complaints they acknowledge that there is a great deal of truth. And our political parties, far from considering them the enemies of the country, vie with each other in championing the evident rights of the workmen, who seek not to resist or overthrow the laws, but only to obtain just legislation by constitutional and legitimate means.

"These considerations, which show that in these associations those elements are not to be found which the Holy See has condemned, lead us to study, in the second place, the evils which the association contends against, and the nature of the conflict.

"2. That there exist among us, as in all other countries of the world, grave and threatening social evils, public injustices which call for strong resistance and legal remedy, is a fact which no one dares to deny—a fact already acknowledged by the Congress and the President of the United States. Without entering into the sad details of these evils, whose full discussion is not necessary, I will only mention that monopolies, on the part of both individuals and of corporations, have everywhere called forth not only the complaints of our working classes, but also the opposition of our public men and legislators; that the efforts of monopolists, not always without success, to control legislation to their own profit, cause serious apprehensions among the disinterested friends of liberty; that the heartless avarice which, through greed of gain, pitilessly grinds not only the men, but even the women and children in various employments, make it clear to all who love humanity and justice that it is not only the right of the laboring classes to protect themselves, but the duty of the whole people to aid them in finding a remedy against the dangers with which both civilization and social order are menaced by avarice, oppression and corruption.

"It would be vain to dispute either the existence of the evils, or the right of legitimate resistance, or the necessity of a remedy. At most a doubt might be raised about the legitimacy of the form of resistance, and of the remedy employed by the Knights of Labor. This, then, is the next point to be examined.

"3. It can hardly be doubted that, for the attainment of any public end, association—the organization of all interested—is the most efficacious means—a means altogether natural and just. This is so evident, and besides so conformable to the genius of our country, of our essentially popular social conditions, that it is unnecessary to insist upon it. It is almost the only means to invite public attention, to give force to the most legitimate resistance, to add weight to the most just demands.

"Now, there already exists an organization which presents innumerable attractions and advantages, but with which our Catholic workingmen, filially obedient to the Holy See, refuse to unite themselves; this is the Masonic Order, which exists everywhere in our country, and which, as Mr. Powderly has expressly pointed out to us, unites employers and employed in a brotherhood very advantageous to the latter, but which numbers in its ranks hardly a single Catholic. Nobly renouncing advantages which the Church and conscience forbid, our workingmen join associations in no way in conflict with religion, seeking nothing but mutual protection and help, and the legitimate assertion of their rights. Must they here also find themselves threatened with condemnation, hindered from their only means of self-defense?

"4. Let us now consider the objections made against this sort of organization.

"(a) It is objected that in such organizations, Catholics are mixed with Protestants, to the peril of their faith. Naturally, yes; they are mixed with Protestants at their work; for, in a mixed people like ours the separation of religious creeds in civil affairs is an impossibility. But to suppose that the faith of our Catholics suffers thereby is not to know the Catholic working men of America, who are not like the working men of so many European countries—misguided children, estranged from their Mother, the Church, and regarding her with suspicion and dread—but intelligent, well-instructed and devoted Catholics, ready to give their blood, if necessary, as they continually give their hard-earned means, for her support and protection. And, in fact, it is not here a question of Catholics mixed with Protestants, but rather that Protestants are admitted to share in the advantages of an association, many of whose members and officers are Catholics; and, in a country like ours, their exclusion would be simply impossible.

"(b) But it is asked, instead of such an organization, could there not be confraternities, in which the working men would be united under the direction of the clergy and the influence of religion? I answer frankly that I do not consider this either possible or necessary in our country. I sincerely admire the efforts of this sort which are made in countries where the working people are led astray by the enemies of religion, but, thanks be to God, that is not our condition. We find that in our country the presence and direct influence of the clergy would not be advisable where our citizens, without distinction of religious belief, come together in regard to their industrial interests alone. Short of that we have abundant means for making our working people faithful Catholics, and simple good sense advises us not to go to extremes.

"(c) Again, it is objected that, in such organizations, Catholics are exposed to the evil influences of the most dangerous associates, even of atheists, communists and anarchists. That is true, but it is one of those trials of faith which our brave American Catholics are accustomed to meet almost daily, and which they know how to face with good sense and firmness. The press of our country tells us, and the president of the Knights has related to us, how these violent, aggressive elements have endeavored to control the association, or to inject poison into its principles; but they also inform us with what determination these machinators have been repulsed and beaten.

"The presence among our citizens of those dangerous social elements, which have mostly come from certain countries of Europe, is assuredly for us an occasion of great regret and of vigilant precautions; it is a fact, however, which we have to accept, but which the close union between the Church and her children that exists in our country renders comparatively free from danger. In truth, the only thing from which we would fear serious danger would be a cooling of this relationship between the Church and her children, and I know nothing that would be more likely to occasion it than imprudent condemnations.

"(d) A specially weighty charge is drawn from the outbursts of violence, even to bloodshed, which have accompanied several of the strikes inaugurated by labor organizations. Concerning this, three things are to be remarked—first, strikes are not an invention of the Knights of Labor, but a means almost everywhere and always resorted to by the working classes to protect themselves against what they consider injustice, and in assertion of what they believe to be their just rights; secondly, in such a struggle of the poor and indignant multitudes against hard and obstinate monopoly, outbursts of anger are almost as inevitable as they are greatly to be regretted; thirdly, the laws and the chief authorities of the Knights of Labor, far from encouraging violence or the occasions of it, exercise a powerful influence to hinder it, and to retain strikes within the limits of good order and of legitimate action.

"A careful examination of the acts of violence accompanying the struggle between capital and labor last year leaves us convinced that it would be unjust to attribute them to the association of the Knights of Labor, for this association was but one among the numerous labor organizations that took part in the strikes, and their chief officers used every possible effort, as disinterested witnesses testify, to appease the anger of the multitudes, and to hinder the excesses which, therefore, in my judgment, could not justly be attributed to them. Doubtless, among the Knights of Labor, as among the thousands of other working men, there are to be found passionate or even wicked men who have committed inexcusable deeds of violence, and have instigated their associates to the same, but to attribute this to the association would, it seems to me, be as unreasonable as to attribute to the Church the follies or the crimes of her children against which she strives and protests.

"I repeat that, in such a struggle of the great masses of the people against the mail-clad power, which as it is acknowledged, often refuses them the simple rights of humanity and justice, it is vain to expect that every error and every act of violence can be avoided; and to dream that this struggle can be hindered, or that we can deter the multitudes from organizing, which is their only hope of success; would be to ignore the nature and forces of human society in times like ours. Christian prudence evidently counsels us to hold the hearts of the multitudes by the bonds of love, in order to control their actions by the principles of faith, justice and charity, to acknowledge frankly what is true and just in their cause, in order to deter them from what is false and criminal, and thus to turn into a legitimate, peaceable and beneficent contest what might easily, by a course of repulsive severity, become for the masses of our people a dread volcanic force like unto that which society fears and the Church deplores in Europe.

"Upon this point I insist strongly, because, from an intimate acquaintance with the social conditions of our country I am profoundly convinced that here we are touching upon a subject which not only concerns the rights of the working classes, who ought to be especially dear to the Church which our Lord sent forth to preach His Gospel to the poor, but with which are intimately bound up the fundamental interests of the Church and of human society for the future. This is a point which I desire, in a few additional words, to develop more clearly.

"5. Whoever meditates upon the ways in which divine Providence is guiding mankind in our days cannot fail to remark how important is the part which the power of the people takes in shaping the events of the present, and which it is evidently destined to take in molding the destinies of the future. We behold, with profound regret, the efforts of the prince of darkness to make this power dangerous to the social weal by withdrawing the masses of the people from the influence of religion, and impelling them towards the ruinous paths of license and anarchy. Hitherto our country has presented a spectacle of a most consolingly different character—that of a popular power regulated by love of good order, respect for religion, by obedience to the authority of the laws, not a democracy of license and violence, but that true democracy which aims at the general prosperity through the means of sound principles and good social order.

"In order to preserve so desirable a state of things it is absolutely necessary that religion should continue to possess the affections, and thus rule the conduct of the multitudes. As Cardinal Manning has well written, 'A new task is before us. The Church has no longer to deal with Parliaments and princes, but with the masses and with the people. Whether we will or no this is our work; we need a new spirit and a new law of life.' To lose influence over the people would be to lose the future altogether; and it is by the heart, far more than by the understanding, that we must hold and guide this immense power, so mighty either for good or for evil.

"Among all the glorious titles which the Church's history has deserved for her, there is not one which at present gives her so great influence as that of 'Friend of the People.' Assuredly, in our democratic country, it is this title which wins for the Catholic Church not only the enthusiastic devotedness of the millions of her children, but also the respect and admiration of all our citizens, whatever be their religious belief. It is the power of this title which renders persecution almost an impossibility, and which draws towards our Holy Church the great heart of the American people.

"And since it is acknowledged by all that the great questions of the future are not those of war, of commerce or finance, but the social questions—the questions which concern the improvement of the condition of the great popular masses, and especially of the working people—it is evidently of supreme importance that the Church should always be found on the side of humanity—of justice towards the multitudes who compose the body of the human family. As the same Cardinal Manning has wisely written, 'I know I am treading on a very difficult subject, but I feel confident of this, that we most face it, and that we must face it calmly, justly, and with a willingness to put labor and the profits of labor second—the moral state and domestic life of the whole working population first. I will not venture to draw up such an act of Parliament further than to lay down this principle. These things (the present condition of the poor in England) cannot go on; these things ought not to go on. The accumulation of wealth in the land, the piling up of wealth like mountains, in the possession of classes or individuals, cannot go on. No commonwealth can rest on such foundations.' (Miscellanies, Vol. 2, p. 81).

"In our country, above all, this social amelioration is the inevitable programme of the future, and the position which the Church should hold towards it is surely obvious. She can certainly not favor the extremes to which the poor multitudes are naturally inclined, but, I repeat, she must withhold them from these extremes by the bonds of affection, by the maternal desire which she will manifest for the concession of all that is just and reasonable in their demands, and by the maternal blessing which she will bestow upon every legitimate means for improving the condition of the people.

"6. Now let us consider for a moment the consequences which would inevitably follow from a contrary course—from a course of want of sympathy for the working class, of suspicion for their aims, of ready condemnation for their methods.

"(a) First, there would be the evident danger of the Church's losing in popular estimation, her right to be considered the friend of the people. The logic of the popular heart goes swiftly to its conclusions, and this conclusion would be most pernicious both for the people and for the Church. To lose the heart of the people would be a misfortune for which the friendship of the few rich and powerful would be no compensation.

"(b) There would be a great danger of rendering hostile to the Church the political power of our country, which has openly taken sides with the millions who are demanding justice and the improvement of their condition. The accusation of being un-American—that is to say, alien to our national spirit—is the most powerful weapon which the enemies of the Church can employ against her. It was this cry which aroused the Know-Nothing persecution thirty years ago, and the same would be used again if the opportunity offered. To appreciate the gravity of this danger it is well to remark that not only are the rights of the working classes loudly proclaimed by each of our two great political parties, but it is not improbable that, in our approaching national elections there will be a candidate for the office of President of the United States as the special representative of the popular complaints and demands.

"Now, to seek to crush by an ecclesiastical condemnation an organization which represents more than 500,000 votes, and which has already so respectable and so universally recognized a place in the political arena, would, to speak frankly, be considered by the American people as not less ridiculous than rash. To alienate from ourselves the friendship of the people would be to run great risk of losing the respect which the

Church has won in the estimation of the American nation, and of forfeiting the peace and prosperity which form so admirable a contrast with her condition in some so-called Catholic countries. Angry utterances have not been wanting of late, and it is well that we should act prudently.

"(c) A third danger—and the one which most keenly touches our hearts—is the risk of losing the love of the children of the Church, and of pushing them into an attitude of resistance against their Mother. The world presents no more beautiful spectacle than that of their filial devotion and obedience; but it is well to recognize that, in our age and in our country, obedience cannot be blind. We would greatly deceive ourselves if we expected it. Our Catholic working men sincerely believe that they are only seeking justice, and seeking it by legitimate means. A condemnation would be considered both false and unjust, and, therefore, not binding. We might preach to them submission and confidence in the Church's judgment; but these good dispositions could hardly go so far. They love the Church, and they wish to save their souls, but they must also earn their living, and labor is now so organized that without belonging to the organization it is almost impossible to earn one's living.

"Behold, then, the consequences to be feared. Thousands of the Church's most devoted children, whose affection is her greatest comfort, and whose free offerings are her chief support, would consider themselves repulsed by their Mother, and would live without practising their religion. Catholics who have hitherto shunned the secret societies, would be sorely tempted to join their ranks. The Holy See, which has constantly received from the Catholics of America proofs of almost unparalleled devotedness, would be considered not as a paternal authority, but as a harsh and unjust power. Surely these are consequences which wisdom and prudence counsel us to avoid.

"7. But, besides the dangers that would result from such a condemnation, and the impracticability of putting it into effect, it is also very important that we should carefully consider another reason against condemnation, arising from the unstable and transient character of the organization in question. It is frequently remarked by the press and by attentive observers that this special form of association has in it so little permanence that, in its present shape, it is not likely to last many years. Whence it follows that it is not necessary, even if it were just and prudent, to level the condemnations of the Church solely against so evanescent an object. The social agitation itself will, indeed, last as long as there are social evils to be remedied; but the forms of organization meant for the attainment of this end are naturally provisional and short-lived. They are also very numerous, for I have already remarked that the Knights of Labor is only one among many labor organizations.

"To strike, then, at one of these forms would be to commence a war without system and without end; it would be to exhaust the forces of the Church in chasing a crowd of changing and uncertain spectres. The American people behold with perfect composure and confidence the progress of our social contest, and have not the least fear of not being able to protect themselves against any excesses or dangers that may occasionally arise. Hence, to speak with the most profound respect, but also with the frankness which duty requires of me, it seems to me that prudence suggests, and that even the dignity of the Church demands that we should not offer to America an ecclesiastical protection for which she does not ask, and of which she believes she has no need.

"8. In all this discussion I have not at all spoken of Canada, nor of the condemnation concerning the Knights of Labor in Canada; for we would consider it an impertinence on our part to meddle with the ecclesiastical affairs of another country which has an hierarchy of its own, and with whose social conditions we do not pretend to be acquainted. We believe, however, that the circumstance of a people almost entirely Catholic, as in lower Canada, must be very different from those of a mixed population like ours; moreover, that the documents submitted to the Holy Office are not the present constitution of the organization in our country, and that we, therefore, ask nothing involving an inconsistency on the part of the Holy See, which passed sentence *'localiter et juxta exposita.'*

"It is of the United States that we speak, and we trust that we are not presumptuous in believing that we are competent to judge about the state of things in our own country. Now, as I have already indicated, out of the seventy-five archbishops and bishops of the United States, there are about five who desire the condemnation of the Knights of Labor, such as they are in our own country; so that our hierarchy are almost unanimous in protesting against such a condemnation. Such a fact ought to have great weight in deciding the question. If there are difficulties in the case, it seems to me that the prudence and experience of our bishops and the wise rules of the Third Plenary Council ought to suffice for their solution.

"Finally, to sum up all, it seems to me that the Holy See could not decide to condemn an association under the following circumstances:

"1. When the condemnation does not seem to be justified either by the letter or the spirit of its constitution, its law and the declaration of its chiefs.

"2. When the condemnation does not seem necessary, in view of the transient form of the organization and the social condition of the United States.

"3. When it does not seem to be prudent, because of the reality of the grievances complained of by the working classes, and their acknowledgement by the American people.

"4. When it would be dangerous for the reputation of the Church in our democratic country, and might even lead to persecution.

"5. When it would probably be inefficacious, owing to the general conviction that it would be unjust.

"6. When it would be destructive instead of beneficial in its effects, impelling the children of the Church to disobey their Mother, and even to enter condemned societies, which they have thus far shunned.

"7. When it would turn into suspicion and hostility the singular devotedness of our Catholic people towards the Holy See.

"8. When it would be regarded as a cruel blow to the authority of bishops in the United States, who, it is well known, protest against such a condemnation.

"Now, I hope the considerations here presented have sufficiently shown that such would be the effect of condemnation of the Knights of Labor in the United States.

"Therefore, I leave the decision of the case, with fullest confidence to the wisdom and prudence of your Eminence and the Holy See."

J. Card Gibbons,
Archbishop of Baltimore.

Rome, February 20, 1887.

11 Edward McGlynn

AN INSURGENT PRIEST'S DEFENSE OF COMMON PROPERTY IN LAND

In 1886, this eloquent and civic-minded pastor of St. Stephen's Church in New York, openly and zealously supported the mayoralty candidacy of Henry George on a platform favoring land socialization. His course displeased Archbishop Michael A. Corrigan, who suspended him from his ministry and secured his excommunication (lifted in 1892). At the Academy of Music in Brooklyn on March 29, 1887, Father McGlynn defended his position in a sermonic lecture entitled "The Cross of a New Crusade," which was distinguished for its oratorical power. That all the children of God should have free and equal access to the land was to McGlynn a truth as certain as the laws of Newtonian physics. While he discussed in simplified terms the chief points in the "single-tax" economics, he was primarily concerned with his relation as a priest to the movement.

Like the crusades of old the "new crusade" was a religious movement in its inspiration, justification and consummation. Its source was God; it was not only outside of man, it was above man. McGlynn defied any man or set of men to forbid him or any other person from crusading for common property in land, which cause was eminently consonant with the highest Christian truth and the best Christian justice and never condemned by Christ or the highest tribunal of his Church.

Ladies and Gentlemen: I stand to-night upon a not very familiar platform. It is true that I may have appeared once and again on this or similar platforms to plead what may not inappropriately be called a political cause. I have spoken occasionally to promote great public interests—of charity, of virtue, of temperance and of law. Yet scarcely one among you needs to be told to-night that I have been exceedingly more familiar with another place, and with another platform, and for many long years—it was twenty-seven years last Friday—I have been ministering before Christian altars and preaching from Christian pulpits. And if I am not permitted to-day to

---

Edward McGlynn, "The Cross of a New Crusade," *The Standard*, April 2, 1887 (excerpts).

preach the truths that I preached only because I knew them to be truths, and to minister before altars before which I reverently bowed only because I believed them to be the altars of God, and to administer the holy sacraments, of the sanctity and beauty of which I preached, and the frequent receiving of which I inculcated only because I believed them to be Christ's appointed medicine to man, I shall not so stultify myself as to permit anyone to say that, because of this suspension from the faculty of preaching in Christian pulpits and ministering before Christian altars I have changed one tittle or jot of my belief in those truths, or lost any of the reverence that I cherished in my heart of hearts from my youth for the beauty of the house of God and the place where His glory dwelleth.

And if I shall not be permitted to preach those truths from those familiar pulpits, I shall preach them as best I may wherever I may be permitted; and while I shall not be guilty of the indiscretion or of the indecorum of obtruding upon a promiscuous audience the sacred and peculiar dogmas or the holy mysteries of the church that I love, yet, so help me God, wherever I stand, upon a political platform, whether I discourse of political economy or of great public interests, I shall never say anything contrary to the great leading truths of Catholic theology. . . .

The cross of the new crusade is not raised in hostility to the cross of Christ. The very thought of a crusade and of the honored badge of a crusade—the holy ensign of the cross—is entirely borrowed from Him. The crusades of old, that brought a good thing, and with it a new name into the world, were inspired by tenderest reverence for the cross of Christ and affection for the places, even on the sea sands, on the mountain side, and at the city gates, where He had walked and slept and suffered and taught and died. It was the enthusiastic love of the cross, and of the magnificent teachings of the cross, that fired the hearts of men and made them undertake and carry on for centuries the old crusades. . . .

When the first crusade was proclaimed at the council of Clermont the happy thought—no doubt inspired—seized upon the multitude of making the Cross of Christ, no matter of how rich or cheap material it might be, the badge of the holy war. And so women rent their garments, and men took off their raiment, and making strips of them formed crosses with which to deck the breasts of the soldiers of the cross. And it was this badge of the cross of Christ, the ensign of the holy war, that gave to all our modern languages the word crusade.

And so the cross of a new crusade need not be any material emblem, but it stands for the acceptance by men and women, by whomsoever will hear, of the call, the trumpet blast, that invites them to forget themselves, to set aside their wretched strifes, to utterly renounce the injustice in which they may have been engaged, and to take on a new enthusiasm of humanity in believing, in working, in battling, in suffering, and, if need be, in dying, for the right, for a great truth that I shall not be guilty of the indiscretion of calling a new truth, for a truth that, like all great truths, must in its germ and in its essence be as old as God himself in eternity, and as old as the world, or the race of men in time. And so it is a new crusade, to which you are invited, for the proclaiming, the propagating, and the enforcing of an ancient truth—a truth that is eminently consonant with the great truth of Christianity itself—and, properly understood, resolves itself into the very essence, the very core of all religion, as taught us by Him, who spake as never man spake before or since, and in homely accents, and in simple parables, taught the poor, the lowly and the oppressed the comforting doctrine, so full of truth and light, of the fatherhood of one God and the universal brotherhood of man.

This new crusade then, while, to use a modern phrase, there is nothing sectarian about it, is necessarily a religious movement. And permit me to say, and I am not at all singular in the saying of it, if it were not a religious movement you might at the very outset count me out of it; for I think that any cause, any movement, any object that enlists the thought of men and the affections of the hearts of men must have a religious inspiration, a religious justification and a religious consumation, or the cause is not worth wasting our breath, our time and our strength upon. It were useless to prate about truth and beauty and goodness and justice and humanity, and the brotherhood of man, if this truth and justice and goodness and beauty, and this universal brotherhood found not their source and their center, their type, their ideal, their justification, in God himself.

That all great causes must necessarily be religious was not hidden from the sages of pagan antiquity any more than it is hidden from us. For whatever fires the heart of man—in the sense in which the heart of man means affection, love, forgetfulness of self, enthusiasm for something outside of self—in this sense whatever fires the heart of man must come from a source that is not only outside of man, but above man. . . .

The crusade that we have chosen to call a "new crusade" is for the enforcing of one of those great truths of which I have already spoken to you—the truth that, with diversity of natural gifts, God has given an equality of essential rights to all His children just because they are His children; that for every mouth He sends into the world to be fed, He sends, with rare exceptions, a pair of hands to feed it; that He has made us land animals, and not fishes or birds, and therefore that He has made us to live upon the land and not to fly in the air or swim in the water, and that because He has made us land animals, and because He has made us at all, He has given us the right, with these two hands somehow or other to dig for a living in order to feed these mouths; and that any man or set of men, who shall by law or in any other way deny, impair, diminish or restrain the equal right of every human being, to the possession of the general bounties of nature, the sunlight, the air, the water and the land, is guilty of blasphemy against the goodness of the universal Father. They are perverting under the name of law the right of men; they are desecrating the holy name of law to sanction a monstrous injustice. Under the name of right they are doing a horrid wrong; under the pretense of guarding the best interests of society, they are opposing the very germinal principle of rightly ordained society. They are guilty of the monstrous crime of making hundreds of thousands, yea, millions of God's creatures feel that this life is a wretched mistake, or worse than that, the joke of some most hateful fiend, rather than the gift of an all-wise and all-loving Father.

It is not for nothing that He who came to save the souls of men did so much to minister to the relief of their bodily wants. He healed their diseases; He raised their dead; He cured their distempers; He bore their sorrows; He felt compassion for the multitude, lest they should faint by the wayside. He miraculously supplemented the laws of nature and fed them with miraculous loaves and fishes in the wilderness. He did all this, because doing it He knew full well that the bodies of men as well as their souls are the creatures of God, and that their bodies and the capacities of those bodies are but signs and symbols of the spiritual things within, even as all the vast universe of God is but His garment, is but the sign and symbol and the thin veil that surrounds Him, through the rifts in which we catch on every hand glimpses of God and of heaven.

The heavens are telling the glory of God. There is a greater heaven here, vaster and more wondrous than the physical universe, in the intelligent mind and the affectionate heart of the least of God's creatures. All the multitudinous and multifarious beauties and glories of the physical world are not equal to the dignity and the sanctity of the mind and the heart of the least of God's children; and therefore it is that Christ tells us that at the very peril of our souls we must look after the bodies of these little ones; we must feed the hungry;

we must comfort and, as far as we can, heal the sick; we must provide shelter for the homeless; we must look after the weak, the blind, the halt, and the insane. Is all this a mistake? No; it is a part of true religion, because it is the sign and the symbol of spiritual things. It is because of the proper care of the bodies of men, of the proper feeding of those bodies, of the proper sheltering of them, that we make it possible for human nature to expand as a beautiful flower under the influence of genial warmth and refreshing breezes and showers, and so the lilies and flowers of every virtue may the more readily expand if the mind and the heart of the child are able to look up and to feel that God the Father has not been entirely unmindful of the wants of the child.

This is the word of an apostle of Christ: "This is true religion—to visit the widow and the fatherless in their affliction, and to keep one's self unspotted from the world." So it is necessarily a part of true religion to insist on what is essentially the equality of man, regardless of the comparatively trifling differences in their gifts and acquirements. This is the political economy, the teaching and reducing of which to practice are the core and essence of this new crusade. All men, inalienably, always, everywhere, have a common right to all the general bounties of nature; and this is in perfect and beautiful keeping with the other law of labor that every mouth has two hands with which to feed itself, a necessary corollary of which is that these hands must have equal direct or indirect access to the general bounties of nature out of which to make a living. That is the whole of the doctrine of this new crusade in a nutshell, that the land as well as the sunlight, and the air, and the waters, and the fishes, and the mines in the bowels of the earth, all these things that were made by the Creator through the beautiful processes of nature, belong equally to the human family, to the community, to the people, to all the children of God. The law of labor requires that these natural materials shall be brought into such relations with men that they shall afford to them food, raiment, shelter, for the erection of works not merely of utility, but of ornament, that out of these materials the children of men shall have equal, indefeasible rights to pluck, to catch, to delve, in order not merely to satisfy the necessities of the animal body or to keep it from the inclemency of the blast, but to do more than this—to make the very shelter itself a thing of beauty, to make the home a kind of temple in which there may be a family altar, to erect great public works that shall serve not merely purposes of utility, but shall educate the eye and the fancy, and shall gladden the habitations of men during their brief temporal abode, to add something to the mere garments that shall clothe and preserve the body from the inclemency of the atmosphere, to make even the raiment of man a work of art, to give a charm and a grace and a dignity even to the mere feeding of the animal. All men then have this right; and it is a part of the gospel of this new crusade that while we may make much allowance for the ignorance in which these great cardinal truths are too often forgotten, the barbarism and the slavery in which because of might right went under and stayed under for centuries; while we may be very indulgent to the errors and even be willing to forgive in some measure the crimes of the past, we hold aloft the banner upon which is inscribed this truth, that ever and always in the past, the present, and the future, the earth and the fulness thereof were given by God, and therefore should belong to all the children of God. . . .

How are we going to give back to the poor man what belongs to him? How shall we have that beautiful state of things in which naught shall be ill and all shall be well? Simply by confiscating rent and allowing people nominally to own, if you choose, the whole of Manhattan Island, if it will do them any good to nominally own it; but while they have the distinguished satisfaction of seeming to own it we are going to scoop the meat out of the shell and allow them to have the shell. And how are we going to do that? By simply taxing all this land and all kindred bounties of nature to the full amount of their rental value. If there isn't any rental value then there won't be any tax. If there is any rental value than it will be precisely what that value is. If the rental value goes up, up goes the tax. If the rental value comes down, down comes the tax. If the rental value ceases, then the tax ceases. Don't you see? It is as clear as the nose on your face.

. . . . We would simply tax all these bounties of nature, where there is a scramble for them, to the full rental value. In a new community, where the people are few, land is comparatively limitless; there is no such thing as rent; the land is pretty equally distributed; there is no choice; it would be a senseless thing for men to quarrel about it; there is land enough for all. What is the law of rent? Where there is competition for a larger or choicer portion of the common bounties, for a portion of land that is nearer a river, that is next to the junction of two great rivers, that is near to a great city, for a corner lot, say at the corner of Broadway and Wall street, or at Broadway and Twenty-third street, there rent exists. And how is the competition for the use of such land to be decided? Simply by allowing it to go to the highest bidder. Thus would be provided, through the exercise of the taxing power, a fund for the common treasury, a munificent fund growing with the growth of population and civilization, supplied by a beautiful providential law, a simple, economic law that works with the same simplicity and the same regularity as the law of gravitation itself—a magnificent ever-increasing fund to supply the wants of increasing civilization and increasing population.

This magnificent fund would go to support all public burdens; it would do a great deal more than is done at present by the tax levy; you would have larger, more beautiful and more numerous parks; you would be able to sweep away the greater part of the wretched rookeries that, under the name of tenement houses, are a sin and a shame, and a blot on the fair name and fame of this beautiful city, and instead of those the best class of houses will be built, and we will have parks, with trees and flowers and the singing of birds, to make glad and beautify this island and God's children, and will thereby add enormously to the value of the surrounding land; and then it would no longer sound Quixotic to talk of building free rapid transit railroads on solid foundations, on which trains could travel at the rate of thirty miles an hour for twenty, thirty or forty miles into the suburbs, to give homes to all the people, from which they could come and go every day, and in which they could enjoy some of nature's life, by which they could get the sun and the air, green fields and flowers. This is no fancy sketch; it is entirely feasible and in every view it could be brought about if a majority of citizens, convinced of the truth of this doctrine, would carry it into practice and deposit their ballots in the ballot box in favor of this thing.

One of the greatest beneficial consequences of this just and necessary reform, of this restoration to all of what belongs to all, would be this: The artificial value that is now given to land, even beyond this enormous value which we have just discussed, would cease; the giving to individual men what God never intended they should have—the absolute ownership of land—would cease. If there was no individual ownership in land then there would be no such thing as speculative value in land. Then no man would be such a fool as to pay rent to keep land fenced in from year to year, preventing everybody else from doing anything with it. That man, if he nominally owned it, must pay the full rental value of it. Even if he were a fool, he would soon see there was no fun in that kind of thing, and he would give it up and let somebody else take it. You see what would be the result. There would be a consequent increase in the building trades, houses would spring up all over the city of New York, and the tenement houses would be depopulated, and the owners would be glad to sell them cheap to the city, so they could be destroyed to make breathing places for the people.

Capital will then find nothing to invest in except human labor and its products. Don't you see the general demand for human labor that would result? In every society there is capital, and it is the instinct of men not to keep capital lying idle if they can use it, and the only manner in which they can use it is by producing something, so that there will be a steady demand for labor. But a more steady demand for labor comes from something else. It comes from the law of hunger, of cold, of the need to have some soft spot to lie down and sleep, and so whether capital employs labor or not, you may be sure, if labor gets a chance, it will employ itself. The average man is not going to lie down and die of hunger if he can get any kind of a fair chance to dig in the soil for food; the average man is not going to perish by the winter's cold if he can get a chance to provide himself shelter; not to freeze if he can get access to raw materials to make clothes for himself. And so in this beautiful condition of things there will always be a demand for labor, and then it will be strictly true and proper to say to any able bodied man or woman that comes begging: "Why, you are not sick—why should you beg?" "I can't find work." "Oh, that is not true; in this community there is always enough work for all; there is always a demand for labor exceeding the supply."

And that leads us to another beautiful consequence—high wages. Oh, that is a grand thing for us labor people. How does that come about? Why, by a reversal of the terrible law that at present makes wages always keep tending down. Why? Because with the increase of population comes this increased value of land. Don't you notice how great fortunes are accumulating, here as they have accumulated in England and elsewhere? They are becoming amassed more and more in the hands of a few.

Now, all this will be changed; it will necessarily have to be changed by this beautiful and simple law that we have just spoken of. These enormous fortunes will be distributed, and wages will become higher. Why? Because then it will be the capitalist that will have to be running around after the laborer and begging him to be kind enough to work for him, and not the laborer that shall be running after the capitalist and begging him as if he were a divinity to give him a chance to live.

So, then, we laboring men shall enjoy this unutterably comforting spectacle of reversing the present order of things by seeing not seven poor devils of workmen running after one lord of a capitalist and begging him to employ them, but the seven poor devils of capitalists running after one workman and begging him to work for them. And he will put on lordly ways and feel that he is the lord of creation, the joint owner of the soil, and that he has something in his muscular and sinewy arms, in his well-preserved health, preserved by chastity, sobriety and healthy muscular exercise, that the poor capitalists have not; that he has got something more precious that these capitalists can't do without, and so he dictates his terms, and he says, "Now, how much will you seven people bid for my labor?" And one poor capitalist says, "Well, for a starter I will say $3 a day." "No, no," "$3.25," "$3.50," "$4," "$4.50," "$5," and finally, when the capitalists begin to thin out in that competition, he knocks himself down to the man who will give him five, or six, or seven dollars.

What will be the proper wages resulting from that competition of the seven capitalists for the labor of that one man? Do you know what the wages will be? Just precisely what they ought to be—exactly, neither one cent more nor one cent less. How does that come about? By that law that works just like the law of gravitation. What are economic wages? In the very essence and nature of things what are wages anyhow? They are what the workman produces by his labor out of the materials to which he has legitimate access. What he has put into that raw material is his, and he sells it to somebody else, and for what should he sell it? for a perfect equivalent. And so the wages of the man will be an absolute and perfect equivalent for what he has done, for this transmutation of his nerves, of his brain, of his sinews, of his time into something new and strange, rich and rare, that he has developed out of that raw material and so economic wages will be a perfect equivalent for the time and muscle, and so on—that he has put into that thing and that will determine itself as a matter of course, just as water finds its level. Directly or indirectly in a true system of economic government every man shall have absolutely his own, a free field and no favors, but absolutely justice to all, favoritism to none. . . .

So the trouble is not overproduction but it is the unjust arrangements of society by which so large a portion of the people either cannot get work at all or have to work at starvation wages. And because when there is a so-called overproduction and underconsumption there comes commercial depression—stagnation in trade—a large portion of the people are thrown out of work and in their misery are willing then to work for lower wages—for anything that will keep them from starving and from perishing. Then there is a revival of trade. Then people say: "Now is a good time to get in the goods, because they can be got so cheap—because labor is cheap. Now is a good time to build, because labor is cheap." And so gradually there is a cessation of this commercial depression, and times begin to get a little better, and then they begin to get what is called good, and the moment the times begin to be good and business begins to prosper, then the man that is sitting there, neither working nor spinning, but eating and drinking, begins to say: "Ha, ha, times are good. Business is prospering. Real estate will go up." And so it does. Land will go up. There is a need for building more houses. There is a need for more factories and land goes up, and so a large and constantly increasing portion of the profits of both capital and labor goes to pay the unjust rent to the landlord. But when we shall have appropriated to the common treasury the economic rent, all that condition must necessarily cease, and as men will be able to get steady employment or steadily to employ themselves, and will get the highest wages that the very law of wages itself will permit, they will not be so foolish when the wants of their bodies are admirably supplied as to work themselves to death, to continue to degrade themselves into mere working machines. And so with the increase of general wealth, the raising of wages, and the general well being will commence, voluntarily and naturally, a shortening of the hours of work. It doesn't require any law of the legislature, or any strike, or any rule of a trade union or any similar society to determine these things. Men will then be more free than they ever have been before, to work or not to work as they please, to work long hours or short hours, as it suits best their tastes, their desires and their convenience. If a man wants to work, very good. If a man does not want to work there will be nobody to coerce him, and so we shall restore in a great measure individual liberty. We shall restore what hitherto has been singularly characteristic of our country, but is fast ceasing to be so characteristic of it—the magnificent individualism of Americans. . . .

Take up, then, the cross of this new crusade, and I, for one, dare to say here, before this vast audience, that I have taken it into my head and heart, and never shall I see the day as long as I live that I shall pluck it out from the one or the other. It were a sad thing indeed to think that any man or set of men should forbid you and me to believe these truths of God, to teach them, to preach them, to love them with a religious enthusiasm or to sacrifice even our very lives in the noble work of making them cheap and common among men; and I stand here and say, without fear of reasonable denial, that all that I have said tonight is eminently consonant with the highest Christian truth and the best Christian justice, and that no condemnation of this truth has ever been heard from the blessed lips of Christ, nor from the highest tribunal of his church. Nor is there any more danger or possibility of such condemnation of so clear and salutary an economic truth than there is of the condemnation of the proposition that two and two make four.

I will read to you as an appropriate summing up of many of the things that I have said a poem by Charles Mackay, entitled "Clear the Way."

Men of thought, be up and stirring
    night and day.
Sow the seed, withdraw the curtain,
    clear the way.
Men of action, aid and cheer
    them as we may;
There's a fount about to stream,
    there's a light about to beam.
There's a warmth about to glow,
    there's a flower about to blow;
There's a midnight blackness
    changing into gray;
Men of thought and men of action,
    clear the way.

Once the welcome light has broken
    who shall say
What the unhidden glories of the day?
What the evil that shall perish
    in the ray?
Aid the dawning tongue and pen,
    aid it, hopes of honest men;
Aid it paper, aid it type, aid it
    for the hour is ripe.
And our earnest must not slacken
    into play.
Men of thought, men of action,
    clear the way.

Lo! the cloud's about to vanish
 from the day.
And a brazen wrong to crumble into clay;
Lo! the right's about to conquer! Clear
 the way.
With the right shall many enter,
 smiling at the dawn.
With the giant wrong shall fall many
 others, great and small,
That for ages long have held us
 for their prey.
Men of thought, men of action,
 clear the way.

12 Thomas M. Mulry

THE SOCIETY OF ST. VINCENT DE PAUL IN THE CHARITY ORGANIZATION MOVEMENT

One test of a genuine interest in social welfare is the amount of willingness shown by major religious bodies to cooperate with one another and with secular and non-sectarian agencies in the support of social causes. A trend of this sort definitely emerged during the 1880's and took form in the cooperative effort made by various agencies to ameliorate labor conditions and improve the moral climate in general. Charity also offered a most fruitful field for the cooperative endeavors of these groups. A significant development at this time was the entry of the Catholic Church into many working relationships with the new Charity Organization Societies.

The pioneer in this endeavor from the Catholic side was Thomas M. Mulry, New York businessman and guiding figure in the St. Vincent de Paul Society of that city. By his patience, tact, and unswerving dedication to the welfare of the poor, this "American Ozanam" dispelled suspicion and distrust and demonstrated that Catholics as well as non-Catholics had much to gain and nothing to lose from systematic and large-scale cooperation in charity. His story of the New York effort—clear, candid, and convincing—was widely read and no doubt furthered similar types of cooperation in many parts of the country.

The following paper was read in April before the Catholic club of New York city, and published later in the Catholic Reading Circle Review. *It has attracted wide attention, and its interest justifies us in making an extensive excerpt from it. The experience of Mr. Mulry and his fellow-workers in New York is one which is being duplicated in every section of the country and is a trustworthy index of the hearty sympathy in philanthropic effort which is to-day bringing catholics and protestants into effective co-operation without compromising honest differences of opinion and method.*—THE EDITORS [*of Charities Review*].

In this paper, I propose to give a few reasons why catholics should co-operate more actively with people of other religious denominations in doing charitable work, because of the mutual advantage to be derived from such co-operation. One of the greatest hindrances to this work in the past has been the distrust and suspicion of each other's motives, which actuated the different charities.

Thomas M. Mulry, "Catholic Co-operation in Charity," *Charities Review,* VIII (October 1898), 383–386.

All the non-catholic societies were not actuated by this feeling, but the activity of those in that field made catholics suspicious of the others.

There was certainly a strong feeling of prejudice against catholics, and whether this was due to ignorance or to malice, there was no question of its existence. This also tended to widen the distance between catholics and non-catholics.

Add to this the prejudice of many of our people, brought from other lands, where they were persecuted for their faith, and the task of bringing together people so diametrically opposed to each other seemed a very hopeless one. With this state of affairs it was useless to look for any concerted effort.

The strange spectacle was presented of charitable societies working, each in its own way, for the good of the poor, and yet violating every principle of charity and religion in their intercourse with each other.

This spirit of antipathy and opposition could not fail to be destructive in its results. It created a sort of piracy among the charities. One was constantly poaching on the other's domains and the professional pauper, the designing beggar, and the avaricious were reaping a harvest over the disputes and the rivalries of the contending sects. A catholic to-day, a protestant to-morrow, and a Hebrew the day after, he could carry on this trade with impunity. There was no danger of discovery while the charities kept so far apart. He applied to all and received help from all. His accommodating conscience enabled him to live in greater comfort than he could hope to enjoy from honest labor, so he labored not, but prospered more.

We were not wholly free from blame, however. It is true we could not compete with our separated brethren in wealth or resources. They had the wealth; we had the poor. We were continually in sore straits to provide for the many who looked to us for help, and yet the catholic layman made no serious attempt to remedy this evil, but stood either idly or stolidly by, leaving to Providence and an overworked clergy the solution of the problem.

In 1882, or thereabouts, the charity organization society was started in New York city. The objects of the society were to prevent the indiscriminate giving of relief, to evolve a system that would be acceptable to all, and to bring the various charities closer together.

The organization gave no relief, but acted as a sort of charities exchange, where all information could be obtained, and where people applying for assistance would be investigated and referred to proper relief societies. There was something repugnant to the catholic idea of charity in this new scheme. It seemed like dragging the worthy poor before the public, and there was nothing to appeal to our people in an organization which expended *all* its receipts in salaries and expenses, none going to the poor.

We refused to co-operate with them, but after a few years a better understanding developed itself. It was seen that there was a good side to the work.

After the organization had been in existence a few years, the attention of some of the members of the society of St. Vincent de Paul was called to the large number of catholic children attending the various protestant missions and Sunday schools. Immediately the charity organization society was looked upon as the cause.

It happened that the work of investigating the matter was assigned to me. I called upon the committee of the charity organization society. What did I find? A body of ladies and gentlemen earnestly endeavoring to do something to help God's poor, and most anxious for our moral support and co-operation.

There had been some catholic gentlemen's names used, but they had taken no active part. I found letters had been sent to clergymen, to conferences of the society of St. Vincent de Paul, to the various charitable organizations; but in most cases the letter had been thrown into the waste basket, the requests to assist ignored; and yet the people needed care and looking after.

Despairing of obtaining assistance from catholic sources, other people took on themselves the care of helping the families, with the result that, in many cases, the children were weaned from the Church.

We saw at once the field this work opened for us. We saw also the danger of neglecting this great means of doing good. Therefore, several catholic gentlemen became actively connected with the association. We soon made our people familiar with its purposes; we also received a warm welcome from the charity organization society. Our assistance was valued very highly and our advice appreciated.

From this beginning has spread a better feeling, a closer relation between the various charities than we had ever hoped for. It will certainly contribute more than anything else to that Christian unity which our beloved, august, and respected Pontiff so earnestly recommends. Perhaps the grand spectacle of a body of laymen devoting their leisure time, the world over, to visiting and relieving the poor has excited the admiration of our non-catholic friends more than anything else;—no paid agents, no class distinction, no petty social differences, all working gratuitously for God's poor, following the same rule, and practicing the same methods.

I have dwelt somewhat at length on the relations of the society of St. Vincent de Paul with the charity organization society because that society has been the great means of accomplishing this co-operation and of extending all the other charities.

It is true, there are many points on which we do not agree. In fact, there are points on which we will never agree, until they come over to our way of thinking. But we have learned to tolerate each other's opinions, to give to each the freedom of thinking as each may think fit, and to do this without compromising one jot or tittle of the faith we value above all else.

To-day catholics are identified with the national conference of charities, with the associated charities of New York city, and there never was a better understanding between all the charities. If the state board of charities, or the state charities aid association, or any other organization, wishes to have some bill introduced in the legislature, all the charities are called together and, if opposition is shown by any one, every effort is made to make the measure acceptable to all before acting upon it.

When we first started in this work of co-operation, people were found willing to sell themselves and their children to any religious sect that would pay the price. This traffic has been almost entirely stopped, and if the abuse exists in any shape at all, it is because of our neglect, as catholics, to enter the field in larger numbers, to guard the interest of our children.

The rights of each are respected, the evil of proselytism has received a great check, and it is but a question of a short time when there will be found the very best of feeling between the charities of all denominations, including those which were most antagonistic to us in the past.

With our associates on the various district committees of the charity organization society, we compare notes, find those of our own people who are attending other churches, report to proper parties, have them turned over to us, and in this way bring them to the notice of the various pastors and charitable societies. When we make our report or notify the proper parties that the people they are assisting belong to us, they at once take their hands off.

In looking over the crowds of children going to summer homes in the country, we found that a large number of them were catholics, and that most were sent to protestant homes, where, for the time being, they were compelled to attend the religious services. Not having any fresh-air vacation society under catholic auspices, we felt it a difficult matter to handle, but as some of those associations were non-sectarian, and as the charity organization society had much to do with them, we complained that this vacation business was drawing many of our children away from the Church. We were very quickly informed that if catholic homes could be found in the country, willing to take children, ours would be sent to them under the same conditions as the others were being sent.

The St. Vincent de Paul society took up the work of finding such homes. One of the members made a tour of the state each spring. Each year homes are found among catholic farmers in which the children are kept for two or three weeks free of charge. The country clergy enter with great interest into this work. Without their help, of course, nothing could be accomplished. Last year 400 catholic children were so placed. The *Tribune* fresh-air fund paid for all the transportation, and the agents of the charity organization society accompanied the children to the various places, and returned with them to their parents at the end of the vacation. All this work was done without any cost to us.

We have learned that much of the opposition ascribed to bigotry against our institutions is not due to that cause at all, but to a difference of opinion as to the best means of dealing with the poor. In our intercourse we receive many valuable hints, and in return give them new ideas. We always have this consolation, that, no matter what may be their defects, and we know they are not perfect, our catholic institutions compare favorably with any others, whether they are public or private.

13 Baltimore Catholic Congress

FOR SOCIAL REFORM AND AMERICANIZATION

The convening of the first lay Catholic Congress, in Baltimore in 1889—there was a second one at Chicago in 1893—

marked formally the transition of the Catholic laity from passive to active participation in the life of the Church—an activity which aimed not at controlling the clergy, as in the early nineteenth century trustee movement, but at aiding them and cooperating with them. The motivation and purposes of the new laity movement may be gleaned from the Resolutions of the Congress. These were mainly concerned with mobilizing the laity behind the philosophy of Catholic action set forth in the Pastoral Letter of the Third Plenary Council of Baltimore. A resolution was made to help solve the labor question along the lines of Cardinal Gibbons' Memorial to Rome on the Knights of Labor.

More significantly, perhaps, the Congress stressed the need for greater cooperation between Catholics and non-Catholics "in general philanthropic and reformatory movements" in both the public and the private sphere, and thus presented a Catholic version of social liberalism. The Resolutions, as did also the papers read at the Congress, soft-pedaled divisive issues like the school question and the restoration of the Pope's temporal sovereignty.

The meeting of the first congress of Catholic laymen in the United States, to celebrate the hundredth anniversary of the establishment of the American hierarchy, is an event of the greatest importance to our church and country. It would seem eminently proper that we, the laymen of the church, should meet and renew our allegiance to the doctrines we profess; that we should show to our fellow countrymen the true relations that exist between the church that we obey and love,

---

Proceedings of the First American Catholic Congress, in *Souvenir Volume Illustrated. Three Great Events in the History of the Catholic Church in the United States,* William H. Hughes, compiler and publisher (Detroit, 1889), pp. 62–63.

and the government of our choice; that we should proclaim that unity of sentiment upon all subjects presented to us, which has ever been the source of Catholic strength, and that in a spirit of perfect charity towards every denomination, we should freely exchange our views in relation to all matters which affect us as members of the Catholic Church.

In the first place, then, we rejoice at the marvellous development of our country, and regard with just pride the part taken by Catholics in such development. In the words of the pastoral issued by the archbishops and bishops of the United States, assembled in the third plenary council of Baltimore: "We claim to be acquainted both with the laws, institutions, and spirit of the Catholic Church, and with the laws, institutions, and spirit of our country, and we emphatically declare that there is no antagonism between them."

We repudiate with equal earnestness the assertion that we need to lay aside any of our devotedness to our church to be true Americans; the insinuation that we need to abate any of our love for our country's principles and institutions to be faithful Catholics.

We believe that our country's heroes were the instruments of the God of Nations in establishing this home of freedom; to both the Almighty and to his instruments in the work we look with grateful reverence, and to maintain the inheritance of freedom which they have left us, should it ever—which God forbid—be imperilled, our Catholic citizens will be bound to stand forward as one man, ready to pledge anew their lives, their fortunes, and their sacred honor.

We cannot, however, shut our eyes to the many dangers that threaten the destruction of that social fabric upon which depends our peace, our liberty, and our free institutions. Although our wealth has increases and prosperity abounds, our cities have multiplied and our states increased, we find, under the shadow of this system, incipient pauperism, discontented men, women, and children, without the benefits of education, without the advantages of religion, deprived of any share in that abundance of participation in those blessings which, through our free institutions, God Almighty designed for the people of our land.

As to the heed to be paid to the rights of the individual, we favor those means, measures, and systems by which these are to be secured.

We recognize next in importance to religion itself education as one of the chief factors in forming the character of the individual, the virtue of the citizen, and promoting the advance of a true civilization. Therefore, we are committed to a sound, popular education, which demands not only physical and intellectual, but also the moral and religious training of our youth.

As in the state schools no provision is made for teaching religion, we must continue to support our own schools, multiply and perfect colleges and universities already established and others, so that the benefits of a Christian education may be brought within the reach of every Catholic child in these United States.

We also recognize among the three great educational agencies, besides the church and school, the Christian home. "The root of the commonwealth is in the homes of the people." Whatever imperils its permanency, security, and peace, is a blow aimed, not only at individual rights, but is an attempt to subvert civil society and Christian civilization.

Therefore, we denounce the existence and development of Mormonism, and the tendency to multiply causes of divorce *a vinculo,* as plague spots on our civilization, a discredit to our government, a degradation of the female sex, and a standing menace to the sanctity of the marriage bond.

We likewise hold that it is not sufficient for individual Catholics to shun bad or dangerous societies, but they ought to take part in good and useful ones. The importance of Catholic societies, the necessity of union and concert of action to accomplish aught, are manifest. These societies should be organized on a religious, and not on a race or national basis. We must always remember that the Catholic Church knows no north or south, no east or west, no race, no color. National societies, as such, have no place in the church in this country; but, like this congress itself, they should be Catholic and American.

We commend the plan and form of the St. Vincent de Paul Society as a typical Catholic society. It is impossible to enumerate all the societies whose labors have done so much in the past to succor the poor and alleviate human misery; and it must, therefore, be left to individual action, to select the field in which each shall aid in religious and charitable work.

As our young men, however, are the hope of the future, we especially commend their societies to the support and encouragement of Catholics. As these were commended in a special manner by the plenary council, we recommend the establishment of these societies throughout the land, and urge upon the laity the importance of supporting them by every means within their power.

We recommend the extension of societies designed to assist the widows and children of deceased members, societies for the relief of the poor and distressed, not forgetting measures tending to improve the condition of inmates of our penal institutions.

Another danger which menaces our republic is the constant conflict between capital and labor. We, therefore, at all times must view with feelings and [of?] alarm any antagonism existing between them, because thereby society itself is imperilled.

With the church, we condemn nihilism, socialism, and communism, and we equally condemn the heartless greed of capital. The remedy must be sought in the mediation of the church, through her action on the individual conscience, and thereby on society, teaching each its respective duties, as well as rights;

and in such civil enactments as have been rendered necessary by these altered conditions. As stated by his eminence, Cardinal Gibbons: "Labor has its sacred rights, as well as its dignity. Paramount among the rights of the laboring classes is their privilege to organize or to form themselves into societies for their mutual protection and benefit. In honoring and upholding labor, the nation is strengthening its own hands, as well as paying a tribute to worth; for a contented and happy working class are the best safeguard of the republic."

We disapprove of the employment of very young minors, whether male or female, in factories, as tending to dwarf and retard the true development of the wage earners of the future.

We pledge ourselves to cooperate with the clergy in discussing and in solving those great economic and social questions which affect the interests and well-being of the church, the country, and society at large.

We respectfully protest against any change in the policy of the government in the matter of the education of the Indians, by which they will be deprived of Christian teaching.

The amelioration and promotion of the physical and moral culture of the negro race is a subject of the utmost concern, and we pledge ourselves to assist our clergy in all ways tending to effect any improvement in their condition.

We are in favor of Catholics taking greater part than they have hitherto taken in general philanthropic and reformatory movements. The obligation to help the needy, and to instruct the ignorant, is not limited to the needy and ignorant of our own communion; but we are concerned, both as Catholics and as Americans, in the reformation of all the criminals and the support of all the poor in the country. By mingling more in such works of natural virtue, as our non-Catholic citizens are engaged in, and taking our proper share in the management of prisons and hospitals, we might exert a Catholic influence outside of our own body, making ourselves better known, and infuse into those good works something of supernatural charity, at the same time that we are solacing the unfortunate and reforming the erring; and we should be able to insist on Catholic inmates being freely ministered to by their own clergy. We must assert and secure the right of conscience of Catholics in all institutions under public control.

There are many Christian issues in which Catholics could come together with non-Catholics, and shape civil legislation for the public weal. In spite of rebuff and injustice, and overlooking zealotry, we should seek alliance with non-Catholics for proper Sunday observance. Without going over to the Judaic Sabbath, we can bring the masses over to the moderation of the Christian Sunday. To effect this we must set our faces sternly against the sale of intoxicating beverages on Sunday. The corrupting influence of saloons on politics, the crime and pauperism resulting from excessive drinking, require legislative restriction which we can aid in procuring by joining our influence with that of the other enemies of intemperance. Let us resolve that drunkenness shall be made odious, and give practical encouragement and support to Catholic temperance societies. We favor the passage and enforcement of laws rigidly closing saloons on Sunday, and forbidding the sale of liquors to minors and intoxicated persons.

Efforts should be made to promote Catholic reading. It is our duty to support liberally good Catholic journals and books, and acquaint ourselves with Catholic doctrine and opinion on the important questions constantly coming to the front and demanding right answers and just, practical solutions. There are comparatively few Catholics who cannot afford the cost of a Catholic journal, or do not spend much more for a story-paper or novel than the price of one. We not only recommend Catholics to subscribe more generally for Catholic periodicals, quarterly, monthly, or weekly, but look with eagerness for the establishment of daily Catholic newspapers in our large cities and a Catholic associated press agency. If our Catholic literature is not equal to the standard by which we measure it, this is due, at least in part, to the slight encouragement now given to Catholic writers of the better type. If the best Catholic books were extensively purchased and read, more would be written which we should be proud of. We recommend, therefore, the work of Catholic circulating libraries and reading circles, and also efforts to have the best Catholic books and periodicals introduced into public libraries. But we do not call all books Catholic that are written by Catholics, nor a journal which is Catholic on one page and infidel or immoral on another.

As fast as practicable we hope for the introduction of proper church music in all our churches where other music is now heard. The music should help devotion at the divine service, and [not] be such as tends to divert the mind from heavenly thoughts. Efforts should be made to have the congregation join in the singing—a Catholic custom formerly, but practiced only in a few churches nowadays.

We cannot conclude without recording our solemn conviction that the absolute freedom of the Holy See is equally indispensable to the peace of the church and the welfare of mankind.

We demand in the name of humanity and justice that this freedom be scrupulously respected by all secular governments.

We protest against the assumption by any such government of a right to affect the interests or control the action of our Holy Father by any form of legislation or other public act to which his full approbation has not been previously given, and we pledge to Leo XIII, the worthy pontiff to whose hands Almighty God has committed the helm of Peter's bark amid the tempests of this stormy age, the loyal sympathy and unstinted aid of all his spiritual children in vindicating that perfect liberty which he justly claims as his sacred and inalienable right.

The report of the committee on resolutions was unanimously adopted.

14 Peter L. Foy

A CATHOLIC VERSION OF THE GOSPEL OF WEALTH

In his paper on "The New Social Order," read at the First American Catholic Congress in Baltimore during the centennial celebration of the American hierarchy, Peter L. Foy, a St. Louis journalist, called attention to the advent of great fortunes, to the social problems they caused, and to courses of remedial action. The centralization of wealth and power, he maintained, was less the result of natural law (science and technology) than of civil law: the state positively had given to the few a large part of the public domain and many other favors, and, negatively, had failed to repress class usurpation or to maintain a healthy balance between millionaires, the toiling masses, and the public at large. He recommended that the state now seek a new equilibrium through labor legislation and public philanthropy: employer liability for industrial accidents; an extension of education along physical, technical and artistic lines; and public hygiene, including sanitary tenements and factories. These social services should be financed by a small tax on all high personal and corporate incomes. A fair distribution of wealth and income being an impossibility for the present and the foreseeable future, society could at least provide provisional or empirical relief for existing evils. According to Foy's version of the "gospel of wealth," the possessors of great fortunes could not and should not be divested of their ill-gotten gains, but they should be forced to contribute liberally to the support of the victims of their rapacity.

Although he stressed public philanthropy, he did not over-

look other ameliorative factors, notably the influence of a properly organized and educated labor movement. The fact is, Foy's paper brought into coordinated focus virtually all aspects of the social question in a vividly painted picture. As such, it served in a sense as a blueprint for the probing discussions of social problems in the two Catholic Congresses and in other Catholic agencies for the diffusion of opinion and knowledge.

The same highly organized industrial and commercial system which extends over western Europe and Germany, overspreads this country also. The field of skilled labor and manufacturing enterprise is wide and varied, and the living and mechanical forces, and the intellectual activities operating in it and through it are manifold. Their fecundity of production in united action is so great that the statistician's figures in that branch of political economy which deals with production and consumption, are a good deal like the astronomer's, when he tells us of the distances of the heavenly bodies and the number of the invisible stars. This power will grow, for new discoveries will be made and new machines invented. Commerce follows manufactures, in spite of all impediments. What is the culmination and grand result of all those agencies of production and distribution? I answer, The creation and concentration of boundless wealth in the cities, and a corresponding increase, concentration, and condensation of the children of toil at the same points. Wealth beyond all that fables yet have feigned flows into the spacious reservoirs of Dives. Landlords, bankers, brewers, distillers, railroad owners, mill owners, iron and steel manufacturers, mine owners, patent owners, and

---

Peter L. Foy, "The New Social Order," Fourth Regular Paper, *Proceedings* of the First American Catholic Congress, in *Souvenir Volume Illustrated. Three Great Events in the History of the Catholic Church in the United States,* William H. Hughes, compiler and publisher (Detroit, 1889), pp. 36–43 (excerpts).

various other denominations of monopolists and privileged count their fortunes by millions and tens of millions. Those high priests of Mammon have apparently no higher mental endowment than other men, and the sinister contingent of them have no moral worth, and not a few belong to the category of dicers and blacklegs. The thimble-rigger and the market-rigger are birds of a feather. The millionaires are not a numerous class. Half the wealth of the United States, for instance, belongs, it is said, to 30,000 persons, the other half to the 64,970,000, who have been so largely instrumental in producing the whole. Whether this be so or not the disparity is monstrous, and we may be sure, it is still more so in the old countries. I but repeat a primary precept of the moral law when I say that we all have equal rights to equal or unequal things, as the case may be; and state but a commonplace of political economy when I say that the interests of capital and labor are the same in the long run. But whether by the operation of natural occult causes, or by human design (chiefly by the latter, I believe), the inequality of things may be too extreme because unjust. In the partition of the net product of industry between labor and capital, for instance, either may get more than its proper share, to the detriment of the other necessarily, as well as of the general interests. The favored one will prefer immediate to remote gain. Unfair division must have been the rule in the past, or the contrast between the two great divisions of society, the rich and the poor, would not be the astounding spectacle it is. The contrast is too violent. The positive pole is too much of a *plus* and the negative too much of a *minus* quantity. Undoubtedly this condition has been partially brought about by statutory enactments and other artificial means. Centralization is unquestionably a law of the industrial as well as the political movement, but the accelerated speed of the centripetal tendency in recent times is attributable not to natural, but to civil law. Capital and enterprise gravitate to certain favorable points, bringing the multitude in their train. Wealth and population increase, but wealth more than population, and distress more than wealth. The great city lifts its tower-crowned head and becomes a centre of attraction powerful as the mountain magnet in the Calender's tale, a seat of science and art, a scene of fashion, luxury, and pleasure, and too often a hot-bed of licentiousness. The centralizing tendency of things in general is stimulated by the lucrative privileges which wealth never fails to win from the government. The cities are the foci of the new ideas and of the intellectual activities and enterprise which essay to realize them in action and object. They possess subtle powers unknown to the rural population which are periodically called into play in the policy of the state for the benefit of private or corporate interests. Capital, in alliance with the most influential political party, whose leaders it never fails to corrupt, always obtains the franchises and privileges which it covets. The centripetal tendency, as it is revealing itself at the present, is manifestly the resultant of a composition of forces, not the least potent of which are the acts of congress, the state legislatures, or the city councils. That the maximum of the movement is not yet attained, is deducible from what is happening every day. The formation of "trusts," in which the unit is an aggregation of millions of capital, and the trust itself a confederacy, is the latest development, but who shall say it is the ultimate one? . . .

The questions now before the American people (they are less political than social) are the most important since the slavery question was decided. In England, the combined socialist and labor movement is the most important since the era of the "Great Rebellion;" in France, since the revolution; in Germany, since the Napoleonic conquest. The accusation and indictment which the proletariat urge in the forum of all nations is that the capitalists, in the broad sense of the definition take or get more than their due proportion of the fruits of the earth and all industry, and in addition the whole unearned increment, whether coming from land or other monopolies. I am bound to say the charge is but too well founded. All the facts and phenomena testify to it. How else could there be squalid misery and an infinite amount of it at one end of the scale and excessive riches at the other? It will not do to attribute the condition of the poor to themselves—to their improvidence, idleness, and intemperance, etc. The proletariat, as a body, are not demoralized, for they are willing and able to work, and live by work when it can be got. Their occasional lapses from sobriety and thrift, and the dissipated habits of some, are in no small degree caused by their wretched, sordid environment, which has been built around them in iron circles by the same blind destiny that flung the golden fleece round their antipodes in the social sphere. If the question of morality should be raised between the two, the debate would never end. Each has its own sins to answer for, and those of each may be put into the scale against the other's; but when the few, trailing their vast possessions, are weighed against the naked many, the landless, the moneyless, the thirty thousand against the twice thirty millions, the scales no longer balance. The thousands, loaded down with the world's goods, are heavy, the million, light. The gold outweighs the flesh and blood and, *a fortiori,* capital outweighs labor. To adjust or readjust the balance, to establish a permanent equilibrium between capital and labor, or more broadly, between the millionaires, the toiling masses, and the public at large, without infringing on the just rights of any is the chief problem of political science in this, our day and generation. The undue preponderance of one class in public affairs and society movements generally, like the unconstitutional preponderance of one branch of a government at the expense of the others, is the fruitful cause of morbid unrest, chronic agitation, and revolutionary change. The people are instinctively opposed to plutocratic ascendancy more than to any other, because plutocracy never hesitates to employ bribery for the attainment of selfish ends, and leans on corruption as its most powerful auxiliary. Furthermore, undue aggressive prominence, inordinate covetousness, loud ostentation, overweening pride, and frivolous exclusiveness—the most marked characteristic of the *nouveaux riches*—are universally disliked, and the caste themselves bitterly envied and loudly cursed. Class pride and the vices inherent in caste have brought down old aristocracies, and are darkly dangerous to the new in the new democratic and industrial era. To restore and maintain the equilibrium of the different powers of the state, of the different classes of the population, is simply to restore and maintain the healthy condition of the state and secure the stability and improvement of its institutions. This rule applies to the natural body as well as the body politic. The harmonious workings of the different organs, the maintenance of the equation of waste and nutrition, are the conditions of health. The frequent disturbance of these normal relations—the feebler action of some organs, the excessive activity of others—means disordered functions, the decay of the organism, and dissolution. To wisely coordinate the special and public interests, to place and maintain each part of the community in its proper place and in just relation to the whole, or, more correctly, to repress all class usurpation, whether the class be workers or employers, is, I repeat, the desideratum of the new statesmanship and the problem of the age. Mere party politics are passing out of date into the limbo whither have fled the ghosts of slavery and the alien and sedition laws. The democracy has the severest of its Herculean tasks before it, for the great social question which is the integral of the labor question, the educational question, the state charities question, and the temperance question will dwarf all other issues, and on the satisfactory solution of it the welfare and healthy progress of the American people depend. . . .

The powers of the state are commensurate with its duties. It possesses the taxing power which is the vital thing in working out the problems of the education question, the labor question, and the charities question. The three are most intimately related, but the last can never be placed on a proper footing or have fair play until the two others are permanently adjusted, which will not be until they are fairly adjusted. Though her ministrations shall continue whether the state act or not, yet it is only when the state has done its part, that voluntary charity can hope to be mistress of the work she has to do—a work that will end only with the consummation of all things, for the world, the flesh, and the devil shall not fail to take toll of the generations on their pilgrimage to eternity. The enemy shall continue to sow tares among the wheat. The vicissitudes of fortune, the tragedies of passion shall continue to leave their marks on character and life. Catastrophes, natural and human, shall continue to strew earth and ocean with wrecks and ruins; and "the blind Fury with the abhorred shears" will not hold from slitting the thread of life, separating husband and wife, robbing children of their parents and parents of their children. The sphere of charity we may be sure will not be circumscribed within too narrow bounds by the action of the state, however broad and beneficent that action may be. . . .

Charity apart, I venture to say that the labor movement, which at first sight seems a selfish struggle between classes, takes the foremost place among those developments which promise to reduce the sum of human misery and promote the comfort and well-being of the greatest number. It is, therefore, in substance philanthropic, and in its philanthropic aspect it demands patient and candid examination by this enlightened assembly. . . .

The liability of the employer or public carrier for the injury or death of the employee or other victim, though partially recognized in law, is continually challenged in the courts to the scandal of American jurisprudence. Every claim of this kind is contested, entailing all the penalties of tedious litigation on the unfortunate claimant. Some summary process for overcoming what is practically a denial of justice by railroad and other corporations is urgently needed. It is estimated that the number of railroad fatalities annually is about 2,500. The serious accidents are many times that number. Over 3,000 sea-faring men on English ships (or one out of every sixty) are drowned every year, owing to the overloading, undermanning, and neglect of repairs.* We do not lose so many because our ocean-going marine is such a speck that no binocular glass can find it on the high seas. Is it not self-evident that the widows and orphans, and the maimed and disabled should receive ample and immediate compensation from those in whose service life and limb were lost? That accumulated wealth and capital, besides furnishing liberal compensation in cases of fatality and dismemberment should also contribute to the support of the men whose disabilities and infirmities have been incurred in the production of it, is a proposition that cannot well be disputed, and we see that in one great country at least it is the groundwork of a new system designed to meet the necessities of the working classes, when disability from whatever cause, accident, illness, or old age, supervenes. The plan adopted by the German government is insurance by the joint contributions of employers, employed, and the state, each contributing a third. But manifestly the premiums ought to be paid exclusively by the employers, because then the tax would be added to the price of the article produced or deducted from the compensation for the service performed. The workman, if he contributes, should have the right to withdraw the amount of his contributions at stated periods. There are 3,861,560 skilled workmen, of whom 259,977 are railroad men, now insured in Germany. There are also 6,978,579 agricultural laborers insured. Denmark and Austria have begun to establish similar systems. This Bismarckian measure is to me an economic fact of the deepest significance—a precedent, I would say, of inestimable value. It is a partial reading at least of the terrible Sphinx riddle of the age. The German law does not, indeed, cover the whole ground, but it brings the whole ground

* This statement was repeatedly made at the Seaman's Congress held last month at Cardiff.

within the domain of "practical politics." An insurance policy of similar character here would be a matter exclusively between the employers and the workmen. The state should do nothing more than exercise the same supervision over it that it does over insurance in general.

The state recognizes its philanthropic duties, but only in a half-hearted, niggardly spirit. As a matter of fact many of the burdens which properly appertain to the state are shifted on the cities, whose local charities in addition are abused by the selfishness of rural communities, which like some foreign countries are but too well inclined to expatriate their paupers and imbeciles. But state philanthropy should not be confined to the erection and maintenance of some asylums. These are of course indispensable, but other institutions are needed. No outdoor relief of any kind is provided in any case for any one. The hospitals, which are too limited in number, for the most part belong to the city, or private foundations, or religious charities. Prisons and reformatories are not charities, but public safeguards, but charity should find free entrance to them and all other penal institutions, for nowhere else are her visits more needed.

Apart from charities public and private, and the labor movement, the philanthropic activities of the day include the sanitary, the temperance, the educational, and the peace (international) movements. The last may have and I am sure has our sympathy, but it has not the practical interest for us that it has for the European peoples. With regard to labor, it is evident, if I have not unhappily spoken in vain, that not only the condition of the proletariat, but public policy demands a more equitable distribution of the joint productions of land, labor, and capital. In no country, as far as I can see, is there any decentralizing action in the regions of industry and commerce at all comparable to or commensurate with the centralizing movement. Cooperation would furnish the panacea, perhaps, but that system is but of very limited extent or application thus far, and is evidently of too slow growth to meet the exigencies of the day. The everlasting cry is for more trade, increased output, new markets! Not a word is said about a just dispensation of profits. Our manufactories, by some political art and craft, are now to overleap all tariff barriers and shake their cornucopiae over Central and South America. So far so good, but the gains are to flow back in the same old channels, and settle in the same old reservoirs of the plutocrats. If we are yet so backward in economics and social dynamics, or let us say in scientific politics, as to be incapable of starting an outflow by automatical agencies the equivalent of the inflow, or in other words, if we are yet incompetent to provide for a fair division of the fruits of industry betweeen the different factors of production, we are at least able to provide provisional or empirical relief for the evils of the existing state of affairs—for the maladies most in sight—for the eruptions and spasms which attest the disordered constitution. First of all, we should extend education. Education is not a remedy for every evil under the sun, and a purely secular education is seriously, even vitally, deficient, for it furnishes no sanction for morals or conduct, and good conduct is more than half the battle of life; but any training of the mental faculties is so much added to the ability of the individual. Free night schools for adults, free reading rooms, free libraries, and free technical schools for industrial training now that apprenticeship is a thing of the past, should be established in our cities, and free museums of art, antiquities, and natural history in our metropolitan cities and in all high schools and universities. Mechanics' institutes would advance the cause, but these should be founded and maintained by the mechanics themselves. All these things would promote popular education and morally would stand as a chain of fortresses against the saloon, the dance-hall and the low variety show. But physical education and public hygiene should also have a place in the new system. Free swimming baths, gymnasia, and open spaces abounding in shade and shelter, should be established wherever needed. Skilled and unskilled labor have an equal interest in these important matters, as they also have in the sanitary condition of their dwellings and the shops and establishments in which the workmen congregate. If the workmen used their ballots to good purpose every shop and every factory, every dwelling, however humble, every living room in the tenement house, would be perfect in plumbing, sewerage, and ventilation. Boards of health and building inspectors pay very little attention to what they deem small matters. It is to be hoped the time will come shortly, when landlords and employers will be compelled by law to maintain the salubrity of their tenants' habitations and the work-quarters of their hands. Education should be supplemented by organization, but this is a matter in which American labor is pretty well schooled, though I believe American working women have not yet fully caught the inspiration. Organization, enlightened by education and governed by sound principles, will be able to give effect to all the legitimate demands of labor. As far as I can see, all these demands are legitimate and practicable. Reduced hours, better wages, increased pay for overtime, the special protection of minors and women, and of that terribly abused class, the sailors, the unlimited liability of employers in cases of fatality, the extension of technical and manual training—these constitute a platform in which nothing is abstruse, unjust, or visionary. When the means for accomplishing these results are canvassed there is, however, no unanimity. Strikes and lockouts are poor expedients at best, and if accompanied by intimidation, are illegal and immoral. Mutiny is death. A man has the right to work for whom he will if he has the right to live. The one is the corollary of the other; and when he is deprived of that right through terrorism or black-listing he is the victim of confederate barbarism as well as criminality. Arbitration is beginning to play a leading part in labor disputes, and it may be that the long-sought solution and synthesis is to be found in it. In any event, the laboring community, when properly organized and instructed, can exact their rights either directly by their own action within themselves, or indirectly through the medium of the state. Democracy, the ruler of us all, is ready to carry out their behests, as soon as convinced that they are reasonable and judicious. Any behests, for instance, calculated to drive away or destroy capital—the wage fund—or to intimidate the non-unionist, or black-list the unionist, would not be reasonable or judicious, but offensive to gods and men alike, and rebellious to democratic rule.

That the temperance movement, which has claims on every member of society, has peculiar claims on the sympathy and support of Catholics is all but self-evident. The great apostle of temperance was a Catholic priest and his mission lay among a Catholic people. On the other side there are very many Catholics engaged in the dangerous liquor traffic. It is not my province to dwell on the subject, but I take the liberty of applauding the wise and comprehensive utterance of the late plenary council held in this city, on it. I will add that whether higher license be the secular solution of the question or not, there are localities in all cities in which no saloon should be permitted—localities in which any form of local option is but a farce or a fraud. There are men, too, of such evil notoriety that no license should be granted to them under any circumstances. The saloons are altogether too many and too flagrant. The temperance question is also a religious question—a fact which the advocates of extirpation too often forget. Any vital reform of the individual must spring from the conscience. No code, however wisely framed or vigorously administered, will suffice of itself to abolish inebriety, while the attempt to do so might cause serious detriment to public morality by superinducing illicit traffic and giving sanction to hypocrisy.

The question is now, I suppose, on every tongue: Where is all the money to come from for those enlarged public charities, those new educational institutions and appliances, those free lyceums, libraries, swimming baths, gymnasia, parks, public gardens, and establishments for giving temporary refuge and relief to the able-bodied destitute and for utilizing their temporary labor to that end? Nothing is to be more deprecated than the abuse of outdoor relief, and I acknowledge it is perpetually liable to abuse. The creation of phalansteries of official lazzaroni living on forced contributions from the industry and property outside were a consummation to be dreaded and abhorred, but such a paradise of pauperism has not the consistency of a madman's dream, and is an impossibility even in the Utopias of socialism. The question of the ways and means is susceptible of a simple solution. The money should come from the superabundant riches of the plutocrats—from the thirty thousand who own half the wealth of the country and in the production of which the physical disabilities of the poor and their consequent helplessness were in the main contracted. An income tax would solve the problem—an impost from which salaries, commissions, and professional incomes should be exempt and also all incomes from whatever source below a certain round sum.* The fund

* If we ask how the great modern fortunes have been acquired in this country, the answer is not far to seek. The federal government, in the first place, has been giving rich mining lands away for nothing, or next to nothing, reserving no power to compel the payment of royalties. It has also given many, many millions of acres as gifts to railroad corporations, especially to the Pacific Railroad Corporations, to whom it has also given public money to the extent probably of $150,000,000. If you ask who are the millionaires of the Pacific coast you are told they are miners and railroad men. The Pennsylvania and New England millionaires are the creation of our tariff laws. The tariff laws account also for a good many of the merchant millionaires of New York. Railroad and transportation monopolies, the "unearned increment" of real estate, city franchises and bank privileges, usury, account for most of the rest.

Wherever you go, you find the millionaires whom you hear of have gas stocks, railroad stocks, street railroad stocks, patent rights, immense tracts of government lands, mines, all of which have come through the government, federal, state, or local, and which were originally vested in the people. It is not suggested that the fortunate possessors should make restitution to the public of their gains, ill-gotten or otherwise, but that they should contribute more liberally than they do to the support of the victims of their rapacity.

thus obtained would be practically a fund for the compensation of damages inflicted on individuals and society by the industrial system, and indirectly by the law. To levy a small percentage, say on all incomes of $10,000 a year and upwards, would be no hardship to Midas rioting in superfluity, and no injustice to the class of capitalists and rich men. That small percentage would furnish the state with ample means to carry out the policy outlined here. Perhaps all monopolies and public corporations, enriched by gifts from the federal government, the state or the city, which pay no royalties, should also be taxed the same as a "natural person," care being taken, however, not to tax the same property or person twice. Taxation should be equitably distributed, and therefore no *single tax* can be an equitable one. Every kind of property should bear its proper quota of the public burden, and no one or two kinds the whole burden. But I am not formulating a legislative measure, I am merely advocating a policy founded (I think) on justice. If the monopolist, the cattle king, and the lord of the "unearned increment" on the surface or in the bowels of the earth, would be wise in time, they must not resist the forthcoming demand for an income tax, which demand I predict will be loud and at last irresistible. True, they have "charters" and "vested interests," and these must be religiously respected so long as the maintenance of them endangers not the foundations of the fabric. Their hoards should be left intact. Spoliation of any kind, in any form, however tempting at the moment, is fatal to the general welfare in the end. But it should not be forgotten how the slaveholders were laid low. In this country more than any other—

> Not heaven itself upon the past has power,

but the state can make laws to take effect from and after their passage. We may not make *ex post facto* laws, but I refuse to believe that the people of the United States have bound themselves perpetually in withes which they cannot untie by the patient constitutional processes familiar to the genesis of our form of government—that they cannot free themselves from self-imposed restraints—which in course of time have become chains of iron and bonds of slavery—without having recourse to force, that is to revolution. I prefer to think that for every wrong there is a peaceful remedy, and that the by no means hopeless task of the statesman is to search for that remedy, and apply it as soon as the public are ripe for it. Things nowadays ripen fast, and ideas which are unjustly stigmatized as socialistic by the "vested interests" (these have ever stood as lions in the path of progress) are ripening fast into party policies and social reforms. He who is not wilfully blind can see that the future, uncertain and dark in other respects, belongs to organized labor, unless in the intoxication of new power, it loses its head and degenerates into socialism, communism, or other anarchical and deadly devolution.

15 Condé B. Pallen

A CONSERVATIVE VIEW OF THE CHURCH'S SOCIAL MISSION

From about 1890 until his death nearly four decades later Condé B. Pallen, journalist and editor, voiced the conviction that the Catholic Church should narrowly construe her social mission and steer clear of social movements. He argued that the ratio of increase in poverty was less than the ratio of population growth. He insisted that society could be improved only as its constituent individuals were perfected because social conditions were nothing more than the aggregate results of the perfections and imperfections in every individual member of the social body. There was indeed a social problem, but it involved only the weak, the unfortunate, and the vicious—persons crushed or pushed aside by social and economic change. The only remedy was divine charity as manifested in the manifold works of mercy of the Catholic Church.

Pallen was a tireless publicist. During the 1890's he fought the social program of the Catholic Congresses and ridiculed the Americanist crusade. His labors as managing editor (1904-1920) of the Catholic Encyclopedia *did not greatly diminish his anti-reform propaganda. Later, as chairman of the National Civic Federation's department of subversive movements, he insinuated that the Bishops' Program of Reconstruction (1919) was Marxist inspired (See Document 24).*

. . . As Christianity had freed the individual from the slavery of the State, so Christianity now sought to liberate the individual from the thraldom of his own passions. In old Rome we have the *Thesis,* or the statement that society is its own end; in Barbarism we find the *Antithesis,* or the statement that the individual is his own end, and in Christianity the *Synthesis,* or the statement that neither the State is the end of man, nor yet that he is his own end; but that in society the individual is to find a means to his own end, and that the end is in something other than himself—in God, his Creator. Rome had declared that the individual is a slave to the State; Barbarism had declared that the individual is a slave to himself; Christianity declares that the individual is neither a slave to the State nor yet a slave to himself. Rome had declared that man is a social being only; Barbarism asserted that he is not a social being at all; Christianity teaches that he is a

---

Condé B. Pallen, *The Catholic Church and Socialism. A Solution of the Social Problem* (St. Louis: B. Herder, 1890), pp. 18–21, 29–32, 40–47.

social being, but that he is also more than a social being. Rome was all government; Barbarism was no government; Christianity is government founded upon the inalienable right of every individual to life, liberty and the pursuit of happiness, in view of his eternal end in God. Rome was Socialism; Barbarism was Individualism, and Christianity is Individuality. . . .

In protestant Christianity we have had the assertion of the *Antithesis.* The Antithesis is fast expending itself, and now we are witnessing in the declaration of Physical Science the formulation of the *Thesis.* Protestantism has declared that there is no unity; Physical Science asserts that there is nothing but unity. Protestantism is the reactive or negative force in the direction of Socialism or State Supremacy; Physical Science is the positive force in the same direction.

Such is the genesis of the socialistic movement of the day. Its inevitable trend is toward State Supremacy, and unless it find some check it will ultimately culminate in a supreme State, fundamental in kind with old Rome. For underlying Socialism is the same conception of the universe as the product of an impersonal Force, and of man as only a phenomenal phase in the blind processes of its action. It declares that man is a social being and a social being only.

. . . . These are factors in the case which the modern Socialist overlooks, or else, if he considers them at all, desires to get rid of, because he entirely misapprehends their meaning. He does not understand that the real inequalities lie beneath the surface. He imagines that the surface of the ocean is higher in one place than in another, and this seems unnatural to him. But it is in human nature that inequalities primarily exist not in the social body itself. It is in the individual, not in the community, that the differences are to be found; and if there are to be found expressions of inequality in social conditions themselves, it is because these conditions are the aggregate result of inequalities in the units of society.

Overlooking this fact entirely, or else misapprehending its meaning, the Socialist seeks a remedy for these inequalities in a change of social conditions. It is the social conditions that make the inequalities, he declares; the remedy, therefore, will lie in changing these conditions. But the very reverse is the case; it is the inequalities in the individual that make the unequal social conditions. If the Socialist ever expects to bring about his dream of social equality, he must begin by eliminating all differences in the individual units of the social body; and it is because he has gone to the science of Political Economy for an answer to his problem that he has entirely overlooked the individual. There he finds no recognition of the individual as such, but only of social factors, as parts of the social whole.

When, therefore, the Socialist tells us that the poor are growing poorer and the rich richer, his obvious meaning is that the poor are growing poorer because the rich are growing richer; and this is the case, he asserts, because the prevailing social conditions are unequal. But this is an inference not deducible from the facts of the case; and moreover, the statement of the Socialist is false in its expression. What should be said is this: There are more poor people now than there were fifty years ago, not relatively, but absolutely; the rich are richer now than they were fifty years ago, not relatively, but absolutely. That is to say, as the population increases there are actually more poor now than there were before, although, in proportion to the increase, there are now fewer poor than there were before; that as the wealth of the world increases, there are more rich people than before, and these are richer than before; although in proportion to the general increase of wealth, the rich are no richer than they were fifty years ago; and this is due, not to the unequal social conditions, but to the inequalities in human nature itself—or those inequalities which exist in human character; that is, in the individual.

. . . . If men desire only the necessaries of life, only the necessaries of life will be produced. If they desire more than the necessaries of life, then more than the necessaries will be produced. Upon human desire, therefore, does the production of wealth depend. If men desire only the production of trousers, only trousers will be produced. If they desire only a certain kind of grain, only that kind will be produced. Hence, the differentiation of human desire will differentiate production, and so differentiate wealth. Differentiation in kind or in degree is differentiation in quality and in quantity. If human desire differentiates in kind and degree, it differentiates in quality and quantity; and differentiation in quality and quantity means inequality. Upon inequality in human desire, therefore, depends the differentiation of production, and, therefore, the differentiation of wealth.

Human desire, we have seen, is the final end of production. To human desire, therefore, as final end, must the product go in the shape of the useful thing or wealth. In this, then, do we find the law of distribution. But it is only as final end that human desire is the first cause of production. Therefore is it the first, or initial force in production, without whose initiation no other industrial force would be put into action. We see, then, that the very law which governs the distribution of wealth is the same law which governs its production. In the one case it is human desire as final cause; in the other it is human desire as first cause. As long, therefore, as there are inequalities in human desire, so long must there be inequalities in the distribution of wealth; and when the Socialist seeks to get rid of the factor of inequality in the distribution, he must first get rid of the same factor in the production of wealth.

. . . . To have a perfect society, we must have the perfect individual, and only then will we arrive at the perfect State. It is, therefore, in the regeneration of the individual that social perfection is to be sought, and in Christianity only is this regeneration to be found, as only in Christianity are the essential means to be found of bringing it about.

In his relations to God will the individual find all his other relations. As in union with God he finds his personal perfection, so there will he find his social perfection. In the City of God will be found the perfect man, and only in the perfect man will be found the perfect social being. The better citizen a man is in the divine polity, the better citizen he will become in the human polity; for the lesser is ever included in the higher. If we look out upon the world to-day, where do we find the best form of government? Is it not among Christian peoples? If we compare the Christian world with the pagan world as it was and as it is, where do we find the highest form of government, the best citizen, and the greatest liberty?

Yet all this is not perfect, and the nations we call Christian are as far from social perfection just in proportion as they are distant from the Christian ideal in the individual members of their several polities. In their social conditions, therefore, will be found many imperfections and defects, and among those ills, to which flesh is heir, is to be found poverty.

Is there any remedy for this in Christianity? We partly answered this question when we said that the perfect individual will make the perfect social condition. But this is not true in an absolute, but only in a relative sense; for just as it is impossible for the individual to become absolutely perfect, so is it impossible for human society to become absolutely perfect. Human nature is finite, and therefore limited in its perfection. It may reach its complete perfection and yet not be infinitely perfect. In human nature we cannot, therefore, expect to find a perfect social state, and as long as the social conditions are not perfect we are certain to find limitations in the workings of the laws which govern human society. One of the effects of social limitations is poverty, or the lack of wealth, in the individual. I do not mean that poverty may not be mitigated, but simply that it can never be completely and perpetually eradicated as long as human society exists.

But is this the final word of Christianity to this problem? To abandon it here is only half a solution. It is true that in the Christian view poverty is not an imperfection in the individual himself; nor is his perfection to be found in the possession of wealth. On the contrary the very opposite may be the case, and the individual may find his salvation in a state of poverty, and in wealth his destruction. But when the individual is crushed out by the working of the social and economic laws—when the weak and the unfortunate, and even the vicious are thrust out beyond the pale, or trampled in the dust under the feet of the nations as they march onward—has Christianity no answer for this difficulty besides the one already given here? Yes, it has an answer, and a ready answer; and not only a ready, but a practical answer.

Christianity is here for a two fold purpose: First to strengthen and perfect human nature as far as it is perfectible. Secondly, to assist the weaknesses of human nature, and where men find their natural limitations, to supplement their work—to make man stronger than himself—to lift him up to the supernatural life of God. Where, therefore, men through their limitations fail, and where society through its limitations fails, Christianity should find within itself the doctrine and the power of supplying these natural deficiencies. The doctrine we have already touched upon, the doctrine of the supreme value of the individual, which we have seen is a Christian doctrine and a Christian development.

In view of this doctrine, the weak, the unfortunate, and the vicious are as precious as the strong, the fortunate, and the virtuous. The practical application of this doctrine is through the law of divine charity. Charity is the love of God; and in the love of God, the love of each and every human creature made in the divine likeness. But it will not suffice to merely teach this doctrine, it must have practical force and exemplification. In the Church herself, as in Christ Himself, is its highest exemplification; for in the Incarnate Word, and in His Church, do we find the highest expression of God's love for man.

In the Church, therefore, we should find the special manifestation of the law of charity. In what way do we find it? It will manifest itself according to the special needs of time and circumstances. Accordingly, when we look over the Church's history, we discover springing up within her pale innumerable organizations and associations, designed to meet the special wants and needs of human nature, in relation to the peculiar times and circumstances which may have developed them; such societies are the Dominicans, Franciscans, Capuchins, Carthusians, Lazarists, Jesuits, Redemptorists, and the innumerable other congregations of men and women, which have sprung into existence throughout her varied history; some lasting as the need of them lasted, and passing away as they ceased to be of use, to make way for other associations to meet the new exigencies and to correspond to different sets of circumstances. All of these have been founded upon the divine law of charity and have sprung from the womb of the Church, as children from their mother. From her they have derived their divine life, and are the special fruits of her divine charity. They were, or are, all addressed to the task of meeting, in some special way, human infirmities, whether corporeal or spiritual. They have been established to feed the hungry, to give drink to the thirsty, to give shelter to the stranger, to clothe the naked, to visit the sick and the captive; for in the hungry and in the thirsty, in the sick, in the naked, in the stranger, and in the captive, they see Jesus Christ Himself according to the words: "Inasmuch as you did it to one of these, My least brethren, you did it to Me." The least of these is an immortal creature, with an eternal destiny, and infinitely precious in the sight of the Master, who redeemed them in His blood, and, therefore, in the sight of His Church, which daily perpetuates that redeeming act.

In our own day, witness her life in charity. See her innumerable institutions daily and hourly devoted to works of mercy. Through them she nurses the sick, feeds the poor, cares for the orphan, suckles the abandoned babe, shelters the deserted old, rescues the fallen woman, embraces the leper, houses the homeless. And she does all this, not merely through the inspiration of private charity, or the pitying impulse of the moment, but through an organized system of charity, finding its expression in innumerable institutions carrying on their work thoroughly and harmoniously in the power of a unity which she alone can give. Witness her Sisters of Charity, her Sisters of Mercy, her Sisters of the Good Shepherd, her Sisters of Providence, her Sisters of St. Mary, her Little Sisters of the Poor, and a host of others; witness the labors of her St. Vincent de Paul Society; cast even a cursory glance at their work. What are they doing? Are they not caring for the weak and the unfortunate; are they not supplementing the work of human society where it fails? Where the working of the social laws have crushed out the individual, the weak and the unfortunate and the vicious, are they not extending the hand of succor to them—lifting them up from the dust, and bestowing upon them, in the divine spirit of charity, what society cannot give them? And why is all this? Because the Church appreciates the supreme value of the individual, and loves with a divine love the least of her Lord's brethren.

What would become of the abandoned babe, the orphan, the helpless, the deserted old, the Magdalen, the unfortunate, and the destitute, if, in the ardor of her love, she did not thus take them to her divine bosom? What became of them amongst the pagan peoples of old Rome? Of what value are they to society? What do they contribute to the welfare of society? What claim have they, therefore, upon society? The pagan world mercilessly answered, "None;" for Charity had not then been born in the person of Christ, and the world knew nothing of the infinite value of a single human soul. The weak, and the unfortunate, and the helpless were cast out to perish. Sparta strangled the puny or maimed infant, for he could never have any value as a citizen. Aristotle and Plato, the noblest intellects of the pagan world, tell us that only the strong and healthy should be permitted to survive; and the Roman father could expose his infant at will, if he thought it likely to be weak or sickly. When the unfortunate of either sex and any age, in the pagan world, were found to be of no further service to society, they were left to shift for themselves and die. Without Christianity, they would to-day be left to perish according to the law of the survival of the fittest. But what society refuses to do, or fails to do, that Christianity supplements by the divine law of Charity. This is our problem and this is its only solution.

16 Bishop James A. McFaul

GRIEVANCES REDRESSED BY FEDERATION OF CATHOLIC SOCIETIES

Many Catholics wished to emphasize problems outside the areas of social or industrial concern, for example, that of the defense of the constitutional rights and legitimate religious interests of Catholic citizens. Catholic rights were allegedly ignored or minimized in public education, state eleemosynary institutions, and in the governing of our overseas possessions. These aggrieved Catholics launched the American Federation of Catholic Societies through which they sought to rally the great body of the faithful behind a nonpartisan political program. They found a dedicated and eloquent spokesman in James A. McFaul, Bishop of Trenton, two of whose many articles are here reprinted.

The Federation movement may be viewed as the Catholic reaction or response to the proscriptive anti-Catholic crusade of the American Protective Association (APA). It was also a covert reaction against the socially liberal and Americanist program of the Catholic Congresses and similarly disposed groups. While not opposed or indifferent to social reform, the Federationists moved slowly and cautiously; they were quick to denounce anti-Catholic trends toward materialism, socialism, anarchy, and divorce, and slow to advance remedial measures of a positive and constructive character. They sought harmony and understanding among the various ethnic groups, they did not insist on immediate Americanization.

CATHOLIC GRIEVANCES—THEIR REMEDY

The editor of the Ecclesiastical Review has requested me to initiate a discussion on the best manner of redressing the religious grievances suffered by Catholics in the United States. It will not be necessary to enter again upon the ground already passed over in my addresses and articles relating to the existence of the grievances themselves. The light of public opinion has been strongly focused upon them, and whatever ignorance existed regarding them has now been dispelled.

Fortunately the press has given great assistance. Newspapers and periodicals, Catholic and non-Catholic, religious and secular, have eagerly participated in the discussion. Criticism, whether favorable or unfavorable, has been very conducive to the dissemination of the truth—the main object proposed from the outset of the agitation. A campaign of education was begun and continued with such earnestness and unanimity on the part of Catholics, that there are now very few, even among

---

James A. McFaul, "Catholic Grievances—Their Remedy," *Ecclesiastical Review*, XXIII (December 1900), 572–578.

non-Catholics, who do not realize that our grievances are many and weighty—such as demand serious consideration, and the adaptation of effective means towards their redress. Briefly, they are: Freedom of conscience in public institutions, the public school question, the treatment of Catholic Indians and the like, along with other numerous evils already in existence or certain to arise in our new possessions.

Up to the present the public attention has been occupied with the exposition of grievances. Their remedy has been referred to, but not presented in any definite plan.

It is surely not necessary to accentuate the need of organization for the purpose of executing any plan selected. Nevertheless, it may not be out of place to touch upon the subject. While bigotry is not by any means dead in this country, most of us will agree with Mr. James E. Wright, who, in the August number of *Donahoe's Magazine,* expresses the opinion that the "careful exclusion of Catholics from any of the Commissions" (to our new possessions) "has not been instigated by bigotry, but . . . is a carefully considered move in the political game . . . under the instruction of astute advisers." Reëlection was of the first importance; everything else must be subservient to it "Had there been appointed," continues Mr. Wright, "even one prominent representative American Catholic on each of the Commissions to the Catholic peoples of the new possessions, the reports submitted . . . would quite likely have been different, and probably would have led to considerable public discussion upon the subjects of education, of marriage, and of the various complex questions arising from the abrupt severance of Church and State. All danger of this was avoided by the selection of exclusively non-Catholic Commissioners. For a similar reason . . . Protestant superintendents of schools have also been appointed for each of the new territories. If American Catholics were chagrined at their ostracism, anti-Catholic sentiment . . . was profoundly elated. . . . In a word, taking all the circumstances of the situation into account, the course followed . . . was doubtless considered carefully, and it seems to have been a shrewd one from the viewpoint of the mere politician whose chief object is an election."

In other words, during a presidential or other campaign it is quite safe to ignore Catholics. And whom have we to blame but ourselves? It has, then, come to this, that politicians looking over the field and weighing the factors on which success will necessarily depend, do not find that the interests of Catholics, as American citizens, must be taken into consideration. What a sad commentary upon the policy of silence to which we have been so long and so tenaciously devoted!

In my opinion organization should be substituted for this policy of silence. For years we have been trifled with and deprived of our rights, often for no other reason than that we are Catholics, and it is high time to devise and to apply a remedy. A sad experience has convinced us that individual effort is useless, except in very rare instances. Even when those eminent in religious or secular affairs have sought redress they have secured very little, if any—precisely because they were supported by no tangible, organized body which commanded attention and urged just concessions.

As regards freedom of conscience in public institutions, Catholics are better off, perhaps, in New Jersey than in many other States of the Union; yet I have been placed in a similar humiliating position when seeking due representation on the boards of management of public institutions, so that the full religious rights of the Catholic inmates might be obtained, exercised, and protected. "Thrice is he armed that hath his quarrel just," I found had but a very remote application. The authorities greeted me with exuberant courtesy, but my requests for the enjoyment of undoubted rights were often futile, and probably were not conceded serious attention. The rights of citizenship do not so strongly appeal to the reigning politician as his own interests, and they are dependent upon the political party which he has espoused. At the present time there are not a few in political life who are concerned solely with whatever will either advance or prove an obstacle to their political ambitions.

It was not thought wise, when giving publicity to our grievances, to anticipate public opinion among Catholics by offering, at the same time, a definite plan or remedy. Therefore, in my letters and addresses to societies composed of Catholics, even organization was referred to only in a tentative way. It was suggested that if societies composed of Catholics retaining their identity and pursuing their own aims independently of one another, touched at certain points, the resulting bond of union would enable them to exert concerted influence, possessing value whenever and wherever bigots attempted the invasion of our rights. Care was taken to state clearly that no movement, purposing to advance Catholics, as Catholics, to political office would be serviceable. In the United States, political office cannot be claimed by the adherents, as such, of any form of religion. Nevertheless, an American citizen should not be discriminated against simply because he is a Catholic, or because he has aided Catholics when there was question of their constitutional rights. Moreover, it was emphatically announced that no organization directed against any political party, merely as a party, could be regarded with favor; that it was not contemplated to interfere with party affiliations. Catholics, in their political and civil relations, must be guided and controlled, of course, by the laws of morality; they cannot admit that there is one code of ethics, one interpretation of the Ten Commandments for the individual and another for the nation. The words of the Saviour are as true to-day as when He uttered them nineteen centuries ago: "Render, therefore, to Cæsar the things that are Cæsar's, and to God the things that are God's." The ballot must be cast in the light of moral principles and conscientiously. Adherence to these principles, however, will not forbid us to oppose ignorant, presumptuous bigotry, or to prevent its followers from entering political life in America.

The object desired is evident enough, although we may not

so clearly perceive the means leading up to its attainment. We may learn a lesson from our Protestant fellow-citizens. They stand up courageously in defence of their rights. If the National Administration, the State Legislatures, or local boards, attempt to interfere with the smallest claim of the sects, their protests are heard in clarion tones throughout the length and breadth of the land, and delegation after delegation of their representative laymen besiege the halls of legislation. As a rule they have been victorious. Very few politicians care to withstand determined public opposition. In fact, public sentiment, properly manifested, is often necessary to enable them to obtain justice for their constituents. The advice given by General Grant, when President, may serve as an illustration: "These people get together, call meetings, get up petitions, and send deputies down here, and thus they often secure their object. Now, that is what you Catholics should do. Get together, make out a statement of your case, and back it with as much force as you can muster." This is good advice; it is brief and right to the point. It is likewise in perfect harmony with our form of government. The citizen is acting strictly within the rights of citizenship when he resorts to such measures to obtain or to defend his rights. Indeed, he may be justly accused of neglect if he does not exercise this prerogative when the occasion demands.

This is the goal to be reached; in what manner can we best advance towards it? The federation of all societies composed of Catholics has been debated for several years, and certain leaders among the laity, belonging to the principal organizations, have even taken steps towards its consummation by calling meetings and by outlining constitutions. This movement has not been primarily inaugurated for the redress of grievances; there are many other reasons given why such a union is desirable. Through federation we would have at hand a body of men trained by experience in the management of organizations, many of whom are anxious and ready to employ their knowledge for the purpose suggested. Shall the movement which they have begun be assisted and directed, or shall it be allowed to run its course and probably expire, mainly because it has not received that counsel and encouragement which would have brought success?

It is alleged that the difficulties and dangers connected with societies would be multiplied in a general organization. If we are to be discouraged by obstacles which, after all, are not insurmountable, then we have departed far from the spirit of our heroic ancestors, who sacrificed life itself rather than surrender either religious or civil rights. But why should we fear? American Catholics are worthy of their forefathers. Point the way; let legitimate, constitutional, prudent means be selected, and they will give most cheerful support. No one can deny that the American Catholic possesses the courage of his convictions.

It is well to remark that any organization taking up the redress of religious grievances must be under wise control, else many mistakes may be made, and it cannot hope to enjoy, what is very necessary, the confidence of conservative, prudent leaders among the clergy and laity.

In some places diocesan unions already exist. Shall federation be accomplished by the formation of other unions, and their aggregation, all leading up to archdiocesan unions, all under spiritual direction, and culminating in a national union? Such a union having been accomplished, religious grievances existing only in a State, after all ordinary means had been exhausted, could be brought to the attention of the diocesan unions within the same, for the benefit of their combined action. The influence of all the societies constituting the national union would be exerted in a question possessing national importance.

Should this plan not meet with favor, might the end be attained by a national board elected by the societies of the United States, this board being under a spiritual director? Again, if the latter plan is not suitable, would the following prove satisfactory? The International Truth Society, of Brooklyn, N. Y. is already organized. The society has selected several boards for special duties. One board, composed of prominent archbishops, bishops, priests, and laymen, is kept informed of the work of the society, and consulted in all important matters.

The work in which the society is engaged may be briefly summed up as follows:

1. The refutation of all misrepresentations, calumnies, etc., against the Catholic Church; 2. The creation of a demand for Catholic literature; 3. The distribution of Catholic literature in sparsely settled districts, among Catholics and non-Catholics, by requesting Catholics to re-mail their Catholic papers and magazines.

This society is willing also to assist in remedying injustice when called upon, and its executive committee will gather together all data relating to a case presented, obtain legal advice, and, when satisfied that action is necessary, quietly bring the question before the proper authorities. Should this prove futile, the matter will be brought before the directors of the society. When their approval has been obtained, a formal protest, previously submitted to them, shall be sent to the chief officers of every Catholic organization in the United States. These having been made aware of the justice and urgency of the case, and the authoritative source whence the protest arises, could sign it. Such a protest, representing the sentiments of the thousands of members belonging to Catholic organizations would, beyond doubt, have very great weight, and effect that which individual effort had been unable to obtain.

It will be seen that this plan is substantially the same as the others. It possesses, however, an advantage which should not be overlooked, viz., an organization already formed, and capable of immediately entering upon the work. It may be well to observe that, while this society is independent of the federation of Catholic societies, it could employ that organization in the accomplishment of this special work.

Again, it has been suggested that a Truth Society might be established in every archdiocese, and diocesan branches added as might be found feasible, all tending to a national organization formed for the same ends, and employing methods similar to those of the International Truth Society.

It will be noticed that the plans here outlined are merely suggestive, and that they require development. This would naturally come after the adoption of a specific plan. In the object to be obtained they agree and their methods are alike. They differ only in the formation of the organization.

It is possible that none of these plans may meet with universal favor. Let, therefore, others be proposed. Every Catholic, ecclesiastic and layman, recognizes the need of a remedy. Let us have an earnest discussion of the subject, give it our best thought, and, having found a legitimate, honorable, and wise solution of the problem, reduce it to practice and prosecute it to a successful consummation.

THE AMERICAN FEDERATION OF CATHOLIC SOCIETIES

This is an age of organization and concentration. Never before was the saying: "In union there is strength" so thoroughly appreciated and so practically demonstrated. Nations unite for the advancement of their interests commercial, political and financial. Within the borders of the same country we find similar efforts. Recently a great impulse has been given to combinations in the same trade or profession because less expense is required with consequent lower prices and greater profits.

James A. McFaul, "The American Federation of Catholic Societies," *Donahoe's Magazine,* LII (July 1904), 87–90.

In America the benefits derived from union are very important and attractive. The very air we breathe excites activity, and we grasp at everything which will contribute to our welfare. This partly accounts for the rapid spread of modern life-insurance. On all sides there have arisen hundreds of companies, large and small, good and bad. Among others we find organizations formed to supply what is called "Cheap Insurance," in comparison with the premiums paid to the great companies, such as the Mutual Life Insurance Company, of New York.

Non-Catholic societies have connected with the insurance plan a species of "*secret work*," including an oath and a ritual closely resembling Free-Masonry. Organizations have grown up also in the Catholic body to compete with this "*Cheap Insurance*" for mutual assistance, and to keep Catholics out of either nominally condemned or forbidden and dangerous societies.

Federation proposes to unite all organizations composed of Catholics, whether they possess the insurance, the beneficial, or the religious feature, to add even the representative members of parishes who belong to no special society, and eventually to combine the entire Catholic people of the United States in a great organization and thereby to advance the interests of Catholics as members of the Catholic Church and American citizens.

This central organization was founded several years ago. Very much has been spoken and written regarding its scope and methods, yet they are far from being understood throughout the United States. Let us therefore draw attention to some of the ends which Federation intends to attain. The Catholic Church in America is composed of various nationalities, speaking different languages. One generation, and in some instances, two and even three generations, will be necessary, owing to racial traits, locality, and numbers, before this difference of language will cease to retard a full grasp of and co-operation in American life. During this formative process, these nationalities suffer great disadvantage as regards the progress and the elevation of themselves and their children.

In recent years, this condition has been emphasized. Take large cities, such as Buffalo, Chicago, etc., you will find, within their territorial limits, colonies of thousands of Poles, Bohemians, and other races. They have settled down like an immense flock of migrating birds; houses, churches, schools, halls, etc., have been erected, and newspapers published. All these are either owned by them or under their control. In a word, a portion of Poland and Bohemia, etc., has been transplanted to America. The people retain all their native customs, having very little intercourse with Americans. Undoubtedly temporary segregation has advantages; it protects, to some extent, religion and the race. It is impossible, however, that such a status should continue. The friction resulting from association with other races will gradually disintegrate these colonies, and their members will sooner or later be merged into and assimilated by the general population of the nation.

The importance of having all these nationalities touch, at certain points, with the great Catholic body therefore is apparent. Thus they will be united more closely to the religious life of the Catholic Church in the United States, and to our national life. The distrust arising from race prejudices and race peculiarities, which has been and is so detrimental to the progress of the Church in this country, will slowly disappear as Catholics of different nationalities are brought into closer contact by the constant intercourse which will result from the meetings of the Federation.

The readiest and best method of accomplishing this central organization has been indicated by experience, viz., to take the present Catholic societies as a basis, and bring them together in a great association, without in any way trespassing on their autonomy, aims or objects. It is proper to accentuate the fact that a Catholic political party is neither contemplated nor desirable. Anyone acquainted with America understands that Catholics as Catholics cannot engage in *partisan politics.* Such a course would be very detrimental to our interests.

It is often asked: What is the use of Federation, if it doesn't engage in politics? Is it not votes that count? In reply I would call attention to the term *partisan politics.* Federation cannot be swayed in favor of any political party. If, however, the School Question, Divorce, etc., are to be solved satisfactorily to Catholics, politics in this broad sense must form a very important feature of Federation. To illustrate: about a year ago, a bill was brought before the New Jersey Legislature. The text of the bill was ambiguous and offered a loop-hole for taxing our parochial schools. Several Catholic gentlemen called upon the introducer of the bill and requested that this ambiguity be removed. They were treated courteously, of course, but all their pleading was in vain. The matter was then taken up by the New Jersey Branch of the Federation. A committee representing both political parties, and different nationalities, was appointed to wait upon a committee of the Legislature, and state the objections to the bill. As soon as the majority-leader of the House of Assembly heard of the movement on foot, the committee of Federation was immediately assured that there need be no misgivings regarding the bill and any change Federation desired would be made in its phraseology. This is the kind of politics Federation intends to engage in, and it is certainly high time that this method was resorted to. Our non-Catholic friends have been attaining their ends by these methods for a long time. We have been crying out against grievances, and have been too timid to exercise the prerogatives granted every citizen by the state and nation.

It is proper that all Catholics should know that those who are calling out Politics! Politics!! when Federation is mentioned, are either those who have given very little attention to the literature of the movement, or are interested, scheming politicians, who for selfish ends oppose it, recognizing that it is a factor which they cannot hope to influence and control. The broad-minded politician and statesman recognizes that Federation, in educating Catholics to use the rights of American citizenship, for their civil, social and religious advancement, is performing a very laudable and highly necessary work.

Non-Catholics, as a rule, in the United States are justice-loving, and anxious to dwell in peace and harmony with other citizens, irrespective of creed or nationality, and such a combination would render them suspicious, and perhaps make them our enemies. They have, indeed, many prejudices, handed down from a bigoted ancestry, which are cultivated and perpetuated by unscrupulous ministers, and very many of them are profoundly ignorant of Catholic doctrine, faith and morality. The policy we must adopt is that which will enable them to understand us and be our friends. Let, therefore, the teachings of the Church be brought home to them. In this work the missions to non-Catholics, preached in almost every diocese of the country, are an important factor. Federation can give much assistance along similar lines by discussing the problems of the day and disseminating their Catholic solution. Further, its influence on Catholic societies composed of Italians, Poles, Bohemians, Hungarians, Greeks, etc., will be of immense benefit; it will protect them from the onslaughts of proselyting Protestants and bring them into intimate relationship with their fellow-Catholics.

We may here ask what has Federation already accomplished? In a short time it has done noble work. It has formed Catholic public opinion on the great topics of the day; it has compelled the attention to the views of Catholics on them, so that the public ear eagerly awaits the proceedings of its National Conventions. These proceedings are published in the Catholic press, and scattered broadcast by means of the secular press. There can indeed be no doubt, that since the foundation of Federation, the Catholic solution of modern problems, the Catholic doctrine on education, divorce, socialism, etc., have been announced with an effectiveness never before experienced in the history of the Republic. This is encouraging, when it is considered that many of the grievances to which Catholics have been subjected in America must disappear before an enlightened, forcible public opinion, such as is created and developed by the Federation. There is besides another hopeful sign of progress in the fact that the National Conventions are gradually growing into great Catholic Congresses, assembled in our largest cities, attended by thousands of Catholics and non-Catholics, and addressed by the ablest ecclesiastics and laymen in the United States.

As practical results of the influence of Federation may be mentioned the concessions made in the Philippine difficulties; the present amicable relations existing in Porto Rico; the changed aspect of the Indian Schools; and the clear light thrown on the solution of the vexed Public School question. Other agencies were at work, it is true, but Federation performed its full share in every problem presented to it. It may not be amiss to state here the position of Federation on the Public School Question. The American public schools are supported by general taxation. No religious teaching is given therein, and, therefore, Catholics cannot conscientiously send their children to them. In consequence, they are obliged to erect their own parochial schools, to support them, and at the same time pay a tax for the support of the public schools. The injustice of this is evident; for as Catholics we must bear a double burden, and that a very heavy one, nevertheless the majority of non-Catholics are adverse to any change in the situation, pleading that it is impossible to satisfy all in a country where so many religious sects co-exist.

Heretofore, Protestants have been very much excited whenever anything was said against the public schools. This was due to ignorance of the Catholic position, and the evils following from the present system. As very few Catholics were able to give a rational explanation of their position, our enemies remained in darkness. Now, thanks to Federation, a solution has been proposed which is commended on all sides for its justice and practicability. It is as follows: 1. Let our parochial school property remain in the possession of the Church; 2. Let the pupils be taught by the Sisters and Brothers just as at present; 3. Let no public moneys be paid to any school for religious instruction; 4. Let the children in the parochial schools be examined, and if it is found that they have received the secular education required by the State, let the State pay for it, just as it does in the public schools.

This solution has found favor with many non-Catholics on account of its fairness. In truth, since Federation has begun agitation on the school question, it has been discussed by the public press everywhere, and non-Catholic educators and ministers of the sects brought to realize the evils arising from the divorce of secular and religious education, have proclaimed that "the Catholic position is correct," the present public school system vicious, productive of irreligion and immorality, a menace to the welfare of the individual, society, and our free institutions. This is certainly making progress; and all due to the efforts of the Federation.

An advance, too, has been made against the evils of divorce and socialism, which is destined to become more powerful as this organization increases in numbers and its aims are better comprehended. Then it will be able to stimulate further public discussion on all these important questions.

The friends of the movement will be glad to learn of the power which it already possesses. Let them try to realize what it means to have close on a million and a half of male Catholics enrolled in its ranks. This accounts for the enthusiasm manifested in our National Conventions, the representative character of the delegates, and the large attendance on the part of the public.

The next National Convention will be held in Detroit, August 2, 3, and 4. It opens under the brightest auspices and under the patronage of so notable an American prelate as he who presides over the diocese of Detroit, the Rt. Rev. John S. Foley; its deliberations will be noteworthy in the history of conventions.

What has been said of a previous National Convention can be safely anticipated regarding the Detroit Convention. "In the representative and magnificent attendance; in the universal sentiment of harmony permeating the whole body; in the messages by letter and telegram of encouragement and confidence from prelates, priests, and laymen, throughout the country; in the unlooked-for but most satisfactory solution of the grave problems associated with the plan of organization; in the harmonizing of mistrustful and conflicting race feelings; in the unmistakeable evidence of the firm bond of union finally effected; in the wise, conservative, yet manly and outspoken resolutions officially voicing the Convention's judgment; in the public measures deeply affecting Catholic interests, in the calm deliberate wisdom of the entire work—in view of all these results, we cannot but believe that the soul-inspiring acclamation of other times is as applicable to Federation as it was to the Crusaders of old: 'God wills it.' "

Lest those who are timid regarding Federation and hesitate to join lest it may transgress the legitimate field in which alone safety can be found and inopportunely precipitate the practical solution of problems which are still immature, it will suffice to add that Federation includes on its Advisory Board some of the most eminent, the most prudent and conservative members of the Hierarchy, and no important step can be taken without their consent. In due time the organization hopes to have the whole Hierarchy acting in the capacity of Advisers. In questions affecting an archdiocese, or a diocese, the Archbishop or Bishop respectively will be the principal member of the Advisory Board; and in national questions the Board of Archbishops. Laymen will thus be guided in the proper channels, and there will be no danger of injury to our interests, arising from misdirection or misapplied zeal.

Federation will endeavor to redress grievances wherever they exist, employing means suggested by wisdom and experience. The redress of grievances, however, is only a small portion of its plan of campaign. Broadly stated its objects are: 1. The unification of the Catholic nationalities in America; 2. The voicing of Catholic public opinion on all the important questions of the day; 3. The destruction of divorce; 4. The banishment of socialism; and 5. The union of religious and secular education. If Federation enables us to solve only the last, it will have entered the wedge deeply into the others and merited well of both Church and country.

17 John A. Ryan

THE "LIVING WAGE" PHILOSOPHY

Even before he completed his graduate studies at the Catholic University of America early in the twentieth century, the Reverend (later Monsignor) John A. Ryan won recognition as the foremost Catholic specialist on the ethical and economic aspects of the wage system. In the article here reproduced, Father Ryan defended the thesis that the personal dignity of the laborer, or his right to lead a decent human life, entitled him to a family living wage. In return for a normal amount of work performed in a reasonably conscientious manner, every laborer should receive a wage sufficiently high not only to meet his personal needs but also to enable him to marry and rear a family in reasonable and frugal comfort. Ryan disagreed sharply on industrial ethics with most Catholic authorities, who derived the worker's right to a living wage from other principles, for example, from the necessity of repairing the labor energy expended, or from a "common estimate" of a just price for labor. The worker could have his energy restored, Ryan retorted, by a payment considerably less than a truly living wage. Nor under modern conditions was there any sure way of arriving at or enforcing the just price principle of the mediaeval Schoolmen.

Ryan insisted that the right to receive and the duty to pay a family living wage had the uncompromising sanction of strict or commutative justice. He was therefore unwilling to rest either the personal or family living wage on such vague and undefined concepts as "equity," "general justice," or "social justice" as expressed in profit-sharing, legislative aids and the like. However desirable in themselves, these measures could not substitute for the right of the worker, in return for a reasonable amount of work, to have access to the requisite amount of subsistence goods in the form of wages. Whether the employer, or the employer plus society, should pay the wage were questions Ryan did not attempt to answer in this article. But in other articles and in his books, notably in A Living Wage: Its Ethical and Economic Aspects *(New York, 1906), he dealt with all phases of the wage problem.*

All Catholic writers on the ethics of wages now maintain that if the laborer does not receive at least a living wage he receives less than his due. They do not all, however, reach this conclusion by the same process of reasoning. The right to a living wage is derived by some from the necessity of repairing the labor-energy expended; by others, from the "common estimate" of a just price for labor; by still others, from the personal dignity of the laborer, or his right to live a decent human life.

Father Antoine, S.J. holds that there ought to be an "ob-

John A. Ryan, "The Laborer's Right to a Living Wage," *Catholic University Bulletin,* VIII (April 1902), 156–174.

jective equivalence" between the labor performed and the pay received.[1] In order that this objective equivalence may be had, the laborer must receive a wage sufficient to replace the energy that he has expended in the service of his employer. Although this formula makes a certain show of exact and rigorous justice, it can be interpreted reasonably, and applied in such a way that the "equivalent" compensation will be less than a living wage. "Restoring expended labor force" can have no other intelligible meaning than paying a man sufficient to enable him to continue at his work. Indeed, this is the sense in which it is understood by the author himself. But any wage that reaches the level of bare subsistence fulfills this requirement. A laborer who has no other means of livelihood than his wages, and who does his work day after day, is "ex hypothesi," getting sufficient compensation to keep up the energy required for that work; yet his wage may be the very lowest. His habitual subsistence may not be capable of repairing a great amount of energy, but it repairs all that he actually expends.

The truth of the matter is that the energy which the laborer puts forth is always *determined* by and furnished by his wages, be they ever so meager. The men and women in the "sweating" trades get enough wages to maintain them continuously at work, and consequently to replace their daily output of labor-force. Hence the rule that Father Antoine lays down is even now enforced throughout the world of industry. Therefore it can afford no rational basis for more just conditions. It would work very well side by side with the "iron law of wages." It demands a subsistence wage for the laborer, but says nothing concerning the quality of the subsistence.

Other authors base the right to a living wage on the principle of just price.[2] Following the Schoolmen, they maintain

[1] "Cours d'Economie Sociale," Paris, 1899, p. 601.

[2] Cf. Vermeersch, S.J., "Questiones de Justitia," Bruges, 1901, Theses 25, 28, 29.

that every purchasable commodity, whether goods or labor, has a certain price that is just. This is merely a particular application of the general principle that in an onerous contract, *i. e.*, one in which neither party intends to confer a favor on the other, there must be equality between the things exchanged. This is of the very essence of the idea of justice.[3] Now equality between the thing given and the thing received, means in the case of economic goods equal gain for each side. Both parties reap an advantage from the transaction; and each wishes to gain at least as much as the other. If the gains are equal, the contract will be just; if not, one of the parties will be treated unjustly. For he is unwillingly deprived of something to which he has a right, namely, an equal share of the advantage arising from the contract.

Now, since economic goods can be exchanged and measured only by means of what is called their *value*, equality of gain must be expressed in terms of value. Therefore, if an exchange is to be just the goods exchanged [they] must be so valued as to bring the same amount of advantage to both sides. The value that is attributed to the goods must be determined and formulated in strict accordance with this purpose. Evidently, the value of goods in this sense is before all else an *ethical* quality. It is measured and assessed by reference, not merely to economic facts, but to an objective ethical standard. This standard is equality of gain.[4] If for example, one coat is exchanged for two pairs of shoes, and if the resulting gains are unequal, the goods have not been rightly valued, and the contract is not in accordance with ideal justice. Consequently justice is not had by

[3] St. Thomas "Summa," 2a, 2ae, p. 77, a, I.

[4] Although he criticises the scholastic doctrine of just price, because he incorrectly assumes that it took no account of the fact of human desire, M. Tarde adopts in so many words the scholastic standard of determining contractual justice. That price, he says, will be just, "qui donnerait une satisfaction égale aux deux." "Psychologie Economique," Paris, 1902, II, p. 44.

exchanging goods at any valuation that the contracting parties see fit to attribute to them, nor at any other valuation whatever, except the valuation that is just, the just price.

But who is to decide in any exchange the valuation that will allow both parties to obtain the same amount of gain? In other words, who is to fix the just value or just price in the concrete? It cannot be the parties themselves; for they are likely to be biased in their estimates; and the stronger bargainer will be tempted to use his power at the expense of the weaker. On the other hand, no general rule of valuation can be devised that will enable each contracting pair to gain equally from the exchange of any given kind of goods. Different men may purchase the same goods from the same merchant at the same rate, and yet the personal advantage accruing to the buyers may not, in fact, most probably will not, be equal in any two cases.[5] The Schoolmen had this fact in mind when they declared that the just price of goods was incapable of exact determination, but consisted in a "certain estimate" (quadam æstimatione). The just price, they said, had three grades, lowest, medium and highest. This approximately just valuation of goods could, in their opinion, be most reasonably and fairly made by the community as a whole. In this way individual bias and individual selfishness (against which the whole doctrine of just price was chiefly directed) would exert a minimum of influence, since they would be subject to so many counteracting forces. True, there were certain objective elements that the community was morally bound to consider in forming its judgment regarding the price of material goods. These were chiefly the cost of production, the general utility, and the scarcity of the goods estimated. Still the proximate determinant of the just price of either goods or labor was always the "communis æstimatio hominum."

This exposition represents correctly, I think, the main fea-

[5] Cf. Hobson, "The Economics of Distribution," New York, 1900, Chap. I; Tarde, op. cit., II, pp. 10–22.

tures of the doctrine of just price, and the rational basis on which it was founded. The modern writers whom we are now considering employ this doctrine to establish the laborer's right to a living wage. Their argument runs thus: the laborer should always receive a just price for his labor; the just price of any kind of labor is the price fixed by the common estimate, or the social judgment, of what is fair; but the social judgment holds that a man's wages should never be insufficient to afford him a decent livelihood; consequently the just price of labor is never less than a living wage.

The champions of this argument are careful to point out that this ethical social estimate is not identical with the economic social estimate of value. In the latter sense the social estimate of the value of anything, for example, labor, is merely an unconscious resultant of the strife of bargaining. It is formed by the "higgling of market," and is always expressed in market wages. On the other hand, the ethical estimate is a conscious pronouncement of the social judgment, or social conscience. It declares the wages that ought to exist, not the wages that do exist. Thus understood, the social estimate, we are told, holds that whatever wages men may be paid in fact, they ought not to receive less than a living wage. And since the social estimate is the proximate criterion of contractual justice, its decision concerning a living wage must be accepted as final.

Theoretically, this rule of pay according to the true, or just, value of labor performed is a very comprehensive and obvious ethical standard. It is comprehensive because it fits the case of every wage worker of whatever condition, and because it gives a general answer to the question, what is a just wage? It is obvious because—on the supposition that labor has a just value—it is merely an ethical truism. By itself it says no more than "give the laborer his due."

Practically, this standard is inadequate either as a justification or as a measure of a living wage. The laborer's due, the just value of his labor, is determined, we are told, by the social estimate, and the social estimate, it is asserted, always appraises labor as worth at least a living wage. Now, the "social estimate" is a rather vague criterion. It is capable of several different interpretations. It is the unanimous, or morally unanimous, judgment of the community—what the older writers called the "sensus communis"? or is it what is known in this country as public opinion? Is it custom? or again, is it the deliberate judgment of a body of men chosen from the various classes, social, industrial, and religious, of the community? With the exception of the last named, none of these "social estimates" is adequate to serve as a satisfactory practical measure of just or unjust wages. The pronouncements concerning a living wage made by these authorities are necessarily either uncertain or untrustworthy, or both.

First, the "sensus communis," it may be conceded, sanctions the *principle* of a living wage. Our knowledge of the average man's sense of right and wrong entitles us, perhaps, to assume this much. Further than this, however, the "sensus communis" can give us nothing definite. As to the amount of subsistence-goods comprised in the idea of a decent livelihood—the precise content of a living wage—its decision will lack unity. The only conclusion that can be derived from it will be some sort of compromise of a multitude of individual or class estimates. Assuming, however, that an average or compromise estimate is objectively deducible, how can it be brought to our knowledge? The "sensus communis" is not a deliberative body, promulgating formal rulings on matters of this kind. While therefore we admit that the "sensus communis," or social conscience, does adjudge the laborer as worthy of a living wage, we deny that it can provide us with any definite and specific concept of what it means by a living wage. And even if it could, we have no satisfactory assurance that its estimate would be in harmony with right reason. In judging of the more general questions of moral conduct, the "sensus communis" is sufficiently trustworthy; but in details, in regard to particular human actions, its judgment is easily perverted by the influence of bad and long established custom.

Second, that somewhat capricious form of the social estimate called *public opinion* is vitiated by defects similar to those just enumerated. Its verdict as to the content of a living wage must necessarily be general and not knowable. Moreover, public opinion is essentially variable and therefore untrustworthy. Indeed, if we accept the press as its mouthpiece it has not declared in favor of even the principle of a living wage.

Third, *custom* may be acknowledged to furnish a fairly definite standard of right and wrong in this matter of wages. But it is not a reliable standard. Custom to-day sanctions wages that are insufficient to afford the conditions of a decent livelihood—witness the remuneration of the "sweated" classes. The canonist Reiffenstuel accepted custom as the practical criterion of justice, and arrived at the conclusion that a just wage need not rise to the level of a living wage.

Fourth, the pronouncement of a carefully selected representative congress or committee would, no doubt, be sufficiently definite and trustworthy. If the social estimate, thus understood, declared that every laborer should have a living wage, and defined what it meant by a living wage, its decision would probably satisfy all reasonable minds. However, as no such judicial body exists, no argument can be drawn from its assumed decisions.

To sum up, the standard of pay according to the true value of labor as determined by the social estimate, affords no valid basis for the living wage doctrine, because it gives no satisfactory answer to the following questions: What is meant by the social estimate? How can it give decisions sufficiently precise to be of any value? How can its decisions be known? Assuming that they are known, what assurance have we that they conform to the objective requirements of justice?

This argument from just price and the "communis æstimatio" has been dwelt on at some length because these concepts and formulas played a great part in medieval thought and industry, and because they are quite common in the Catholic ethical literature of to-day. For centuries the Schoolmen, one after another, asserted and expounded the doctrine that every commodity, be it labor or material goods, that men buy and sell had one just price. Accordingly, they maintained that individuals did wrong when they attempted to take advantage of their fellows to buy or sell at any other price. The doctrine is incontestable. For when we assert that it is possible for a commodity to be sold at an unjust price, we tacitly assume that it has some other price that is just. An action can not be adjudged wrong or unfair except by reference to some ethical standard. The ideal just price of a thing may be impossible of determination, but it exists if only as an ideal.

So much is clear concerning the doctrine. The method of determining just price, the "communis æstimatio," served very well for the small communities and simple economic relations of the Middle Ages.[6] When masters and workmen lived together in relations "like unto that between fathers and sons"; when the whole body of consumers and producers interested in the fixing of any scale of wages or prices, was grouped within the limits of a small town; when the classes of goods and services that were to be appraised were few in number and simple in character; and when the standard of living was nearly uniform for all,—under these circumstances the "communis æstimatio" of the just price of labor was apt to be more or less precise, and could easily be made manifest to all concerned. Besides, the "communis æstimatio" quickly became crystallized in custom. Thus, it was not only definite and patent, but more or less constant during long periods of time. It was likewise in fairly close conformity with ethical ideals, since

[6] Cf. Ashley, "Economic History," London, 1894, 3d ed., I, p. 138.

it was formed under the direct and powerful influence of moral and religious teaching. "No such sustained and far-reaching attempt is now being made," says Professor Ashley, "either from the side of theology or of ethics, to impress upon the public mind principles immediately applicable to practical life."[7]

In the highly complex industrial life of our own time, the criterion of "communis æstimatio," seems, for the reasons above given, to have outlived its usefulness.[8] The "doctrine" of just price is as true and vital as ever, because it is a fundamental principle of justice. What is required is a new method or formula for applying it to modern conditions. And if some of the present-day disciples of the Schoolmen would but imitate the example of their masters by trying to find such a formula, they would do a greater service to the memory of the Schoolmen, as well as to the needs of the present generation, than by clinging to an outworn criterion which the Schoolmen, were they with us, would probably be the first to reject. To transplant the Scholastic formula of "communis æstimatio" into an environment for which it was never intended, and to give it an interpretation that is so elastic as to be unmeaning, is to bring discredit upon the doctrine of just price and involve the whole question in confusion.

Finally, we come to the third argument, which deduces the laborer's right to a living wage from his personal dignity and his right to a decent livelihood.[9] In common with all other

[7] Op. cit., II, p. 388

[8] Cf. Castlelein S.J., "Institutiones Philosophiæ Moralis et Socialis," Brussels, 1899, p. 369.

[9] Pottier, "De Jure et Justitia," Liège, 1900, pp. 220–265; Verhaegen, "Le Minimum de Salaire," Ghent p. 21. Pope Leo XIII in "Rerum Novarum": "The preservation of life is the bounden duty of each and all, and to fail therein is a crime. It follows that each one has a right to procure what is required in order to live; and the poor can procure it in no other way than by their wages."

men, the laborer is endowed with the right to a decent livelihood in the abstract. In the concrete, this right must conform to the usages and possibilities of the industrial organization in which he lives. In order to make his right effectual, valid here and now, he must do all that is reasonably within his power towards acquiring for himself the goods that are essential to subsistence. This he does by expending his labor power under the direction and employment of others. To the general work of production, therefore, he has contributed all that can reasonably be asked of him, and his claim against his fellows for a decent livelihood, from being abstract, negative, and potential, has become concrete, positive, and actual. In return his fellow men (whether "fellow men" in the concrete means his employer or his employer plus society, need not be discussed now) must, by putting the requisite amount of subsistence goods practically within his reach, enable him to realize this right. According to the usages and institutions of our industrial society, these goods can come to him only in the form of wages. In order that his right may become effectual, therefore, in order that he may come into actual enjoyment of it, his wages must be sufficient for a decent livelihood. No other way of realizing his right is open to him. Humanly speaking, there are no unappropriated goods within his reach, and if there were his duties as a wageworker leave him no opportunity of securing them. To sum up the argument in the form of a syllogism: the laborer has a right to a decent livelihood; but in the present industrial order his sole means of realizing this right lies in his wage; therefore he has a right to a living wage.

If it be objected that, as a matter of fact, some laborers have other resources of living besides their labor power, the answer must be that such laborers are quite exceptional. Whether they also have a right to a living wage is, after all, of comparatively little importance. Still it may be observed that the question would seem to merit an answer in the affirmative. In the first place, these men, it is assumed, put in the same amount of time as their less fortunate fellows: distributive justice, then, would seem to require that they should obtain the same remuneration. In the second place, the continued payment of smaller wages to certain individuals in any occupation tends to lower the wages of the whole group. Finally, the unquestionable advantages arising from a more general diffusion of wealth, furnish a very strong social reason why the persons whom we are considering should be paid a living wage, even if it be conceded that they have no strict individual right thereto. Other considerations drawn from social utility, such as the wisdom of rewarding individual initiative and thrift, point to the same conclusion.

The laborer's right to a living wage stands out in clearest light once we lay firm hold of two fundamental facts concerning man's nature and his essential relation to the earth's resources. The first of these is the fact that the laborer is by nature—prior, consequently, to any contract—a person, a being endowed with certain indestructible rights. "Indestructible" by other men, be it always understood. While the precise matter of his wage-contract is a certain amount of labor-force, this labor-force is not something standing apart with an existence of its own. It is inseparable from the subject in which it inheres, and that subject is a person. It cannot possibly be dealt with, contracted for, without affecting the personality of the laborer. It must be dealt with, then, in such a way as not to violate this personality. In other words, the labor-contract must be so framed as to conserve and safeguard the laborer's dignity. The latter is a fact anterior to the contract, a previous condition that the contract must take into account if it is just and reasonable. The subject of the labor force must be dealt with, not as a thing, but as a person. As a person he has an indestructible right to a decent livelihood.[10]

The other important fact to be kept in mind is that the earth is intended by the Creator for the common use and enjoyment of all his children. "Nature," says St. Ambrose, "made all

[10] Cf. Antoine, op. cit., pp. 317, 318, 319.

things common" (De Officiis, I, 28). There is nothing in the nature of the earth to show that any portion belongs to one man rather than to another. Nor is there anything in the nature of men to indicate any difference in their primary claims upon the earth's resources. On the contrary, as persons, all men are equal, and have by nature equal rights of access to the means of subsistence. This common right of property is, it cannot be too often repeated, the *primary* right of property. To enable men to realize in the most convenient way this primary right is the sole purpose of the right and institution of *private* property. The private right is, therefore, only a means to the common right. It is consequently always subordinate to, and limited by, the latter. Private rights of property must always be exercised in such a way that the common right of no individual will be infringed upon. Now, the common right of property includes in the case of every individual at least a decent livelihood. In the case of the laborer this means a living wage. Hence private rights of property must be so interpreted and exercised as to conserve and safeguard this particular common right. When they are not so exercised; when they are interpreted in such a way as to withhold from the laborer his living wage, the true order of rights is violated. The order established by nature and reason is reversed, since an attempt is made to place private and secondary rights above common and primary rights. In this way men are treated as unequal in the field in which nature made them equal. Men are not equal in all respects, nor is it reasonable that they should possess equal amounts of property. But they are equal as persons, and as such have equal rights to a certain reasonable minimum of property—the means of a decent livelihood.[11]

[11] It is perhaps worth while to point out that the whole doctrine of just price rests ultimately on this equality of rights to the use of the world's goods. The right to equality of gain from an exchange is derived from the equality of men as persons, and their consequent equal rights to the conditions of personal development; namely, the bounty of the earth. Cf. Castelein, op. cit., p. 208.

A word concerning the wage-rights of women and children. From the principles above laid down it is evident that those women who are obliged by circumstances to earn their own living have a right to what is for them a living wage. Since their sole means of living is their wages, the latter should be sufficiently large to enable them to live decently. Women who can live without working for hire, and women who receive a partial support from other sources, form a comparatively small proportion of the whole number of female wage workers. For the reasons advanced above regarding men who have outside sources of income, these similarly-placed women would seem to be entitled to receive a living wage.

Women doing the same work with the same degree of efficiency as men in occupations where men are employed in considerable numbers, have a right not merely to a woman's living wage, but to the same wage as their male fellow workers. Distributive justice would suggest that equally efficient workers should be treated equally in the matter of wages. Besides, if the women receive less pay than the men the latter are gradually driven out of that particular occupation.[12] Unless we are prepared to admit that an increase in the proportion of women workers is desirable, we must acknowledge that the evil seems serious enough to require the remedy of uniform wages for the two sexes in occupations where they are equally efficient.[13]

Children of either sex who have reached the age at which they may, without detriment to themselves or society, become wage-earners, but who cannot perform the work of adults, have a right to a wage sufficient to afford them a decent living. The time of life which may be regarded as normal for children to

[12] Cf. Smart, "Studies in Economics," London, 1895, chapter on Women's Wages.

[13] Cf. Fairbank's "Introduction to Sociology," New York, 1896, p. 148.

begin working for wages is another question; for the present it will suffice to note that there is such a normal starting point, and that it is considerably above the age of many children now employed. As the case of the latter, that is, of all working children under the proper age, is abnormal, a discussion of their wage rights would be unprofitable and productive of confusion. Children who have arrived at the normal working age are entitled to a living wage because their wage, generally speaking, is their only source of living.

A living wage for children means compensation sufficient to enable them to live decently as members of a family. It does not mean the requisites of boarding-house life, for this is not the average condition in which working children are found.

Finally, children of either sex who perform the work of adults ought to receive the wage of adults of the corresponding sex engaged in that work. The reasons for this statement are similar to those given in connection with women who are equally efficient with men.[14]

Thus far I have treated of the right of every wage-worker, man, woman, and child, to a wage sufficient for his reasonable *personal* needs. It is evident that one class of laborers, namely, married men, ought to earn something more than the equivalent of personal subsistence. If they do not their wives and young children will be unprovided for. Again, if the adult male laborer who is not married receives only a personal living wage he is precluded from entering the conjugal state. Hence, it would seem that the wage of an adult male should be large

[14] In speaking of a living wage, whether for men, women, or children, it is assumed that they are employed, or, at least are in a condition to be employed, during the whole of the working time of the year. Hence women who are obliged to devote all their attention to household duties for a considerable portion of the year, and children who attend school, are not entitled to a year's living wage. Their right to a decent livelihood, as we shall see, must be secured in another way.

enough to supply not only his own reasonable needs, but also the reasonable needs of his wife and children. Such remuneration is called a family living-wage.

Catholic ethical writers of to-day are practically unanimous in the belief that the adult male laborer ought to receive a wage capable of maintaining decently himself and his family. This much they hold is due him by a title of justice. But, just as in the question of a personal living wage, they arrive at a common conclusion by different roads. According to some of them the laborer's claim to a family wage is not based on strict or commutative justice, but on legal or social justice; or, again on general justice or equity. Others, on the contrary, contend that the question involved is one of commutative justice, as defined by the "social estimate"; while still others start from the concept of man's personal dignity and natural rights.

Father Antoine argues thus:[15] In any rightly ordered society, the father is the family's natural provider. Since the laborer's ability to discharge this duty depends upon his wage, social welfare requires that his wage should be adequate for this purpose. If it is not, the inevitable result is social confusion and social injury. Hence the rights and obligations involved in the payment of a family wage lie within the field of social justice. They have no direct concern with strict or commutative justice. That is to say, the laborer's claim to a family wage is not founded on an equality between the things exchanged—the labor and compensation. Such equality does not necessarily exist in a labor-contract stipulating the payment of a family wage; for the labor may not be worth that much. We know that the value of labor is always equivalent to at least a subsistence capable of replacing the energy expended; that it may, indeed, rise above this minimum—but we cannot say that it is necessarily commensurate with a family wage. The family does not figure in the contract directly. Its needs therefore, are not the true measure, either of labor's value, or of

[15] Op. cit., p. 606.

the wage equivalent to that value. Hence the laborer's claim to a living wage does not rest upon the principles of commutative justice.

The positive part of this argument is sound. Considerations of social utility and consequently of social justice, do make it imperative that the laborer's wage should be capable of properly maintaining his family. The contention that these are the only considerations that are pertinent is based on a false assumption. This assumption is that the minimum wage should be measured solely by the standard of labor-force. The writer gives as an expression of the relations of justice involved in the wage-contract, this formula: minimum wage = labor-force = personal subsistence. Now, it has already been pointed out that the labor-force of a human being cannot in reason and justice be regarded in this abstract way. Human labor-force must be dealt with as the attribute of a person. The human dignity of the laborer gives rise to certain rights and obligations that must be secured and assumed in the wage contract; and these as we shall see presently, have a direct bearing on the sustenance of his family.

It is the view of Father Castelein that the laborer's right to a *personal* living wage is based on commutative justice, while his right to a *family* wage is sanctioned merely by general justice or equity.[16] The value of a man's labor, he holds, is always equivalent to the former, but not necessarily to the latter. After the laborer has received this just equivalent, and after the other factors of production have been fairly remunerated, there will remain, in the normal conditions of industry, a certain gross profit which ought to be divided between himself and his employers. Such division is demanded by the principles of general justice, or equity. If this rule is fairly carried out the result will be, generally speaking, proper provision for the laborer's family.

This opinion, it will be observed, is very similar to Father

[16] Op. cit., pp. 376 sq.

Antoine's, the only difference being that "general" is substituted for "social" justice. It is likewise true as far as it goes, but it does not go far enough. "General justice or equity," is a very insecure basis for a prerogative so important as the right to a family-wage. That the profits from an industry in excess of fair personal wages for employes and fair returns to employers, ought to be shared by both classes is a valid principle; but that the family's natural right to a livelihood should be wholly dependent upon a contingency of this kind, seems inconsistent with the moral dignity of human beings. The sustenance rights of wives and children, and the family-wage rights of the father, rest upon a broader and more enduring foundation. As a matter of fact, when the writer turns from his perplexing and ineffective discussion of the kind of justice involved, and engages in the formulation of positive arguments, he appeals to more solid principles. In the order established by Divine Providence, he says, a family wage is due the laborer because of his dignity as a man (p. 388).

According to Father Vermeersch, the right to a family living wage is derived from the principles of commutative justice. He maintains that the social estimate, which is the proximate determinant of the just price of labor, regards the labor of the head of the family as worth at least a family living-wage.[17]

Father Vermeersch, conscious that there are objections to this teaching, does not content himself with this particular line of argument. Like Father Castelein, he has recourse to the proof drawn from the order of nature, or of Divine Providence.[18] If the laborer (the adult male, it is always understood) does not get a family-wage his personal independence, or personal dignity, is ignored; the exercise of some of his most essential powers and faculties is hindered; his common right to the use of the world's goods is violated.

[17] Op. cit., thesis 29.

[18] Ibid., pp. 560–563.

The latter argument, which starts from considerations of the laborer's personal dignity, is the only one that rests securely on the fundamental principles of natural justice. It may be stated, thus, as a sort of double syllogism: Every man has a natural right to all the external conditions of normal and reasonable self-development; but one of these conditions is the effective opportunity of marrying; therefore every man has a natural right to the effective opportunity of marrying. Now the effective opportunity of marrying means, in the case of the laborer, a family wage; therefore, the laborer has a natural right to a family wage.

The first proposition, that man has a natural right to all the external conditions of reasonable self-development may be taken for granted. Since rights are at bottom human actions, or opportunities of human action, they are always measured and determined by the rational end of human action. This principle is admitted by all schools of ethical writers. The rational end (earthly) of human action, we saw, is the normal and reasonable development of the individual. The individual is not a mere means to the welfare of the social organism. Nor is any particular individual a mere means to the end of other individuals. All human individuals are ends in themselves. They are specifically equal in the end toward which they move —the normal and reasonable development of a human person—and in the human faculties by whose exercise this end is attained. They are therefore of equal dignity and importance as pursuers of this end. *In se* and in the sight of the Creator, it is as important that one man should have the means of attaining his end as that another should. It follows therefore that if men are to act reasonably toward one another, if they are to treat one another in accordance with nature and reason, they must recognize this supreme fact that men have equal claims to the conditions of normal, reasonable self-development. They must so act towards one another, and so use the resources of the earth, the common inheritance of all, that all shall have effective access to the minimum amount of freedom and material goods required for this purpose.

Now, among the conditions—to repeat the second proposition—required for normal and reasonable self-development, is the effective opportunity of marrying. Humanly speaking, this is true of all men. And "effective opportunity" means not merely absence of legal restraint, but positive, immediate access to the material goods necessary for the marriage state. It means for the head of the family the possession of the goods that will properly maintain his family. Every man has a natural right to that much, at least, of the world's bounty.

A "natural right," that is, a claim upon his fellows, springing from his nature as man, and conditioned only by his willingness to contribute all that can reasonably be asked of him toward supplying the general needs of society. A right to "at least" the means of maintaining a family, because this much of the earth's resources is indispensable for normal human life.

To live a normal human life is to exercise one's essential faculties, supply one's essential needs, and develop one's personality—all in a reasonable and moral way. Now, among man's faculties, one of the foremost is that of propagating his kind. Among his needs one of the greatest is the longing for the permanent love and companionship of a person of the opposite sex. The marriage state is not, indeed, so imperatively necessary for right living as is security of life and a decent personal livelihood, but it is nevertheless of primary importance. Abstracting from a supernatural vocation, the average man cannot properly develop his personality outside of conjugal life. This does not mean that the man without a religious vocation cannot be celibate and at the same time chaste —only the foul of mind or the cowardly of will assert or believe this infamous doctrine—but it does mean that for the average man, celibacy is not the normal condition. The man whom poverty forces to accept it supports an unnatural and unjustifiable burden, and is deprived of one of the chief means of normal self-development. Outside of the religious life, the man who deliberately embraces celibacy from lofty and generous motives is somewhat exceptional; while the man who does so from any other kind of motives goes through life with, at least, an egotistic and stunted personality. We may conclude then that, in whatever circumstances the average man may find himself or place himself, conjugal life is, humanly speaking, one of his most primary and persistent needs, and an essential condition of right human life.

So much for the positive side of the right to the material goods needed for family life. Under its negative aspect, the right of one man morally restrains all other men from hindering its realization. Consequently when a man is prevented by his fellows, whether through social institutions or individual selfishness, from enjoying this right he is the victim of injustice. The adult man, therefore, who is willing to contribute his reasonable share to the service of society, has a natural right, an unconditional claim upon his fellows, to the means of properly maintaining a family, because this is an essential condition of normal and reasonable self-development.

Now, in the case of the laborer, "the means of properly maintaining his family," can be nothing else than the family-wage. In the existing industrial order there are morally speaking, no other resources within his reach. In his wage, if anywhere, his right to the effective opportunity of marrying must be realized. In his wages it *will* be realized if justice and social order are observed; for it is a claim that is conditioned only by his readiness to contribute his reasonable share to the service of society. This condition he fulfills by his daily labor. To resume the entire argument: the laborer has a natural right to a family wage because this is the only way in which he can exercise his right to the means of maintaining his family, and he has a natural right to the means of maintaining his family because this is an essential condition of normal human life.

It has been objected that according to this reasoning the

laborer has also the right to a wage sufficient to support his infirm and needy parents. Since he is in duty bound to care for them, and since he has an unquestioned right to accept that duty, it follows that he has a right to the one means available for this purpose, an increased wage. But there is no true parallel between these cases. In the first place, the right to a family wage is not derived from the duty, as such, of maintaining a family. This duty occasions the right to a family wage, not simply because it is *a* duty, but because it is this particular duty, that is, because it is necessarily involved in the exercise of the right to marry. The right to marry, not the duty of maintaining a family, is therefore the true *cause* of the moral claim to a family wage. Now the right to marry is essentially different from the right to support infirm parents. The former is necessary for normal and reasonable self-development, and thence creates the right to the material goods required for its exercise. The latter responds to no such necessity and carries with it no such resultant claim. In the normal relations of life the laborer is not as a rule called upon to provide for his parents during their later years. Generally speaking, they will have, or should have, themselves taken precautions against such a contingency. To be sure, occasions may arise in which the laborer ought to forego marriage rather than allow his parents to suffer. This course may in the circumstances be the one most consistent with right living. However, this is not according to the normal order of things; it is not what usually happens or ought to happen. It is not therefore to be taken as the standard and cause of natural rights and natural justice.

Some have thought that, since the immediate purpose of the family wage is the maintenance of the laborer's family, it should vary with the size of the family. The conclusion does not follow. For the sake of convenience in reckoning, and for the reason that the laborer's daily or monthly wage is more or less uniform while he remains in full vigor, the cost of bringing up his family should be considered as a unit. The total life needs of the family divided by the total working time of the father during the adult period of his life, gives the family living-wage.

In accordance with this rule, the laborer who is not yet married has a right to the average family wage, and not merely to remuneration for his present needs. The excess is assumed to be put by as a provision for marriage. It is to be reckoned, therefore, as furnishing a part of the total resources needed for family maintenance.

The right to a family living-wage is the prerogative of every adult male laborer, married or unmarried. Rights must be interpreted according to the average, normal conditions of human life, and the average, normal conditions of the laborer is that of the head of the family. If individuals wish to remain unmarried they are privileged to do so, but they should not be compelled to make such a choice.

Moreover, there is a strong social reason for treating the married and the unmarried alike in this respect. If employers were morally free to pay single laborers less than a family wage, they would as far as possible try to engage these only. And they would be strongly tempted to insist upon non-marriage classes in labor contracts. Thus a premium would be placed upon a very undesirable kind of celibacy.

Although the argument for a family living-wage has in the foregoing pages been drawn solely from the natural rights of the individual, there has been no intention to ignore the validity of social considerations. The latter are evident at a glance. Without a family wage, the laborer can neither be a good citizen, contribute his normal share to the increase of population, nor properly rear such children as he does cause to be born. In each of these respects the damage to society is very great. Our chief concern in this place, however, is to define the indestructible rights of the individual. It is in the incontestable facts of man's nature—man's personal dignity and his essential needs—that we have found the right of the laborer to a family wage if he is to live a normal and reasonable human life.

18 Peter E. Dietz

A "LABOR" PRIEST'S PLEA FOR SOCIAL REFORM

At the outset of his stormy career the Rev. Peter E. Dietz, as first editor of the English section of Central-Blatt and Social Justice, *the Central-Verein's social reform journal, wrote several perceptive articles on the social question. In the one reproduced here he urged German-American Catholics, after the example of Catholics in Germany, to study and support the social reform movement. The great need, he felt, was social legislation, a field in which America was relatively backward. In order to secure the enactment of welfare measures, wrote Father Dietz, Catholics would have to support the trade union movement and cooperate with all reform groups, religious and secular.*

In this spirit Dietz formulated a comprehensive social reform program and secured its adoption by the Central-Verein and the American Federation of Catholic Societies. Ceaselessly active throughout the Progressive period, Dietz proved himself a resourceful organizer, with his Militia of Christ to influence trade unionists and his American Academy of Christian Democracy for Women for the training of social workers.

When the traveler sets out on his journey, the limitations of the lowland forbid a larger view. The ideals on the heights,

"The Metamorphosis," *Central-Blatt and Social Justice,* II (July 1909), 7–10.

indeed, beckon him not to count the dangers and hardships of the ascent, but to hasten his steps, determinedly onward and upward. As he rises higher, his effort is amply rewarded by the larger view and he may be permitted a moment's rest to scan the paths he trod and the panorama invisible in the valley. May it give him higher aims!

Not so long ago, the voices were not few that, dissenting, endeavored to recall the Central-Verein from the upward paths of social progress that it meant to follow. The pessimist shouted: idle dreams; the sluggard: vain endeavor; the timid: rash presumption; but the optimist shouted: forward, and forward they went. What of it if our laity be not as well educated as the laity abroad? What of it if our press be not as strong? What of it if our organization be not as thorough. Everywhere in the world weak beginnings were the sign of big achievements. The grapes are sour only to the fox that slinks away in failure.

For a long time we have had social ideals preached to us in glowing terms. We grew tired of the glare of oratory. What good is the ideal unless it becomes real; the test is the shaping of it in reality. The absence of reality makes the ideal worthless. It is of little consequence which method we follow. There are many and entirely different methods, but it does matter that something be accomplished worthily. It is well for us that our development should spring from the roots in which we have our being. At Dubuque in 1907 the watchword was given out: "Transformation of the Central-Verein into the American Volksverein." At Cleveland in 1908 the various plans suggested, were sifted and endorsed. Indianapolis, 1909, will find them under way.

Ignorance and corruption are the ills; education and religion are the remedies. The key to the situation is the honest and intelligent vote. There is a fable told by Æsop in the olden days that runs like this: "A man came into the forest and made a petition to the trees to provide him a handle for his axe.

The trees consented to his request and gave him a young ash-tree. No sooner had the man fitted from it a new handle for his axe than he began to use it, and quickly felled with his strokes the noblest giants of the forest. An old oak, lamenting when too late the destruction of his companions, said to a neighboring cedar: "The first step has lost us all. If we had not given up the rights of the ash, we might yet have retained our own privileges and have stood for ages."

To all practical intents may we not compare the members of the Central-Verein with the trees in the forest? They are all American citizens; each one has a mind of his own; each one has his legitimate place in the Republic. Every single one of them has all the rights and liberties and duties of the American citizen. As a public-minded, patriotic citizen of a country that he dearly loves, he is interested in the public affairs of his country. It becomes his part to participate in the making and administration of the law. No one will question the propriety of doing this and no one will be able to dispense him from the duty of doing it.

A man comes into this forest with an axe. He is the professional vote-getter; the politician. He has an axe to grind. But not only that—he wants a handle for his axe. The trees in the forest are to furnish him this handle. They are to give him their vote; their greatest civic prerogative as sovereign Americans. We will not be misunderstood. We have no grievance with the politician as such, least of all with the politician of honor. It is his right as truly as it is ours to solicit the votes of a constituency. The point, however, is this: we are to furnish the handle. For what? We must know before we furnish it. It is the first stroke that counts. It is the first step that may lose all. We must know, because we want the noblest giants of the forest to remain standing. We want our Catholic Faith, that has withstood the shock of the ages, to endure. We want our history, our racial traditions, our Catholic principles and convictions, not only to stand in the face of the modern world, but we want them to be the parent stock from which springs a new and healthy undergrowth.

We are told that we must hang our heads in shame when we compare the social legislation of most civilized countries with our own. We are told, moreover, that we American citizens of German extraction have done little to compare worthily with the social action of our brethren abroad, manifesting itself in press and pulpit, club and parliament. Both charges are at once true and false. It is true that we have little legal provision for the problems of industrial hygiene, trade diseases and accidents, employers' liability, and the arbitration of industrial disputes—and these are the great problems that must engage the present attention of all agents of social reform—but it would be false to say that as a nation we have been unconcerned about social legislation.

On the contrary, considering the newness of our land—for what are a hundred years compared with the ages of civilization in Europe—and the rawness of our populations, gathered from every part of the globe, we have much reason to be grateful for what has been achieved. The foundations for social legislation are laid deep and broad in the institutions of our civil liberty. While Europe has been wresting the ballot from its undemocratic governments—a task by no means accomplished even now—we have enjoyed the power of the ballot from the beginning. While in Europe the state is still largely above and apart from the people, with us the state has always been the people only. In principle, at least, we have a government of the people, by the people and for the people. We, ourselves, are the government, and by using the sovereign prerogative of the ballot we have achieved much fundamental legislation that Europe is still struggling for under more adverse conditions. We are optimistic enough to believe that the constitution of the nation is still hale and hearty and that it will eliminate one by one the harmful features that mar our public life and threaten our vitality. We have planned our national life broadly and deeply; it remains for us to build the superstructure.

As to the other charge, it is true that as American citizens of German extraction we have done little to compare with the social achievements which are the glory of our Catholic brethren abroad. There is no field of human and public interest in which they do not toil by organization a hundredfold. The Volksverein and the Centre-Party stand as the spirit and incorporation of them all. If to-day the German Catholics are well schooled in the public issues before the country, they owe it to the Volksverein for the Promotion of Social Education. And if to-day German Catholics take a very leading and intelligent part in the making of the law, the preservation of all true national ideals, and especially in championing above all others the cause of the workingman, they owe it to the Centre-Party. Let us exalt their example before the world and keep it before our own eyes as the luminous cloud that by night led the faltering people of Israel out of the bondage of Egypt. We in America have had problems of our own, more pressing for the first. We have had language, church and school problems; we have had a large share of the problem of adding another province to the commonwealth of the Church Universal, laying out the territory, clearing away the wilderness of prejudice and antipathy and breaking a new soil from behind the Catholic plough. These problems have largely been solved, and with all the good-will in the world and with all the rock-ribbed conviction of Catholic Faith in our hearts we turn with enthusiasm to the newer problems of social legislation. We know that we are in duty bound to contribute the best that is in us for social service and we are determined to acquire the qualifications that religion and patriotism alike impose.

We hear the call of the child; the wail comes to us from the cotton mills and mines; from the glare of the city street after dark; from the byways and alleys of the slums, so-called; from workshops and homes overcrowded and infested with disease; and we remember that its guardian angel ever stands before the face of the heavenly Father ready to accuse us if we heed not the call!

We hear the call of the young inexperienced and perhaps giddy girl; separated by untoward conditions from home and friends; torn away but too often from all the ideals and associations that would make of her a woman after God's own heart; we hear the cry of the girl working on starvation wages and in despair almost ready to sell her soul for the comforts of life; the agonizing cry of the white slave, bartered in human traffic; and the slumbering fires of chivalry break forth again from the embers of the ages of Faith when man's honor was the best protection of woman, and we pledge ourselves to be their champions.

We hear the call of the woman; the mother, like Rachel crying for her children; the mother's heart, like the pelican bleeding itself for its young ones; we hear the call of the woman for larger civic and social influence to show a practical sympathy to her sister, the drudge—a sympathy unknown and unknowable to the heart of man; we hear this call and may God defend that we turn a deaf ear to it!

We hear the call of the invalid and the aged; the unemployed and the unorganized; the laborer whose limbs are lacerated and torn while taking the risks inseparable from his work and the gaining of a livelihood; who in death bequeaths to the world at large a broken-hearted widow and a half dozen healthy and hungry children; we hear all this agony wrenched from the depths of humanity, and may it be permitted us to hope that on the crack of doom, in the day of judgment, the Savior of mankind will say to us: "Come, you blessed of my Father, possess the kingdom prepared for you from the beginning of the world. For I was hungry and you gave me to eat; I was thirsty and you gave me to drink; I was a stranger and you received me into your house; naked and you clothed me; sick and you visited me. For as long as you did it to one of the least of these my brethren, you did it to me."

We are determined to approach these problems not only in

an individual way, but by organization. We will approach them not only with personal sympathy pure and simple and the disorganized help it can give, but with the ballot in our hands. Preventative measures are more charitable, just and economic than remedial ones, and therefore we will realize our American power as voters to its fullest capacity. We will vote intelligently. We will furnish the handle to the axe, but only to the axe that will cut down the rotting growth of abuses that exist in order to make way for the new and healthier undergrowth of true social legislation. We will appeal to the sense of justice inborn to the soul of man and keep it aroused at all times, before voting, while voting, and especially after voting.

To accomplish this great aim the Central-Verein must develop first-class leadership and an appreciative and enthusiastic following. By the action of its Central-Bureau for the Promotion of Social Education several stipends have been granted to enable advanced students to complete practical courses in the social sciences under the direction of the Volksverein Bureau at Muenchen-Gladbach, in Germany. It would be too long here to digress into a disquisition on the nature and work of the Volksverein. Most readers are familiar with it; but for the benefit of those who are not we will treat of it in a succeeding issue. Suffice it to say that the Volksverein is the strongest Catholic organization in the world and that the Holy Father has recommended it as a pattern to the Catholics of Italy and of the world. It is here at the headquarters of the Volksverein, from which a network of invisible threads extends over the whole empire, that our representatives will get their principal training to prepare for the leadership that will devolve upon them.

In the meantime we have not been remiss. Social lectures were given in nearly all our large cities last winter, with the result that the popular appreciation for the social program has grown remarkably. In several cities Catholic workingmen's associations have been formed, not in competition with the labor-unions, but to fit the Catholic workingman for his proper sphere in the labor-union. This popular interest is further served by the hearty support which is everywhere given to the official organ, "The Central-Blatt and Social Justice." In the beginning, when discussing the advisability of putting such a publication under way, a prominent Catholic wrote us: "I am not much in favor of a particular social reform publication for Catholics. It is needed badly—but it will not be supported nor read. I say this not including Germans, for I am not so well posted on them." The fact that the "Central-Blatt and Social Justice" has now about 8,000 readers, with subscriptions coming in at the rate of 1,000 per month, speaks volumes for the up-to-dateness of one out of ten of the members of the Central-Verein.

As the reports come in one after the other of the various Staats-Verband Conventions, we cannot conceal our joy at the social tinge given to the proceedings. Everywhere there are discussions on the labor problems, civic duty, social service, divorce legislation, abuse of liquor, legislative enactments, etc. The Ohio Staatsverband, perhaps, more than any other, has left the beaten track to open up new fields for social activity. The delegates felt that the time had come to break the narrower circles in which their work had been confined all too long and to enter the broader arena of public life.

The Social Institute to be held at Oberlin, Ohio, in conformity with the recommendations of the Cleveland (1908) Convention of the national body, was heartily endorsed by the Staatsverband, and the discussion that followed the introduction of the motion assures the success of the course. A number of delegates, notably from Cincinnati and Cleveland, pledged themselves to the representation of their societies at the courses. Furthermore, the legislative committee of three, which had been created a year ago to fight an obnoxious school bill, has been enlarged to five, representing every district of the state. Its program is no longer defensive purely, but it will also consider the constructive side of social legislation.

The plan to co-operate with the American Association for

Labor Legislation was discussed and endorsed, and the appointment of two delegates determined upon to represent the Staatsverband in the State Council. This is justly regarded an important step forward, and it is along this line of cooperation that we are going to look for results in the near future. In Europe, as mentioned elsewhere, the Catholic ferment in the work of the International Association for Labor Legislation is very marked. It is commendable, surely, for us to cherish a similar ambition here.

An amendment was offered to the Constitution of the Staatsverband, which by modifying the order of business will make the yearly State Convention a Social Institute at the same time. The amendment provides for a course of three lectures on a specified social topic—the first for the Sunday evening mass-meeting, the other two distinctively for the delegates. These latter two to be given as soon as the general body reconvenes at the hall on Monday and Tuesday mornings. After the lectures general discussion will be in order and the consensus of opinion embodied in the resolutions.

There were several other topics broached on the floor which unfortunately did not find public expression and the benefit of the discussion that would surely have followed. The one related to the trade-union movement and the other to the farming interests. It was suggested that the Catholic trade-unionists of the Staatsverband form a trade-union section of the yearly convention. A number of delegates who happened to be members of trade-unions, one of them a city president, heartily endorsed the suggestion to ascertain as far as possible the names of the leading trade-unionists of the Central-Verein in the State of Ohio and to endeavor to bring them to the next convention at Columbus, 1910. The sentiment was prevalent that the application of Catholic principles would go a long way to safeguard and strengthen the trade-union movement, and that especially in view of the ordeal of fire that unionism seems to be destined to undergo in these days. It is a matter of no mean consolation to the writer that the best applause given him in his address to the delegates at Hamilton, Ohio, was in response to the following quotation from John Mitchell: "It is a pity that there are many who, failing to understand the fundamental principles and the lofty ideals of trade-unionism, condemn, *without investigation,* the motives and policies of those whose sole desire is to alleviate suffering, to redress wrong, and to raise to a higher standard a class of people handicapped in the race of life, and who, acting in their individual capacities, are as helpless and defenseless as a rudderless ship in an ocean storm."

Undoubtedly labor-unions may do wrong and have done wrong; but let that human institution that has never done wrong cast the first stone! On the whole it may truly be said that the American labor unions have been the most solid bulwark of the rights and interests of the American working-man and at heart they offer the proper, real and Christian solution of many of our labor difficulties. And, therefore, it is eminently proper that Catholics at large identify themselves *actively and effectively* with the labor-union movement in order to vanquish the secret conspiring forces that are sapping its vitality from within and to lead it to new and larger successes. In the very nature of things this work appeals to the Central-Verein and seems destined to play an important role in its future course.

The other topic mentioned was one of agricultural interest. It was noted that after all it was the farmer that made the backbone of the country. That in the conservatism of his spirit and his relatively higher regard for morality was to be found one of the mainstays of the country's continued prosperity; that, moreover, he had problems of his own, immediate and pressing, that should have all the assistance that true Christian organization could offer. Is it hoping too much when we anticipate a Central-Verein farmers' section at our State Conventions? In this case, as in every other, God's interest is also true self-interest. The Central-Bureau is anxious to receive communications from Catholic farmers in this matter.

In conclusion, we may say that we want *all classes* represented in this movement. In the Catholic bosom there is no necessary conflict between the rich and the poor; the employer and the employe; the trade-unionist, the laborer and the farmer. What is to the interest of one is to the interest of all. "That all may be one" was the Savior's greatest prayer. In view of the peculiar state organization of the United States, the State Conventions of the Central-Verein have a more important significance than many of us realize, and we are determined with might and with main to build out the program of the state organizations. Onward and upward! It is the first stroke that counts.

PART THREE

Social Education and Organization

19 William J. Kerby

SOCIAL SCIENCE A PART OF THEOLOGICAL STUDY

Most Catholic thinkers assumed that the clergy must give direction to the social movement, and this conviction was explicit and central in the thought of the Reverend (later Monsignor) William J. Kerby who, on his return from the University of Louvain in 1897 with a doctorate in social and political science, began a forty-year professorship in sociology at the Catholic University of America. In an early essay he brought his powers of analysis and classification to bear on the relationships that properly existed between the priesthood and the social movement. Pushed aside by the onrush of the industrial revolution, Christianity, thought Father Kerby, through its association with the labor movement and with statesmen, scholars, and reformers, was gradually regaining its influence by the teaching of humane ideals, the enactment of social legislation and the strengthening of conscience. He believed that in step with this evolutionary process, social science should be included as a seminar subject in the theological training of the clergy, offering accurate, honest, reasoned, and complete knowledge of the field. This would prepare the few highly gifted priests to show the world what the Gospel means to society, and would thoroughly acquaint a large number of the clergy with the scope, methods and spirit of the social sciences in order that they might render greater service. Finally it would encourage the majority of the clergy, those members who were too occupied with the cares of the ministry to have much time for social thought, to bring intelligent sympathy into their dealings with social problems.

Kerby's essay on the priesthood and the social movement and other of his writings marked the entry of social science into Catholic theory and practice. The author was renowned for his advocacy of scientific charity. A founder of the National Conference of Catholic Charities in 1910, he served as its secretary during its first decade.

Much is being written at present about the relation of the Gospel or Christianity to the social movement. That a great amount of what is written should be vague and very general results from the situation. Neither the Gospel nor the social movement is a fixed quantity in the minds of observers. We have Catholic and Protestant Christianity, each radically unlike the other; we have many phases of the social movement, which at best is something difficult to define. While my purpose is to write specifically of the relation of the Catholic Priesthood to the social movement, for the sake of exposition, I use the word Christianity, taking it to mean what is conveyed by the term to the average mind. I then take the social movement to mean the whole democratic tendency in general, but in particular, that part of it whose center is in the labor movement from its conservative to its radical side.

There is no doubt that the two recognize their influence on each other. Each feels that the other means much to it, in the purposes for which both are working. Christianity is attracted to the social movement by the latter's idealism, its pronounced ethical character, and its sustained effort to realize itself in actual institutions. It is repelled by the aspect and fact of radicalism, impatience, an irreligious and antichristian character, and short-sightedness. Christianity has outlived so many similar movements and has learned by experience of so many dangers and illusions that lurk in them, that it can not help taking a conservative attitude. Then the social movement is attracted to Christianity because the ideals of the former

---

William J. Kerby, "The Priesthood and the Social Movement," *Catholic University Bulletin*, VI (January 1900), 18–28.

find their highest expression and a consecration in the pages of the Gospel; and Christianity is permeated with effective sympathy for the poor and suffering. In addition, its history shows it to have been the mother of many great reforms, made in the interests of humanity. But the social movement at times mistrusts Christianity somewhat and mistakes its conservatism for enslavement to institutions and interests against which the movement is directing its whole force. They can not avoid nor evade each other.

The situation has been brought about in a large measure by immediate social questions which absorb attention everywhere. We commonly claim and rightly, too, that civilization is Christian; that the best understanding of human dignity and rights is found in the Gospel, as is also their surest guarantee; that the wisest guidance of social life is taken from the Gospel; that much of the progress of our twenty centuries is due to Christianity, and that many great reforms have been effected by the Church. Now that our *unsolved* social questions attract so much attention, Christianity is called to account. The human rights, so grandly taught, are only in part a reality; massive evil and no end of wrong mar our social life; opportunity for mental, moral, and even physical development is denied vast numbers of our social population. The social movement is a reaction against this condition. It is asking a two-fold question, which directly bears on Christianity, a question which will never disappear till answered effectively. Is our civilization Christian? What is Christianity worth? If we sum up the countless minor questions springing out of the situation, we can more easily realize the directness and earnestness with which the interrogation is made. The following will suggest the trend of these questions:

a) Are the *social conditions and tendencies* of modern life Christian: pauperism and social crime with accompanying degradation; the centralization of wealth; the stratification of society into classes which so often make a mockery of human equality and fraternity; the gradual elimination of conscience from business, politics, and legislation?

b) Are the *methods* of modern life Christian; methods in business, in social and industrial life, in politics and legislation? Do we find in them the legitimate product of the spirit of the Gospel? Can a business man easily be honest?

c) Are the *principles* of modern social and economic life Christian? competitive industry, manufacture for profit, private ownership of land and capital, monopoly, state individualism, and the struggle for existence?

d) Are the *ideals* of modern social life Christian? Society is shifting to an economic basis, emphasizing the economic idea in life, and its ideals correspond. Can we find the Gospel conception of the character, grandeur, and destiny of man in the successful man of to-day?

The questions are honest and earnest. They merit serious thought and a definite reply. It matters not that in many of them there are exaggerations, false assumptions of fact, and an unwarranted pessimism. In general, they are justified, and in every way worthy of all attention. Nor does it even matter that Christianity is in no way accountable for the actual condition of things; that they would be inconceivably worse except for it. The questions are there, and Christianity is vitally interested in their solution.

Replies have been made to the questions, or at least attempts have been made to formulate replies and inaugurate movements which would accord with their tenor. We may say in fact, *quot capita, tot sententiae*. While prejudice, creed and school have played their part, for our purpose of exposition we may reduce them to four principally.

A first view may be roughly stated in this way. The Gospel is supernatural and divine. It is capable of regenerating society and successfully directing it; but we have heretofore not understood it. The Gospel condemns the ideals, principles, methods and tendencies of modern social life and emphatically protests against these conditions. They are entirely unchristian. Brotherhood in Christ is the ideal—the Golden Rule is the law; yet we live in a state of semi-savagery. The Gospel condemns competitive industry, manufacture for profit, private monopoly, private ownership of land and individualism, and it commands co-operation, common ownership of wealth and socialism. This is, in substance, the reply of the Christian Socialists, taking the term in a strict and correct sense. They trace their origin to Maurice and Kingsley in England. Many who share that view are to be found in the United States. The Rev. Mr. Sprague, Bliss and Herron, all ministers, are well known as representatives of it. The view sometimes comes to expression in the secular press, and it cannot be denied that a sentiment in favor of the view is growing.[1]

A second reply may be thus formulated. The Gospel is divine and properly understood in principle. It does not condemn the principles of modern social organization as such. It does condemn many tendencies and methods and unchecked institutions and it protests against conditions which characterize modern social life. But these are due largely to political and economic principles on which our social organization rests and

[1] See, for example, the article on Christian Socialism in Bliss' Encyclopedia of Social Reform. The word is there taken in a broad sense, including every organized effort of a Christian church to further the cause of social reform. Sprague's Christian Socialism and the lectures of Rev. Mr. Bliss and Herron are authentic expressions of the view. The last named has just resigned as Professor of Applied Christianity in Iowa College, Grinnell, Iowa. He was practically forced out on account of his radical views. His letter of resignation may be found in the Chicago *Commons,* October 31, 1899. Mayor Jones of Toledo, the Golden Rule candidate for Governor of Ohio, in November, is the exponent of a view much like that under discussion. He received 106,721 votes.

to a philosophic movement which has hindered Christianity from exercising its power. Christianity is not all sufficient; it cannot coerce nor change human nature. Supposing proper and wise co-operation, it can regenerate society. This may be called the attitude of the majority of Christians; particularly of the Catholic Church. It finds expression in documents, such as papal encyclicals, episcopal letters and in the attitude of the Church toward actual problems.

A third view is that of the average non-Christian or anti-Christian socialist. The Gospel is false and Christianity a human invention. Human, not divine brotherhood is the ideal and the law. Competitive industry, private monopoly, social classes, etc., violate human rights and hinder human development. Hence they are wrong independently of any consideration of the Gospel. Christianity, as an institution, is not the friend of the oppressed, it is rather their enemy.

The fourth view may be summarized in this way: The Gospel or Christianity has not much direct bearing on the question. Yet, judged by it, our civilization is not Christian. Reform can be brought about chiefly by economic and political action of the suffering classes. This view is found in the active labor movement, very widely shared among statesmen, students and reformers. A great majority are Christian and they sincerely welcome any assistance in reform work offered by the churches. Some believe that the Gospel is divine but that its representatives "are opposed to any practical effort to advance the cause of the poor and oppressed" and that they "are against the poor and allied to the plunderers."[2]

No one of these replies has won universal recognition, and no one of the numberless replies, more or less resembling these, has fared better. As regards the social movement, the great problem is still unsolved, the value and power of the Gospel,

[2] From a letter written to me by a student of social conditions. See Catholic University Bulletin, January, 1899, p. 50.

its relation to the social movement, is still an open question. Appeal to the past is of no avail. That Christianity has revolutionized society and has effected stupendous reforms is forgotten. The temper of the time is peculiar. What is alone in question is the value of Christianity to the present. A final reply, which will for all time or even for any epoch meet the question, is in the nature of the case not to be expected. It would suppose a unity of faith, a rearrangement of the perspective of life, and a social revolution. The situation resolves itself into a question of more or less. Social evils and sin, defective human institutions and social maladjustments there will be while man is man. There is a sad philosophy in the lives of Judas and Peter.

The first of the replies enumerated—that of the Christian Socialists, fails, I think, to understand the Gospel. Manysided study is necessary to reach an understanding of the scope and meaning of it. The personality of our Savior, the conditions in which He worked and which He tolerated, attitudes which He took, the processes and limitations which He recognized in supernatural life, the laws of social growth, individual man and social nature, human limitations and the historical interpretation of the Gospel, all these elements must be taken into account before we can safely claim to have understood the rôle of the Gospel in life and its relation to the problems of society. I think the interpretation of the Christian Socialists fails here. At any rate it has not become a factor in the situation.[3]

The third reply need not be discussed here since it calls into question the divine character of Christ. The view is current only among one class of socialists.

The fourth reply, if we may so call it, is the expression of a

[3] The limitations to which the realization of the Gospel may be subjected are admirably though briefly described in the letters of Cardinal Newman published in the *Contemporary Review,* Oct., 99. Tolstoi's life, work, and failure are suggestive in this connection.

widely shared view. But even here we find the admission that reform by ballot is worse than nothing if the ballot is taken to be all sufficient. Law without conscience is useless, and the world does not trust in conscience without Christianity. At any rate, professed Christians who are actively interested in the labor movement, do not believe that much can be accomplished independently of religion, that is, of Christianity.

The second reply—that of the majority of Christians—particularly of the Catholic Church, is the only one, I think, that is warranted by the serious and unbiased study of the Gospel, of the history of the Church and of the economic, political, and religious history of the past three centuries. As a matter of fact the social system in which we live has not had a fair trial; we have seen its worst and not its best. Economic forces were turned loose a century and a quarter ago when the industrial revolution came. Political philosophy cleared away all legal barriers, and the disintegration of religion weakened the moral forces of society. The economic development carried all before it, and our social problem is the result. The whole reform work of the century reduces itself to the teaching of humane ideas and the checking of economic forces by legislation, and to strengthening conscience. Political and economic institutions and ethical interpretations are being slowly adjusted. Here lies the path of progress. Only when political, economic, and religious forces have done their best, may we declare our institutions bankrupt and seek a radical revolution. This, I think, is the basis of the position taken by most Christians and in particular by the Catholic Church, to which I now confine consideration.

The attitude of the Church is not correctly understood by the social movement; when it is understood, it will hardly be accepted and acted upon spontaneously. It is necessary that the Church turn her energies to the situation, understand it, and effectively demonstrate the wisdom of her course. As the historic Church, as the one true custodian of the Gospel, as the vast organization possessing the accumulated wisdom of the ages, she has this duty to the social movement, to human society. Here lies the duty, the matchless opportunity, the responsibility of the Catholic Priesthood. The situation is clear; the point needs no demonstration. Hence I take up some practical phases of the question.

A general reply to the questions asked by the social movement is not sufficient. Only when the priesthood understands the social movement, its philosophy and its goal, its temper and its limitations,—only then will the Church win over the movement to her view. The theological sciences, as commonly taught in our seminaries, are not enough. The priest must know human society, its structure, laws, forces, and institutions; he must also know its history and its tendencies. True enough much of this is learned in our courses in moral philosophy, in theology and in history. But I think that their spirit and method are not entirely in sympathy with the actual situation; at least not as much so as might be. The knowledge needed is philosophical and scientific,—that is, accurate, honest, reasoned, and complete knowledge. It must be based on an actual acquaintance with social conditions; cursory reading of magazines and newspapers is worse than useless. It must be honest; free from professional bias and party spirit. There must be no fear of the truth. If investigations show that we are anywhere at fault, we can best afford to be the first to know it and profit by it. The honest service of truth is the only ambition worthy of a scholar who is a man. Our knowledge should be reasoned. Too much present-day opinion springs from feeling and sympathy, and often effectually hinders progress. Our knowledge must be relatively complete. Moral, religious, economic, political and social forces combine in producing the social phenomena which we study—no one-sided view of them is ever safe. A railroad train is in a sense an epitome of social history and economic conditions, just as the postage stamp on my desk is synoptic of the philosophy of the material universe. We may go as deeply as we wish in our social studies—any phenomenon we investigate is many-sided; strikes, crime, labor organizations, the factory, machinery, social classes suggest problems which no genius can, as yet, successfully meet.

The priesthood has exceptional advantages for the study of social sciences. The mind of the priest is formed according to a solid, consistent, philosophical system of truth which gives it a constructive tendency, evenness, and correctness of view. A complete theory of human existence, human society, and revelation in their organic relations is kept constantly before his eyes. He possesses, too, a complete and satisfactory philosophy of sin, human passions, liberty, and grace, of the central facts of history, of the root of social problems, and the element of limitation in every human institution. The position, duties, and influence of the priest give him unequalled opportunity to understand the conditions and the temper of those for whose sake reforms are generally undertaken.

What is now needed is a slow adjustment of college and seminary courses to this situation. The horizon must be widened and the social sciences must be received into the system as an integral portion of it. They must become part of the theological formation, though necessarily submitting to the limitations which healthy traditions, and the actual situation impose. This need be only a continuation of the work already begun in the teaching of Ethics and Moral Theology. Both take account of modern conditions, as they are now taught. We must merely differentiate the social sciences, let them assume, at least an individuality and a name, and later, a proportion in keeping with their importance.

It may be well to anticipate some difficulties which could be urged, though the purpose of this paper is rather to suggest a problem, not to solve it; to stimulate, not to direct.

It is, of course, impossible for every priest to pursue such work as is here outlined. Time, talent and taste are necessary, and, needless to say, not all have them. But I am speaking of the priesthood rather than of the individual priest. The priesthood is a divine institution interpreting revelation to life and directing life by revelation. The social intelligence must be formed in the theoretical truths of revelation and the social will must conform to its practical truths. Life, social life at least, resolves itself into intellectual, political, social and religious movements; the priesthood should understand them. The organic view of it, as a divine institution, shows its plenary responsibility to every phase of social life which comes into contact with divine revelation. The individual priest should measure duty and direct activity by this view. It gives us apostles, raises up leaders, inspires thinkers and fits the priesthood to all times, classes and conditions.

Once this view of the relation of the priesthood to the social movement enters our traditions, and the study of society has its place in the process of theological formation, our students in general will have a sufficient knowledge of the social sciences. Then there will gradually arise among them those with peculiar talent for this work; men who may become thinkers of the first rank in Economics, Political Science, Sociology. This is the process which has given us our thinkers in Dogmatic and Moral Theology, History, Canon Law, the Languages, and Scripture. It is the brilliant few that we need—the dozen great minds which shall furnish us a safe leadership in uncertain social conditions, and show to the world what the Gospel means to society. Next to them, the great number, who are to be, at least thoroughly acquainted with the scope, methods and spirit of the social sciences and who may render great service to the cause. Then the greater number, so occupied with the cares of the ministry as to be able to give little time to social thought, can at least bring intelligent sympathy into their dealings with social problems, as is largely the case now. All in all, the traditions in which the priesthood is formed would thus adjust themselves to the times, and an effective reply to the great question of civilization and Christianity would, *nolens volens,* be forced on the world.

The work has been admirably begun in Germany, France,

Belgium and Italy, where the priesthood has practically taken over the leadership of the Catholic people in the social movement. They are writing on Economics, Sociology and Political Science, entering politics, organizing labor unions and reform parties. Conditions made it imperative. The Catholic laity is doing a noble work in these countries; it can do a great work here, but the laity alone cannot accomplish the result we seek. They have not and cannot easily have a theological formation. Truth is organic, is one; revealed and natural truth differ rather in the way of knowing than in quality. In the condition I am discussing the theological formation is necessary. When bishops and priests lose the theological spirit in their reform work, they harm rather than help the cause. This was seen in France a century or more ago; instances on the continent nearer our own time are not lacking. We must be assisted by Catholic thinkers, men who are more or less well acquainted with theological truth. No one else can do their work. But it is not reasonable to expect them to do too much.

There is a practical difficulty in the fact that there is no room in our college and seminary courses for this study as outlined. But we need not hesitate for that. Our courses enjoy no immunity from human conditions and their consequences. The situation will force the adjustment some time; the only danger is that we may be too slow. The recognized place of physiology and psychology in Ethics and Moral Theology, and the actual attention given to Economics, assure us that practical obstacles will eventually be overcome. An educational system that has overcome difficulties without number, and achieved results, great as ours has done, need never find reason for hesitation.

In urging the introduction of the social sciences into the process of theological formation, I justify myself by an organic view of the priesthood, and by the example of the Holy Father. He has studied and written on our social problems with a success and sympathy which are a source of congratulation. The encyclical on the study of philosophy touches fundamental questions of thought; the encyclical on marriage treats a group of specific social questions; those on the constitution of civil society and the origin of power, are professedly studies in political philosophy from a Christian standpoint; that on liberty is a study of the rights and duties of citizens; that on the condition of labor is an admirable review of the social situation, and a platform for religious, social, legal, and political reform. This organic view of the priesthood is one of two great thoughts for which our University stands. It aims to serve the Catholic cause, to equip Catholic priest and layman for a life which shall be at once, serviceable to God and Country,—*Deo et Patriae*. The University stands against the fatal process of excessive specialization—it represents a synthetic thought. It is to serve in equipping priests and laymen who will stand for the unity of truth, faith and science. What is this but the Christian idea! The true concept of life assumes continuity between present and future existence. The future is to be determined here—we are part and parcel of the world and society. Christ founded His Church primarily to accomplish the work of sanctification and salvation; neither knowledge nor earthly prosperity or happiness is her direct purpose. Yet there is an essential harmony in things. In serving the future, the Church best serves the present. The Church will, therefore, never be indifferent to temporal prosperity. She is directly interested in social problems and reform. She has a message for the age, and she depends on her priesthood for its effectual presentation.

20 Charles Patrick Neill

THE NEED FOR TRAINED SOCIAL WORKERS

The National Conference of Catholic Charities could not have designated a person more qualified to discuss new trends in

Catholic charity than Charles Patrick Neill, who held a doctorate from the Johns Hopkins University, and had been professor of political economy in the Catholic University of America, a member of the District of Columbia board of charities, and Federal Commissioner of Labor (1905–1913). In his paper, read at the third convention of the Conference in 1914, he explained why adequately trained lay charity workers were necessary. The task of the charity worker was to diagnose the causes of personal and family destitution and to prescribe remedial measures. Inasmuch as rehabilitation involved moral uplifting, the problem facing the charity worker was often more subtle and baffling than the one confronting the physician. Moreover, success in remedial charity was often contingent on preventive charity, that is, on social reforms, and this was an additional reason for specialized training for charity workers.

This biennial gathering of Catholic charity workers and students here is at once significant and symbolic—not only the Conference itself, but the place of its meetings. To my mind, it compares in importance and in meaning to the annual regathering that marks each year, the opening of the University in whose halls we meet. For in charity and in education have been played two of the great historic rôles of the great historic Mother Church; in these two fields have been two of her great contributions to the development of civilization. But today, everywhere, a strong and steady effort is going on to take away from her influence as much as possible, both these fields of activity, to secularize education and charity alike. And so, although we had already many great universities, this new

---

Charles Patrick Neill, "Training for Social Work," *Proceedings*, National Conference of Catholic Charities (Washington, D. C., 1914), pp. 55–60.

University was founded so that in the very highest lines of study and of research, in all the present day educational needs, opportunity might be afforded to have the work carried on under Catholic auspices, guided by Catholic principles, and consecrated and spiritualized by Catholic motives.

So, in the same way, although we have annually a number of well organized and important charitable conferences in which we join with those of other faiths, and of no faith, we have also founded this Catholic Conference, not only to furnish still another occasion to keep abreast with the ripest thought dealing with the many complex and baffling problems in new fields of social activity; not only to study and discuss the most effective ways that experience suggests of grappling with these problems in their concrete form; but also to furnish a meeting place in which even the most recently developed forms of charitable endeavor shall be studied and discussed in the light of distinctly Catholic principles, and to insure as far as we can that such work shall still be carried on consciously in the name and in the spirit of Him who taught us, if we gave but a cup of cold water, to give it in His name. For we believe, no matter how imposing or how efficient a secularized system of so-called charity may seem, that unless it is permeated by religious zeal, it must ultimately become a dead mechanical thing, a mere material corpse from which has fled all trace of the motive that originally gave it birth and of the spirit that lent it beauty.

At bottom, the principle of Charity is one of the great distinguishing marks between the ancient civilization and ours of today. It is the vital, the spiritual, characteristic of our civilization, it is the contribution to that civilization which the Church of Christ has made, it is the soul of the social body that the Church has supplied. So inwoven in our social structure have the motive and principle of charity become, so much a part of our mental process has it been, that its influence would probably for a considerable time, continue to endure even if works of charity become altogether secularized and divorced from religious motive. But eventually if the spiritual motive be cast out, the spirit of charity as we have known it, must wither and perish; efficiency must again become the sole end, and civilization at heart again become pagan.

It is because we believe this that we are gathered here, we Catholics, religious and laymen and laywomen alike, determined on building up a great National Conference of Catholic Charities that shall in every field of activity give renewed impetus to the teachings of charity of our Church, and to renew our loyalty to those teachings; to furnish an opportunity periodically to acquaint ourselves with one another, and with the new phases of charitable work in the different parts of our vast country, to benefit by one another's experiences and to aid each other by discussions of the means and methods best adapted to success in every field of activity, old or new. We have started this movement to stimulate the study of Catholic principles of Charity so that there may be no field of charitable endeavor in which we shall not be efficiently represented; no field in which there shall not be well equipped workers, inspired by spiritual and Catholic motives; in a word, no field in which there shall be a possibility that the spirit of charity should become so secularized that the badge of the Cross might come to be no longer the symbol of Calvary and its teaching, but merely a conventionalized design without spiritual significance.

But if we are to realize this high aim, if we are in the future to carry on the Church's mission of Charity as she has so nobly done in the long centuries of the past, if we even hope to do our full share in the field of charity in the future, we must not only put heart and soul in the work, but we must see to it that we understand every phase of our complex charitable problems of today and we must be prepared, if necessary, to build up new forces to meet new needs. In the past, the Church has not only preached and taught the principles of charity as the true basis for our individual and our social life alike; but she has also built up great institutions, and within what we may broadly call her ecclesiastical structure, she has created great and enduring organizations of men and of women through which the principles she taught might flower into concrete expression; and through which she also might give to her children opportunity wholly to consecrate their lives and their very being to works of charity. Thus she has her organizations which care for the foundling and the orphaned; she has set up institutions to care for the needy sick and mentally defective; she has havens of refuge for the morally sick in her reformatories, inebriate asylums and homes of the Good Shepherd; and she has her homes for the needy, the aged and the infirm. The need for work in all these fields continues as much as ever; but in addition, new demands for systematic charitable effort are constantly arising of a sort for which our existing organizations were not formed and to which they are not adapted, and which call for a kind of work for which we must develop specialized lines of lay activity. I am not unmindful of the splendid and many sided activities of the noble organization of St. Vincent de Paul; but we cannot unload upon one single lay organization every form of social or charitable effort to which our religious organizations are unadapted.

What we need today is lay workers, trained workers, who can give their lives to certain outside lines of work, just as our religious do to their traditional lines of work. The need of *trained* workers is obvious to anyone at all familiar with the many complex, subtle, baffling problems growing out of the mere fact of poverty and destitution in all our great congested centers of population. This is a form of poverty that because of the environment it necessitates, exposes its victims, and especially the children, to moral as well as physical disaster; and the problem of how to deal with it is one that grows increasingly vexatious. If the problem were simply one of hunger and clothing, it would be very simple. It would be merely a mathematical and not a moral one. It would be like feeding an army in time of peace. One ration multiplied by the number of the needy would be the answer. But we all know that mere material relief alone will not cure the trouble; in many cases it may aggravate it. Doing nothing but giving such relief is only too often no better than it would be to feed a suffering patient morphine and let the treatment stop at that. Too often our poverty case is complicated by the lack of some moral quality, the restoration of which is necessary to effective, permanent "relief." The charity worker among the poor of our great cities particularly, has often no easy task in diagnosing and locating the real cause of a family's distress. And when it is found, it all too frequently calls for a moral as well as an economic and physical upbuilding.

We all know that our moral upbuilding is more difficult than physical upbuilding, just as moral education is often more exacting than mental education. The charity worker has often a harder job than the doctor. The diagnosis is often as hard. In one case the patient helps the doctor as far as he can while in the other case he too often mistreats and deceives the worker seeking the real cause of his condition. Given a correct diagnosis, the doctor much of the time has a more or less established rule as to what treatment or prescription to use. But with the charity worker each case may be a test of personal judgment, and success in helping it may depend entirely on the worker's individual skill. In every case, the charity worker must seek resources in the particular "patient" that will respond most effectively to this or that appeal, to this or that influence; and, what is often more important, as to how long any given influence will continue to work. The charity worker must go entirely outside the individual into the home, and neighborhood, and even the whole environment to know whether these forces can be made to work for the "patient," or whether they work against him. In a word, without in any way minimizing the complexities and the elusive elements with which the physician has to grapple, or the requirements of personal training and ability that condition his success, it remains true that only too often the character of the task before a charity worker is really more subtle and baffling than the one before the doctor and calls for at least as much judgment, experience and training.

And yet, not every one may practice medicine. Zeal for the cause of health or devotion to the sick is not accepted as a sufficient basis to turn any one loose as a healer. But too often zeal in the cause is all that is expected in the charity worker. The unintelligent, untrained charity worker can, in spite of disinterested zeal, often cause as much moral havoc as a result of his or her ministrations as an untrained practitioner of medicine could cause of a physical sort.

The work of the teacher, too, requires training. The children entrusted ordinarily to a teacher are normal types; they are carefully classified and graded; the lessons to be taught them are carefully planned and adapted to their mental capacity. None of this is left to the individual teacher. The pupils are selected and classified for the teacher, and the lessons to be taught them are put into her hands. Moreover, each teacher is merely doing for the children just what was once done for him or her; each has been through the same mental process as the pupil whom he or she is teaching. The teacher's own experience therefore is of great assistance in the work. And the child furnishes a plastic, receptive mind and responds consciously and willingly to the teacher's efforts. A charity worker on the other hand has the task of moral training; is trying to educate not mind but character; is dealing, not with a normal type, or with one whose experiences could be recalled in his or her own life by the charity worker, but with something other than the normal type, each case presenting a separate problem; is dealing, not with a young plastic, receptive mind or character, but with a character grown and set, and with an individual who too often works against rather than with the efforts put forth in his or her behalf. We require now not only a good education, but we demand a special course of technical training in the art and science of teaching before we permit any one to enter upon the work of teaching in our schools. But we turn over the harder and more baffling task of the charity worker too often to anyone willing to undertake the work.

Not only has the charity worker the problem of the individual to deal with, but very often it develops that the distress is partly or wholly due to social maladjustments, too often it is the community that is delinquent as much as the individual sufferer. The problem of charity then takes on a new form. Thus the charity worker not only faces the need of reforming an individual but also of securing changes in the social system as well. It may be challenged that this is leading outside of the field of "Charity," but this is not at all the case. In its wider aspects the term charity is as broad as the modern form "social service."

In its beginnings charitable work has usually been individual and remedial. In this it has been like the earlier phase of medical practice, it ministered only to the economically and the morally "sick." Its work was to alleviate existing distress, and to nurse back to economic health when possible. But like medical practice, charity work soon finds a larger and even more important field of activity in preventive work; and in this field, charitable activity takes on the character of "social service." This has been an easily explained development. No one sees more clearly or at closer range the sad results of some of the defects of our social and industrial system than the charity worker. No one sees more clearly how the delinquencies of the community visit their penalties on the helpless and unoffending individual or family. And so the charity worker finds his field naturally expanding into the work of specific social reforms.

Difficult as is the task of working a change in the character of the individual, still harder is the task of bringing about social readjustments. To work successfully in this larger field of preventive charity calls for a broader and a deeper training, a keener and more analytical judgment, a riper experience, and a more forceful type of man or woman than does "remedial" charity dealing primarily with the individual. This is, therefore an additional reason for specialized training for charity workers.

Although, as has already been said, the field of charity is and historically has been always one of the great fields of activity of the Church, and although the most complex relations exist between our charities and our religious and moral philosophy, and our individual and our social ethics, it yet seems to be the one field of important activity that we Catholics seem *in practice* to feel, needs no particular training for its workers. In our colleges and universities we have taught law and medicine and engineering and a host of other things to equip our young men for successful works in various fields of the work of the world. But until within a year or two, practically no Catholic college provided any adequate study of Charities in its curriculum, and in consequence heretofore any Catholic layman or laywoman who wished to devote himself or herself to this field of social work, and sought specialized instruction, has had to seek it from non-Catholic sources. A beginning has been made, and as will be shown by the later papers on this evening's program, systematic courses in charity are becoming available in Catholic institutions. But our colleges and universities will not have done their full duty to the Church and to its mission, nor their duty to society, until every Catholic college and university shall give place in its curriculum to regular courses related to charitable, or social work. Just as we furnish practical courses to those who wish to go in for law, medicine, engineering, etc., so for those who wish to go into social work special courses in Catholic philosophy must be offered that shall apply its principles, not speculatively, but in their concrete application to the present day needs in this field of work. Related fields of knowledge must be embraced in such courses so that relief and preventive charity work may be carried on, not in a haphazard way, but in correlation with the principles and laws that govern social life, social processes, and social growth. Only in this way may we hope to build up a body of Catholic charity workers, and a Catholic literature on our present day charitable problems that will compare with the secular literature in this field which is daily growing larger and larger.

At intervals of two or three years, courses of the kind to which I refer, are regularly given in this University and Trinity College. Reports of courses inaugurated in the past two years will now be presented to you. Let us hope that the near future will see our representative colleges and our special schools in charity sending forth graduates equipped to do the exacting work of social service, with skill that shows understanding and practical mastery, and with consecration that shows divine grace and social sympathy united in this noble work.

21 Henry Somerville

THE TENSION BETWEEN VOLUNTEERS AND PROFESSIONALS IN CATHOLIC CHARITIES

The problem of regulating Catholic charities so as to make them properly effective is a perennial one. St. Vincent de Paul faced it in the seventeenth century, and it was painfully acute in America during the first quarter of the twentieth century when new needs and new methods in the charity field clamored for evaluation and adoption. To this problem Henry Somerville, active in the English Catholic Social Guild, addressed himself in a luminous commentary on the fourth meeting of the National Conference of Catholic Charities. He was particularly informative on the ideas and attitudes of lay women, organized in a vast array of leagues, societies, and guilds, and of laymen and their great family-relief organization, the Society of St. Vincent de Paul. The organizers of the women's groups, viewed as "progressives," favored the scientific methods of charity administration, which included budget plans for dependent families, the keeping of case-records, the use of the confidential exchange, the employment of salaried workers and a closer cooperation with non-Catholic agencies. The laymen's groups, the "conservatives," on the other hand, feared that many of the new methods were not in keeping with the spirit of Catholic charity.

Somerville did not think that Catholic charitable workers should cling stubbornly to the old ways or accept uncritically the new. He thought they should study and experiment, judge every method by the results it yielded, and steer clear of abstraction and mere theory. This should be the attitude especially of the more practical and experienced workers, the members of the Society of St. Vincent de Paul, who should give attention to the science as well as to the art of charity. Research and experiment should rule not only in family rehabilitation, but in other fields as well—child care, for example, an area in which a bitter battle raged between the respective advocates of the orphanage and the foster home. By a process of experiment and testing, Catholic charitable workers should discover if, under what conditions, and to what extent the orphanage and the foster home succeeded or failed. The approach which Somerville suggested came to prevail widely in the post-World War I period. Although Somerville all but ignored the Sisterhoods, it was they who most widely applied his ideas.

Nations have always had their "social problems," and the millions of souls who throughout the Christian centuries have felt it their vocation to devote their lives to the performance of

---

Henry Somerville, "The National Conference of Catholic Charities," *Catholic World*, CV (August 1917), 587–597.

works of charity have been rendering social service in the best sense of the term. The seven spiritual and the seven corporal works of mercy comprise the whole programme on behalf of those two great categories of our neighbor in need, whom the sociologist calls the dependent and the delinquent. In this country at the present time social service has become, if not the vocation, at least the avocation of a host of persons who now constitute a distinct professional class. I have seen it stated in one of those labor union journals which are not friendly to that class, that "organized charity" is now the sixth largest industry in the country. I don't know what kind of activities were reckoned as organized charity in order to get that estimate, but I fancy it is not so greatly exaggerated as the ordinary reader might think. In New York City there are over four thousand salaried social workers employed by private philanthropic agencies, and in one case at least the salary amounts to ten thousand dollars a year.

No doubt the professionalizing of social work is less ideal than the consecrated service of religious, but it is a fact which Catholics must accept and reckon with. Catholic charity can no more remain independent of the developments of modern philanthropic method than Catholic schools can be indifferent to the systems and standards of the secular educational institutions of the country. Catholic charitable agencies are inevitably brought into connection—and sometimes into collision—with non-Catholic agencies, both public and private. A large part of our present problems arise from the fact that we have to work with those who differ from us in motives, methods, and principles; and often enough we have to use machinery that we have not fashioned and which is ill-adapted to our special ends. But of course not all our difficulties arise from the non-Catholic and anti-Catholic elements with which we have to deal. Charitable work of its own nature always presents problems that can only be solved by hard study, and after repeated experiment and error. The Church teaches us the principles of charity, but we often make mistakes in their application. Saints and doctors from very ancient times have been aware of the abuses by which almsgiving tends to produce not good but evil, by subsidizing imposture and idleness; yet no one has found an infallible and practicable safeguard against this abuse. St. Vincent de Paul pointed out that charitable acts, though inspired by the loftiest motives, could be entirely ineffective if they were not well regulated. How to regulate our charitable activities so as to make them properly effective is one of the greatest problems that Catholics can concern themselves with in America today.

The wide field and the multitudinous forms of charitable enterprise may be seen from a glance at the contents of the *Report,* just published, of the Fourth National Conference of Catholic Charities held at Washington last September. There are still many good people who think of charities as merely a matter of almsgiving, orphanages, and homes for the aged poor. The *Report* under review will show the National Conference of Catholic Charities dealing with such questions as the legal minimum wage, public and private employment agencies, types and causes of feeble-mindedness, the rôle of legislation in the field of relief, the availability of parochial schools and parish halls as social centres, juvenile delinquency, and the social needs of Catholic young women. To reprint a complete list of the titles of all the papers read at the Conference would give an idea of the diversity, but not of the unity, of the Conference discussions. Only those who are intelligently as well as actively engaged in charitable work can see the ramifications of the most commonplace relief problems. The daily work of the ordinary member of the St. Vincent de Paul Society, for instance, presents questions about which there is voluminous debate. The principal work of the St. Vincent de Paul Society is to visit and relieve the poor in their homes. It is, or should be, what scientific philanthropy calls family rehabilitation, that is, to secure for the family a certain minimum standard of living;

and whenever possible, and as far as possible, to make the family provide for its own needs by its own affairs.

The largest section meetings of the Conference were those held by the Committee on Families, the committee which dealt with the problems of family rehabilitation. Perhaps the best way of showing the kind of work done at the Conference will be to describe the programme at one of these section meetings.

At the first meeting of the Committee on Families three papers were read: one was on *Adequate and Inadequate Relief*, the second was *The Meaning and Limitations of Records in Relief Work*, and the third was *Difficulties and Objections in Making Records in Relief Work*. At the second meeting of the Committee on Families there were three more papers: on *Personal Service in Relief Work*, on *The Practical Responsibility of Parents for the Education, Health and Faith of their Children*, and on *The Family Budget*.

Although read at different meetings the papers on *Adequate and Inadequate Relief* and *The Family Budget* were both on the one subject, and it is more convenient to take them together. It is not unjust to say that the average St. Vincent de Paul conference does not pretend to follow out a consistent programme of giving "adequate" relief, that is, relief sufficient to maintain the relieved family according to a certain settled standard of life. What a conference usually does is to make a weekly allowance, the amount of which is roughly proportionate to the resources of the conference, and to the deserts as well as to the needs of the relieved family. Sometimes the total income of the family is thus made to exceed what is strictly necessary for decent maintenance, but more often the relief is less than adequate, after taking other known sources of income into account, to supply the necessaries of reasonable living. The family is expected to manage somehow on less than a sufficiency. If an outsider asked a Vincentian why more relief was not given, the first reply would most likely be that the conference funds would not allow it. But I believe that most Vincentians have the impression that, apart from the questions of conference funds, the giving of relief that leaves the applicant skimped is a practical way of stimulating him to strive to better his condition by his own exertions. Moreover, relief that seems inadequate in view of the known resources of the family may be fully adequate with the real resources, of which the conferences does not know all. There is no question here of fraud on the part of the family, of deliberate concealment of resources. The fact is that most families have resources of income, which are comparatively important, but of which they are scarcely conscious. Perhaps the children earn a few coppers by running errands for neighbors, somebody may be giving the family cast-off clothing, or broken food, or firewood, and even coke and coal are often obtained gratis in various ways. It is a familiar saying that one-half the world does not know how the other half lives. It is literally true that we don't know how our next-door neighbor lives, and many of us don't know how we live ourselves.

Scientific philanthropy is very impatient with such incomplete knowledge of the families relieved, and with such rough and ready modes of allotting relief; and it seeks to insure that the relief given is exactly proportionate to needs. In this attempt to secure exactness many things are involved. First, it is necessary to determine what are the requisites of a proper standard of life for a dependent family. Certain lists of such requisites have been drawn up and the money cost of the commodities taken into account, thus getting a "budget statement" of what a dependent family needs, and relief is given accordingly. Of course the budget will vary for different families according to the number and ages of the children, the health of the members of the family, the level of prices in the neighborhood, and other circumstances. The budget plan had some strong advocates at the Conference. One of the speakers said:

All families are identical in this, that they require a certain amount of food, and of clothing and a decent shelter, without which they cannot hope to exist. Through careful study an "irreducible minimum" has been worked out. It is the norm whereby a family of five may live and enjoy health and even some small measure of comfort on a limited income. . . . The allowance for rent gives the family decent quarters with proper sanitation and ventilation. It is the duty of the Friendly Visitor to see that each family is housed as healthfully as possible for the money allowed for that expenditure. In New York City the average rent for a family of five in all districts of the Borough of Manhattan is $12.50 per month. The cost of fuel and light ranges from two to three dollars per month in summer to four or five dollars in winter, so the allowance for these items throughout the year is $3.75 per month. . . . In the estimation of the food allowance the Atwood standard has been found practical. The dietary has been agreed upon by many authorities in various parts of the country, and it has been checked up by Professor H. C. Sherman of Columbia University, according to the most exact laboratory standards. The dietary now in use for the average family of five provides the following foods: Milk, 14 quarts; eggs, 1 dozen; butterine, ½ pound; cheese, ½ pound; chuck steak, 2 pounds; flank steak, 2 pounds; cod fish, 1 pound; bread, 12 pounds; oatmeal, 3 pounds; macaroni, 1 pound; rice, ½ pound; sugar, 3½ pounds; beans, 2 pounds; carrots, 4 pounds; onions, 4 pounds; potatoes, 15 pounds; tomatoes, 1 pound; apples, 1 pound; prunes, 2 pounds; dates, 1 pound; cocoa, ½ pound; tea, ¼ pound; coffee, ½ pound.[1]

The budget plan requires, not only that a detailed statement of the families' needs be drawn up, but that there be complete knowledge of the families' own resources so that the relief given as a supplement to those resources will be just sufficient to make up the amount required for the budget. This complete knowledge of resources necessitates skilled and searching investigation of the circumstances of the family. Further, the agent of the relief society who visits the family must see that the money is spent in accordance with the budget directions. The whole plan would be made useless if the family doubled its consumption of meat at the expense of the milk and vege-

[1] *Report,* pp. 161, 162.

tables, or if it spent on candies the appropriations for fruit.

Obviously, there may be acceptance of the principle of the budget plan but disagreement about its details. Some of the speakers at the Conference bluntly denied that any private charitable organization ever can or ever does continue to give "adequate" relief to all the families with which it deals. An objection to the budget principle as it is advocated and practiced by secular charitable societies, was that it establishes between the charity worker and the recipient of relief a relation which is not that of friendly help but of dictatorial supremacy. Poor persons are given relief only on condition of their surrendering the right of managing their own households. The following remarks were made by a speaker at the Conference:

> I think that a distinction is necessary between families that are entirely dependent and those that are dependent only in an emergency or intermittently. In a family of the latter type the mother has a certain kind of self-reliance and resourcefulness which must be taken into account. Perhaps her methods may not approve themselves to the charity worker, nevertheless they are her own. It seems to be assumed that one who applies for relief is absolutely worthless and capable of standing only when one holds him up. I myself, in many years of work in charity, have never met that type. Persons of that description ought to be in an institution.[2]

Another burning question discussed by the Committee on Families was that of the keeping of case records in relief work. Such records are defined as "repositories of information concerning the social relations of individuals." In more concrete terms, they are records of all the facts concerning a dependent which may possibly have a bearing on the condition of dependency. An advocate of record keeping enumerated some of the particulars which ought to be recorded:

> Why is the family in a state of destitution? How long has it been so? Are the causes within the family, or external to it? Do the conditions arise from sickness, loss of work, drunkenness? What is

[2] *Ibid.*, p. 167.

the source of the information obtained? If from the family itself has it been checked by independent testimony? What public agencies can or should be invoked to remedy some of the conditions discovered? Is the family a chronic or an "acute" case? Have other organizations been engaged upon it? What private aid, outside the organization itself, can be enlisted? These and many other questions of detail should be investigated and answered, before a record is made, if the organization is to accomplish any really efficient work.[3]

The value of records is urged from the standpoint of the individual relieved and from the standpoint of the community. The record preserves the results of investigations. The purposes of records are stated as follows:

1. To preserve for reference in the records of the organization a memorial of the facts ascertained and the relief given.
2. To economize the labor of subsequent investigators in dealing with the same family.
3. To serve as the basis of an annual or other periodic report to the supporters of the organization, thereby promoting further interest in the work.
4. To furnish confidential information to other charitable organizations dealing with the same family in return for similar favors.
5. To furnish data for a study of the causes of dependency, with a view to their amendment or removal.[4]

The advocates of "records" were in the majority among the speakers at the Conference. The word is put in inverted commas because records of some kind are kept by the most old-fashioned charitable societies, including all conferences of the St. Vincent de Paul Society. But the details recorded in the minute books of St. Vincent de Paul conferences are not rec-

[3] *Ibid.*, p. 133.

[4] *Ibid.*

ords in the sense that scientific philanthropy uses the term. Records mean the ascertainment and preservation of all kinds of facts about the economic, social, educational, moral, mental and medical history of a family. The St. Vincent de Paul Society has never tried to obtain or to keep such records. The arguments in favor of records are implied in the statement given above of the purposes of records. Records are objected to by opponents because they are often unreliable, because their compilation means the diversion of a large proportion of charitable funds from the direct relief of the poor to clerical and investigation expenses, and because, it is said, they violate the confidential relation that should exist between the giver and the receiver of charitable relief.

It is not the business of the present article to discuss the value of these various arguments, but only to show the questions at issue relating to the administration of such ordinary charitable works as are undertaken in nearly every parish of the country by the St. Vincent de Paul Society. There is one very important point that is worth particular notice. The adoption of the two policies under consideration, the budget plan and record keeping, would both require charitable workers with far greater skill and knowledge, and with much more time at their disposal, than the great majority of Vincentians possess. In other words, these policies would require a great extension of the employment of trained salaried workers in Catholic charitable work. This is another question that causes controversy, for it is urged by some that the tendency of the salaried worker is to push out the voluntary worker from the field of active charity.

There are two schools of opinion, which have been called the "conservative" and the "progressive" among Catholic charity students and workers. The differences betweeen them are not sharply defined, but they are clearly discernible. The progressives are disposed to favor many of the methods of organization and administration that distinguish modern secular philanthropy, as the budget plan for dependent families, the keeping of case-records, the use of the confidential exchange, the employment of salaried workers, and close cooperation with non-Catholic agencies. It was the present writer's personal impression, when attending the Conference last September, that the members of the women's societies present showed themselves distinctly progressive, whilst the men, or at least the laymen, nearly all of whom are Vincentians, were for the most part conservative.

If I may mention another personal impression, it is that the progressives had the advantage in the discussions of being more articulate. They had perhaps less experience in practical work, but they were more acquainted with the literature of relief, they were more accustomed to regarding methods of charity as subjects for argument, and they were more skillful in dialectical statement. The assertions of the progressives were often a distinct challenge to the conservatives, but the challenge was not taken up on the Conference floor. Yet the conservatives were not convinced; they stick to the old ways. I do not by any means believe that this is altogether due to mere prejudice or to the human tendency to stay in a rut. It is, I think, due to a feeling that the new methods are not in keeping with the spirit of Catholic charity. The feeling may be all wrong, or partly wrong, or it may be quite right.

It is important to have the question thrashed out. The National Conference of Catholic Charities is helping us to get the question thrashed out. Without the National Conference we might despair of ever having the question settled, or even intelligently discussed. The conservatives whose views have been formed by experience rather than by theoretical study, will not be able to make themselves vocal and give their proper contribution to the discussion until they take more interest in what may be called the theory of charity administration, in the study and comparison of methods, and in the observation and recording of results. We are all acquainted with persons who are very proficient in the art of a thing without being interested in the science of it. Many an excellent writer cannot tell others the rules of good style. Many an efficient teacher would be a poor informant on pedagogy. The questions at issue in regard to the practice of charity cannot be determined by merely abstract reasoning; there will be no satisfactory verdict on the value of a method except the verdict of experience. What is necessary is that the practical Catholic workers in charity (especially Vincentians, because of their great importance and great opportunities), should be aware of the questions at issue; they should study the new methods in the light of their experience, and they might even test them by experiment. These questions of method in relief work are of vital importance.

Experienced members of the St. Vincent de Paul Society could throw a flood of light on these questions if they would study them as questions of science as well as of practice. Vincentians who have this mental attitude to charity questions will not only increase their practical efficiency, but they will have a power of expressing their judgments on doubtful questions which will be of the most valuable service to the Church and to the cause of charity. Not the least of the splendid accomplishments of the National Conference of Catholic Charities will be just this formation of a mental attitude in charity workers, the cultivation of an intellectual interest in the theory of charity, that will help us in the making of a Catholic science of charity applicable to the conditions of a country like America in the twentieth century.

The treatment of dependent families was only one of the many questions discussed at the Conference, but I have taken it as an illustration because it is a branch of charitable work that has to be done in practically every parish, and which is largely in the hands of the laity. Another of the most elementary and best known forms of charity is the care of dependent children in institutions, usually called orphanages. Recent events have made the general public aware that children's institutions form the subject of heated controversy amongst those who are actively interested in the administration of charity.

The dispute is not as to whether certain institutions are well-conducted or ill-conducted, but whether such institutions should be allowed to exist at all. Some prominent leaders of the new scientific philanthropy say that orphanages should be abolished, and that so far as dependent children of normal mentality and physique are concerned, institutions should be used for their temporary shelter only, until such children can be placed in foster homes or returned to their natural homes. A strenuous campaign is being conducted to educate the public as to the superiority of foster homes over institutional care.

Now there is no doubt that orphanages, like almsgiving, represent a form of charity liable to ready abuse. The trouble about many orphanages is that though they are crowded with children they contain few orphans. The majority of the children have one parent or both parents living, and many of these parents are able, or could be made able, to take care of their own children. This would be good for the children and, still more emphatically, it would be good for the parents. The easy admission of children to institutions contributes to the disorganization of the family which is, I venture to say, the gravest social evil of the present time.

The institutional care of children is a department of charity in which Catholics are simply forced to take account of the modern theories and standards with which scientific philanthropy is familiarizing the public mind. Our institutions in many cases are financially supported out of public funds and the public authority can and does impose conditions on the institutions receiving such funds. The Committee on Children at the National Conference of Catholic Charities naturally gave a good deal of attention to the questions relating to the policy of Catholic institutions in receiving and discharging children, and also with regard to the placing of children in foster homes. The papers and discussions on this subject were eminently realistic. There was a general recognition of the fact that it is useless to adopt an absolute attitude either of pro-institutionalism or anti-institutionalism. Both institutions and foster homes are needed. Much of the talk against institutions is based on theorizing and not on experience. To prove that the family home in the abstract is better than the institution in the abstract, does not help us with the concrete question as to whether the actual foster-homes available are better places than are our institutions for the actual children that we have to care for. The most ardent friends of institutions will admit that we can make use of all the satisfactory foster homes that may be found. Defence of the institution does not mean hostility to the foster home, but it means that if we make comparisons, we must compare the concrete institution with the concrete foster home, and not waste time debating about abstractions.

It would be well if the National Conference of Catholic Charities were to encourage such research as would enable us to show the actual accomplishments of institutions, as to what happens in afterlife to the children discharged. There should be research also into the actual accomplishments of foster homes taken as a whole. It is not sufficient to give the results only of those foster homes that have proved satisfactory. Catholic charitable agencies of all kinds are subject to constant and searching criticism from investigators making all sorts of surveys, and surveys are generally undertaken to prove that established ways of doing things are wrong, and that new ways are the best ways. It would be worth while to have many of these investigations investigated, and to use the same statistical methods of testing the new philanthropic agencies as are employed in criticism of the old.

It is very noteworthy that the question of "delinquency" was considered big enough to deserve the attention of a general meeting of the Conference instead of being dealt with by a section committee. The increase of juvenile delinquency during recent years in North America constitutes not only a difficult social problem, but a most disquieting social symptom. A general scrapping of old methods of dealing with delinquents has not prevented a steady deterioration in conditions. There are now juvenile courts and staffs of probation officers in nearly every city, but juvenile lawlessness increases. What is the cause and what the remedy? In much of the discussions at the Conference there was a note almost of desperation in speaking of this subject. A multitude of measures was suggested as likely to be helpful in limiting delinquency, but there was no robust confidence in any of them. "Church and State and community must in one way or another divide responsibility for delinquency," said one speaker. More truant officers, more playgrounds, more social centres, more sodalities, more Sunday-schools, more religious education, more vocational guidance, more "big brothers" were all asked for. It made me think of a remark I once heard from an Archbishop: "In the United States," he said, "the Family has been given up. It is lost sight of. The social workers and writers do not take it into account." Surely in the question of juvenile delinquency the Family is an institution of some consideration, not less than Church and State and community. It may be predicted that at no distant time social and charity workers will be brought back to the ancient view of the Family, of its natural functions and its natural liberties. When that times comes many of the policies most in favor at the present day will be cast aside as profoundly anti-social, and every measure will be judged according to its effect on the weakening or strengthening of family ties. The doctrine of the Family will be one of the corner-stones of that modern sociology that we hope to see builded, and for which the National Conference of Catholic Charities is collecting invaluable materials.

22 The Sisters' Conference

A PROGRAM FOR CATHOLIC CHILDCARING HOMES

Not unlike the Society of St. Vincent de Paul in relief work, the Catholic sisterhoods until World War I cultivated their vast field of institutional charity along traditional lines. After the war, however, they brought to the social scene their own version of scientific charity. Their special contribution was the small group system in child care. The small group system attempted to utilize the advantages of existing types of child care: the small cost of the old-fashioned orphanage (the "congregate" plan), the personal emphasis of the cottage plan where a sister or two lived in a separate building with not more than forty children, and the domestic atmosphere of the foster home. In the small group system the large building (or buildings) of the orphanage was divided into apartments to which were assigned a small number of boys and girls under the supervision of a Group Mother, the whole "population" of the orphanage coming together for school, chapel, and special educational purposes.

The small group system derived its first great impetus from a report in 1923 to the National Conference of Catholic Charities. The report showed not only how small groups should be set up and managed, but also the ways in which they could make a major contribution to family rehabilitation. As the small groups multiplied, many of them participated actively in family case work through their own trained workers and in cooperation with Catholic and community agencies.

FOREWORD

Ideals

Emulating the kind example of the Son of God, the Catholic Church has in every age and every clime engaged in works of charity for the children of the poor. She has inspired her most devoted members to leave the world and its treasures and consecrate their lives to the care of the motherless and the fatherless. For centuries her religious have sheltered and reared abandoned, destitute, neglected and delinquent children. Her chief aim has been to prepare their souls for eternal life, but at the same time she has made every effort to develop their minds and their bodies so as to make possible a useful, happy life in this world.

God has endowed every child with varying talents. Each child should be given the opportunity to develop his talents fully. The supernatural motive underlying Catholic charity demands that in the care of her children the Church not only keep up with advancing standards of health, education, recreation, and social life, but be in the vanguard with all genuine improvements. Accordingly, at this time when the Nation is everywhere extending its activities in the field of child welfare, it is but right that we who are doing the work of Christ in Catholic Child-caring Homes should review the manner in which we are caring for His children, and set before ourselves a practical form of modern child care.

A Work Worthy of Our Best

The care of needy children is the noblest work undertaken by our religious orders. In no other field are we called on to

---

Committee on Standards, Sisters' Conference, National Conference of Catholic Charities, *A Program for Catholic Childcaring Homes.* (Washington, D. C.; 1923), pp. 5–10, 14, 18, 20–22.

assume the duties of Christ so completely. Our children need more than teachers and nurses: they look to us for everything in life. Truly may it be said that they are what we make them. With the saving of souls is bound up the training of minds, the development of character and the building of bodies. These children, who are peculiarly Christ's and "our own," deserve our care more than the children of the rich or of the middle class. No true mother will deny to her own children the best she possesses, nor will the superior who truly appreciates the work fail to assign to her child-caring homes the ablest members of her community.

Preservation of Family Life

Yet our Homes are only substitutes for the medium of care instituted by God—a child's own family. They are established to care for little ones whose families have been broken by death, disease, sin, or misfortune. No one can dispute that the best guardians and moulders of a child's life are its own parents, when faithful in their duties. They possess the four great essentials for proper child-care, namely, an intimate knowledge of each child, a deep affection, a flexibility of treatment providing for each child according to its own special wants, and the ability to give a practical, concrete training in religious, moral and economic principles. We should, therefore, make every effort to keep children in their own homes, when these are normal and happy or when they can be made so by financial assistance or efficient, family welfare work.

Each Child an Individual

Every mother knows that children differ from one another in disposition, character, habits, desires and ability. To treat all alike would be a mistake resulting in discontent, lack of ambition and often in utter failure. Individuality must be encouraged and routine adjusted so as to make place for it.

Though uniform procedure is laid down in the various sections of the following program, it must always be borne in mind that the child-caring home does not exist for itself but for the children.[1]

PROCESS OF ADMISSION

Application

If we are to maintain family life, children should be admitted to our Homes only after it has been clearly proven that they cannot be properly cared for in their own homes. Therefore, before accepting a child, every child-caring home should require a thorough study of family conditions.

Investigation

The investigation should be undertaken with a view to finding out what is necessary to build up the family life. Where conditions can be improved by the rendering of material assistance, employment or medical service, these should be supplied. It may, however, become evident that the best interests of the child require separation from his home, at least temporarily. Then the full facts should be gathered as to the history and conditions of the parents and relatives, and the school, health and religious record of the child.

Agreement

The arrangements for the admission of the child should include a signed agreement by which the relatives who are able promise to pay a just share of the cost of support—the family budget to be made the basis of payment—and to permit both an investigation of their home conditions prior to the discharge

[1] Proceedings of Special Conference of Religious—1920; p. 24.

of the child and the maintenance of supervision after its discharge. The records made at the time of admission should be very carefully kept, because the Home will depend upon them to determine the type of care needed by the child and to keep in touch with the family.

Records

The practice of having a separate folder to hold the records and documents pertaining to each child has been found most advantageous.

A complete set of records is being prepared, as stated in the letter of transmittal, and can be secured on application at the National Conference of Catholic Charities, Washington, D. C.[2]

In some States the law requires that in addition to the above records a record book be kept, containing the following facts: the name of the child, sex, color, place and date of birth, place and date of baptism, and last residence; the following facts concerning the father and mother: residence, if living, birthplace, religion and occupation; the reason for nonsupport by the father, if living; the reason for nonsupport by the mother, if living, and such other information as may explain the dependency of the child. Such book is conveniently indexed and the records so arranged, either by means of a card index or otherwise, that an accurate roll call of the children present at any time can readily be made from them. The record book is desirable, because it gives the chronological order of admissions and has a character of permanency not insured by other record cards or sheets.

In cases where children are accepted from the Poor Law officers or a court, the information necessary for the social, school, religious and physical history of the child should be requested from the committing officer.

[2] See also Proceedings of the Special Conference of Religious—1920; p. 14.

The proper records require health records, dental records and school records, besides the social records mentioned.

Physical Examination

On admission the child should be given a complete physical examination by the house physician and the results noted on a standard record form. Special attention should be paid to eyes, ears, nose and throat, dental and orthopedic defects. The services of specialists should, if possible, be secured for this work. Any defects discovered should be followed up and corrected, before discharge from quarantine, if at all possible. The tests for venereal disease should not be omitted, and if there is a suspicion of mental defect or abnormality, a mental test should be given where possible.

Quarantine

To avoid the spread of contagious diseases, a special period of quarantine should be observed from the time the child is admitted until the attending physician is satisfied that there is no danger of contagion. This period is generally two weeks, and during this time the child eats, sleeps, plays and is cared for in separate quarters. During quarantine a study of the child should be made to determine his proper school grade. Plans should be laid to overcome retardation and to provide the child with vocational work adapted to his intelligence. The previous school record is essential for grading and should be secured in every case. Much can be done during the period of quarantine to remedy previous neglect of religious training by teaching the child the catechism, prayers and his duties toward God.

If a spirit of tender affection permeates the quarantine quarters, the little ones, so recently taken from their family, will realize that they have come among devoted friends and have found anew a mother's care.

METHODS OF CARE, ORGANIZATION AND EQUIPMENT

Inasmuch as these subjects are cognate, it was considered desirable to treat them in one chapter.

There are three systems of care: the *Cottage System,* the *Congregate System,* and the *Small Group System.* For some time it was thought that in order to avoid mass treatment it was necessary to adopt the *Cottage System,* with twenty-five or thirty children in each house and each house a separate unit. Many orphanages, however, found it impossible to adopt this system because they could not afford to discard their present buildings and erect new ones.

Group System

Progressive superintendents feel that the family spirit must be carried into the procedure and administration of child-caring homes. The molding of a child's character demands intimate personal contact between each child and those who take the place of his parents. Such contact can hardly be present where children are handled in large masses as under the old Congregate System. With the passage of years there has come into existence a third type of care known as the "*Group System.*" It is adaptable to buildings built on the congregate plan. Its aim is to bring to the children those advantages that are to be had only when they are cared for and educated in small groups. Experience has shown that almost every child-caring home can adopt this method of caring for its children without assuming an intolerable burden. Very often a rearrangement of rooms with a slight decrease in the population and a few extensions is sufficient to provide the facilities needed.[3]

[3] Proceedings of Special Conference of Religious—1921; p. 7.

The Group Mother

Let us visualize one of our Catholic homes conducted under the Group System. The children are divided into groups of about thirty. A Sister or Group Mother is placed in charge to act as mother and confidant to all the boys or girls of her group. She is responsible for their conduct and behavior at all times except when they are in school. She learns each child's strong and weak points and is able to award praise or blame. Her little family forms a separate unit with its own living room, dining room, bedroom, and bathing and lavatory facilities. She encourages the children to keep in touch with their relatives and friends and allows the relatives to visit frequently under direction from the office or the Sister Superior, if there be no central reception room. She sees that an accurate record is kept of the names and addresses of all visitors. . . .

It cannot be doubted that the family spirit engendered in a Home conducted under the Group System, as we have described it, will be a potent influence in the lives of its children. Prudence dictates that those desiring to adapt a congregate home to the Group System ought to do so gradually. First, the children may be divided into groups, based either on their class in school or on the policy of keeping children of the same family together and mixing older with younger children. Then a few living-rooms may be set apart, and later separate dining rooms and bedrooms, until the system is completely installed. . . .

Discipline

While order and system are necessary in the administration of a home they should never be permitted to become a fetish. Children are naturally spontaneous and vivacious. Restrictions appropriate to adults may well result in undue repression.[4]

[4] Proceedings of Special Conference of Religious—1920; p. 32.

Marching in lines, silence at meals and too great confinement to household tasks tend to fetter the freedom of childhood. Well-directed and active play during the periods of recreation will help to work off those excess energies which give rise to restiveness.

Athletic contests help greatly to develop cooperation, intense striving, a willingness to sacrifice self for the general welfare, and a spirit of fair play. Masculine leadership seems necessary for the proper development of boys over 12 years of age. If these older boys are grouped together, a male group leader should be in charge of them for their recreation and physical and vocational training.

Positive building up of character depends far more on providing the proper incentives than on the infliction of punishment. More and more the feeling is becoming prevalent that corporal punishment, privation of food, prolonged isolation, and humiliating penalties are more hurtful than corrective. If corporal punishment is necessary it should be administered by the Superior or Superintendent and a record kept as a protection for the child and the Home. Where penalties are required the resourceful Group Mother will secure obedience and good conduct by the imposition of minor tasks and the privation of minor privileges such as participation in games, attendance at moving pictures or other entertainments, trips to places of interest, and—when a merit system is in use—by a loss of credits.

Ability to control their own lives and the lives of others may be developed by a thoughtful distribution of responsibility. Among the older children the groups may well be divided into smaller units of eight or ten, with lieutenants in charge of each unit and all reporting to an elected group leader. Specific household tasks, supervision over younger children in play, in manners and at prayers may be considered as rewards for good conduct and used to strengthen directive ability.

Group rivalry may be used to inculcate habits of cleanliness, study and order. A banner given to the most proficient group will inspire its members to extra care. Pressure thus brought to bear by the members themselves on other members of the group will have greater effect than if it came from the Group Mother. . . .

DISCHARGE, PLACEMENT AND AFTER-CARE

Reinvestigation

Periodical reinvestigation of the family will prevent the permanent severing of the tie between parents and child, and will help to make the parents realize that they have not been freed entirely from their responsibility. Where children are admitted in order to tide over some emergency, the family should be closely watched and an effort made to help it rehabilitate itself so that the child may return home as soon as possible.

Free Home Placement

As soon as a child is permanently committed to an institution by court procedure or voluntary surrender, its name should be entered upon the list of placeable children, in a special book or record. Periodically the superintendent should go over the records of the other children to find those eligible for placing out. By "placing out" we mean the placing of a child in a family not related to it within the second degree, for the purpose of providing a home for such a child. An institution should not undertake to place a child in a home unless definitely authorized to do so through voluntary surrender of the child by the parents or under the existing laws of the State or judicial procedure. The placing out of a child is a serious task requiring painstaking and conscientious work. It is essential in selecting the child that definite information be secured as to its family history, its baptism, and its physical and mental condition.

Nor should a foster home be approved until after a thorough investigation and visitation of the applicants and their homes. Investigation should be made by a trained social investigator. Afterwards, duty demands that we follow up the placement with supervision of the child and the home until such time as the child no longer needs supervision. Ordinarily, supervision should not cease until the boy or girl has reached the age of twenty or is adopted. Except for special reasons, consent to legal adoption should not be given until the child has been in the foster home not less than one year, and longer if it is the practice in your community or under the direction of the State law, and only after careful supervision has shown that the placement is satisfactory.

The records of investigation and supervision should be completed and kept in such a way as to make it possible to secure promptly full information concerning all children placed and the foster-parents with whom they have been placed.

In their placement work, child-caring homes should adhere strictly to the standards described in Mr. Edmond J. Butler's article: "Standards of Child Placing and Supervision," which is given as Appendix B of the present work.

After-Care

Children should not be discharged from Homes, where they have been watched over and carefully trained, until the family conditions into which they are to enter have been thoroughly investigated and found fit for them. Every child-caring home owes it to the children to see that their future is not blighted by indiscriminate discharges. Where family conditions have been such as to warrant the separation of childern from their family, they should not be returned until it is morally certain that they will be well cared for.

An even greater duty is owed to those children who have no relatives to go to. A boy or girl of 15 or 16 should not be turned loose to people who come to the door of the Home asking for a child. Very often such applicants have little regard for the child's future and are thinking only of the service they can exact. Their fitness ought first to be ascertained by thorough investigation of their home and of their references.

Nor does the task end on the day of discharge. Every conscientious superintendent should see to it that supervision and visitation of discharged children, even when discharged to their parents, is kept up for a period of from 2 to 3 years, or until the child is well-established in its new home. Only too often have boys and girls been released to uncles and aunts who tired of them within a few months and then sent them adrift to fall into the dangers which beset the way of the unguarded. The lack of proper after-care in years gone by was responsible for most of the sad occurrences which have helped to give a false impression of the value of institutional care.

23 Monsignor Robert F. Keegan

DIOCESAN ORGANIZATION IN CHARITY

As Catholic charities multiplied and became increasingly scientific in purpose and method, they realized that their respective efforts required coordination and a degree of over-all supervision on the local level. In response to this need, about thirty diocesan bureaus of Catholic charity were formed in the more highly urbanized centers during the 1920's. In describing these agencies at the convention of the National Conference of Catholic Charities in 1932, Monsignor Robert F. Keegan, New

York Secretary of Charities, pointed out that they performed a coordinating function not only among Catholic charities but also between these and non-Catholic community agencies, public and private. Success in such difficult work was contingent on professionally trained directors and personnel in the diocesan bureaus. Keegan also insisted that Catholic charity organization deal with health, housing, minimum wages, social insurance, and social legislation in general, that is, with the preventive as well as the more obvious remedial aspects of charity. This was counsel easily accepted in the depths of the Great Depression.

The development of Catholic organization to meet present day needs is not new. It is a continuous task, one which the Church has undertaken in century after century, and in country after country. In America today, she faces a unique challenge. Any attempt to forecast how she will meet that challenge must call to mind her guiding principles, view her history, study recent trends, and then set all this against a background of the industrial and social conditions now existing in this country.

Charity is individual. Charity is organic. The Church emphasizes the personal obligation contained in the divine words, "By this shall all men know that you are My disciples if you have love one for another."[1] But, in addition she has always

---

Robert F. Keegan, "Developing Catholic Organization to Meet Present Day Needs." An address delivered at the National Conference of Catholic Charities in Omaha, September 1932, by The New York Secretary for Charities. Reprinted with permission from *Catholic Mind,* The Monthly Review of Christian Thought and Documentation, 106 W. 56th St., New York, N. Y. 10019.

[1] John xiii, 35.

recognized the organic nature of charity as part of her corporate life. As the mystical body of Christ, she has been conscious "that if one member suffer anything all the members suffer with it."[2] Constantly she urges her children to "be of one mind, having the same charity."[3] This unity of thought she would have flower into unanimity of action "with all humility and mildness, with patience supporting one another in charity."[4]

ORGANIZED CHARITY IN THE CHURCH

Here in the new world the Church has been true to her traditions. It is indeed a far cry from the little orphanage established by the Ursulines in New Orleans in 1727, to the 607 Catholic children's homes and agencies which today care for thousands of her children. Glancing at the meager beginning of the Mullanphy Hospital established by the Sisters of Charity in St. Louis in 1828, who could have prophesied that today there would be more than 560 Catholic hospitals in the United States? Little did the founders of the first St. Vincent de Paul Conference in St. Louis in 1845 think that today their society in this country would number 20,000 members and would expend three and one-half million dollars in a single year.

Truly has the Church in America responded to the command of Christ, "So let your light shine before men that they may see your good works and glorify your Father Who is in heaven."[5] The true spirit of charity is restless. It cannot, in the nature of things, be complacent. If the Charity of Christ presseth us, then it must engender within us what Dr. Kerby has aptly called, "the Passion for Perfection."

[2] 1 Cor. vii, 26.
[3] Phil. 2.
[4] Ephes. 2.
[5] Matt. v, 6.

Today we look out upon a world disrupted, disordered, and disillusioned, upon multitudes with savings gone, menaced by the specter of hunger, cold and sickness. Today, as in Galilee, the heart of Christ has "compassion on the multitudes."[6] Once again Christ calls on the members of His mystical body to support one another. Can we allow that call to go unheeded?

THE POPE'S LEADERSHIP

God in His Providence has given us a Pope to whom the whole world turns for inspiration and leadership. His stirring Encyclical "Quadragesimo Anno" has moved the hearts of men as have few documents in history. He searched and found the hidden causes of the present conditions. He saw clearly the need for reconstructing the entire social order. He has boldly enunciated the principles on which such reconstruction must be founded. He calls upon mankind to establish a juridical and social order based on social justice, having for its soul, social charity. Justice and charity, says the Holy Father, working hand in hand, must sternly and uncompromisingly control the headstrong and vehement power of economic supremacy which has wrecked the peace and happiness of the world.[7]

Directed by the words of His Holiness, we assert that Catholic charitable organization must have a two-fold objective. First, intelligent and adequate care for those in distress, directed toward restoring self-support wherever possible. Second, positive, definite and concerted action to eliminate the causes of unemployment, sickness, accidents, family dependency and the host of other challenges which we meet in our daily work. These two objectives may be viewed as the remedial and preventive aspects of Catholic organization. We take them up in order.

[6] Matt. xv, 32.
[7] *Quadragesimo Anno*—Barry Vail Edition—page 37.

REMEDIAL ASPECT

The remedial work of the Church in this country until recently has been largely the responsibility of the parish, of religious communities, and of individual groups of the laity. In the last two decades there has been a growing recognition of the need for planning a further development of Catholic charitable work upon a diocesan basis. In diocese after diocese, our Bishops have appointed Diocesan Directors of Charity and have delegated to them varying degrees of authority over the charities of their territory.

1. Diocesan Plan

The orderly development of our charitable work requires continued extension of this diocesan responsibility. Such an extension includes leadership by the Bishop in meeting the charitable needs of his diocese and the integration of the various institutions and agencies already existing. Moreover, diocesan responsibility implies the guiding of future development and extensions according to a well considered plan. I do not for a moment contend that one form of organization for Catholic Charities will fit every diocese. Local conditions, the presence of other private and public agencies, state legislation, and varying Catholic traditions and resources make it essential that each diocesan plan be adjusted to the actual situation within the diocese. Before any plan is determined upon, however, the entire situation should be carefully considered by those equipped with training and experience, the needs and resources carefully charted, objectives agreed upon, and practical steps for their attainment set forth.

It will be found that some functions, particularly those in the relief of families, may be wisely delegated in whole or in part to the parish and its auxiliaries. Other functions such as those concerned with the care of children, the sick and the aged, transcend parish bounds and extend either to a section or to the whole diocese. Negotiations with city and state authorities and with Community Chests or private organizations, must be conducted by Catholic representatives in the name of the Bishop and must reflect his mind. The coordination and the fostering of these parochial, district and diocesan-wide programs constitute the main work of the central diocesan charities.

In developing and executing a diocesan plan, it is essential that the central diocesan charities be considered as an extension of the diocesan secretariate. The appointment of independent local Catholic representatives in various sections of the diocese to cooperate with neighboring organizations may sometimes work successfully but it may also militate against diocesan unity, and can hardly serve to maintain close contact with the Bishop, from whom authority in the diocese proceeds.

2. *Personnel*

It seems hardly necessary to say that a Diocesan Director of Charities needs professional training. The Bishop is accustomed to consult with canonists and theologians, with financiers and architects. He is convinced of the necessity for a trained diocesan school superintendent. In the same manner he needs someone who is trained in the administration of social work, who is acquainted with the complexity of laws relating to social welfare, and who is in touch with the civic agencies dealing with these problems.

The successful development of Catholic charities also requires careful preparation and training of the workers in the field. Consciousness of the need for professional standing has been growing among social workers. The movement toward state registration is advancing. Social workers are seeking recognition somewhat similar to that afforded to nurses, doctors and lawyers. The further this movement is carried forward, the more necessary it becomes that Catholic workers be properly trained. Unless the Church keeps in step with it, the separation between charity and social work will grow greater and our Catholic agencies will be hindered in their participation in public or semi-public funds, in tax support, and in the Community Chests of the country.

The demand for trained service dictates that our religious communities, which operate so many Catholic works should place new emphasis in their novitiates on training in modern standards and methods of charitable work. If our Catholic women's colleges were to insert in their curriculum, preparatory courses for social work, they would stimulate many recruits for the field. Our Catholic schools of social work are few. We need more. Those we have can render a great service to the Church, if they will only keep their standards high. Catholic charitable work needs leaders. We have many privates now. We need above all, a few who will qualify as staff officers.

In the increasingly important field of public social work, the number of outstanding Catholics is small. Catholic philosophy and Catholic thinking should have greater influence in such public social work. In both public and private agencies, there is need for Catholic leadership. To get leaders, we must have training centers which will properly qualify them. Every Catholic Charities' office should meet the minimum requirements as a training center for field work.

Father LeBuffe, the distinguished Jesuit editor and writer, says: "Social service is reasoned and reasonable charity. That it may be cold and may be inhumanly scientific is admitted. But so may medicine, and so may be the law. That it is frequently unbaptized is also readily granted, but that it is unbaptizable, that it cannot be vivified and ennobled by the sweet flavor of God-inspired love is a distinctly mistaken contention."

So training is required of those who would do the work of the Lord well in the field of charity. For, as Father LeBuffe well puts it "Charity must be reasoned, based on facts, and worked out in terms of all that has been discovered for the relief of human woes."

Let us not wait until there is a frontal attack on the Church, or close our eyes to the daily sniper. Let us hope that the day of meekly following, of having standards of care forced upon us, are over.

Bishop Turner has well said that "science has its place in religious charitable work and no one deplores it, no one would have it otherwise. We realize that science can be made the handmaid and need not be the mistress in the spirit of charitable work."[8]

3. *Cooperation*

The development of Catholic charities according to a diocesan plan and with a proper personnel requires the wholehearted cooperation of all groups within the diocese. Without common understanding there can be no unanimity of thought or unity in action.

Nowhere is cooperation more necessary or effective than in the financing of our Catholic charitable works—an ever present problem. Where this task is left entirely to the ingenuity of many separate little groups, the difficulty is multiplied. Some sort of universal appeal to every Catholic within the diocese seems essential. If unanimity of thought and action are to be preserved, all the people within the diocese should feel that they are sharing in the Church's work of charity. While the parochial spirit has accomplished great things for the Church, we all know that it has its limitations. At least once during the year, Catholics should be reminded that they have a diocesan charitable responsibility. Diocesan fund raising, properly conducted, results in a growth of diocesan spirit, in a closer drawing together of clergy, Religious, and laity, and in a better understanding of the needs of our people and the vast activities of the Church in the field of charity.

The development of Catholic organization in the remedial

[8] Social Mission of Charity.

field therefore requires the active leadership of the Bishop exerted through a central diocesan office in close touch with all the charities of the diocese. This development calls for a personnel, trained, alert, and loyal to the teaching and traditions of the Church; it demands cooperation among Catholic groups and with all fair-minded non-Catholic groups. It requires the intelligent participation of all the clergy and all the laity. Such development should be positive, not casual; orderly, not haphazard; uniform, not disjointed. So much for the remedial. What about the preventive aspect of the work?

PREVENTIVE ASPECT

It is axiomatic that our efforts should extend beyond remedial functions. Here as elsewhere, "an ounce of prevention is worth a pound of cure." Many of the difficulties of the poor are due to social, agrarian, and industrial conditions which they cannot control. Wherever possible our leaders should strike at the roots of poverty and distress. The securing of social justice through strong local and national policies of social action is an important objective for Catholic organization.

SOCIAL LEGISLATION

Social legislation is not a panacea for all ills. But when it is wisely drawn and efficiently administered it can do much to further the ends of justice. In the words of His Holiness Pope Leo XIII: "The more that is done for the working population by the general laws of the country, the less need will there be to seek for particular means to relieve them."[9]

The state "is not founded for the purpose of men's merely

[9] *The Condition of Labor,* Paulist Press, page 18.

living together, but for their living as men ought to live."[10] No arguments are needed at a National Conference of Catholic Charities to justify the legislation which has taken so many children out of industry, and which has set up humane children's courts and public departments to deal with their problems in an understanding manner. We all know where Mothers' Aid Laws are properly administered, the great good which accrues to thousands of widows and children. We realize the tremendous amount of distress avoided yearly by the hundred and fifty million dollars distributed under Workmen's Compensation Laws.

Who then should be more interested than we in the promotion of public health and of proper housing? These measures will reduce the costs of relief and of correction. Sickness is at the root of much of our poverty. Congested slum conditions contribute largely to delinquency. If we strike at the roots of these problems we will not only promote the welfare of our fellow citizens, but in the long run save the community greater expense.

In these days of rapidly falling wage scales, we cannot overlook the plea of His Holiness Pope Pius XI, that all fathers of families receive a wage sufficient to meet adequately ordinary domestic needs. The Pope's words are strong, "Intolerable," he says, "and to be opposed with all our strength, is the abuse whereby mothers of families, because of the insufficiency of the father's salary are forced to engage in gainful occupations outside domestic walls to the neglect of their own proper cares and duties, particularly the education of their children."[11] The Church through her Bishops has declared in favor of legislation to effect a decent minimum wage scale as follows: "The several states should enact laws providing for the establishment of wage rates that will be at least sufficient for the decent

[10] Aristotle, *Politics,* Book 3, Chapter 9.

[11] *Quadragesimo Anno,* page 30.

maintenance of a family, in the case of all male adults, and adequate for the decent individual support of female workers."[12] I quote from the program for social reconstruction.

Neither is there any mincing of words in the statement of the Bishops' program on the important question of social insurance: "The state should make comprehensive provision for insurance against illness, invalidity, unemployment, and old age."[13] To date seventeen of our states have written into their statute books an old age security act. On the other hand, only one state, Wisconsin, has demanded that industry should supply compulsory unemployment insurance.

PROCEDURE OUTLINED

If Catholic organization is to be effective in the field of prevention we must see clearly and teach unremittingly the obligations of the community by reason of these principles of social justice. Our Holy Father has set forth two fundamental steps which must be taken:

1. Preparation of our priests to take an active part in social reform. His words are clear: "No easy task is here imposed upon the clergy, wherefore all candidates for the sacred priesthood must be adequately prepared to meet it by intense study of social matters."[14]

2. Preparing our Catholic laity to apply the principles of Catholic teaching. In this connection His Holiness says: "In order to bring back to Christ these whole classes of men who have denied Him, we must gather and train lay apostles, amongst working men and amongst employers."[15]

Some promising steps have already been taken. The holding

[12] Bishops' Program of Reconstruction.

[13] *Ibid.*

[14] *Quadragesimo Anno,* page 58.

[15] *Ibid.,* p. 58.

of regional meetings of the Catholic Conference on Industrial Affairs in various parts of the country should serve to arouse the interest of our people. The College Department of the National Catholic Educational Association has recently sent to 163 Catholic colleges and universities a "Syllabus on Social Problems in the Light of Christian Principles," which carries with it a resolution adopted at its meeting in Cincinnati last June to the effect that "colleges be urged to encourage those students who have not had a course in social problems, to take such a course if possible during the coming school year."[16] It further recommends that such a course be made a requisite for a bachelor's degree.

The diocesan director of charities should keep closely in touch with the social legislation which is being proposed in his state and community. In many dioceses he can recruit and guide the efforts of forceful members of the laity who will be interested in this work. Here again it will be necessary to co-operate with groups which are outside the Church. As citizens our obligation is to the entire social body. Our striving for social justice must be integrated with similar efforts on the part of our fellow citizens who are of a different faith. Prudence dictates that there are limits to such cooperation, but good-will and devotion to a common cause demand that we work hand in hand with all who are sincerely striving for sound measures of social, agrarian, and industrial reform.

OUTLOOK FOR THE FUTURE

What of the outlook for the future? There are those in this country who believe the amelioration of present evils can be accomplished only by revolution. This method is contrary to our American way of doing things. Our faith counsels sane, orderly processes of reconstruction. Yet we must face the facts.

[16] *The Catholic News,* August 20, 1932.

So far we have had in this greatest of depressions, an acceptance of conditions by men who have lost their jobs through the operation of policies that were to abolish poverty. Ten million and more unemployed have been quiet because they have been fed, clothed, and sheltered—not very well, but after a fashion. Let us not be deluded by this apparent complacency. Reorganization and reconstruction are necessary.

Our Holy Father has laid down an exceptionally broad and fearless program to guide legislative and voluntary action looking toward better conditions for both capital and labor. Trite as the statement is, the only sound remedy for unemployment is employment. Inordinate greed and huge profits during one turn of the economic wheel and appalling conditions of unemployment affecting millions during another, must come to an end. The intolerable effects of widespread unemployment must be planned against—first, through the recognition on the part of employers and employees of their mutual interdependence, the realization that disaster to one means catastrophe to the other; second, the acceptance of the fact that as long as the farm industry of our country is sick, just so long will the economic recovery of our workers in the cities be delayed; third, through the adoption of the principle that a healthy, decent, normal standard of living cannot be based on economic law solely, but must bring into it, God's eternal principles of justice and charity.

What part will Catholic leadership play in this all important crisis? Looking back over the history of the Church in America we have reason for hope. Great things have already been accomplished by the development of Catholic organizations which are daily fulfilling the commandment of love. This has been done while the Church has been under a severe strain to erect churches, schools and colleges. In large measure it has been done by Catholics endowed with little of this world's goods. Today in many parts of the country members of our faith have risen to positions of prominence and the Church enjoys a security and a prestige far beyond what it had in earlier decades. The time has arrived when her social mission can be more adequately fulfilled. If we can but marshal our resources, if we can but rally our Catholic people under the leadership and inspiration given by His Holiness, a new era is at hand.

With the watchwords justice and charity ever in mind, spurred on by divine faith and unwavering patriotism, Catholic charitable organization in America can become a mighty force in both remedial and preventive action for the welfare of all the people.

24

THE BISHOPS' PROGRAM OF SOCIAL RECONSTRUCTION

Two essays written in 1919 and 1920, each by a priest experienced in the social apostolate, afforded exceptional encouragement and guidance to Catholic thought and action in the years that followed, especially during the New Era Twenties and the New Deal Thirties. John A. Ryan was the author of the first document, entitled "Social Reconstruction: A General Review of the Problems and Survey of Remedies." When a committee of bishops of the National Catholic War Council adopted the statement, it was immediately dubbed the Bishops' Program of Social Reconstruction or, more simply, the Bishops' Program.

The Bishops' Program proved to be a provocative document. In the drive for "normalcy" after World War I the changes envisaged by the document were damned as subversive and revolutionary, more Marxist than Christian in inspiration and purpose. In the wake of the Depression Thirties both friend and foe have generally looked upon the Program as a precursor, even a blueprint, of the New Deal and the Welfare State. Yet the language of the document does not justify these opinions. The program, it is true, called for "ultimate and fundamental reforms" designed to transform the majority of wage-earners into "owners, at least in part, of the instruments of production." But this modification, even abolition, of the wage system was to be achieved not by socialistic political action but by voluntary industrial cooperation in the form of producers' cooperation and partnership arrangements. The New Deal, as is well known, had little place for these types of social reconstruction in its legislative program. Like the New Deal, the Bishops' Program sought to improve labor conditions by legal enactments. Unlike the New Deal, it expected the states, not the federal government, to guarantee minimum wages, social insurance, and proper housing. Conscious of constitutional limitations, the bishops minimized the role of the Federal government.

In most respects the Bishops' Program was more reminiscent of prewar Progressivism than anticipatory of the New Deal. Nevertheless, it was rightly viewed as a forward-looking document; it clearly and courageously called upon public authority to assume responsibility for social welfare, and for these reasons it had the power to encourage social thought and action.

FOREWORD

The ending of the Great War has brought peace. But the only safeguard of peace is social justice and a contented peo-

---

Bishop's Program of Social Reconstruction. A General Review of the Problems and Survey of Remedies. National Catholic Welfare Council ("Conference" after 1922), Washington, D. C., 1920.

ple. The deep unrest so emphatically and so widely voiced throughout the world is the most serious menace to the future peace of every nation and of the entire world. Great problems face us. They cannot be put aside; they must be met and solved with justice to all.

In the hope of stating the lines that will best guide us in their right solution the following pronouncement is issued by the Administrative Committee of the National Catholic War Council. Its practical applications are of course subject to discussion, but all its essential declarations are based upon the principles of charity and justice that have always been held and taught by the Catholic Church, while its practical proposals are merely an adaptation of those principles and that traditional teaching to the social and industrial conditions and needs of our own time.

PETER J. MULDOON, *Chairman*
Bishop of Rockford
JOSEPH SCHREMBS
Bishop of Toledo
PATRICK J. HAYES
Bishop of Tagaste
WILLIAM T. RUSSELL
Bishop of Charleston

SOCIAL RECONSTRUCTION

"Reconstruction" has of late been so tiresomely reiterated, not to say violently abused, that it has become to many of us a word of aversion. Politicians, social students, labor leaders, business men, charity workers, clergymen, and various other social groups have contributed their quota of spoken words and printed pages to the discussion of the subject; yet the majority of us still find ourselves rather bewildered and helpless. We are unable to say what parts of our social system imperatively need reconstruction; how much of that which is imperatively necessary is likely to be seriously undertaken; or what specific methods and measures are best suited to realize that amount of reconstruction which is at once imperatively necessary and immediately feasible.

Nevertheless it is worth while to review briefly some of the more important statements and proposals that have been made by various social groups and classes. Probably the most notable declaration from a Catholic source is that contained in a pastoral letter, written by Cardinal Bourne several months ago. "It is admitted on all hands," he says, "that a new order of things, new social conditions, new relations between the different sections in which society is divided, will arise as a consequence of the destruction of the formerly existing conditions. . . . The very foundations of political and social life, of our economic system, of morals and religion are being sharply scrutinized, and this not only by a few writers and speakers, but by a very large number of people in every class of life, especially among the workers."

The Cardinal's special reference to the action of labor was undoubtedly suggested by the now famous "Social Reconstruction Program" of the British Labor Party. This document was drawn up about one year ago, and is generally understood to be the work of the noted economist and Fabian Socialist, Mr. Sidney Webb. Unquestionably, it is the most comprehensive and coherent program that has yet appeared on the industrial phase of reconstruction. In brief it sets up "four pillars" of the new social order:

(1) The enforcement by law of a National minimum of leisure, health, education and subsistence;

(2) The democratic control of industry, which means the nationalization of all monopolistic industries and possibly of other industries, sometime in the future, if that course be found advisable;

(3) A revolution in national finance; that is, a system of tax-

ation which will compel capital to pay for the war, leaving undisturbed the national minimum of welfare for the masses;

(4) Use of the surplus wealth of the nation for the common good; that is, to provide capital, governmental industries, and funds for social, educational and artistic programs.

This program may properly be described as one of immediate radical reforms, leading ultimately to complete Socialism. Evidently this outcome cannot be approved by Catholics.

Program of American Labor

Through its Committee on Reconstruction, the American Federation of Labor has issued a lengthy program of reform proposals and demands which may be grouped under the three heads of trade union action, labor legislation and general industrial and social legislation. The principal demands under the first head are: the legally guaranteed rights of the workers to organize and to carry on the normal activities of trade unions; a living wage; no reduction in present scales of wages; the right of labor to fix its hours of work; the eight-hour day; equal pay for equal work by the two sexes; exclusive reliance by labor on trade-union effort to maintain fair wages; establishment of coöperative stores; and no organization of a political party by the workers. Labor laws demanded are: prohibition of wage working by children under sixteen years of age; abolition of private employment agencies; prohibition of all immigration for two years; and vocational education which will fit the young for life in an industrial society. By implication both the eight-hour day and the living wage are declared to be subjects for trade union action, not for legislation. Among the measures of general social legislation recommended are: a special tax on "usable land" not cultivated by the owner, and taxes on land values which would make the holding of idle land unprofitable; government housing; government ownership and operation of docks, wharves and water powers; taxes on excess profits, incomes, and inheritances; and limitation of the power of the courts to declare laws unconstitutional.

While this program is more practical and more moderate and reasonable than that of the British Labor Congress, its proposal for taxing land into use could easily involve confiscation. On the other hand, it does not give sufficient consideration to the case of the weaker sections of the working class, those for whom trade union action is not practically adequate; nor does it demand or imply that the workers should ever aspire to become owners as well as users of the instruments of production.

British Quaker Employers

Probably the most definite and comprehensive statement from the opposite industrial class was put forth several months ago by a group of twenty Quaker employers in Great Britain. In outline their program is as follows: A family living wage for all male employees, and a secondary wage in excess of this for workers having special skill, training, physical strength, responsibility for human life; the right of labor to organize, to bargain collectively with the employer and to participate in the industrial part of business management; serious and practical measures to reduce the volume and hardship of unemployment; provisions of such working conditions as will safeguard health, physical integrity and morals; the reduction so far as practicable of profits and interest until both the basic and the secondary wage have been paid, and transfer to the community of the greater part of surplus profits.

The spirit and conception of responsibility that permeate every item of the program are reflected in this statement: "We would ask all employers to consider very carefully whether their style of living and personal expenditure are restricted to what is needed in order to insure the efficient performance of their functions in society. More than this is waste, and is, moreover, a great cause of class divisions."

American Employers

The only formal statements on the subject of social reconstruction that have yet come to our attention from an important group of American employers, are a declaration of principles and certain proposals by the National Chamber of Commerce. The declaration of principles was made at a convention of the organization, in Atlantic City, December 6, 1918. Beyond a general commendation of peaceful and friendly relations between employers and employees, it included nothing of importance on the labor phase of reconstruction. It condemned government operation and ownership of railroads, telegraphs and telephones, and demanded more moderate taxes and a modification of the Sherman Anti-Trust Law. More recently the executive officials of the Chamber have submitted to a referendum vote of its membership a statement, "with a view to furnishing a basis on which American industry can build a national labor program." The main specific proposals in this statement are: recognition of the right of workers to organize; adequate representation of both parties in the determination of employment conditions; a decent home and proper social conditions; no reduction in wages until all other costs of production have been brought down to the lowest possible level; and a system of national employment offices. Inasmuch as this organization represents more employers than any other association in the country, the vote of its members on these proposals will be of the greatest significance.

An Interdenominational Statement

In Great Britain an organization known as the Interdenominational Conference of Social Service Unions, comprising ten religious bodies, including Catholics, spent more than a year formulating a statement of Social Reconstruction. (See the summary and analysis contained in the Catholic Social

Year Book for 1918.) This statement deals with principles, evils and remedies. Presuming that Christianity provides indispensable guiding principles and powerful motives of social reform, it lays down the basic proposition that every human being is of inestimable worth, and that legislation should recognize persons as more sacred than property, therefore the State should enforce a minimum living wage, enable the worker to obtain some control of industrial conditions; supplement private initiative in providing decent housing; prevent the occurrence of unemployment; safeguard the right of the laborer and his family to a reasonable amount of rest and recreation; remove those industrial and social conditions which hinder marriage and encourage an unnatural restriction of families, and afford ample opportunities for education of all children industrially, culturally, religiously and morally. On the other hand, rights imply duties, and the individual is obliged to respect the rights of others, to cultivate self-control, to recognize that labor is the law of life, and that wealth is a trust. Finally, the statement points out that all social reform must take as its end and guide the maintenance of pure and wholesome family life.

Such in barest outline are the main propositions and principles of this remarkable program. The text contains adequate exposition of the development and application of all these points, and concrete specifications of the methods and measures by which the aims and principles may be brought into effect. In the latter respect the statement is not liable to the fatal objection that is frequently and fairly urged against the reform pronouncements of religious bodies: that they are abstract, platitudinous and usually harmless. The statement of the Interdenominational Conference points out specific remedies for the evils that it describes; specific measures, legislative and other, by which the principles may be realized in actual life. Especially practical and valuable for Catholics are the explanations and modifications supplied by the Year Book of the Catholic Social Guild.

No Profound Changes in the United States

It is not to be expected that as many or as great social changes will take place in the United States as in Europe. Neither our habits of thinking nor our ordinary ways of life have undergone a profound disturbance. The hackneyed phrase: "Things will never again be the same after the war," has a much more concrete and deeply felt meaning among the European peoples. Their minds are fully adjusted to the conviction and expectation that these words will come true. In the second place, the devastation, the loss of capital and of men, the changes in individual relations and the increase in the activities of government have been much greater in Europe than in the United States. Moreover, our superior natural advantages and resources, the better industrial and social condition of our working classes still constitute an obstacle to anything like revolutionary changes. It is significant that no social group in America, not even among the wage-earners, has produced such a fundamental and radical program of reconstruction as the Labor Party of Great Britain.

A Practical and Moderate Program

No attempt will be made in these pages to formulate a comprehensive scheme of reconstruction. Such an undertaking would be a waste of time as regards immediate needs and purposes, for no important group or section of the American people is ready to consider a program of this magnitude. Attention will therefore be confined to those reforms that seem to be desirable and also obtainable within a reasonable time, and to a few general principles which should become a guide to more distant developments. A statement thus circumscribed will not merely present the objects that we wish to see attained, but will also serve as an imperative call to action. It will keep before our minds the necessity for translating our faith into works. In the statements of immediate proposals we shall start, wherever possible, from those governmental agencies and legislative measures which have been to some extent in operation during the war. These come before us with the prestige of experience and should therefore receive first consideration in any program that aims to be at once practical and persuasive.

The first problem in the process of reconstruction is the industrial replacement of the discharged soldiers and sailors. The majority of these will undoubtedly return to their previous occupations. However, a very large number of them will either find their previous places closed to them, or will be eager to consider the possibility of more attractive employments. The most important single measure for meeting this situation that has yet been suggested is the placement of such men on farms. Several months ago Secretary Lane recommended to Congress that returning soldiers and sailors should be given the opportunity to work at good wages upon some part of the millions upon millions of acres of arid, swamp, and cut-over timber lands, in order to prepare them for cultivation. President Wilson in his annual address to Congress endorsed the proposal. As fast as this preliminary task has been performed, the men should be assisted by government loans to establish themselves as farmers, either as owners or as tenants having long-time leases. It is essential that both the work of preparation and the subsequent settlement of the land should be effected by groups or colonies, not by men living independently of one another and in depressing isolation. A plan of this sort is already in operation in England. The importance of the project as an item of any social reform program is obvious. It would afford employment to thousands upon thousands, would greatly increase the number of farm owners and independent farmers, and would tend to lower the cost of living by increasing the amount of agricultural products. If it is to assume any considerable proportions it must be carried out by the Governments of the United States and of the several States. Should it be undertaken by these authorities and operated on a systematic and generous scale, it would easily become one of the most beneficial reform measures that has ever been attempted.

United States Employment Service

The reinstatement of the soldiers and sailors in urban industries will no doubt be facilitated by the United States Employment Service. This agency has attained a fair degree of development and efficiency during the war. Unfortunately there is some danger that it will go out of existence or be greatly weakened at the end of the period of demobilization. It is the obvious duty of Congress to continue and strengthen this important institution. The problem of unemployment is with us always. Its solution requires the cooperation of many agencies, and the use of many methods; but the primary and indispensable instrument is a national system of labor exchanges, acting in harmony with State, municipal, and private employment bureaus.

Women War Workers

One of the most important problems of readjustment is that created by the presence in industry of immense numbers of women who have taken the places of men during the war. Mere justice, to say nothing of chivalry, dictates that these women should not be compelled to suffer any greater loss or inconvenience than is absolutely necessary; for their services to the nation have been second only to the services of the men whose places they were called upon to fill. One general principle is clear: No female worker should remain in any occupation that is harmful to health and morals. Women should disappear as quickly as possible from such tasks as conducting and guarding street cars, cleaning locomotives, and a great number of other activities for which conditions of life and their physique render them unfit. Another general principle is that the proportion of women in industry ought to be kept within the smallest practical limits. If we have an efficient national employment service, if a goodly number of the returned soldiers and sailors are placed on the land, and if wages and the demand for goods are kept up to the level which is easily attainable, all female workers who are displaced from tasks that they have been performing only since the beginning of the war will be able to find suitable employments in other parts of the industrial field, or in those domestic occupations which sorely need their presence. Those women who are engaged at the same tasks as men should receive equal pay for equal amounts and qualities of work.

National War Labor Board

One of the most beneficial governmental organizations of the war is the National War Labor Board. Upon the basis of a few fundamental principles, unanimously adopted by the representatives of labor, capital, and the public, it has prevented innumerable strikes, and raised wages to decent levels in many different industries throughout the country. Its main guiding principles have been a family living wage for all male adult laborers; recognition of the right of labor to organize, and to deal with employers through its chosen representatives; and no coercion of non-union laborers by members of the union. The War Labor Board ought to be continued in existence by Congress, and endowed with all the power for effective action that it can possess under the Federal Constitution. The principles, methods, machinery and results of this institution constitute a definite and far-reaching gain for social justice. No part of this advantage should be lost or given up in time of peace.

Present Wage Rates Should Be Sustained

The general level of wages attained during the war should not be lowered. In a few industries, especially some directly and peculiarly connected with the carrying on of war, wages have reached a plane upon which they cannot possibly continue for this grade of occupations. But the number of workers in this situation is an extremely small proportion of the entire wage-earning population. The overwhelming majority should not be compelled or suffered to undergo any reduction in their rates of remuneration, for two reasons: First, because the average rate of pay has not increased faster than the cost of living; second, because a considerable majority of the wage-earners of the United States, both men and women, were not receiving living wages when prices began to rise in 1915. In that year, according to Lauck and Sydenstricker, whose work is the most comprehensive on the subject, four-fifths of the heads of families obtained less than 800 dollars, while two-thirds of the female wage-earners were paid less than 400 dollars. Even if the prices of goods should fall to the level on which they were in 1915—something that cannot be hoped for within five years—the average present rates of wages would not exceed the equivalent of a decent livelihood in the case of the vast majority. The exceptional instances to the contrary are practically all among the skilled workers. Therefore, wages on the whole should not be reduced even when the cost of living recedes from its present high level.

Even if the great majority of workers were now in receipt of more than living wages, there are no good reasons why rates of pay should be lowered. After all, a living wage is not necessarily the full measure of justice. All the Catholic authorities on the subject explicitly declare that this is only the *minimum* of justice. In a country as rich as ours, there are very few cases in which it is possible to prove that the worker would be getting more than that to which he has a right if he were paid something in excess of this ethical minimum. Why then, should we assume that this is the normal share of almost the whole laboring population? Since our industrial resources and instrumentalities are sufficient to provide more than a living wage for a very large proportion of the workers, why should we acquiesce in a theory which denies them this measure of the comforts of life? Such a policy is not only of very questionable morality, but is unsound economically. The large demand for goods which is created and maintained by high rates of wages and high purchasing power by the masses is the surest guarantee of a continuous and general operation of industrial establishments. It is the most effective instrument of prosperity for labor and capital alike. The principal beneficiaries of a general reduction of wages would be the less efficient among the capitalists, and the more comfortable sections of the consumers. The wage-earners would lose more in remuneration than they would gain from whatever fall in prices occurred as a direct result of the fall in wages. On grounds both of justice and sound economics, we should give our hearty support to all legitimate efforts made by labor to resist general wage reductions.

Housing for Working Classes

Housing projects for war workers which have been completed, or almost completed by the Government of the United States, have cost some forty million dollars, and are found in eleven cities. While the Federal Government can not continue this work in time of peace, the example and precedent that it has set, and the experience and knowledge that it has developed, should not be forthwith neglected and lost. The great cities in which congestion and other forms of bad housing are disgracefully apparent ought to take up and continue the work, at least to such an extent as will remove the worst features of a social condition that is a menace at once to industrial efficiency, civic health, good morals and religion.

Reduction of the Cost of Living

During the war the cost of living has risen at least 75 per cent above the level of 1913. Some check has been placed upon the upward trend by government fixing of prices in the case of bread and coal, and a few other commodities. Even if we believe it desirable, we cannot ask that the Government continue this action after the articles of peace have been signed; for neither public opinion nor Congress is ready for such a revolutionary policy. If the extortionate practices of monopoly were prevented by adequate laws and adequate law enforcement, prices would automatically be kept at as low a level as that to which they might be brought by direct government determination. Just what laws, in addition to those already on the statute books, are necessary to abolish monopolistic extortion is a question of detail that need not be considered here. In passing, it may be noted that government competition with monopolies that cannot be effectively restrained by the ordinary anti-trust laws deserves more serious consideration than it has yet received.

More important and more effective than any government regulation of prices would be the establishment of cooperative stores. The enormous toll taken from industry by the various classes of middlemen is now fully realized. The astonishing difference between the price received by the producer and that paid by the consumer has become a scandal of our industrial system. The obvious and direct means of reducing this discrepancy and abolishing unnecessary middlemen is the operation of retail and wholesale mercantile concerns under the ownership and management of the consumers. This is no Utopian scheme. It has been successfully carried out in England and Scotland through the Rochdale system. Very few serious efforts of this kind have been made in this country because our people have not felt the need of these cooperative enterprises as keenly as the European working classes, and because we have been too impatient and too individualistic to make the necessary sacrifices and to be content with moderate benefits and gradual progress. Nevertheless, our superior energy, initiative and commercial capacity will enable us, once we set about the task earnestly, even to surpass what has been done in England and Scotland.

In addition to reducing the cost of living, the cooperative stores would train our working people and consumers generally in habits of saving, in careful expenditure, in business methods, and in the capacity for cooperation. When the working classes have learned to make the sacrifices and to exercise the patience required by the ownership and operation of cooperative stores, they will be equipped to undertake a great variety of tasks and projects which benefit the community immediately, and all its constituent members ultimately. They will then realize the folly of excessive selfishness and senseless individualism. Until they have acquired this knowledge, training and capacity, desirable extensions of governmental action in industry will not be attended by a normal amount of success. No machinery of government can operate automatically, and no official and bureaucratic administration of such machinery can ever be a substitute for intelligent interest and cooperation by the individuals of the community.

The Legal Minimum Wage

Turning now from those agencies and laws that have been put in operation during the war to the general subject of labor legislation and problems, we are glad to note that there is no longer any serious objection urged by impartial persons against the legal minimum wage. The several States should enact laws providing for the establishment of wage rates that will be at least sufficient for the decent maintenance of a family, in the case of all male adults, and adequate to the decent individual support of female workers. In the beginning the minimum wages for male workers should suffice only for the present needs of the family, but they should be gradually raised until they are adequate to future needs as well. That is, they should be ultimately high enough to make possible that amount of saving which is necessary to protect the worker and his family against sickness, accidents, invalidity and old age.

Social Insurance

Until this level of legal minimum wages is reached the worker stands in need of the device of insurance. The State should make comprehensive provision for insurance against illness, invalidity, unemployment, and old age. So far as possible the insurance fund should be raised by a levy on industry, as is now done in the case of accident compensation. The industry in which a man is employed should provide him with all that is necessary to meet all the needs of his entire life. Therefore, any contribution to the insurance fund from the general revenues of the State should be only slight and temporary. For the same reason no contribution should be exacted from any worker who is not getting a higher wage than is required to meet the present needs of himself and family. Those who are below that level can make such a contribution only at the expense of their present welfare. Finally, the administration of the insurance laws should be such as to interfere as little as possible with the individual freedom of the worker and his family. Any insurance scheme, or any administrative method, that tends to separate the workers into a distinct and dependent class, that offends against their domestic privacy and independence, or that threatens individual self-reliance and self-respect, should not be tolerated. The ideal to be kept in mind is a condition in which all the workers would themselves have the income and the responsibility of providing for all the needs and contingencies of life, both present and future. Hence all forms of state insurance should be regarded as merely a lesser evil, and should be so organized and administered as to hasten the coming of the normal condition.

The life insurance offered to soldiers and sailors during the war should be continued, so far as the enlisted men are concerned. It is very doubtful whether the time has yet arrived when public opinion would sanction the extension of general life insurance by the Government to all classes of the community.

The establishment and maintenance of municipal health inspection in all schools, public and private, is now pretty generally recognized as of great importance and benefit. Municipal clinics where the poorer classes could obtain the advantage of medical treatment by specialists at a reasonable cost would likewise seem to have become a necessity. A vast amount of unnecessary sickness and suffering exists among the poor and the lower middle classes because they cannot afford the advantages of any other treatment except that provided by the general practitioner. Every effort should be made to supply wage-earners and their families with specialized medical care through development of group medicine. Free medical care should be given only to those who cannot afford to pay.

Labor Participation in Industrial Management

The right of labor to organize and to deal with employers through representatives has been asserted above in connection with the discussion of the War Labor Board. It is to be hoped that this right will never again be called in question by any considerable number of employers. In addition to this, labor ought gradually to receive greater representation in what the English group of Quaker employers have called the "industrial" part of business management—"the control of processes and machinery; nature of product; engagement and dismissal of employees; hours of work, rates of pay, bonuses, etc.; welfare work; shop discipline; relations with trade unions." The establishment of shop committees, working wherever possible with the trade union, is the method suggested by this group of employers for giving the employees the proper share of industrial management. There can be no doubt that a frank adoption of these means and ends by employers would not only promote the welfare of the workers, but vastly improve the relations between them and their employers, and increase the efficiency and productiveness of each establishment.

There is no need here to emphasize the importance of safety and sanitation in work places, as this is pretty generally recognized by legislation. What is required is an extension and strengthening of many of the existing statutes, and a better administration and enforcement of such laws everywhere.

Vocational Training

The need of industrial, or as it has come to be more generally called, vocational training, is now universally acknowledged. In the interest of the nation as well as in that of the workers themselves, this training should be made substantially universal. While we cannot now discuss the subject in any detail, we do wish to set down two general observations. First, the vocational training should be offered in such forms and conditions as not to deprive the children of the working classes of at least the elements of a cultural education. A healthy democracy cannot tolerate a purely industrial or trade education for any class of its citizens. We do not want to have the children of the wage-earners put into a special class in which they are marked as outside the sphere of opportunities for culture. The second observation is that the system of vocational training should not operate so as to weaken in any degree our parochial schools or any other class of private schools. Indeed, the opportunities of the system should be extended to all qualified private schools on exactly the same basis as to public schools. We want neither class divisions in education nor a state monopoly of education.

Child Labor

The question of education naturally suggests the subject of child labor. Public opinion in the majority of the States of our country has set its face inflexibly against the continuous employment of children in industry before the age of sixteen years. Within a reasonably short time all of our States, except some stagnant ones, will have laws providing for this reasonable standard. The education of public opinion must continue, but inasmuch as the process is slow, the abolition of child labor in certain sections seems unlikely to be brought about by the legislatures of those States, and since the Keating-Owen Act has been declared unconstitutional, there seems to be no device by which this reproach to our country can be removed except that of taxing child labor out of existence. This method is embodied in an amendment to the Federal Revenue Bill which would impose a tax of 10 per cent on the profits of all goods made by children.

Sufficient for the Present

Probably the foregoing proposals comprise everything that is likely to have practical value in a program of immediate social reconstruction for America. Substantially all of these methods, laws and recommendations have been recognized in principle by the United States during the war, or have been indorsed by important social and industrial groups and organizations. Therefore, they are objects that we can set before the people with good hope of obtaining a sympathetic and practical response. Were they all realized, a great step would have been taken in the direction of social justice. When they are all put into operation the way will be easy and obvious to still greater and more beneficial result.

Ultimate and Fundamental Reforms

Despite the practical and immediate character of the present statement, we cannot entirely neglect the question of ultimate aims and a systematic program; for other groups are busy issuing such systematic pronouncements, and we all need something of the kind as a philosophical foundation and as a satisfaction to our natural desire for comprehensive statements.

It seems clear that the present industrial system is destined to last for a long time in its main outlines. That is to say, private ownership of capital is not likely to be supplanted by a collectivist organization of industry at a date sufficiently near to justify any present action based on the hypothesis of its arrival. This forecast we recognize as not only extremely probable, but as highly desirable for, other objections apart, Socialism would mean bureaucracy, political tyranny, the helplessness of the individual as a factor in the ordering of his own life, and in general, social inefficiency and decadence.

Main Defects of Present System

Nevertheless, the present system stands in grievous need of considerable modifications and improvement. Its main defects are three: Enormous inefficiency and waste in the production and distribution of commodities; insufficient incomes for the majority of wage-earners, and unnecessarily large incomes for a small minority of privileged capitalists. Inefficiency in the production of goods would be in great measure abolished by the reforms that have been outlined in the foregoing pages. Production would be greatly increased by universal living wages, by adequate industrial education, and by harmonious relations between labor and capital on the basis of adequate participation by the former in all the industrial aspects of business management. The waste of commodity distribution could be practically all eliminated by cooperative mercantile establishments, and cooperative selling and marketing associations.

Cooperation and Co-Partnership

Nevertheless, the full possibilities of increased production will not be realized so long as the majority of the workers remain mere wage-earners. The majority must somehow become owners, or at least in part, of the instruments of production. They can be enabled to reach this stage gradually through cooperative productive societies and co-partnership arrangements. In the former, the workers own and manage the industries themselves; in the latter they own a substantial part of the corporate stock and exercise a reasonable share in the management. However slow the attainments of these ends, they will have to be reached before we can have a thoroughly efficient system of production, or an industrial and social order that will be secure from the danger of revolution. It is to be noted that this particular modification of the existing order, though far-reaching and involving to a great extent the abolition of the wage system, would not mean the abolition of private ownership. The instruments of production would still be owned by individuals, not by the State.

Increased Incomes for Labor

The second great evil, that of insufficient income for the majority, can be removed only by providing the workers with more income. This means not only universal living wages, but the opportunity of obtaining something more than that amount for all who are willing to work hard and faithfully. All the other measures for labor betterment recommended in the preceding pages would likewise contribute directly or indirectly to a more just distribution of wealth in the interest of the laborer.

Abolition and Control of Monopolies

For the third evil mentioned above, excessive gains by a small minority of privileged capitalists, the main remedies are prevention of monopolistic control of commodities, adequate government regulation of such public service monopolies as will remain under private operation, and heavy taxation of incomes, excess profits and inheritances. The precise methods by which genuine competition may be restored and maintained among businesses that are naturally competitive, cannot be discussed here; but the principle is clear that human beings cannot be trusted with the immense opportunities for oppression and extortion that go with the possession of monopoly power. That the owners of public service monopolies should be restricted by law to a fair or average return on their actual investment, has long been a recognized principle of the courts, the legislatures, and public opinion. It is a principle which should be operative in competitive enterprises likewise, with the qualification that something more than the average rate of return be allowed to men who exhibit exceptional efficiency. However, good public policy, as well as equity, demands that these exceptional business men share the fruits of their efficiency with the consumer in the form of lower prices. The man who utilizes his ability to produce cheaper than his competitors for the purpose of exacting from the public as high a price for his product as is necessary for the least efficient business man, is a menace rather than a benefit to industry and society.

Our immense war debt constitutes a particular reason why incomes and excess profits should continue to be heavily taxed. In this way two important ends will be attained: the poor will be relieved of injurious tax burdens, and the small class of specially privileged capitalists will be compelled to return a part of their unearned gains to society.

A New Spirit a Vital Need

"Society," said Pope Leo XIII, "can be healed in no other way than by a return to Christian life and Christian institutions." The truth of these words is more widely perceived today than when they were written, more than twenty-seven years ago. Changes in our economic and political systems will have only partial and feeble efficiency if they be not reinforced by the Christian view of work and wealth. Neither the moderate reforms advocated in this paper, nor any other program of betterment or reconstruction will prove reasonably effective without a reform in the spirit of both labor and capital. The laborer must come to realize that he owes his employer and society an honest day's work in return for a fair wage, and that conditions cannot be substantially improved until he roots out the desire to get a maximum of return for a minimum of service. The capitalist must likewise get a new viewpoint. He needs to learn the long-forgotten truth that wealth is stewardship, that profit-making is not the basic justification of business enterprise, and that there are such things as fair profits, fair interest and fair prices. Above and before all, he must cultivate and strengthen within his mind the truth which many of his class have begun to grasp for the first time during the present war; namely, that the laborer is a human being, not merely an instrument of production; and that the laborer's right to a decent livelihood is the first moral charge upon industry. The employer has a right to get a reasonable living out of his business, but he has no right to interest on his investment until his employees have obtained at least living wages. This is the human and Christian, in contrast to the purely commercial and pagan, ethics of industry.

25 Edwin V. O'Hara

A BASIS FOR A RURAL PROGRAM

John A. Ryan's counterpart in the Catholic social movement was Edwin V. O'Hara, who wrote for the Catholic Educational Association the basic document of the Catholic rural life movement, on which much Catholic social thought has been lav-

ished in the last four decades. O'Hara, a Portland, Oregon, pastor, was almost as concerned as Ryan with urban labor and social problems, and was largely responsible for the enactment and early enforcement of Oregon's pioneer minimum wage law for women and children. O'Hara came to the conclusion, however, that rural Catholics should have religious facilities equal to those of urban Catholics, beginning with religious instruction. He contended that the number of Catholic rural schools per capita was only half that of the urban schools, and was convinced that more and better schools in rural areas would help maintain the Catholic population there. The rural count was disproportionately low, being only one-fifth that of the total Catholic population. Many rural families moved into the cities in order to give their children a Catholic education—a tendency O'Hara allowed was of benefit to school-age children but socially and morally perilous to the parents and older sons and daughters.

O'Hara believed, as did the erstwhile Catholic Colonization leaders, that agriculture was the true nursery of moral and civic virtue. Normal rural life fostered self-reliance, initiative and character, a healthy rate of population growth, and vocations to the priesthood and the religious life. Cities made use of these values, but they were relatively powerless to create them. With less emotion and eloquence, and perhaps with no more facts and statistics than Bishop Spalding, O'Hara nevertheless pictured a sharp contrast between town and country. He differed from Spalding and the other colonizers in opposing a mass exodus from the cities, a "back to the farm" movement of urban failures and incompetents. He insisted, instead, that farm life be made attractive to retain on the land those familiar with the traditions and processes of agriculture. Growth in the Catholic farm population should come from its own inherent strength with only such accessions from the outside as could be effectively assimilated to farm life and rural culture. Organic growth would involve, from the religious angle, a more informed, farm-interested and respected rural priesthood, ru-

rally oriented religious orders, summer vacation religious schools, after the Lutheran example, and religious correspondence courses.

In the last half century the urban problem has usurped the first place in the public mind. The rapid growth of industrial centers with the consequent congestion of population in limited areas has given rise to a series of acute industrial and social issues which, affecting as they do the immediate welfare of that section of the population which is best able to give voice to its social needs, have tended to become identified in the popular imagination with the whole of our social problem. The strife between capital and labor in our industrial centers has become so noisy as to assume to be the fundamental social issue. Problems of housing and sanitation, child labor in factories, vocational education, these are only a few of the reform programs which have sprung from the unhealthy warehousing of great groups of families in our big cities and industrial centers.

The best thought in America has set itself to the solution of these urban problems and while the goal of social reform in the cities still lies far in the future, it is a matter of encouragement that the public mind has been educated to a hopeful attitude and that already by education, by organization, and by legislation steps have been taken towards ameliorating the worst social conditions.

As might naturally be expected these urban problems had their religious counterpart, and vastly to her credit the Catholic Church has set herself to the task which has been thrust upon her by the rapid urbanization of our people. The cities

---

Edwin V. O'Hara, "The Rural Problem in its Bearing on Catholic Education," Catholic Educational Association, *Bulletin,* XVII (November 1920), 232–244.

of our land are filled with the institutions and organizations, religious, educational, social, and charitable which stand as an enduring monument to the faith, wisdom and self-sacrifice of the Catholic hierarchy, clergy, and laity. But it has not been sufficiently considered that the rapid growth of urban population has created problems of the first magnitude in the country whence population has been drained, as well as in the city into which it has poured its flood. In social life as in the physical world condensation at one point involves rarefaction at another, and tension and instability are created at both poles. The object of this paper is to indicate that there is a rural problem; that this problem has the gravest religious bearings, and finally to make some tentative suggestions looking towards the solution of the religious rural problem.

I. THERE IS A RURAL PROBLEM

Fundamentally the rural problem in the past has been one of isolation and drudgery. These conditions have rendered the lot of the farmer, of his wife and children, very hard indeed. It is unnecessary to paint the picture of the rural home remote from its neighbors, hardly accessible during long seasons of the year because of impassible roads, cut off from communication with the outside world and devoid of the social life which might mitigate the dreary and monotonous existence of its members. The long hours of physical drudgery in what has been aptly described as the farmer's contest with the force of gravity added to the undesirability of country life. The lack of adequate school facilities still further intensified the problem. Whittier painted an idyllic picture of the rural school:

> "Still sits the schoolhouse by the road
> A ragged beggar sunning;
> And by it still the sumach grows
> And blackberry vines are running."

A more prosaic description would show an unprepared teacher, a disorganized course of study and a short and irregular school attendance.

The past generation witnessed a notable amelioration of these rural hardships. The isolation of the farmer has been diminished by the improved roads, the daily delivery of mail, the rural telephone, and the auto, which have brought farmers into closer social relations with their neighbors living miles away than are enjoyed by city folk with families living in adjoining flats. The drudgery of farm labor has been mitigated by the countless inventions from the self-binder to the corn-husker, which have transformed farming into a machine industry. The movement for the consolidation of rural schools has spread rapidly and has resulted in a vast improvement of the educational opportunities of multitudes of country children.

While these forces were at work for the improvement of rural conditions a new and alarming danger to agriculture has made its appearance in the flight of the farming population to industrial centers. The extent of this migration of population is shown in the following table from the 13th Census Report:

POPULATION OF THE CONTINENTAL UNITED STATES

	No. in 1910	*Per Cent*	*No. in 1900*	*Per Cent*	*Per Cent Increase*
Total number	91,972,266		75,994,575		21.0
Urban	42,623,383	46.3	31,609,645	40.5	34.8
Rural	49,348,883	53.7	44,384,930	59.5	11.2

During the decade of 1900 to 1910 the rural population of twenty-two States either decreased or showed an increase of less than ten per cent. Among these twenty-two were all the northern States east of the Rocky Mountains except the Dakotas.

The dry bones of these statistics are clothed with no pleasant aspect of wholesome flesh when we consider the history of any actual rural community. The rush to the city has robbed the farms of their best cultivators, who have left the least capable behind or have been supplanted by tenant farmers who have a minimum of interest in the social life of the community or even in transmitting unimpaired the richness of the soil which they have undertaken temporarily to till. The wild and unscrupulous advertising of city life by commercial clubs which seem obsessed by the idea that there is some special merit in mere bigness; the natural desire of industrial centers to build up a large labor supply near their factories; the glamour of the city streets and amusement places,—these, and other inducements, have led thousands of capable young farmers to abandon their rural homes to a tenant population.

The farmer pursues the most fundamental, the most dignified profession in the world. He is the primal producer. It is true that not by bread alone does man live, but it is also true that food commodities are not the chief things which the farm produces. It produces a type of citizen which has been in every civilization the substantial foundation of stable social order. The city has undertaken to milk the farm for its own selfish profit. It has gone further and built up a contempt for farm life. The "rube" is the butt of the ignorant urban jest. It is, nevertheless, from the country with its prolific population and its fertile fields that the city must draw both its sustenance and its people.

We are repeating the experience of more ancient civilizations. Read the first volume of Ferrero's *History of Rome,* change the dates and the names and you have a sketch of the large features of our recent history. When the agricultural population decayed Rome ceased to be a free republic, nor to-day shall we be able to predicate democracy of a tenement house population warehoused in great cities. Here, then, is our rural problem—the most important and the most neglected field of social endeavor; namely, the problem of maintaining on the land a sufficient population effective and prosperous in production, and happy and content by reason of a highly developed social and cultural status.

"The back to the land movement" has no significance for the rural problem. To send out of the cities families who have no acquaintance with farming cannot result in enriching the agricultural community either economically or socially. It is essentially a city movement which seeks with wonted generosity to unload on the country groups of individuals who have failed to make a living in the city and who it is mistakenly supposed would become efficient producers on the land and bring down the cost of food-stuffs for the rest of the city dwellers. Farming is not only the oldest and most fundamental of occupations; it also requires a high degree of intelligence for success. The future of the rural community requires above all, that farming be made attractive to the young, able-bodied and capable men and women who have been educated from their youth to a knowledge and mastery of agricultural forces.

II. THE RURAL PROBLEM HAS THE GRAVEST RELIGIOUS BEARING

It is the most obvious of facts that a city population is not prolific. Cities do not tend to reproduce themselves and would be faced with a declining population were it not for immigration. The great growth of our cities has not been due to any pronounced excess of births over deaths; it has been due most largely to the influx of people from the farms and from abroad, and to the prolific tendency of the first generation of families dwelling in the city. It is perfectly true that due to the improvement of sanitation in the city and to its neglect in the country, many cities show a lower infant mortality than the open country. On the other hand, the city with its hotels and tenements, its luxury and feverish excitement, and its large population economically submerged, naturally tends to a restricted birthrate both from voluntary and involuntary causes. The large families are really found in the country. Conditions of life among the city population, no matter what salutary influence may be brought to bear, tend to extinction—as is shown by the fact that relatively few city families have representatives to the fifth generation. In the country, on the contrary, is found the fertile and prolific population, and any influence set to work there grows with the passage of time like the tiny mountain stream which swells into a mighty river as it is joined by the waters from other springs in its course through the plains below. A religious center in the country, consequently, is a fountain bubbling up like Jacob's well, a blessing for future generations. If we take a far-sighted view of the religious problem, we must be impressed with the probably correct estimate that in a century twenty rural families will have a more numerous progeny than a hundred city families. It is therefore a fact worth noting that the future will be with the Church that ministers to the rural population.

We have already presented statistics from the Federal Census showing that in 1910 fifty-three and seven-tenths per cent of the total population of the United States was rural and only forty-six and three-tenths per cent urban. When we turn to the religious census of 1916 we find that of the 15,721,815 Catholics in the United States 5,081,930, or approximately one-third, lived in cities of more than 300,000 population, and 8,888,802 lived in cities of over 25,000 population.

CATHOLIC POPULATION OF U. S.

Total Catholic Population	*In cities of over 300,000*	*In cities of over 25,000*	*In cities of over 25,000*
15,721,815	5,081,930	8,888,802	57.0 *per cent*

While definite figures are not available showing the Catholic population of cities and towns under 25,000 population, a reasonable estimate, based upon the census figures, would indicate that such cities and towns, which are of course very numerous, contain at least twenty-five per cent of Catholic people. We are thus driven to a conservative statement that in the United States eighty per cent of the Catholic population must be classified as urban and twenty per cent, or less, as rural in the sense of these terms as accepted by the United States census reports. In tabulated form the urban and rural percentages of the total and Catholic population of the Continental United States would be as follows:

TABLE SHOWING TOTAL POPULATION AND CATHOLIC POPULATION OF THE CONTINENTAL UNITED STATES IN 1910 CLASSIFIED AS URBAN AND RURAL

	Population of U.S.	*Per Cent*	*Cath. Population of U.S.*	*Per Cent* (Estimated)
Total number	91,972,266		15,721,815	
Urban	42,623,383	46.3	12,684,672	81.0
Rural	49,348,883	53.7	3,037,143	19.0

In the decade 1906 to 1916 the Catholic population showed a decreased proportion in each of the fifteen States in which the Catholic Church was not the leading denomination. (Religious Census 1916, page 114.) This indicates a decreased proportion in rural Catholic population during that decade.

When we turn from the consideration of the total population to the school population we do not find the situation more reassuring. The table given below from the Federal Census showed the following classified school attendance in 1909-1910:

SCHOOL ATTENDANCE IN U. S.—1909–1910

Age Period	*In Urban Communities*	*Per Cent*	*In Rural Districts*	*Per Cent*
Under 6	212,994	2.8	183,437	1.7
6 to 9	2,442,305	32.7	3,236,015	30.7
10 to 14	3,326,340	44.5	4,702,322	44.7
15 to 20	1,330,324	17.8	2,262,898	2.15
21 and over	168,057	2.2	145,199	1.4
Total	7,480,020	100.0	10,529,871	100.0

Thus of the total school population the attendance in rural districts was ten and one-half million as against seven and one-half million in the city; that is, fifty-eight per cent were rural and forty-two per cent urban. In striking contrast to this enormous rural school attendance are figures extracted from the *Official Catholic Directory* which indicates that ninety per cent of organized Catholic schools are urban and only ten per cent rural.

TABLE SHOWING TOTAL AND RURAL CATHOLIC SCHOOL ATTENDANCE BY PROVINCES

	Total	*Rural*	*Per Cent Rural*
Baltimore	53,222	4,359	8.1
Boston	212,008	5,473	2.6
Chicago	164,550	12,923	7.8
Cincinnati	248,122	28,129	11.3
Dubuque	48,549	22,750	46.6
Milwaukee	81,412	18,831	23.1
New Orleans	67,165	20,477	30.4
New York	346,455	10,850	3.1
Oregon City	24,785	3,336	13.4
Philadelphia	209,977	12,175	5.7

TABLE SHOWING TOTAL AND RURAL CATHOLIC SCHOOL ATTENDANCE BY PROVINCES (Cont.)

	Total	*Rural*	*Per Cent Rural*
St. Louis	64,093	16,396	25.5
St. Paul	54,509	19,472	35.7
San Francisco	27,358	1,274	4.6
Santa Fe	17,023	3,014	17.7
	1,619,228	179,459	11.0

The above table shows the Catholic School population as reported in the *Official Catholic Directory* of 1919; rural includes villages and towns which at the last Federal census (1910) had less than 2,500 population. Owing to the growth of towns, many of these places had undoubtedly passed out of the "rural" class by 1918, consequently the showing of 11 per cent of the total as rural school attendance is considerably too large.

But the importance of the rural religious problem is not to be measured by counting heads. The country is the nursery of individualism; it is God's own training school in self-reliance. In a survey made sometime ago of the members of the City Club of one of the greatest cities in America, it was found that seventy-five per cent of the members had been farm boys. This was no fortuitous circumstance. It is not merely that city industrial life, with its monotonous routine kills initiative in the multitude, but city school life is incapable of developing initiative in the children. The city schools have been feverishly experimenting with a thousand makeshifts to develop the motor regions of the child mind and the story of the effort is largely a record of failure. Farm life, on the other hand, supplies this indispensable feature in a balanced educational program. The country boy and girl have an indisputable advantage in the development of self-reliance, initiative, and character. In the city, when we discover a need we telephone for a mechanic or have a delivery boy supply us from the department store. In the country we are thrown upon our own resources and learn a self-reliance in meeting the problems of life that is of the essence of leadership. If we lose the country population we lose not merely numbers, but leaders of the future generations both in county and in city.

An even more direct loss to religion arises from the lack of numbers of the rural Catholic population. We are losing vocations to the priesthood and religious life. In most Catholic countries a very high percentage of vocations comes from the country. Nor is this surprising. Contact with nature is wholesome. Rural life has fewer distractions and the absence of commercialized amusements presents a more favorable field for the development of religious vocations. It is at our peril that we shall neglect to develop a rural Catholic population.

III. THE PROGRAM

The first element in a Catholic rural program is the rural religious leader. The dignity of rural leadership must first be recognized. This recognition will follow only from an appreciation of the critical importance of a rural Catholic population. The country parish will be invested with a new status. It will cease to be a place of exile for those who long for city positions and instead of being a stepping-stone cityward it will be viewed in its true light as a post of honor and of achievement. The rural religious leader will be an anchor for a rural Catholic population. He will be the center of a Catholic colonization program; he will warn his people against the allurements of city life and encourage them to build up a rural culture worthy of the historic profession of agriculture.

Not only is there need of a new status for the rural pastor but there is need, too, for the multiplication of rural religious communities both of men and of women. The rural districts of America from a religious point of view justify the etymological derivation of their name, heathen and pagan. A work of reconstruction in American rural life as vast and as honorable as that wrought by the Benedictines in Christianizing western Europe is awaiting our rural religious communities. Cardinal Newman describes work of this religious community in language that deserves to be quoted:

"St. Benedict found the world, physical and social, in ruins, and his mission was to restore it in the way, not of science, but of nature, not as if setting about to do it, not professing to do it by any set time or by any rare specific or by any series of strokes, but so quietly, patiently, gradually, that often till the work was done it was not known to be doing. It was a restoration, rather than a visitation, correction, or conversion. The new world which he helped to create was a growth rather than a structure. Silent men were observed about the country, or discovered in the forest, digging, clearing and building; and other silent men, not seen, were sitting in the cold cloister, tiring their eyes, and keeping their attention on the stretch, while they painfully deciphered and copied and re-copied the manuscripts which they had saved. There was no one that 'contended, or cried out,' or drew attention to what was going on; but by degrees the woody swamp became a hermitage, a religious house, a farm, an abbey, a village, a seminary, a school of learning, and a city. Roads and bridges connected it with other abbeys and cities, which had similarly grown up; and what the haughty Alaric or fierce Attila had broken to pieces, these patient meditative men had brought together and made to live again."

American rural life cries out for a modern Benedict of Nursia. There is no substitute for the religious community as a vitalizing center for the Catholic rural community. The experience in Australia of a religious community of women who devote themselves to the religious instruction of children in the remotest country districts is full of significance for us in America, and the beginnings which have already been made of similar work in our own country should be encouraged and multiplied.

It is often taken for granted that the bright lights of the city must forever dazzle the eyes of the simple country folk and that we can only sit idly by while the huge serpent of city life first fascinates and then devours its victim. There are many, indeed, who have so succumbed to the glamour of urban life that residence in a rural community seems a dishonorable exile. They can tolerate a week or two of hunting in the country but to live in the country would mean for them supreme boredom and *ennui*. There is a story told of Diogenes the Cynic and of Aristippus who followed in the train of courtiers of a prince "where favors followed fawning." On one occasion these two met in the streets of Athens and Aristippus with lofty condescension addressed the cynic philosopher: "Oh, Diogenes, if you only knew how to flatter princes you would not need to live in a tub!" "Oh, Aristippus," replied the philosopher, with all the scorn of a freeman, "if you only knew how to live in a tub you would not be reduced to flattering princes!" Those who have within themselves resources to enter into the joys of the open country can but pity those who are dependent for stimulation upon the commercialized amusements and feverish streets and artificial gaiety of city life.

In our present organization not only have we neglected to bring religious instruction to the rural communities, but our strong city schools have been a magnet attracting Catholic rural families to the city. All of us who have been city pastors have had experience of receiving into our parishes families from the country, the sole cause of whose migration to the city was to give their children the advantages of a Catholic education. We have uprooted from the soil a flourishing vine, denuding the countryside and in most cases adding little to the city. While the children find their place in school, the father and older boys drift into the ranks of unskilled labor and the girls enter upon occupations where the average income presses close upon the minimum of decent subsistence. It is undoubtedly true that we cannot hope to bring to remote country districts the luxuries of religious education and religious services which are placed at the disposal of families in a large city parish, but it may be safely asserted that it would be immeasurably better that the average successful Catholic farmer should remain on the soil, if he could be assured of the most moderate and modest opportunities for the religious instruction of his children, than that the family should be uprooted from the land and devoured whole in the vortex of industrial life, with all its traditions broken, its habits of life disarranged, facing economic problems for which it is unprepared and, like a plant uprooted, dependent for its life on the generous dews of Catholic schooling.

There are great sections of the country in which the opportunities for religious instruction of country children will remain largely restricted to the summer season. The country Sunday school is universally conceded to be a failure. Replies from rural pastors in every diocese in the United States to my questionnaire on rural religious education voiced with practical unanimity the complaint that the rural Sunday school was utterly inadequate for the religious training of the children.

In many sections the Lutherans successfully conduct rural religious summer schools, choosing a month in the summer vacation when there is a lull in the farm work. They gather the children at the public school building or country church, and give them an intensive course of religious instruction for a month or six weeks, with sufficient review of secular branches to vary the program and prevent the day's work from becoming monotonous. Undoubtedly there are vast possibilities of organizing such summer schools for our Catholic children, and the details should be worked out on a comprehensive plan.

There are possibilities, too, in the training of lay catechists for the country districts, as has been demonstrated in the diocese of Pittsburgh and elsewhere. It must of course always remain true that permanent success in dealing with rural educational problems can be had only by forces which are themselves identified with rural life. In this connection it might be suggested that through the Rural Deans the Church might function in its rural work without the creation of new machinery. It would of course involve a new definition of the scope of their activities.

A field which has been practically untouched is that of the rural Catholic press. It is true that the dogmas of religion do not vary with city and country, but it is equally true that the environment in which the city Catholic lives is vastly different from the environment of his country cousin, and this difference must be reflected in the newspapers and periodicals which appeal to the various groups.

In secular education the correspondence school has inaugurated a new era and thousands of persons who have been denied the opportunity of organized school life are pursuing their studies at home with enthusiasm and success. There can be no doubt that the correspondence school method has great significance for rural religious education. And when capable agencies enter this field the children in thousands of Catholic rural families living remote from their neighbors, will be found studying the Catholic religion through the service of the rural mail delivery. It will require national organization working through convents in every diocese which will set aside capable teachers to supervise the papers of the rural pupils.

I may quote in conclusion a passage from one out of hundreds of similar letters which I have received from country pastors throughout the United States. The writer of this letter has a wide and successful experience in one of the poorest and most isolated regions of the Atlantic coast. He writes:

"There are all over the country many devoted priests who realize the great need of *concerted* action in regard to rural school problems, but as they are most of them buried away in small parishes, like myself, they never come in contact with one another. I myself know of several such, who have expressed to me their desire of just such united campaigning for an improvement of our rural school conditions. If any steps can be taken toward uniting through the country the friends, clerical and lay, of our Catholic rural schools, I shall be ready to join in any such movement and do all I can, by act or writing, to further it.

"There is need, too, not only for work in connection with the rural school proper, but for rural social and catechetical work, distribution of good literature, organization of the children, etc. I have come to certain conclusions on these matters which may or may not stand the test of criticism, but at any rate we need at the beginning of such a work a great plenty of suggestions, and good sense and experience will afterward select those that are most practicable."

To bring to fruition the earnest request of hundreds who are bearing single-handed and in isolation the heavy burden of responsibility in this vast and important field of rural life, I submit to the members of this Association the desirability of entering upon a study of the rural Catholic school problem in the United States, and in the words of a zealous correspondent "urgently request that steps be taken to formulate a national rural school policy to replace the haphazard way in which this vast field is left to the initiative of individuals, enormously handicapped by rural poverty and lack of appreciation of the work on the part of Catholics."

26 Michael J. O'Shaughnessy

A BLUEPRINT FOR ECONOMIC PLANNING

Of the countless plans drawn up during the Great Depression to bring about economic recovery or to reform (or transform) society, none, at least from the Catholic point of view, was more precisely formulated or more cogently and uncompromisingly defended than the blueprint confidently laid before the country by Michael J. O'Shaughnessy, oil executive and industrial publicist. In a carefully prepared pamphlet, published in 1932, he insisted that capital must accept partnership with labor as the only basis for equity and stability in the nation's economy. In the spirit of Theodore Roosevelt's New Nationalism, *O'Shaughnessy argued that the distributist economy and individualistic government of the early Republic had been antiquated by the march of technology and science. The time had come to legalize monopoly and to make it serve all occupational groups and the public generally. He would have the federal government place all major industries under the control of a server of trade associations, made up of an equal number of representatives of capital, organized labor, and consumer groups and empowered concurrently to fix wages, hours, and maximum and minimum prices, and to accumulate reserve funds against the hazards of dividual exhaustion, unemployment, and the technological displacement of workers.*

This arrangement, he contended, would assure adequate "wages" to both capital and labor since nearly all consumers were producers, either directly or indirectly, and stood to gain more than to lose from any price increases that might ensue. Moreover, the consuming public was duty bound to defray the costs of industrial stabilization in return for its manifest benefits. The decisions of the trade associations would be subject to administrative and judicial review. He believed the plan was constitutional under the commerce clause. Pope Pius XI's encyclical Quadragesimo Anno *inspired O'Shaughnessy's plan and his subsequent writings in the field of social justice.*

Indicated Reform

The reforms necessary to save the capitalistic social order from destroying itself are, as stated heretofore, not many nor

---

Michael J. O'Shaughnessy, *Man or Money?* (New York: privately printed, 1932), pp. 20–21, 25–33.

drastic, certainly not radical. The profit urge, prostituted by greed, must be controlled by forcing industry to cooperate and not compete destructively in the conduct of the nation's business. Industry, through legalized monopolies, must be forced to conduct its affairs in the interest of labor and the public, with a minimum of Federal Government supervision. Cooperation in industry must take the place of destructive competition.

Individualism

The founders of our Republic envisaged its future as agricultural (a distributive state) and rugged individualism was made the corner stone of our governmental structure, but the development of modern banking and the concentration of capital and industrial activity in great corporations, accelerated by inventions, machinery and mass production has fundamentally changed the conditions of our national life. These corporations cannot be destroyed without destroying the country. Unintelligent or vengeful regulation can bring them to a point where they cannot maintain themselves and efficiently serve the people. But they must be controlled in a manner to preserve as great a degree of individualism to the citizen as is consistent with the changed conditions of our national life. As desirable as it may be, a return to the ideal of individualism in the Twentieth Century is impossible. Such an attempt would continue the present confusion indefinitely and eventually fail. . . .

In order to preserve its national existence, the first and most important duty of government is to so order the economic life of the Commonwealth as to provide every citizen with the opportunity to earn a decent living. The exact contrary prevails throughout the world. Economic slavery exists on an unprecedented scale. A slave is a human being that has lost his freedom of action to others or to a social system, if you will, in his most elemental right to keep himself alive. It is estimated that there are twelve million unemployed in the United States, with their dependents numbering around forty million souls, that are in this condition, consequently it follows that slavery exists in the social order under which we, in the United States are now functioning. Similar conditions prevail in all the industrial nations of the world.

Duty of the Privileged Class

Enlightened self-interest would suggest that the comparatively few in the world who have most of the money and the power it confers, should take the lead in establishing a social order where both capital and labor would be stabilized. Obviously, no solution can be expected from the under-fed, underclothed, and poorly housed human beings, except by violent destruction of our present social order, and it should be remembered that this class is in the vast majority throughout the world.

It is past understanding that the possessors of great wealth do not realize that the security of their possessions depends upon industry and agriculture in the United States being profitable and it cannot be profitable so long as money is accumulated in so few hands that 95% of the population, that purchases two-thirds of the goods and services of the country, have not sufficient income to buy the products of industry and agriculture in a sufficient volume to make them profitable. The only way to do this is by a more equitable distribution of wealth. The privileged class, the possessors of great wealth, should take the initiative in such a movement, but they are blinded by greed and by obstructing such a program, they are committing industrial and financial suicide. It is futile to criticize without suggesting a remedy.

THE PROGRAM OF REFORM

The outline of a program to reform the capitalistic social order to forestall its disintegration, now rapidly under way, and its eventual destruction, is here presented for the consideration of thoughtful citizens:

A legislative proposal to stabilize industry and finance, to realize social justice and to abolish economic slavery in the United States, based on the principles that:

(a) The citizen has the right to work and is entitled to the protection of the laws in maintaining such right and in demanding an equal share of the employment available in the trade in which he is employed;

(b) That every citizen has the right to own property and earn a decent wage that will enable him to decently support his family;

(c) That money (capital) is entitled to a fair and reasonably assured wage;

(d) That prices for commodities produced by any industry should be such as to provide for fair and stabilized wages for the actual money employed in the industry and fair and stabilized wages for the human beings employed in it and to provide means of subsistence for human beings deprived of the opportunity to work through the introduction into the industry of machinery and improved technical methods, until the opportunity to earn a living for such human beings be provided in new industries or through other means.

To translate these principles into law:

All units in the major industries doing an interstate business and employing over fifty men and/or women, be empowered to form a trade association of all corporations or individuals that compose the industry, to accomplish the following ends:

(a) (1) to insure equal partition of available work among workers in the industry entitled thereto;

(2) to maintain production on a profitable basis;

(3) to fix maximum and minimum prices for raw materials and manufactured products.

(b) (1) All members of such associations to employ by the year, the average number of employees engaged in the industry over the period of the preceding ten years, at wages sufficient to enable workers to realize rights enumerated above; to set aside reserve funds to provide for fair and stabilized wages for workers and for money, based on the operations of the industry in the preceding ten years;

(2) All members of the trade association should be required to standardize their accounting forms, cost systems, earning statements, etc., which information should be continuously available to public inspection.

Management

The directors of the Trade Association to be nine in number, three representing the capital invested in the industry, to be chosen by the managements of its constituent members; three representing labor employed by the industry, to be chosen by labor unions existing or to be formed of employees in such industry; and three, representing the public or consumers, to be chosen by Associations of consumers of the products of the industry concerned.

Federal Government Veto

There should be invested in a Federal agency, the right to veto any acts of the association, particularly in reference to the fixing of prices of raw materials and manufactured products, that might be against the public interest. Such veto to be subject to review by the Federal Courts.

Voluntary Co-operation

All units, in a given industry would be free to join the trade associations or not, as they saw fit, but those choosing to remain out of the association, would be compelled under heavy penalty, to abide by the maximum and minimum prices and wage scales, fixed by the trade associations.

World Industrial Co-operation

The trade associations in each industry should be empowered to make agreements with associations in other industries for the purpose of stabilizing industrial activity throughout the nation and should further be empowered to deal with cartels or trade associations in other countries, looking towards the stabilization of industrial conditions throughout the world, raising the living standards in backward countries and consequently their purchasing power.

Agriculture

The depressed condition of agriculture in the United States is the most important single factor in the dislocation of our economic structure. The drastic curtailment in the purchasing power of the farm population of the country, numbering 30,157,000 souls in 1930, is largely responsible for the present distressed condition of industry. The rural population, whose purchasing power depends on agriculture, in 1930, was 54,000,000, comparing with an urban population of 69,000,000 in the same year, while in 1920, the rural population was 51,000,000 and the urban population 54,000,000. These figures indicate the migration of the population from the rural districts to industrial centers, largely on account of the fact that agriculture offered less attractive opportunities of profit than industry. While every thoughtful citizen realizes that industry cannot be profitable when agriculture is unprofitable and that the entire economic structure of the country is thus thrown into dislocation, the leaders in industry and agriculture have never cooperated to solve the economic problems besetting the country. The fact is that a spirit of antagonism exists between these groups. This tragic condition of affairs must be changed before stability and security can be attained in our economic structure.

Both political parties have, for years, promised relief for the farming community, but actual legislation has largely been undertaken on the theory that by helping industry (business), the farmer will be incidentally benefited. This is putting the cart before the horse. Industry can never be permanently profitable until the purchasing power of the farmers of the country is restored. The agricultural community have been guilty of the same excesses in the way of overproduction and speculation as the entire population in the past ten years. The problems confronting agriculture are generally speaking, identical with those besetting industry. Openminded, intelligent and sympathetic cooperation between industrial, agricultural, financial and political leaders to correct the disparity between the prices which the farmer gets for his products and the prices he has to pay for his requirements, could bring agricultural reform into harmony with the industrial reform suggested in this program.

Transportation—Banking—Utilities

Banks and insurance companies, now regulated under special laws, by the nature of their services, do not come under the scope of this program. The necessity of reforming our banking laws to curb the profit urge of the bankers and protect depositors and investors is conceded by thoughtful citizens and definite action is probable in the very near future.

It would be highly desirable and advantageous to all concerned that the Federal laws regulating railroads, that are extensive employers of labor and indirectly serve all consumers, be amended to come within the spirit of this reform.

The public utility industry, regulated by the laws of the States, prevents some difficulty but when the people of the country are convinced that this fundamental reform is indispensable to their industrial and financial security and stability, it will certainly not be difficult to bring this industry within the beneficial effects of this program.

Two Hundred Corporations Hold the Key

Less than fifty industries need be considered in this program. The assent of the two hundred corporations with less than two thousand directors, that are estimated to control thirty-five to forty-five percent of the business wealth of the United States, (excluding from business wealth that of Government, agriculture and professions), could make this reform effective.

Effects at Home and Abroad

Should the United States attain permanent security, prosperity and social justice along the above lines, its example would likely bring the same blessing to all the peoples of the earth.

The adoption of this program would:

(1) Stabilize industry in the United States and possibly throughout the world;

(2) Permanently stabilize prices for securities on their intrinsic values and permanently stabilize dividends on the capital stock of all industries based on the actual amount of money invested in them;

(3) Stabilize employment, guaranteeing human beings an opportunity to earn a decent living and to own property.

COMMENTS ON THIS PROGRAM

Principle (a).

Man's power of keeping himself alive depends on his right to work. Nature provides this opportunity for all men. Any social order or government that does not safeguard this human right fails in its minimum service to organized society. This does not mean that the Government must provide every man with a job, but it does mean that laws must be such that no class of citizens, natural or unnatural, (corporations) can deny or abridge, for its own benefit, this right to other citizens; for instance, that machinery or technical research be permitted to enrich a few and deprive great numbers of human beings from earning a living. Most civilized nations acknowledge this duty and the discriminatory character of their laws, by sustaining the unemployed through doles from the public treasury. The denial of man's right to work necessitates a reform in our social order and laws, based on justice, for which state or private charity cannot be substituted.

Principle (b).

Man's right to own property is a natural right, possessed by him before any organized society came into existence. It is based on the rights of man to the fruits of his labor and cannot be taken from him by any Government or social order. Inasmuch as nature provides sustenance sufficient for every human being, justice demands that the laws of any Commonwealth be such that all its citizens have the opportunity to earn a decent living; that it is unjust that a few citizens have more than is required to decently sustain them and that others have nothing at all. The very existence of society depends on this right of the individual being extended to his family. If this were not true, mankind could not perpetuate itself.

Principle (c).

Capital (money) and labor applied to land (the products of the earth) provide new wealth, additional capital. They are indispensable to each other. A partnership status should exist between them. They should each receive a fair wage, and share equally in the new wealth their cooperative action creates. It is to the advantage of both labor and consumers that the fair earning power of money (capital) be stable, but this can never be attained until the partnership status with labor is realized. The wages for money, however, must be computed on actual money employed in the industry and not on inflated corporation capitalization based on fictitious earning power, predicated on wages for labor below its living requirements. This is tantamount to money receiving an excessive wage at the expense of labor.

Principle (d).

In the modern economic structure, it is the function of corporation management to distribute equitably the rewards between money and human labor in fixing the prices of consumers' goods. This is practically done by fixing, as above, the wages for money and the wages for human labor. It is just that the people of the country should bear in the price they pay for commodities, the burden of providing fair wages for money and fair wages for human beings engaged in the various industries producing them. It is to the interest of all the citizens that these wages be stable. The vast majority of consumers are engaged, directly or indirectly, in production. In order that they may be able to maintain a satisfactory status as consumers depends upon production being profitable and the only way that this can be brought about is that the price of commodities be such as to provide a fair profit above cost.

Inasmuch as the introduction of machinery and inventions into industry has displaced human labor and deprived many of the opportunity to work, it is consequently just that the prices of commodities include an equitable contribution to taxes to provide funds for the education of unskilled workers in some trade which will eventually enable them to find employment in some or other of the trade associations. Industry should also contribute its equitable proportion with other sources of tax-revenue to a fund to be used in public works for the benefit of all the people, to give employment to unskilled labor that cannot be employed permanently in any industry. As there may still remain an excess number of human laborers, it is just that the prices of commodities include a contribution, in common with other sources of public revenue, to taxes to provide a fund to enable such laborers to acquire and cultivate farm lands, by which they may at least raise enough to feed themselves and their families and not be obliged to accept private or state charity. As the people's commonest feelings of human sympathy and justice will not tolerate a condition where men willing to work starve in the midst of plenty nor can any state long endure in which such a condition exists, it is only commonsense to meet this situation in a practical and businesslike manner, to provide work rather than pay doles that destroy the morale of a large part of the population of the country when millions are periodically reduced to a condition of pauperism and are kept alive only by public or private charity.

This is not paternalism nor is it socialistic. The Government, representing all the people, is responsible for not protecting, through proper laws, a large proportion of the citizenry from being reduced to pauperism through their right to work being denied them. It must consequently assume responsibility and temporarily extend the financial aid necessary to liquidate this social injustice.

Comments on the measures proposed to translate the above principles into law:

Provision (a)—1. The provision to insure equal partition of available work among workers in the industry entitled thereto, again, on account of the disrupting effect of machinery, requires that the work hours per week for each laborer be fixed on the basis of providing work for all.

Provision (a)—2. The fixing of prices scientifically, as indicated above, would insure the maintenance of production on a profitable basis. The elimination of costly waste incident to destructive competition in industry, through cooperation in trade associations and the consequent lowering of cost of producing raw materials and manufactured products, would provide funds to meet all of the above ends at prices for commodities not burdensome to consumers that are regularly employed at wages which would greatly increase the consuming power of the whole population.

Provision (a)—3. The directors of the trade association would be empowered to fix maximum prices for their products to protect the public and minimum prices to protect the various units within the trade association, or others who might elect not to join such trade associations. Both of these prices should be subject to veto by a Federal agency if found to be unfair and against the public interest. These prices would be elastic and made to meet conditions that might develop from time to time, affecting the industry. It should be carefully noted that there is a vast difference between an industry fixing its own prices justified to the public by fullest publicity in the methods used in computing them and subject to the scrutiny of a Federal agency, and the arbitrary fixing of prices by the Government.

Provision (b)—1. This provision is absolutely necessary to bring about gradually a better distribution of wealth through an equitable distribution of the national income. It is the most effective way to create permanent customers for industry. It will obviate the necessity of the semisocialistic provisions for unemployment insurance, etc., and it will eliminate the periodic necessity for state aid or doles and largely reduce the tremendous sum that is raised each year by community chests and other charitable institutions, private and state, for the purpose of taking care of the destitute. It provides for the setting up of surplus reserves to stabilize wages for human beings as well as dividends for stockholders. The necessity for this reform is now largely conceded by employers of labor as absolutely essential to any kind of stabilization.

Provision (b)—2. This provision is to secure the fullest publicity of all the actions of the trade association. No measure will so completely re-establish confidence and none will provide so powerful a curb on greed. Injustice is born and thrives in the dark. No industry honestly conducted in the interest of its various units, its employees and the public, need fear the fullest publicity of all its actions.

Legality

The opinion of Edmund O. Campbell on the right of the Federal Government to regulate the industry of mining coal (Congressional Record, January 13, 1932), indicates a possible method by which the Federal Government might constitutionally impose on all industries through Federal licenses to corporations to engage in Interstate Commerce, conditions which would compel them to adopt some such program as is suggested above.

It apparently would be possible for Congress to authorize the creation of these Trade Associations without modifying the antitrust laws except to define such legalized monopolies, organized on the terms it might prescribe, as not constituting a restraint of trade.

In any case when the people of the country are convinced that such a social and economic reform is necessary to their security, and well-being, there can be no doubt that the Congress has the power to put it in effect.

27 National Catholic Welfare Conference

CONSTITUTIONAL CRISIS AND SOCIAL JUSTICE

The personnel of the Social Action Department in the National Catholic Welfare Conference saw in the "code authorities" set up under the National Industrial Recovery Act a sound foundation on which to erect an occupational group system along the lines of Pope Pius XI's encyclical Quadragesimo Anno. *Shortly after the Supreme Court invalidated the Act the Department prepared and published over the signatures of 131 leading Catholic social thinkers and actionists a pamphlet entitled* Organized Social Justice *which called for an amendment to the federal Constitution to empower Congress to enact all needed labor legislation. The pamphlet contended that a perfected NRA would give wage-earners, farmers, and small business men, as well as the great industrialists, an effective voice in the control of economic life, and by so doing enable the country to rid itself of laissez-faire capitalism without resorting to excessive governmental regulation of the economy.*

Organized Social Justice *proved to be more a tract for the times than a blueprint for the future. The Supreme Court itself resolved the constitutional crisis in 1937 and Congress refused to repeat the NRA experiment.*

ORGANIZED SOCIAL JUSTICE

Now that the NRA is destroyed, a new and better way must be found to abolish the principal injustices that afflict our economic life. This is the first thing needed. The second and more fundamental is to create an economic order which will enable men to do justice readily and in some degree automatically. Without justice we cannot have either industrial recovery or lasting prosperity.

Social Action Department, National Catholic Welfare Conference, *Organized Social Justice. An Economic Program for the United States Applying Pius XI's Great Encyclical on Social Life. 131 Signers* (New York: The Paulist Press, 1935), pp. 3–23.

SOCIAL INJUSTICE

Competition does not explicitly aim at justice. As generally carried on, it endeavors to buy labor for the lowest wage and sell goods for the highest price. It assumes that this "enlightened selfishness" will automatically bring about the maximum of justice for all. It assumes that evil trees will bring forth good fruit.

Of course, it was bound to fail. In the great industries it long ago began to commit slow suicide. Over large areas of the industrial domain it has given way to economic dictatorship. The main elements of the dictatorship are swollen fortunes, concentrated control of investments and credit and industrial arrangements exercising all the essential powers of monopoly.

The evil effects of this dictatorship are manifest, even in times of so-called prosperity. In 1929, a fifth of our families received less than one thousand dollars a year and two-fifths less than fifteen hundred. The right of a family living wage is a fundamental of Catholic social teaching. Yet our industries could have turned out sufficient goods to provide all families with a minimum of two thousand dollars a year. Nor is this all: the potential capacity of our industrial plant was and is far greater than its actual capacity in 1929.

The main cause of the twenty per cent unused capacity and the thirty per cent undeveloped capacity was the unbalanced distribution of the national product. Too much was disbursed in the form of large and very large incomes. Hence too much was converted into instruments of production and too little into consumption. Moreover a considerable part of the excessive incomes was spent neither for finished goods nor in the creation of new capital goods: billions of dollars were "invested" in worthless securities and other unprofitable forms of speculation. Had the masters of industry given a considerably larger share of the product to labor, the latter would have bought sufficient goods to keep our industries going at full capacity, and there need have been no depression.

SOCIAL JUSTICE

In the field of production social justice demands such a use of our natural, technological and human resources as will provide all our people with a decent livelihood and ensure a steady elevation of the standard of living. In the words of Pope Pius XI: "Then only will the economic and social organism be soundly established and attain its end, when it secures for all and each those goods which the wealth and resources of nature, technical achievement, and the social organization of economic affairs can give."

In the field of distribution, social justice demands a far greater measure of equity than now obtains in the United States. According to the estimates of Moulton and Associates in "America's Capacity to Consume" (p. 56), one-tenth of one per cent of American families received in 1929 practically as much as the forty-two per cent of American families occupying the lower ranges of the income scale. Such extremes are impossible of either economic or social or ethical justification.

In more specific terms, social justice demands: wages and hours which will ensure continuous employment, a decent livelihood and adequate security for all workers; the prices of commodities so adjusted and interrelated that the various groups of producers can command the means of a decent and appropriate livelihood; such a reduction in the general rate of interest as will, on the one hand, evoke sufficient saving for the common good, and, on the other hand, permit neither excessive investment nor insufficient consumption. Finally, social justice requires all the economic classes to promote the common good by a reasonable amount of honest labor and service.

NECESSITY OF INTERVENTION BY GOVERNMENT

In 1933 many of the masters of industry professed to be persuaded that the country could never and should never go back to the old economic régime. Now that their fears of economic collapse have been dissipated or mitigated by the recent improvement in business conditions, the most powerful industrialists are clamoring for 'a return to unlimited competition and *laissez faire*.' In 1931, Pope Pius XI declared that, "The whole economic life has become hard, cruel and relentless in ghastly measure." Industrialists who desire a return to the régime are, without realizing it, equally cruel; for they would defeat recovery, make unemployment chronic and indefinitely postpone the coming of social justice.

Government is by right and duty more than policeman. It should see to it that the laws and institutions and the whole character and administration of the country shall be such as of themselves will bring public well-being and prosperity. It should protect the poor, and wageworkers generally, because of their great weakness. Social legislation of a sweeping sort is in its province. The social obligations of ownership it should define and enforce. It should help to establish the form of personal ownership which will best meet the common good, and set up public ownership or control of those industries which cannot safely be left in private hands.

In the United States all these and many other social and industrial obligations of public authority will have to be performed mainly by the federal government. Since industry is national in its scope and effects, it cannot be adequately regulated except by national action and legislation. Unfortunately, this fact is not grasped by all of those who believe in adequate regulation. Some of them desire and hope that the thing can be done by the forty-eight States.

As a matter of fact, the constitutional power of the States to fix wages, hours or prices, or to enact any of the other important regulations of the NRA is so uncertain that it is not worth serious consideration. In half a dozen or more decisions, the Supreme Court has indicated that most State legislation of this character would violate the due process clause of the Fourteenth Amendment to the Constitution. Even if the States had the requisite constitutional authority, they would be unable to agree upon uniform legislative measures for our nation-wide industries and our nation-wide competition. Hence the only alternative to a constitutional amendment enabling Congress to set up standards of industrial and social jusice, is no standards at all. Pope Pius XI called for a just regulation of industry by public authority, but the only public authority competent to do this in our political system is the federal government. Those, therefore, who oppose an amendment to the Constitution which would confer this power upon Congress are, either wittingly or unwittingly, demanding the continuation of the old order—*laissez faire,* individualism, liberalism and unlimited competition.

To be sure, the States and their political subdivisions should be constitutionally authorized to regulate local industries and to set up higher standards in all industries than those established by the federal government. The more progressive States have frequently excelled the majority of the States in their social and industrial legislation. They took the lead and enacted laws which set a good example for the rest of the country. All the States should retain this beneficial power and opportunity.

LIMITATIONS UPON INTERVENTION BY GOVERNMENT

Yet to think of the economic welfare of the people in terms of government only is fatal. The amount of government regulation would have to be progressively increased. Even so, it would not be adequate. Let us consider a few of the most important regulations which have been enacted or are likely to be enacted in the United States.

Social insurance is good; it fills out the living wage and cushions our insecurity; but it assumes that the underlying insecurity and injustice are to be otherwise cared for. Regulation of farm production and special taxes to assure parity of farm prices with other prices have been, it seems, necessary; but underproduction when so many are poor and taxation devices to assure parity are the heroic measures of an unjust society. Low credit for farmers and governmental inauguration of a new kind of homesteading by establishing farmers in land ownership at low interest rates is good; but the production, marketing and credit system will require more and more assistance for them from government. Special governmental commissions or bureaus for the regulation of output, prices, wages, hours and collective bargaining are apparently necessary in certain industries; but this implies an endless battle of government with industries which are not organized for service either of the community or their own workers.

Regulation of securities, stock markets and holding companies has long been needed; but it will be impeded by excessive savings for investment made by the few, so long as the income of the country is not rightly distributed. High taxes on large incomes and inheritances bring wider distributive justice; but they do not correct the bad distribution of the product. Federal regulation of the major movements of the credit market has become urgent because of the underlying unbalanced production and income distribution and the striving for maximum profits.

As things go, the government would have to keep on tinkering. The totalitarian State, fascist or collectivist would sooner or later come upon us from around the corner where now it lurks.

UNIONISM

Organization of employees into free unions is a right and a necessity. A collective bargain, the union representing the employees, is now the only approximately equal bargain; an equal bargain is the only free bargain and the only one that can start with the basic justice of the living wage and move onward toward employment conditions that will tend to secure steady employment and a high standard of living for all. This is true whether the bargainers on the other side are competitive owners, or private dictators, or an NRA or a facist State, or a collectivist State.

Yet if collective bargaining is the sole safeguard of employees, one class of organized owners and creditors lines up on one side, seeking more power and profits, and another class of dependent and propertyless employees lines up on the other, seeking a measure of decent living. The striving for social justice becomes strife, conflict, finally social war and a road to destruction.

ORGANIZATION BY OCCUPATIONAL GROUPS

If the régime of individualism and *laissez faire* is bankrupt (as it surely is) and if no amount of government regulation can bring about an adequate or just economic order, where shall we find a satisfactory solution? In some form of collectivism (either Socialism or Communism) is the answer given by many of our intellectuals. They reject as futile any program of regulation. They completely overlook the middle ground between individualism and collectivism. This attitude is inexcusable for two reasons: first, because it ignores the proposals for reconstructing the social order set forth by Pope Pius XI; second, because it minimizes or misrepresents the important achievement of the industrial codes under the NRA.

The essence of the Pope's program is a system of occupational groups. In each industry the occupational group should include all interested parties: labor as well as capital; employees as well as employers. Employers and labor and the other subdivisions of other occupations would keep their rights of separate assemblage and vote inside the occupational groups and their right of separate organization. These groups, says Pope Pius XI, would "bind men together not according to the position which they occupy in the labor market but according to the diverse functions which they exercise in society." The occupational groups would seek to modify competition by maintaining standards of fairness with regard to wages, hours, prices and business practices; to avoid private industrial dictatorship by enabling labor to share in all industrial policies and decisions, and to exclude political or bureaucratic industrial dictatorship by keeping the immediate and day to day control in the hand of the agents of production. They would be prevented from injuring the consumer or the common good by governmental action, "directing, watching, stimulating and restraining, as circumstances suggest or necessity demands." This form of government control is very different from and very much less than that contemplated by collectivism. Moreover, the consumers could protect themselves through some form of representation in relation to the governing bodies of the occupational groups.

In a word, the occupational group system would aim to bring into industry sufficient self-government to reduce to a minimum the conflicting interests of the various industrial classes, to place industrial direction in the hands of those most competent to exercise it and to permit only that amount of centralized political control which is necessary to safeguard the common good.

Some persons who are sympathetic with an occupational group organization have been confused by references to the Medieval Guilds. The resemblances are, indeed, considerable, but so are the differences. In striving to understand the structure and function of occupational groups it is much more helpful to compare them with institutions within our own experience: the trade associations, the code authorities and the codes of fair practice which functioned under the NRA. If employees had been represented (adequately, of course) in the associations which drew up the NRA industrial codes and in the "authorities" which administered the code provisions, the NRA and its institutions would have been fairly comparable with the proposed occupational groups. Had the NRA been permitted to continue, it could readily have developed into the kind of industrial order recommended by the Holy Father.

Three other modifications of the NRA structure are needed for an adequate and just economic order. (a) Economic self-government should be extended to farmers and to the professions. (b) A council or federation should be formed, of all the organized industries and professions, to handle their relations to one another and to the whole community. (c) Government should have the power not only to prevent wrong but to be a positive agent in promoting the common welfare.

This organized economic life would range over the whole field of social justice—quantity of production, quality, prices, steadiness of work, wages and salaries, hours of work, training of personnel, social insurance, methods of work, capitalization, interest, profits and credit. This régime would be dominated by neither private dictators nor public bureaucrats.

The economic welfare of the people would then be in their own hands. They could seek justice directly, every day, habitually, in a favorable atmosphere and in a suitable social order. They would fufill that duty of social justice which requires them to build an economic order within a governmental order, that will pervade all ownership and all work, in the service of the common good.

Employees would have the knowledge and power to use their organizations for social justice to themselves and social justice in output and prices for all the people. They could pursue their own welfare without an endless future of strikes or suppression and serve the community without fear of betraying their own interests.

Here is the opportunity for the growing numbers who have turned against the poverty, waste and wrong of our time to put dignity, order and justice into the work of their lives. Nor would they be exchanging their present masters for political appointees. Farmers, middle class business groups and the professions would be so organized that they could guide their function in society to their own welfare and to the welfare of others. This is social justice.

A federation of all the functional divisions of the productive, service and distributive activities of economic society would be able not only to prevent the separate divisions from doing wrong but to bring them all into effective cooperation for the common good. Our economic life would be guided by reason. It would correspond to thought and knowledge and become emancipated from both the anarchy of competition and the tyranny of private or public dictatorship. Government would retain its power of preventing injustice and supplementing the work of the organized groups.

A right economic order is a partnership for the common good between government—federal, State and city—and the self-governing, democratically organized membership of the industries, of farming, of trade and of the professions. In the proper functioning of economic life the immediate responsibility rests upon the people, so organized in their industries and professions and in the federation of their organizations as to be able to fulfill their responsibility.

Under an occupational group system it would become practicable to effect a wide diffusion of private ownership, to restore to that institution the position that it once held in American life and American aspirations. Nowhere is the delusion more startlingly evident of trying through injustice to fulfill the

American promise than in the concentration of wealth within a country that was committed less than a century ago to be and remain a nation of owners. Even farmers at an alarming pace are becoming tenants and laborers. A small minority of our people own the greater part of our wealth. Ownership of the means of livelihood is a natural right of man, not that all things must be held in personal ownership nor that personal ownership carries with it absolute rights but that ownership is a right, is personal-social of its very nature and should be the normal possession of normal men. It is a means of liberty and of defense against aggressions of the powerful, whether the powerful be the rich as now, or the State as in a fascist society, or even the far more responsive organized industry or profession in the economic order here outlined. It is the surest title to participation in the common good. It is the surest means of great production and wide distribution.

OBSTACLES

Four great obstacles confront both industrial recovery and the establishment of a right economic order. One is the inadequate organization of some of the most important social classes. Labor unions comprise only a small minority of the wage earners; farmers' cooperative societies are relatively few and feeble; consumers' cooperatives are even fewer and feebler and the quasi-independent middle classes in the cities are for the most part ineffectively organized. The task of remedying these conditions will necessarily be slow and to a large extent will have to wait upon the creation of the framework of the new economic order.

More immediate and more fundamental is the second obstacle. It consists in the opposition of almost all business men, and of a majority of all persons who are neither laborers nor farmers, to those radical and fundamental changes which are necessary in our distributive system. With a few notable exceptions, the masters of industry and finance still look forward to a resumption of unlimited investment, unlimited production and unregulated distribution. They still hope to make at least six per cent on all their investments, past and future. They ignore the twenty per cent unused capacity of our industries in 1929 and the thirty or forty per cent of additional capacity that might have been developed. They do not realize, or do not want to realize, that the cause of all this unused and undeveloped productive power was their failure to put sufficient purchasing power into the hands of the masses who would consume all that the industrial plant could produce.

The remedy is obvious: labor and the farmers must obtain a larger share of the product, while capital must be restricted to a smaller share. A considerable reduction in the rate of interest is essential to both recovery and reconstruction. It is the inevitable counterpart of an increase in the incomes and purchasing power of the wage earners and the farmers. This may be a "hard saying," but it is a true one.

The universal capacity of our industries for overproduction (relatively to existing effective demand) had led many of our economic thinkers to the conclusion that we cannot have a rational economic order without a large degree of compulsory economic planning. Their program would involve a despotic regulation of production by the central government. Happily this is not necessary. If laborers and farmers received adequate incomes,—incomes that are possible with anything like a full utilization of our productive resources—they would be able and willing to consume, with a very few exceptions, all the potential products of all our industries. There would be no need of planning to prevent general overproduction. Particular and temporary overproduction could be adequately dealt with by the federations of the occupational groups.

The third obstacle to reform and reconstruction is the popular hesitation to amend the Constitution. The reasons why an amendment is necessary have been sufficiently sketched in a preceding paragraph. Here it will be sufficient to note that without an appropriate constitutional amendment the country can obtain neither the most elementary regulation of industry, as in the matter of minimum wages, maximum hours and fair business practices, nor an occupational group system endowed with the authority necessary to its various functions. It is greatly to be regretted that men who detest individualism and *laissez faire* are virtually supporting the retention of that discredited régime by opposing an amendment to the Constitution.

The fourth obstacle to industrial recovery, to industrial reorganization and to social justice is the most obstinate of all. It is the most obstinate because it cannot be surmounted by social mechanisms or by information and argument. It consists in the inability of men to perceive their obligations of individual and social justice and in their unwillingness to fulfill these obligations. Following the gospel of "enlightened selfishness," men have easily persuaded themselves that justice comes automatically through self-seeking. Business practices and business ethics have perverted men's ideas of right and wrong, of justice and injustice. In the struggle for a livelihood and security vast numbers of men, possibly the majority, have adopted an immoral philosophy of both ends and means. They have come to look upon the end of life as the making of money and the lawful means thereto as any method that their ingenuity can render at once effectual and safe.

Nor has the industrial depression brought about saner views of life and conduct. The great majority of industrialists look upon the depression as merely an unpleasant interlude or interruption to the business of money making. They want to go back to the old régime and the old methods. Millions of the working population have become embittered by their privations, by their inability to obtain the necessaries of life in the midst of overproduction and plenty. There is no evidence that the passions of greed and envy or the practices of dishonesty, double dealing and extortion are less dominant or less prevalent in 1935 than they were in 1929.

ECONOMIC REFORM AND MORAL REFORM

Appalled by the prevalence and persistence of this crass materialism, some Catholics have lost faith in specifically economic meaures of reform. They recommend that all our energies should be directed toward a reformation of public and private morals. They insist that economic injustice would automatically cease and social justice be automatically realized if all persons would sincerely and intelligently strive to keep the Two Great Commandments. Undoubtedly this judgment is correct. Indeed, it might be regarded as a platitude. If all men would honestly and fearlessly practice the gospel of brotherly love they could achieve social justice within any framework of economic organization, just as they could have civil peace and righteousness in any kind of State.

The issue is one of practical possibilities. It is whether social justice can be more quickly and more extensively attained by moral teaching alone or by combining it with economic reorganization. The answer of experience is clear and compelling. Neither moral reformation nor economic reorganization is alone sufficient. Both are necessary and each supplements the other. A bad economic system and environment can make moral reforms exceedingly difficult. In the words of Pope Pius XI, "nowadays the conditions of social and economic life are such that vast multitudes of men can only with great difficulty pay attention to that one thing necessary, namely, their eternal salvation."

After recounting the abuses and injustices of present day economic conditions the Holy Father declares: "A stern insistence on the moral law, enforced with vigor by civil authority, could have dispelled or perhaps averted these enormous evils." Here is a clear expression of confidence in political as well as moral measures. The fact that the Pope set forth at great length a plan for reconstructing the social order should be sufficient evidence that he does not rely entirely upon moral reformation. He does, indeed, place moral renovation first: "this longed for social reconstruction must be preceded by a profound renewal of the Christian spirit, from which multitudes engaged in industry in every country have unhappily departed." If the Christian spirit were renewed in the hearts and minds of men it would not only enable them to make a more intelligent and more effective application of the moral law to their own economic transactions, but provide them with the most powerful motive for supporting and effectuating plans of economic reform and reconstruction.

CONCLUSION

Many Catholics who believe that we need a new economic order are discouraged over the prospects for an occupational group system. It will not be adopted, they fear, within one hundred years. Nevertheless, it is the only arrangement that will hold America safe from Fascism or Communism. Faced with these alternatives, how can any zealous and intelligent Catholic justify himself in yielding to discouragement or following a course of aloofness and inaction?

Moreover, the establishment of the economic order described in the foregoing pages need not be unusually difficult nor postponed to the indefinite future. If the NRA had not been destroyed it could have been developed and transformed into an occupational group system within ten years. It can be reëstablished through a constitutional amendment within five years. Here is a work that ought to stir the emotions and enlist the energies of all genuine believers in social justice. To sit by with folded hands or to heed the selfish and misleading propaganda of the servitors of plutocracy, is to commit apostasy from Catholic social principles and treason against America.

Not the least of the virtues of the economic order set forth in this pamphlet is its fundamental democracy. Men would be able to order their own economic lives. They would not be regimented by plutocratic or proletarian or political dictators. The intrinsic and indestructible dignity of the individual would be safeguarded against submergence in and subordination to the mass. The significance of the human person as a child of God and a brother of Christ would obtain, for the first time since the Middle Ages, effective recognition in economic institutions. The sacredness of personality has never been formally recognized in the maxims of historical capitalism. It is frankly rejected in the philosophy of Communism. It is treated as an exploded theory by most of our intellectuals. In the occupational group system it would again become a vital element in American thought and life.

Signers:

Sylvester Andriano, San Francisco, Calif.
Rev. W. Howard Bishop, Clarksville, Md.
Rev. John P. Boland, Ph.D., Buffalo, N. Y.
Linna E. Bresette, Washington, D. C.
Redmond Brennan, Kansas City, Mo.
Rev. Nicholas W. Brinkman, St. Louis, Mo.
August Brockland, St. Louis, Mo.
Rev. Charles A. Bruehl, Philadelphia, Pa.
Louis F. Buckley, South Bend, Ind.
Thomas E. Burke, Washington, D. C.
Rev. P. H. Burkett, S.J., Philadelphia, Pa.
Col. P. H. Callahan, Louisville, Ky.
Rev. H. V. Campbell, Denver, Colo.
Rev. J. M. Campbell, Ames, Iowa.
Right Rev. Msgr. John C. Carr, Buffalo, N. Y.
Rev. John J. Casey, Taunton, Mass.
Rev. John M. Cooper, Ph.D., Washington, D. C.

James A. Corcoran, New York, N. Y.
Rev. J. B. Culemans, Moline, Ill.
Rev. Cyprian Emanuel, O.F.M., Cleveland, Ohio.
Dorothy Day, New York, N. Y.
Henry B. Dielmann, San Antonio, Tex.
Rev. James Dolan, Taunton, Mass.
George F. Donovan, Ph.D., Webster Groves, Mo.
Rev. J. B. Donovan, C.M., Webster Groves, Mo.
Rev. John J. Doody, Chicago, Ill.
Rev. Peter B. Duffee, O.F.M., New York, N. Y.
Thomas J. Duffy, Columbus, Ohio.
Howard E. Eagan, Ph.D., Chicago, Ill.
Rev. William J. Engelen, S.J., St. Louis, Mo.
Rev. Sebastian Erbacher, O.F.M., Detroit, Mich.
P. T. Fagan, Pittsburgh, Pa.
James L. Fitzgerald, New York, N. Y.
C. J. Freund, Detroit, Mich.
Rev. Leo C. Gainor, O.P., Oak Park, Ill.
Rev. Hugh A. Gallagher, Mansfield, Mass.
Anna Dill Gamble, York, Pa.
Rev. Francis J. Gilligan, D.D., St. Paul, Minn.
Rev. James M. Gillis, C.S.P., New York, N. Y.
Francis J. Gorman, Washington, D. C.
Rev. Joseph E. Grady, Rochester, N. Y.
Rev. Raphael Vonder Haar, O.F.M., San Luis Rey, Calif.
Very Rev. Francis J. Haas, Ph.D., St. Francis, Wis.
James E. Hagerty, Ph.D., Columbus, Ohio.
John B. Haggerty, Washington, D. C.
Rev. John J. Harbrecht, Cincinnati, Ohio.
Thomas P. Hart, M.D., Cincinnati, Ohio.
Rev. Henry Hoerner, M.A., Sioux Falls, S. Dak.
Jane M. Hoey, New York, N. Y.
Rev. Frederick A. Houck, Toledo, Ohio.
Rev. Joseph Husslein, S.J., St. Louis, Mo.
Sister Mary Ignatius, S.N.D., South Euclid, Ohio.
Harry Jenkins, Philadelphia, Pa.
Rev. Athanasius Karlin, O.M. Cap., Victoria, Kans.
Edward Keating, Washington, D. C.
Rev. Edward A. Keller, C.S.C., Notre Dame, Ind.
Leo E. Keller, Detroit, Mich.
Rev. Franklyn J. Kennedy, Milwaukee, Wis.
Hon. Thomas Kennedy, Harrisburg, Pa.

Right Rev. Msgr. William J. Kerby, Ph.D., Washington, D. C.
Jerome G. Kerwin, Ph.D., Chicago, Ill.
Paul Kiniery, Ph.D., Chicago, Ill.
Rev. J. B. Koncius, Mount Carmel, Pa.
Rev. John LaFarge, S.J., New York, N. Y.
John Lane, Washington, D. C.
John A. Lapp, Ph.D., Washington, D. C.
Rev. Henry B. Laudenbach, Buffalo, N. Y.
George W. Lawson, St. Paul, Minn.
James A. Losty, Ph.D., Chicago, Ill.
Rev. A. J. Luckey, Manhattan, Kans.
Joseph McDonagh, Washington, D. C.
Right Rev. Msgr. Matthew F. McEvoy, Milwaukee, Wis.
John A. McGarry, Chicago, Ill.
Leo A. McGinity, New York, N. Y.
Rev. R. A. McGowan, Washington, D. C.
Hon. Edward F. McGrady, Washington, D. C.
Louise McGuire, Washington, D. C.
Rose J. McHugh, Albany, N. Y.
Thomas F. McMahon, Edgewood, R. I.
John F. McNamee, Cleveland, Ohio.
James H. Mahoney, New Bedford, Mass.
James Maloney, Philadelphia, Pa.
Dr. Julia T. Metcalf, Los Angeles, Calif.
Rev. Virgil Michel, O.S.B., Collegeville, Minn.
Rev. Raymond J. Miller, C.SS.R., Oconomowoc, Wis.
E. E. Milliman, Detroit, Mich.
Parker T. Moon, Ph.D., New York, N. Y.
Frederick A. Moran, Albany, N. Y.
Rev. P. G. Moriarty, San Francisco, Calif.
Elizabeth Morrissey, Ph.D., Baltimore, Md.
Rev. W. F. Mullally, St. Louis, Mo.
Arthur M. Murphy, Ph.D., Leavenworth, Kans.
Daniel C. Murphy, San Francisco, Calif.
Philip Murray, Pittsburgh, Pa.
Rev. George Nell, Effingham, Ill.
Agnes Nestor, Chicago, Ill.
Rev. John M. Nugent, O.P., Oak Park, Ill.
James O'Connell, Washington, D. C.
Rev. John J. O'Connor, Ph.D., Helena, Mont.
Walter J. O'Connor, Ph.D., Washington, D. C.
Right Rev. Msgr. Thomas J. O'Dwyer, Los Angeles, Calif.

Rev. Wilfrid Parsons, S.J., New York, N. Y.
Rev. A. H. Poetker, S.J., Detroit, Mich.
George S. Roche, Pittsburgh, Pa.
Sister Rose de Lima, Convent Station, N. J.
Eva J. Ross, New Haven, Conn.
Right Rev. Msgr. John A. Ryan, D.D., Washington, D. C.
Mae Sargent, Los Angeles, Calif.
Right Rev. Msgr. Arthur J. Scanlan, Yonkers, N. Y.
Rev. Edgar Schmiedeler, O.S.B., Ph.D., Washington, D. C.
Rev. M. Schexnayder, Baton Rouge, La.
Ellis Searles, Washington, D. C.
Mrs. Anna H. Settle, Louisville, Ky.
George N. Shuster, New York, N. Y.
Rev. Frederic Siedenburg, S.J., Detroit, Mich.
Right Rev. Msgr. Matthew J. Smith, Denver, Colo.
Josef Solterer, Washington, D. C.
Olive Sullivan, Chicago, Ill.
Sister Miriam Theres, Oswego, Oreg.
Rev. Joseph F. Thorning, S.J., Ph.D., Washington, D. C.
M. F. Tighe, Pittsburgh, Pa.
Hon. Richard M. Tobin, San Francisco, Calif.
Paul George Toohey, Kansas City, Mo.
Right Rev. Msgr. R. Marcellus Wagner, Cincinnati, Ohio.
Frank P. Walsh, New York, N. Y.
George L. Warren, New York, N. Y.
Rev. Russell I. Wilbur, St. Louis, Mo.
Mary J. Workman, Los Angeles, Calif.
Very Rev. Msgr. Peter M. H. Wynhoven, New Orleans, La.
Cecilia M. Yawman, Rochester, N. Y.
Charles A. Zenkert, Buffalo, N. Y.

28 Aloysius J. Muench

THE EVOLUTION OF COMPANY UNIONS INTO INDUSTRIAL COUNCILS

Only a few Catholic social thinkers spelled out the relationship between capital and organized labor in explicit terms. One of these was Monsignor Aloysius J. Muench, professor of sociology in St. Francis Seminary, Milwaukee, and in later life Bishop of Fargo, North Dakota; Papal Nuncio to West Germany; and finally, Cardinal. Pointing out that in origin and purpose both craft and industrial unions were fighting organizations, Monsignor Muench concluded that they were incapable of promoting solidarity between capital and labor. He called attention to the few ideally constructed employee representation plans—company unions in which employers accorded workers a genuine partnership status. He urged labor leaders and business men friendly to labor to come together and draw up a "standard plan," embodying the successful bargaining agreements, to serve as a stimulus for the formation of "industrial councils" on which both employers and employees would be represented.

In theory and in law, company unionism disappeared from the industrial scene soon after Muench wrote in the mid-1930's. His plan has been widely applied, however, under various forms of union-management cooperation. In appropriating Philip Murray's term, "Industry Councils," for an occupational group system, Catholics adopted a slight variant on Muench's phraseology.

Modern business enterprise rests on an alliance between capital and labor. Capital needs labor, and labor needs capital. Though both are mutually indispensable one to the other, labor has nevertheless been in a position of disadvantage under historical capitalism.

Historical capitalism views labor, not as its partner, but as its servant. Worse, it conceives of labor as a commodity to be purchased and sold on the labor market. Not reasons of justice or

---

Rt. Rev. Msgr. Aloysius J. Muench, "A New Alignment of Capital and Labor," *The Salesianum* [St. Francis Seminary, Milwaukee, Wis.], XXX, No. 1 (January 1935), 1–9.

equity, but the law of supply and demand dictates the negotiations of purchase and sale. This condition of affairs caused Pope Leo XIII to write more than forty years ago: "It is shameful and inhuman to treat men like chattels to make money by, or to look upon them merely as so much muscle or physical power." And Pope Pius XI speaking of the steady pressure of economic and social ideas in the direction of false liberalism as applied to business recently said: "Capital, however, was long able to appropriate too much to itself; it claimed all the products and profits, and left to the worker the barest minimum necessary to repair his strength and ensure the continuance of his class. For by an inexorable economic law, it was held, all accumulation of capital falls to the wealthy, while by the same law the workers are doomed to perpetual want or to a very low standard of life." This statement characterizes concisely and precisely the spirit of capitalism in its relation to labor. The learned Pontiff does not mean to imply that all employers succumbed to this spirit. He desires merely to characterize the essential features of the system as such.

Aware of its condition of subjection labor sought to free itself from a yoke which, to use again the words of Pope Leo XIII, "was little better than slavery itself." The laissez-faire system which was ushered in with the industrial revolution had taken from the worker the protection of both the guilds and the law. Helpless against the onrush of the mighty forces of organized capital, labor sought protection for itself behind the bulwarks of organization. It met organization with organization. The right to organize was not conceded without a struggle. Conspiracy laws were invoked against labor, and at every step it met embattled employers. The spirit of militancy begot labor organizations, and down through the decades to our day the sound of the battle cry has not died away. With one master stroke, Pope Pius XI has again painted for us the picture: "None the less, as things are now, the wage-system divides men on what is called the labor market into two sections, resembling armies, and the disputes between these sections transforms this labor market into an arena where the two armies are engaged in fierce combat." Ideas of warfare mark everywhere the industrial conflict. Only a few months ago President Roosevelt used the term truce in his fireside radio chat, in which he appealed to both capital and labor to lay aside as a temporary experiment the weapons of industrial warfare. The proposal was accepted by both sides, but not without phraseology that indicated that the spirit of battle was not dead.

By the force of organization labor seeks to wrest from capital some of the freedom which it itself enjoys through organization. In his Short History of England G. K. Chesterton writes straight to the point: "The modern trade union was the inspiration and creation of the English expression of the European effort to resist the tendency of capitalism to reach its natural culmination in slavery."

Labor organizations are consequently defense organizations against the growing powers of plutocratic capitalism. They attempt to equalize power. Their historic mission has been to wring from industrial capitalists the right to a living wage, the right to collective bargaining, shorter hours, and better work conditions. History bears testimony to the fact that whatever progress has been made in higher and better standards of work and living of wage-earners has been brought about largely through labor organizations.

Yet, the militant origin and the militant aggressiveness of trade unions, inspired by militant leadership, are precisely the reason why they do not appear to offer the right approach to a cordial and harmonious understanding between capital and labor, and therefore to the corporate reconstruction of the social order according to the ideas of Pope Pius XI. In this connection it is important to remember that trade-unions are by reason of their origin and purpose combatant organizations.

Now, in order to be effective combatant organizations trade-unions must be particularistic. They must concentrate their interests on a particular trade or craft. This, however, makes for a division of interests in the same industry. In the brewing industry, for example, the workers are divided according to their separate crafts and organized accordingly. The teamsters have their separate unions, and so have the bottlers, coopers, carpenters, electricians, and others employed in the same industry. What is the result? Not only are the workers divided among themselves but approach to the management "in a tender of business fellowship," to use the phrase of A. L. Filene, the successful Boston merchant, is made almost imposible. As a matter of fact in hardly any instance has trade-unionism succeeded in making even a near approach to a new alignment of labor to capital. The corporative reconstruction of economic society, in which capital and labor work together as business fellows, is completely out of the purview of labor leaders. Where a fairly good relationship has been worked out between employer and employe on the basis of collective bargaining, as in the Baltitimore and Ohio Plan, or in the Nash Clothing Company Plan, agreements are more in the nature of a truce than of a close merger of common interests in the same business enterprise.

The weakness of trade-unionism on this score has long been felt by those who look beyond the narrow field of objectives of opportunistic labor leaders. Of late there has been considerable agitation among workers to supplant trade and craft unions by industrial unions. Leaders in the American Federation of Labor have looked with much disfavor upon industrial unions, and whatever concessions they have made to industrial unionism have been wrung from them only after bitter fights on the floor of their annual conventions. For years the United Mine Workers of America have been organized along industrial rather than trade union lines. The organization has been very militant, as is attested by the bloody conflicts in mining areas, and perhaps had to be so because of the chaotic conditions of the mining industry and the intransigent attitude of mine owners toward organized labor. Despite factors of economic strength, industrial unions have done little to advance labor toward the goal of an economic solidarity with capital. The fault does not of course lie entirely on the side of labor. Capital also is wary of a corporate reorganization of business in which both the employers and employe own and manage on a basis of mutuality. In plans of this kind the employer is as afraid of domination by organized labor as the employe has been afraid in the past of the domination of corporate capital. Hence, whatever advance labor may make in the direction of establishing a basis of common solidarity is viewed with suspicion and distrust. The atmosphere is still too filled with the smoke of battle to allow capital and labor to see issues clearly. Whatever the explanation the fact remains that industrial unions, relying largely on the building up of class consciousness for the furtherance of their ends, have also made no approach to the new order of things as outlined in the encyclical of Pope Pius XI on the reconstruction of the social order. Like two armies organized labor and capital stand opposed to each other, and "the disputes between them transform the labor market into an arena where the two armies are engaged in fierce combat."

Unfit for a corporative reconstruction of the economic order both trade and industrial unions of the old type have been swept away in countries that have established the corporative state. The corporative idea has spread in Europe from Fascist Italy to Germany, Austria, Hungary, Esthonia, and Portugal. The strong spirit of individualism of the French militates strongly against the establishment of the corporative state in France, although the trend toward it is on the upgrade. It is of no small significance that the Austrian Corporative State set up according to the chief guiding ideas of the Pope's encyclical on the reconstruction of the social order has also done away with the free trade and industrial unions. Perhaps one of the reasons is that Austrian labor organizations were deeply imbued with the Marxian doctrine of class struggle. But there can be no doubt either that labor organizations of either the European or American plan originate in and thrive on class consciousness, and consequently do not fit into the scheme of a corporative state. Instead of welding employer and employe together they separate. No one understood this better than Mussolini, himself an ex-Marxist. Familiar with the virtues and the vices of class struggle, he decided to eliminate it in Italian economic life. The new corporative state which he promulgated in its final form on November 10, 1934, dissolved the old organizations of both capital and labor. Employer and employee, like in the medieval guild system, now are members of one and the same organization, each working for the common good of the business in which he is engaged.

Fascist compulsion no matter of what color would hardly be acceptable to either the American employer or American employe. But is there no basis of a voluntary kind in American industry that could become the foundation of a corporative relationship between employer and employe? There is, and it is to be found in a few ideally constructed employe representation plans.

Employe representation plans have been sneeringly dubbed by labor "company unions." Unfortunately good company unions that meet the approval of labor are all too few in the country. "Employers have indicated in many cases," writes an economic authority recently,[1] "that their main purpose is to use employe representation plans to combat or destroy trade unions. They desire to maintain the competitive advantage of negotiating wages, hours, and working conditions solely with their own employes, since trade unions seek to establish basic standards in wages and working conditions in the plants of all competing concerns. This procedure of the unions cuts off the opportunity of each employer to gain competitive advantage

[1] Arthur E. Suffern in Spahr, *Economic Principles and Problems* (New York: 1934), p. 331.

by cutting wages, increasing hours, and requiring more burdensome working conditions." This description of the attitude of many employers who favor company unions is not an overstatement of the facts. It is not a mere coincidence that after the enactment of the now famous Section 7A, employers engaged in feverish activity to erect company unions as bulwarks of defense against the expected onrush of organized labor.

Organized labor views company unions with contempt. It charges that they are the creatures of employers to enslave still more his workers; that the management controls the election of representatives; that committee men representing workers, fearing they may lose their jobs if they obstruct management plans, are easily intimidated; and that in the event of an industrial conflict workers have neither the power of membership of a large trade union organization nor the financial resources of large labor organizations to support strikers. No one plant, continues the indictment, can individually fight trade practices of an industry as a whole. Greater cohesion than company unions afford is required if labor is to come into its rights. Democratic management of industry is a sham and mockery under a system of company unions.

Generally true, the indictment is nevertheless too sweeping in its scope. In condemning all company unions because of the faulty organization or misdirected purposes of some company unions, organized labor makes the same mistake that industrialists make in condemning all trade union organizations because of the radical policies and corrupt leadership of some trade unions. Organized labor has missed fine opportunities of achieving a greater participation in the management of business by not throwing its full support behind employe representation plans that meet with the aspirations of labor.

A number of companies treat their workers as partners in the business enterprise. Some of the employe representation plans are outstanding examples of what might be accomplished in the field of a corporative reorganization of the economic order. In a number of companies such as the William S. Filene Sons Company, Dutchess Bleacheries, Inc., Boston Consolidated Gas Company, and Louisville Railway Company, employes are represented in the board of directors. An arbitration board composed of employes only settles all grievances of workers in Filene Stores. The Philadelphia Rapid Transit Company and the Columbia Conserve Company permit employes to acquire common stock, own it as a group, vote it as a block, elect their representatives to the board of directors, and, if desired, ultimately to obtain control. The latter Company pays its workers an annual wage, including vacations and unemployment. Other companies, such as the Philadelphia Rapid Transit Company, pay bonuses for efficiency and operate generous profit sharing plans.

A serious mistake has been made by organized labor to include all company unions in its criticisms. And a graver mistake has been made in not including the best features of good company unions in its program for the achieving of a more democratic organization of industry. For, the flat fact is that these unions have given employes a degree of control and ownership which, ordinarily, is not conceived as possible under collective bargaining with unions. Indeed, Col. P. H. Callahan, a Louisville manufacturer, who years ago introduced the famous Ryan-Callahan plan of partnership in his plants writes in a letter to the Editor of the Louisville Courier-Journal, September 5, 1934: "Ten years ago most of my conferees agreed that Union Labor was never intended as the real solution of the Capital and Labor controversy." Careful readers of the Pope's encyclical will come to the same conclusion.

Should labor, then, be expected to give up trade unionism? Not at all. The rights that workers have won through their organizations have been purchased at too heavy a price to expect labor to give up what still remains to it as the most effective weapon of defense against attacks of unscrupulous industrialists.

But organized labor should widen its objectives and change its attitude toward good employe representation plans, and that for its own sake. Certainly an attitude of hostility such as was evinced in the Kohler strike can not be justified. Organized labor should seriously undertake to work out a constructive program for a new alignment of capital and labor, and work with all its efforts to secure good-willed industrialists for its objectives. Unless this is done the ideal of the corporative reconstruction of the economic order will never be achieved. Nothing should be so clear to observers as the truth of the Pope's statement that the present division of capital and labor on the labor market will serve only to perpetuate conflict. Class consciousness can not be organized without class struggle.

What should labor's constructive program be?

First, it should pay open recognition to business men who have made a tender of business fellowship to their employes. Secondly, labor leaders should get into touch at once with these business men with a view to giving them support against competitors that make impossible a better operation of corporative employer-employe plans as to wages, hours, and work conditions. Thirdly, they should seek with the aid of these business men to draw up standards for these plans that are in line with the best experience of a corporative organization of business and have been tested in the practical field of business. In other words, successful features of existing employe representation plans or of collective bargaining agreements might be incorporated into this standard plan. Fourthly, an alliance of industrialists and labor leaders, convinced of the practicableness of this standard, should be formed for the purpose of promoting its extension over as wide a field of industry as possible. Fifthly, industrial councils should be formed in the industries that have adopted the standard plan for the purpose of effecting a high level of cooperation in which employers and employes work together for their common good. Representatives of employers and employes should compose these industrial councils.

An ambitious program? Perhaps. Yet, it can be built on principles and policies that have been tested and tried in the actual business world.

There are only two ways of effecting a corporative reorganization of economic society: the one way is that of fascist compulsion which neither American industry nor American labor desires, and the other way is that of a voluntary merger of common interests in corporate or vocational groups, supported by strong organizations of employers and employes alike.

Grave disorder will continue in society unless men get together on a basis of mutuality of interests. "There can not be question of any perfect cure unless this opposition be done away with, and well organized members of the social body be constituted—vocational groups, namely, claiming the allegiance of men, not according to the position they occupy in the labor market, but according to the diverse functions which they exercise in society." So writes Pope Pius XI, and the problem can not be expressed more succinctly.

29 Charles E. Coughlin

SOCIAL JUSTICE THROUGH PUBLIC OWNERSHIP AND CONTROL

The Rev. Charles E. Coughlin, famed "radio priest," summarized the program of his Union for Social Justice in sixteen points. They reflect his belief that the Great Depression stemmed primarily from private monopoly of natural resources and of money and banking, only incidentally from unjust relations between capital and labor. In both social outlook and oratorical power Father Coughlin was reminiscent of Father Edward McGlynn and the single-tax agitation that preceded him by half a century.

Without comment and just as a matter of record, we give here the principles of Father Coughlin's National Union for Social Justice, as drawn up by Father Coughlin in the following sixteen points: "1.—I believe in the right of liberty of conscience and liberty of education, not permitting the state to dictate either my worship to my God or my chosen avocation in life. 2.—I believe that every citizen willing to work and capable of working shall receive a just and living annual wage which will enable him to maintain and educate his family according to the standards of American decency. 3.—I believe in nationalizing those public necessities which by their very nature are too important to be held in the control of private individuals. By these I mean banking, credit and currency, power, light, oil and natural gas and our God-given natural resources. 4.—I believe in private ownership of all other property. 5.—I believe in upholding the right to private property, yet in controlling it for the public good. 6.—I believe in the abolition of the privately owned Federal Reserve Banking System and in the establishment of a Government-owned Central Bank. 7.—I believe in rescuing from the hands of private owners the right to coin and regulate the value of money, which right must be restored to Congress where it belongs. 8.—I believe that one of the chief duties of this Government-owned Central Bank is to maintain the cost of living on an even keel and the repayment of dollar debts with equal value

---

"The Coughlin Sixteen Points," *The Guildsman* [Germantown, Ill.], III (April 1935), 10–11.

dollars. 9.—I believe in the cost of production plus a fair profit for the farmer. 10.—I believe not only in the right of laboring men to organize in unions, but also in the duty of the Government, which that laboring man supports, to facilitate and to protect these organizations against the vested interests of wealth and of intellect. 11.—I believe in the recall of non-productive bonds and thereby in the alleviation of taxation. 12.—I believe in the abolition of tax-exempt bonds. 13.—I believe in the broadening of the base of taxation founded upon the ownership of wealth and the capacity to pay. 14.—I believe in the simplification of government, and the further lifting of crushing taxation from the slender revenues of the laboring class. 15.—I believe that in the event of a war for the defense of our nation and its liberties, there shall be a conscription of wealth as well as a conscription of men. 16.—I believe in preferring the sanctity of human rights to the sanctity of property rights. I believe that the chief concern of governments shall be for the poor, because, as it is witnessed, the rich people have ample means of their own to care for themselves."

30 Association of Catholic Trade Unionists

STATEMENT OF PRINCIPLES

The Association of Catholic Trade Unionists aimed at more than education and propaganda: It aided trade unionists in maintaining their rights and in performing their duties. When necessary, the members of the ACTU participated in strikes that, upon investigation were found to be just. They furnished also, free of charge, legal aid to union members harassed by Communist or criminal leadership. In their meeting halls the ACTU sponsored "conferences" in which groups of workers drawn from all races and creeds discussed abuses in their unions and planned the strategy to bring about their removal. The first issue of The Labor Leader, *the publication of the Association of Catholic Trade Unionists, appeared in mimeographed form January 3, 1938. Besides indicating the activities of the Association, this first issue stated its purpose very clearly.*

ACTU IN ACTION

Ten months old last week, the ACTU looks back on some real accomplishments in 1937 and consequently faces 1938 with hopes of bigger and better deeds to come.

Granted there was plenty of room for bigger and better deeds in 1937 and plenty of room for improvement in those deeds done. Still and all, if its only contribution to society has been the help supplied in starting the Workers School at Fordham, the ACTU would have more than pulled its weight so far. In addition, however, the ACTU did the following things:

1) It supported strikes at Woolworth's, The Long Island Daily Press, Todd Ship Yards, the Brooklyn Daily Eagle, Weisbecker's Grocery Stores, and the Elmhurst Overhead Station of the Edison System.

In all but the Hershey strike ACTU members marched in picket lines (at the Eagle about fifteen times), usually with signs stating their position. In three strikes ACTU representatives spoke at meetings of strikers, in two at public open-air meetings, for a total of eleven meetings. In nearly every strike,

---

The Labor Leader, Vol. I, No. 1 (Jan. 3, 1938), 3–5.

where it was possible, the ACTU investigated both sides before committing itself.

2) It brought together employer, CIO, and AF of L for a conference at *The Catholic Worker,* which led to settlement of strike at the Schraeger Cigar Stores.

3) Its chaplain, Father John Monaghan, spoke at meetings of three unions on the natural right and necessity for union organization.

4) The ACTU, or members thereof, helped persuade Father Joseph Moody to speak at a Utility Workers mass-meeting called to protest Edison lay-offs, at which he stated the Church's stand on the right to work; helped persuade Father Thomas Conerty to join the Citizens Committee of the Eagle strike; Fathers Edward Swanstorm, William Kelly, and Edward Lodge Curran to investigate the Eagle strike; Father Curran to write a letter to *The Brooklyn Tablet* strongly supporting the strikers, which letter was important in persuading the publisher to sign a contract; Father Bertran Weaver to investigate the Krug Bakery strike; Fathers Moody and Curran to join Father Monaghan in negotiating with Edison executives for settlement of the Elmhurst strike.

5) Issued leaflets protesting the frame-up of George Donahue in Checkers' Local 1346, ILA, distributing two different leaflets seeking action at teamsters' and checkers' meetings; issued another supporting the Transport Workers Union in the BMT election; two others supporting the CIO in general; one refuting Communist leaflets that urged a United Front of Catholics and Communists against Fascism, distributed at ERB offices.

6) Published two issues of "Power & Light," organ of the Edison Chapter of the ACTU, both of which strongly supported the CIO and Utility Workers Local 1212, UER & MWA, thereof and urged Catholics to join same; distributed nearly 10,000 copies of each at ten power plants and office buildings throughout Edison system. Total cost: $130.

7) Further assisted organization of Catholics into bona fide unions by speaking at Holy Name meetings and the like, at Department Store Workers meeting of Macy warehousemen, distributing copies of *The Catholic Worker* to Transport Workers and to employees of The Metropolitan Engineering Company.

8) Supported various miscellaneous causes such as passage of Doyle-Neustein Bill (New York's little Wagner Act): protest of WPA lay-offs; defense of John Brophy, CIO director and good Catholic, from slanderous attacks of Communism in "Our Sunday Visitor"; urging police investigation of New York waterfront unions; peace conferences of CIO and AF of L; support of Republic Steel strike survivors; defense of National Labor Relations Board on Edison decision; condemnation of Fascist suppression of labor organization in Jersey City by Mayor Hague.

[No point 9 listed.]

10) Fought for, single-handed, and won upwards of $2000 in severance pay for 11 women workers at Teachers College Cafeteria discharged after an average of 12, ranging up to 24 years work.

11) Conducted weekly classes on the Labor Encyclicals of Popes Leo XIII and Pius XI and in Parliamentary Law and Public Speaking.

12) Staged an ACTU Dance for purely social purposes, had a good time, and made $15.

13) Held meetings every two weeks (monthly during the summer) to discuss questions of policy and action and to listen to speakers like Fathers Boland, Monaghan, Moody, Conerty, Rice and Hensler of Pittsburgh's Catholic Radical Alliance; and Dorothy Day and Peter Maurin of *The Catholic Worker.*

14) Joined the Nocturnal Adoration Society at the Paulist Fathers Church in a body and completed first of 12 hours monthly watching.

15) Held ACTU Communion Breakfast at Father Mon-

aghan's church, Corpus Christi, on the Feast of Christ the King, with 55 attending.

DEBT TO CW

In all this the ACTU owed, and still owes, a tremendous debt to *The Catholic Worker,* its foster-mother, who not only fostered, but aided, abetted, supported (financially and otherwise), criticized and encouraged its struggling off-spring.

Also in the matter of the Workers School it is greatly indebted to Fathers Robert Gannon, S.J., rector; John Lennon, S.J., dean of the Woolworth Branch; and Ignatius W. Cox, S.J., friend and counsellor; and above all to Father John Boland, who has given generously of his valuable time to fill an important place on the faculty.

THE STAND OF THE ACTU

(reprint of statement of principles authorized by Executive Board and membership in ACTU)

A group of militant Catholic union men, following the counsel of the Holy Father, Pius XI, founded the ACTU (Association of Catholic Trade Unionists) on the afternoon of February 27, 1937, at *The Catholic Worker* headquarters in New York City.

The purpose of the founders was not to organize Catholic unions, as some have thought, but to build up an organization of Catholics side by side with the established unions of America. The New York ACTU, for example, has leaders in 22 different trade unions, about half CIO, half AF of L, and a few independent.

The ACTU stands for a sound trade-unionism built on Christian principles. Its chief purpose is to foster and spread such unionism in the American labor movement by bringing to Catholic men and women in particular and to all men and women in general, a knowledge of those principles and by training leaders and supplying an organization to put them into practice.

A BETTER LIFE

This means that all Catholic workingmen and women should recognize their duty to join a bona fide trade union. It means that all Catholics should inform themselves about and take an active part in the affairs of the union to which they belong, not to win themselves a soft spot in a good business, but to guarantee that truth, justice, and charity prevail in the conduct of that union. In short, they must see to it that their union performs its true function as a necessary means for men to win a better and more Christian life.

The ACTU agrees that no Catholic can remain in a union that is run along Marxist or un-Christian lines, but at the same time it loudly insists that no real Catholic can resign from that union, and thereby surrender it to Marxists or racketeers, until he has made every possible effort to cure the corruption of that union. By "possible effort" we do not include and we intend to oppose any and every Fascist or un-Christian tactic.

WAKE UP AND LIVE!

To sum up, we believe that the only way for all men to win a better life is by a universal recognition and practice of the rights and duties that all men have by the very fact of their humanity.

We shall never gain this recognition or practice until Catholics begin to wake up and live in the Labor movement, until they educate and train themselves for leadership, until they organize and work actively and intelligently for a Christian "reconstruction of the social order."

Basing our stand on the papal encyclicals, the writings of other recognized Catholic authorities, and the basic principles of common sense and justice, we believe that:

THE WORKER HAS A RIGHT TO:

1) Job security.

2) An income sufficient to support himself and family in reasonable comfort.

3) Collective bargaining through union representatives freely chosen.

4) A share in the profits after just wage and return to capital have been made.

5) Strike and picket peacefully for just cause.

6) A just price for the goods he buys.

7) Decent working hours.

8) Decent working conditions.

and that THE WORKER HAS A DUTY TO:

1) Perform an honest day's work for an honest day's pay.

2) Join a bona fide union.

3) Strike only for just cause and after all other legitimate means have been exhausted.

4) Refrain from violence.

5) Respect property rights.

6) Abide by just agreements freely made.

7) Enforce strict honesty and a square deal for everybody inside his union.

8) Cooperate with decent employers who respect rights to bring about a peaceful solution of industrial war by the setting up of guilds for the self-regulation of industry and producer-cooperatives in which the worker shares as a partner in the ownership, management, or profits of the business in which he works.

31 Dorothy Day

DECENT POVERTY THE SOCIAL IDEAL

In the concluding chapter, here reproduced, of her book, House of Hospitality, *Dorothy Day focuses attention on the social philosophy of the Catholic worker movement of which she was co-founder and principal leader. The Catholic workers believed that all Christians, if not indeed all men, should embrace "decent" poverty, that is, be satisfied with a minimum sufficiency of food, shelter, and clothing. Should they do this, they would have the disposition, the material and spiritual strength with which to carry on the works of mercy and thus to lift the destitute poor out of their hopelessness and misery. Miss Day claimed with a breath of serene triumph that the houses of hospitality—soup kitchens, discussion clubs, and reform centers all in one—were true object lessons in poverty's success. The Catholic workers stressed personal rather than State responsibility for the care of the poor. In their unqualified devotion to the labor movement they preferred the picket line to the Wagner Act.*

They did not deny that the State had an enlarging function to perform in modern society. They acquiesced in, if they did not always enthusiastically support, the New Deal relief, recovery, and reform measures. But it was their missionary approach that gave them distinction and enormous influence in later-day social reform.

CONCLUSION

1.

As I read through the foregoing pages, I feel that I have given no adequate account of the work, that it is very much a day by day record of little events, of my own conflicts and meditations.

It is true that at times when much work was being done and progress was being made, little writing was done. There are large gaps in the account of our activities. In telling of the immediate works of mercy, I feel that I have neglected a great deal of our work in the labor field throughout the country from coast to coast. Naturally during those times when I was travelling and speaking before labor groups throughout the country, and when we were participating actively in strikes, there had to be gaps in the record.

Even in presenting a picture of life in a House of Hospitality, the story is not complete. I find the pages crowded with people, but in respecting their situation and their desire for privacy, I cannot go into details about them, what they look like, how they have come to be with us, their backgrounds and their tragedies. I must leave the book as it stands.

We have never faltered in our conviction during these six years of work that hospices such as our Houses of Hospitality are a vital necessity in times like these.

We do not deny that the State is bound for the sake of the common good, to take care of the unemployed and the unemployable by relief and lodging houses and work projects. Pope Pius XI pointed that out very clearly. He lamented that so much money was spent in increased armaments that should be spent on the poor. He urged the "press and the pulpit throughout the world" to fight the increase of armaments, and

---

Conclusion from *House of Hospitality* by Dorothy Day. Copyright 1939, Sheed & Ward, Inc., New York, pp. 257–275.

added sadly that "up to this time Our voice has not been heard."

No, we are not denying the obligations of the State. But we do claim that we must never cease to emphasize personal responsibility. When our brother asks us for bread, we cannot say, "Go be thou filled." We cannot send him from agency to agency. We must care for him ourselves as much as possible.

And we claim that as Catholics we have not sufficiently cared for our own. We have not used the material, let alone the spiritual resources at our disposal. We have not drawn upon our tremendous reserves of material and spiritual wealth. We have scarcely known or recognized that we possessed them.

Approximately twenty-five million Catholics in the United States! It would be interesting to know how many of them are on relief, trusting to State aid. If we took care of our own, and relieved the government of this immense responsibility, how conditions would be transformed! Then indeed people could say "See how they love one another!" Then indeed we would be "bearing one another's burdens." But of course, we would not be limiting our care only to our own. We would inevitably be caring also for others outside the faith.

This would also point the way to a solution of the industrial problem. As Christian masters freed the slaves who had converted them, because they recognized their dignity as men made in the image and likeness of God, so the industrial slaves of today can find freedom through Christianity.

Certainly this is an upside-down way of looking at the problem from a worldly standpoint. But we are fools for Christ's sake. We are the little ones God has chosen to confound the wise. We are the least of His children, yet through us He has done great things. Surely the simple fact of feeding five thousand people a day, in all our houses month after month for a number of years, is a most astounding proof that God loves our work.

We are down in the slums, but we can never be as poor as

Christ, or as those ragged and destitute ones who come to us in the mornings to be fed. We are constantly overcome with a sense of shame because we have so much more than these others.

Christ was a man so much like other men that it took the kiss of Judas to single Him out, as Mauriac says in his *Life of Jesus.* He was a man like those others on our bread line. We must see Christ in each of them.

Our work in the labor field takes place not only in the Houses of Hospitality. To reach the organized and the great masses of unorganized workers we have had to go out on the streets, to the public squares, to the factories, waterfronts and picket lines.

The hardships of the migratory worker and the sweatshop worker are even greater than those who are on the bread lines and in the lodging houses. They are the family men and women who are trying to care for others. They are those who are seeing their dear ones go without essentials in the way of medical care and food, who are seeing their children grow up to find unemployment awaiting them.

In the first chapter I gave a summary of the field covered by Houses of Hospitality. Here is a brief review of some of the labor issues we have dealt with during the past six years.

Again and again we have helped workers on strike regardless of all talk as to whether the strike was just or unjust. We have done this for two reasons: first, it is never wrong to perform the Works of Mercy; secondly, because in a time of industrial warfare it is easy to get in touch with the workers by meetings and by widespread distribution of literature. It is a time when the workers are thinking and struggling; they are enduring hardships and making sacrifices, they are in a receptive state of mind.

The first number of the paper came out in May 1933. In that issue we featured a story of the Negro labor on the levees in the South which was being exploited by the War Department.

We also wrote about women and children in industry and widespread layoffs of men.

In the second issue we took up the farmers' strike in the West and wages and hours of restaurant workers. In the third issue, child labor in the textile industry, as well as a two-page synopsis of labor struggles during the month. In the fourth issue we had front page stories on the coal strike and the milk strike. In these first issues of the paper there were also stories on the race issue and the condition of the Negro in industry and in professional work. In the sixth issue of the paper we were already combating anti-Semitism. In the same issue we showed up some profit-sharing plans of industrialists as a further move to exploit labor.

By the second year, our circulation had jumped from 2,500 to 35,000 copies, and our readers included workers and students throughout the country. In the second year, 1934, the seamen's strike on the West coast, the strike of the rural workers in the onion fields, a silk workers' strike in New Jersey, the textile strike, took up many columns in the paper. In New York City we helped Orbach's department store workers in their mass picketing, and called upon our readers not to patronize a store where such wages and long hours prevailed. We helped to defeat an injunction—one of the chief weapons of the employer to break strikes—which was handed down against the picketers. Our participation in this strike and in the National Biscuit Company strike cost us many readers. Our circulation was by now 65,000, but many church and school groups cancelled their orders because of the pressure of employers' groups. There were 3,000 on strike in the National Biscuit Company factory on 14th Street, and every day there were mass picket lines and scuffles with the police.

In the March 1935 issue there was printed a speech in regard to the Child Labor amendment which Dorothy Weston, Associate Editor, had made over the radio. Our endorsement of the Child Labor amendment also cost us many subscribers, as a majority of Catholics were opposed to it, for fear of government interference in the education of our youth. But in spite of the consistent opposition (which, as we have always pointed out, is very good for the clarification of thought), our circulation rose to 100,000 at the beginning of the third year.

When the Borden Milk Company the next year attempted to foist a company union on their workers, the editors took up their cause and called public attention to the unethical conduct of the employers. We called attention to the intimidation of Borden drivers by gangsters and thugs, and urged our readers not to use Borden's milk while unfair conditions prevailed. As a result of the story we ran, the employers attacked *The Catholic Worker* in paid advertisements in the *Brooklyn Tablet* and the *Catholic News.* This dispute also cost us some thousands of subscribers.

A few months later the spring strike of 1936 started among the seamen on the East coast. Because we had moved into our larger headquarters on Mott Street we were able to house about fifty of the seamen during the strike. In the fall strike, we not only housed some of them, but also fed thousands of them daily in the store we opened on Tenth Avenue, which we kept going for about four months. At that time we printed our "Stand on Strikes" which has been widely circulated in pamphlet form among labor unions throughout the country.

By publicity and moral support, we encouraged the organization of the steel industry when the C.I.O. began its activities. In the same year, our workers assisted the marble workers' strike in Vermont, the fishermen in Boston, the sharecroppers in Arkansas, the auto workers in Detroit. We covered the sit-down strike in Michigan, and the five and ten cent store strike in New York, the steel strike in Chicago. We also helped in the organization drive of the stockyards in Chicago.

That was the tragic year when ten workers were killed and scores more wounded in the Memorial Day massacre. One of our staff had a friend killed in that tragic episode. Our workers in Chicago had been helping in the soup kitchens and marching on the picket lines as well as distributing literature.

Many of these strikes I covered personally, in order to get a complete report to our readers, and also to speak to the workers at their meetings. I was one of the few newspaper reporters allowed into the Flint Fisher Body plant to visit the hundreds of sit-down strikers who had been in the plant for forty days. By this time we had groups of Catholic Workers in many big industrial centers throughout the century.

In the labor field the Pittsburgh group was most prominent, headed as it was by Fathers Rice and Hensler. They were the first priests to go out on the picket line and on sound trucks at street corners. Their example led many other priests to become active in the labor field.

The Lowell textile strike was interesting from several angles. When our workers began to distribute *The Catholic Worker* to the strikers and the public, and to start a food kitchen, the officials of the town telephoned the Chancery Office in Boston to find out if we were all right and were assured that we could go ahead. (On the other hand, we know of an occasion when a speaking engagement at a church in Jersey City was cancelled because of Mayor Hague's opposition to the paper.) The local paper proclaimed in their headlines that the entrance of *The Catholic Worker* into the Lowell strike marked the turning point in the conflict and led to prompt negotiations between the workers and the employers.

Often the immediate work in the House of Hospitality in caring for the unemployed kept us from work farther afield. It was of course impossible to answer all calls for help or to supply lay apostles wherever they were needed. We could only do the work which came to hand.

At the same time, we covered a pretty wide field. I notice in looking back over the old issues that Eddie Priest put in some months in a machine shop in Brooklyn, John Cort in a brass factory in New York, Julia in a five and ten cent store, where she did a good deal of indoctrinating and organizing by the distribution of literature and attendance at union meetings. Stanley Vishnewski covered many picket lines and Bill Callahan covered the Newspaper Guild strike in Brooklyn and the auto strike in Michigan.

We tried to cover not only city industrial plants, but also country plants. Certainly the Seabrook farm of four thousand acres in New Jersey with their own canning plant, is an industrial setup. The plant is so huge that two airplanes are used to fly over the fields to spray them against insects.

There is not much difference between this farm and the collective farms of Russia except that the latter are owned by the State. The Communists would make no changes in setup, admiring "bigness" as they do. They would merely take them over, they say, and run them for the benefit of the workers.

Some of the boys from *The Catholic Worker* farm in Easton went down to Seabrook and worked for a while, talking with union officials and workers and spreading literature. During the summer we plan to repeat this venture more intensively, giving almost a complete issue of the paper to discussing corporation farming as opposed to "farming as a way of life," and upholding the small landowner and co-operative owner against the State as well as against the industrialists. It is not only in California and in the South that horrible conditions exist for migratory workers and relief workers. We have them here in New Jersey, just outside the door.

An article on the natural and supernatural duty of the worker to join his union, appearing in the September 1937 issue found a widespread circulation. In New Orleans, where organization activities were bitterly fought at the time, it was circulated by the thousands, also in New England among the textile workers.

During this last year the truckdrivers' strike, the sharecroppers' strike, the Newspaper Guild strike in Chicago, the tanker strike and the miners' strike have been covered.

In the past six years we have had many interviews with

Catholic industrialists and many of them were not too cheering. Not wishing to increase class war attitudes, we did not publish many of them.

During these past years, former Governor Murphy's stand in the auto strikes, and Sheriff Boyle's and Mayor Michael Sewak's stand in the steel strike in Johnstown were highlights. By moral force rather than by armed force, these men prevented violence and bloodshed and stood out not only against the industrialist but against a campaign of public vilification and condemnation. Because they resolutely refused to use armed guards against the workers, and insisted upon arbitration—because they upheld human rights above property rights—they were termed spineless and yellow-livered, not only by atheistic capitalists but by many of their fellow-Catholics. Their courage and leadership in public life have been an inspiration to others and a message of hope to the workers. May God raise up other men like them.

The great problems in the labor movement today are the conflict between the A. F. of L. and the C.I.O., and the unemployment situation. It is still a struggle to organize; in many industries only small beginnings have been made

There is too much agitation about Communism in trade union ranks. This situation can be remedied only by education of the rank and file and by earnest and unambitious participation of Catholics in their trade unions. By "unambitious" we mean a participation which does not look towards personal advancement and official positions. There has been too much of that already on the part of Catholics in politics and trade unionism.

The day calls for a new technique. We must make use of the spiritual weapons at our disposal, and by hard work, sacrifice, self-discipline, patience and prayer (and we won't have any of the former without the latter), work from day to day in the tasks that present themselves. We have a program of action and a philosophy of life. The thing is to use them.

We have been criticized for holding up the counsels of perfection as norms of human conduct. It is sad that it is always the minimum that is expected of lay people. On the other hand, we get too much praise from some for performing work which is our plain duty. If we have a vocation for the work (and the joy we take in it is one of the proofs of our vocation), then we deserve no credit. Indeed we deserve censure for not having done more, and for doing what we have done so badly, given the opportunities we have had. Through the help of His friends, God has given us the means and the opportunities to be closer to the poor and the outcast and the worker than any other group in the country today. That we have not effected more with those we have reached is our fault, which we must acknowledge and recognize without discouragement. We must make a greater use of prayer.

As Léon Bloy wrote: "There is only one unhappiness, and that is—*not to be one of the Saints.*"

And we could add: the greatest tragedy is that not enough of us desire to be saints.

2.

It is a hot summer night, nearly ten o'clock. Here on Mott Street, the noise of children, of grown ups and of radios will continue until after midnight, so I might as well sit up and write. The telephone bell keeps ringing and visitors keep coming in, but Gerry Griffin and Joe Zarrella are downstairs to attend to both and I can sit upstairs here and finish this account. *Finish* is scarcely the word, however. An account of this kind is never finished. The work goes on, the little work of feeding people, and clothing them and housing them and talking to them. It continues here and in all the other houses throughout the country in one form or another. We may meet with failure on every side, but still the work goes on. And when I speak of failure, I am not cheerless about it. We have the failure of the Cross always before us. After all, we are sowing the seed and why should we be looking for any results. It may not be for us to reap a harvest. We are told to cast our bread upon the waters, which may seem a most profligate way of sowing, but we are assured that it will bear bread, so it is up to us to have confidence and to go ahead.

Gerry and Joe carry most of the burden of the New York house. Bill Callahan makes up the paper and does a lot of speaking; Eddie Priest has charge of the printing of pamphlets and leaflets and has gotten out 20,000 in the last year; Peter Carey and Victor Smith have charge of the Union of Unemployed which is made up of men from the bread line and has been going on for the past year. Through their Monday afternoon meetings they have kept a credit union going (a miracle when you consider it is made up of men who have come in from the bread line) and have started three cooperative hostels, one of which is named after St. Joseph and the other after St. Patrick. The men are off relief and support themselves by odd jobs, helping each other out in every way they can. Frank Datillo, Jim Smith and Kate Smith take care of the circulation department and right now Shorty, Kate Travis and John Pohl take turns in the kitchen. Peter Clark and a group of other men have charge of the bread line. But everybody helps everybody else and men come and go to take jobs and others take their places. Still, the ones I name have been with us for quite a time now.

The greatest inconvenience we suffer is lack of space. Out in the back yard these summer days we have set up a shoe repair shop and supply the leather and tools for each man to mend his shoes. We have a tailor who sets up his machine in any corner he can find and mends suits. The barber also operates in the back yard in the summer and in the store in winter. The card files, the letter files, the editorial office, the library, the reception room, are all one and the same apartment on the first floor and often it has to be a bedroom too when the house is crowded.

But somehow the work goes on. Here and everywhere is Peter Maurin, the guide, the teacher, the agitator. He has no office and shares his room with Joe and Gerry. He has a book case but no desk. He carries on his indoctrinating wherever he happens to be, in the office, on the street corner in the public square or on the lecture platform. These past eight months he has been travelling constantly throughout the far west and the south, and when the winter comes he will set out again, "stirring up the people." People are not the same, after meeting Peter. They read his book, *Easy Essays,* which is made up of many of his writings for *The Catholic Worker,*—or they hear him speak, and he stirs them to think, to read and to act. He never stirs them to unthinking action. The new social order with him is based on the knowledge and practice of the teachings of the Church and the study of the Gospels, history, and tradition.

One of these days we are going to write a book about Peter and call it "Conversations with Peter." All of us will write it and we will give the background of those conversations, the people with whom he is talking, the situations that have arisen to bring forth those conversations.

But right now as I contemplate the unanswered letters on the desk, the copy for the next issue which is coming out next week, the proofs for this book, a retreat on the farm in August for members of all the groups who can make it by the thumb route, a trip South in the fall and another to the far Northwest this winter,—it is hard to figure out when that piece of work will be done. I have scarcely written twenty-five pages in this note book the past year.

A few weeks ago I returned from a month's trip through the middle west where I visited fifteen of the houses. There has been news recently of two more houses opening in Baltimore and Buffalo and I shall have to visit them. Even now I have not visited the Troy and Burlington places.

I have found many things to cheer me on the way. For one thing, the utter poverty of the houses. They all depend on the voluntary and occasional contributions of the readers of the paper in those particular cities. In some cities there are only a few active workers who can contribute their time and some of the money they earn. For instance in Washington, the Blessed Martin House is run by a Negro, Llewellyn Scott, who works for the Government and earns about twenty dollars a week. Out of this he supports a mother and sister in a little apartment where they take in a roomer who helps bear the burden of the rent. He also supports the House of Hospitality there, putting up as many as twenty-five men and feeding about fifty every day. There are not only colored men but white men in the house. It is miserably poor and ramshackle and he somehow manages to find the twenty-five dollars a month rent. He wrote us the other day that just as all the food in the house gave out he went down to the alley where the entrance of the house is to tell the line of men that there was nothing else for them. And there just inside the door he found a big box of sandwiches that someone had left!

In Harrisburg the House of Hospitality has been used to shelter evicted families until they could be sheltered elsewhere. Mary Frecon who has charge of it is sheltering a mother and two children in her own home in addition to having the care of the House on her hands.

The House in Harrisburg sheltered Lucille, too. She was a colored girl, twenty-three years old. She was found dying in an empty house next door. She had grown up on the streets. She and her brothers and sisters had just prowled around, living as best they could. For the last few months, ravaged with syphilis and drink, Lucille had been cared for by an old colored man who lived in an abandoned shed down an alley. He gave her his cot—that and a chair were the only things he had—and he slept on the floor and waited on her as best he could. But the flies were eating her alive, huge horse-flies, and in her agony she crawled out and sought shade and relief in an abandoned house next to ours where another old colored man camping there had taken care of her. He too knew the uselessness of appealing to agencies. Then the neighbors told Mary Frecon about it and she found Lucille moaning and crying and trying to beat the flies away that fastened themselves upon her open sores.

She was brought to the clean bare rooms of the House of Hospitality and taken care of by the women of the Harrisburg group.

Not a hospital in Harrisburg would have her and it was only after five days that the doctor got an ambulance and sent her to the House of the Good Shepherd at Philadelphia where they deposited her without a word and no papers about her case. The House of the Good Shepherd is not a hospital, but it is for such girls as Lucille had been. So they took her in, nursed her and there she died not many weeks later.

While she was lying in the Catholic Worker house she had been baptized and anointed by one of the priests at the Cathedral. Our slums are full of Lucilles.

In Cleveland there are two Houses and the one on the East Side in the Negro district was woefully poor. They had to pay twice as much rent as the House in the white neighborhood—this is always the case—and they didn't have one third of the room. The men there were sleeping in the cellar for lack of bed space upstairs and heavy rain had caused an open sewer pipe to overflow, filling the place with stench. As I went down the stairs to this desolate dormitory a rat brushed across my ankle. I was dizzied by the smell and by the contact with the rat and sat down on the edge of one of the neatly made-up beds. They had put linoleum down on the cement floor, and they had cleaned and whitewashed the place. They had put broken glass in the rat holes about the basement but even so as I sat there two more rats dashed across the room. It seemed unbelievable that these men, mostly colored, should welcome such a hole as a shelter. It indicated what they had been forced to accept before.

Poverty is one thing, and destitution still another. We have always made that distinction. Some of our houses have a decent poverty, which means that the men are reasonably fed and sheltered in a certain amount of poor comfort which they mainly make for themselves. The Houses in Toledo, Akron,

Milwaukee, Chicago and St. Louis are a sample. There, through the work of the men themselves, who have come in to get help, the places have been improved. Plumbing has been repaired, heating has been provided through the mending of dilapidated furnaces, windows have been made fast,—and in some cases so much work has been done by the jobless that those who come to visit the houses think the men are living in too much comfort!

They do not see them as they come in, ragged, haggard and hopeless. They see only the comfortable House that they have made, they see now men who are halfway decently clothed and fed, men who bear some semblance to their own fathers and brothers and husbands, and they say,

"What are these men doing here, enjoying this comfort? Why don't they go away to make room for the destitute?" They do not realize that these same men were the destitute only a few weeks before.

It is true that these men have been removed from the class of the destitute. Now they are able by their initiative and their hard work, to feed and help others. They are the ones who keep the houses up, who do the cooking, the cleaning, the repairing.

In his book, *The Poor and Ourselves,* Daniel Rops points out clearly the distinction between the destitute and the poor. The destitute are so hopeless, so removed from ordinary life, that it is as though they had a wall around them. It is impossible to reach them, to do anything for them except relieve a few of their immediate needs. As soon as they have begun to work, to think, to read,—no matter whether they are penniless or jobless, they are removed from the ranks of the destitute.

Yes, there are many things that cheer me, as I travel around the country. Down in Missouri, one of the CIO unions bought a piece of land for the evicted sharecroppers and has enabled them to make an experiment in cooperative farming. Here is an experiment in mutual aid, in personal responsibility, in education.

In Southern Illinois, a Chamber of Commerce in a little town has bought an abandoned mine, and removing some of the machinery which is expensive to operate, has put the miners back to work, giving them a chance to buy back the mine by deducting the price from their pay. Evidently this is being done with the cooperation of the miners' union, and is another example of mutual aid and personal responsibility.

Not everyone in the country is looking to the Federal government for help.

Certainly, leaving out of account Divine Providence, revolution is inevitable. But trusting to Divine Providence, may we not work with hope, that despite politics and the gigantic bureaucracy which is built up throughout the country, the people will themselves settle their problems?

Certainly without poverty, without an acceptance of poverty, and by that I mean decent poverty, without sufficient food, shelter and clothing, we cannot get out of the morass we are in. Certainly too, we can do nothing without the works of mercy—an expression of our love for our neighbor to show our love for our God.

So we come back again to Peter Maurin's fundamental ideas. "Reach the people through voluntary poverty (going without the luxuries in order to have the essentials) and through the works of mercy (mutual aid and a philosophy of labor)."

It is hard for us ourselves to become simple enough to grasp and live with these ideas. It is hard for us, and hard for our readers and friends throughout the country. We still are not considered respectable, we still are combatted and condemned as "radicals."

"We are fools for Christ's sake . . . we are weak . . . we are without honor . . . we are made as the refuse of this world, the offscouring of all, even until now."

And following St. Paul, I am certainly praying that we continue so, because this is indeed "the downward path which leads to salvation."

PART FOUR

The New Pluralism

32 Mortimer J. Adler with Walter Farrell, O. P.

DEMOCRACY THE BEST AND ONLY JUST FORM OF GOVERNMENT

John Stuart Mill in his Representative Government *demonstrated on Utilitarian principles that democracy was the best and only truly just form of government. A like enrichment of political theory from a neo-Scholastic angle was made by Mortimer J. Adler and the Reverend Walter Farrell, leading neo-Thomists, who reached the conclusion, after an exhaustive (and some would say needlessly tedious) analysis, that only immature, abnormal, or criminal persons were justly excluded from the franchise and from an equal voice in government. Mixed forms of government such as Aristotle's polity, which combined oligarchy and democracy, and St. Thomas'* regimen regale et politicum*—a blend of despotism and constitutionalism—were philosophically indefensible.*

With a few exceptions, Catholic philosophers did not respond outwardly to Adler's and Farrell's thought. If they were unconvinced by the argument, they yet made no serious effort to refute it. They probably saw in democracy the only satisfactory alternative to totalitarianism and welcomed a theory which lent to democracy the strength of impregnable truth. They must have realized also that Catholic acceptance of the Adler-Farrell viewpoint would improve the social image of the Catholic Church in the United States.

I am grateful to you for the opportunity of addressing you on this occasion—grateful not only for the honor, but for the

---

Mortimer J. Adler, "The Future of Democracy," American Catholic Philosophical Association, *Proceedings for the Year of 1945,* pp. 1–22 (excerpt).

pleasure of being able to harangue fellow-philosophers at a time when good food and good manners prevent them from talking back; and grateful also because the topic of our general discussion at these sessions is the philosophy of democracy. Yet in this last respect, I must confess, my gratitude is mixed with other emotions as I stand before you.

I cannot help recalling the Fifteenth Annual Meeting held in Washington in 1939. It was devoted to the philosophy of the state. One of the papers presented on that occasion claimed to demonstrate the proposition that democracy is morally the best form of government because the most just; or, stated more strictly, that democracy is the only perfectly just government, and hence that the political community can attain its due perfection only through democratic institutions.[1] As I recall the paper, I also remember murmurings and mutterings which spread through the philosophical corridors after it was delivered, voices of dissent from so radical a thesis, voices of doubt about the steps of the proof, and, last but not least, voices of disapproval over the fact that the author of the paper had said—not by implication, but explicitly, and without apology—that the political philosophy of Aristotle and St. Thomas fell short of the whole truth, both by reason of serious inadequacies and because of grave errors.

I was one of the few who agreed with that paper six years ago. I was not shocked by the criticism of Aristotle and St. Thomas, because it has always seemed to me that political philosophers must suffer the blindnesses of their limited historical perspectives. Aristotle did well enough for a Greek, and St. Thomas well enough for a thirteenth century man, but neither could do well enough for all time. As Don Sturzo has

[1] See the *Fifteenth Annual Proceedings of the American Catholic Philosophical Association*, pp. 122–165.

recently pointed out in a brilliant paper,[2] no competent moralist today could take the Greek or mediaeval view of slavery, or war, or nationalism. So no competent political thinker today could take the Greek or mediaeval view of the forms of government, and of democracy among them.

I said that I was one of the few who agreed with the demonstration of democracy given six years ago. I still do, with greater assurance and for stronger reasons. An elaborate series of articles on the theory of democracy, written collaboratively and published in *The Thomist,* has removed what few doubts I may have had at the time.[3] These articles have solved what

[2] "The Influence of Social Facts on Ethical Conceptions," in *Thought,* XX, 76, March, 1945: pp. 97-116. Writing of slavery, which he regards as "an unnatural institution" which "should be frankly condemned as wholly indefensible," Don Sturzo says: "So long as the system continued in fact, ethical conceptions did not escape its influence. It is true that moral discussion sought to limit the immoral consequences of slavery, by insisting on the Christian duties of mutual forgiveness and charity among owners and slaves. Nevertheless, the question of principle was left untouched even by those who regarded the abolition as an ideal (to be realized only in the very distant future) *and, still more, by those who sought to justify the seemingly inevitable practice on the ground that it was not really contrary to nature or even that it was a legitimate deduction from the natural law*" (pp. 98-99, italics mine).

[3] "The Theory of Democracy" appeared in the following issues of *The Thomist:* III, 3, pp. 397-449; III, 4, pp. 588-652; IV, 1, pp. 121-181; IV, 2, pp. 286-354; IV, 3, pp. 446-522; IV, 4, pp. 692-761; VI, 1, pp. 49-118; VI, 2, pp. 251-277; VI, 3, pp. 367-407; VII, 1, pp. 80-131. The series was left incomplete with three or four more installments to come, when one of the collaborators went into active service as a naval chaplain. It will probably not be completed as originally planned, but the whole may be forthcoming entirely recast. As I understand it, the four parts to come would have dealt with the following topics: the absolute injustice of

difficulties I could raise against the thesis. They have convinced me that every principle on which the demonstration rested was sound, and that every step of the proof was valid. They even helped me to understand how the truth about democracy on the natural plane and in the temporal order is thoroughly consistent with the truths of Christian faith about the supernatural life and the eternal destiny of man.[4]

Some of you may have read the articles I refer to, although perhaps not; they were unduly long and hard to read.[5] Simple

---

slavery; the absolute injustice of subjection; the problem of the relative justification of unjust forms of government, such as despotism and oligarchy, by reference to historic circumstances; and the future of democracy.

[4] See especially Parts II and III dealing with the theory of the political common good in itself and in relation to natural and temporal happiness and to eternal and supernatural salvation (*The Thomist,* III, 4; IV, 1, 2), in which it was proved that the political common good is a means to temporal happiness and that temporal happiness is truly an end in the natural order, inferior in perfection to, but not subordinated as a means to, the beatitude of the blessed in heaven.

[5] My guess that these articles were either not read or not read well enough was completely substantiated by the discussions I heard at the Milwaukee meeting both before and after I delivered this paper; discussions in which questions were raised as if *de novo* although these articles had already raised and answered them, and in which positions were taken as if irrefutable although these articles had already considered and refuted them. For example, the one hundred and thirty page analysis of the modes of happiness (Part III of "The Theory of Democracy") adequately explained why the supposition that man has only a supernatural end is utterly unthomistic as well as contrary to all the facts of nature; yet this supposition was frequently broached by persons who showed no acquaintance with an analysis that met all their difficulties and

points were often labored and the documentation often seemed unnecessarily painstaking or, perhaps, painful. The authors obviously labored under the impression that they had to work against long unchallenged prejudices and venerable, because unexamined, verbalisms in traditional political theory. Nevertheless, the articles seemed clear to me; more than clear, demonstrative and unanswerable so far as they went.

Perhaps I am not alone in thinking that the argument was unanswerable and the theory unobjectionable. No serious objections or irrebuttable refutations have appeared in the journals or come to my notice, with one slight exception—a little flurry on the common good in relation to the doctrine of the person, which has been ably dealt with by Father Eschman;[6] and which, in so far as it was relevant to the theory of democracy, Father Farrell completely disposed of in his paper this morning.[7] On the record, then, maybe there is more agreement now than there was six years ago.[8]

One other fact tends to suggest that the general tenor of opinion may have changed with the times. It is the simple fact that this meeting is devoted to the philosophy of democracy. Considering that fact, I ask myself: To what other form of gov-

---

objections, or who talked as if they had the authority of St. Thomas for their extraordinary view that the composite natural substance, man, has no *telos* proportionate to its *physis*.

[6] "In Defense of Jacques Maritain" in *The Modern Schoolman*, XXII, 4 (May 1945), pp. 183–208.

[7] "Person and the Common Good in a Democracy," published elsewhere in these Proceedings. Cf. the analysis of the common good given in Part II of "The Theory of Democracy," *The Thomist*, III, 4.

[8] Unfortunately the printed record does not seem to be an entirely reliable sign of philosophical work done or undone. See fn. 5 *supra*.

ernment would this Association devote a whole session? To oligarchy, even when eulogistically called "aristocracy"? Hardly. To despotism or absolute government, even when masquerading under the less offensive name of "monarchy"? Just as unlikely. The only possibility I can think of is the so-called "mixed regime." But even then, if all the confusions were eliminated, and the mediaeval *regimen regale et politicum*—an accident of feudalism—were separated from the Aristotelian mixed constitution, we would not devote a whole meeting to its discussion, because we are a philosophical, not an historical, association. Royal and political government belongs entirely to the past. It has no present existence. It has no future. And, what is more important, it is obviously an historical anomaly which cannot be defended in principle.[9]

Of course, it is true that democracy has no present existence either; or, at best, the inchoate existence of something just coming to be. But democracy does have a future—a future in the order of right political desires, not merely in the order of predictable fact. That, I take it, is why we are concerned at these meetings with the philosophy of democracy, as we would be with no other form of government. That is why I have chosen to talk to you this evening about the future of democracy. Let me explain this choice a little more fully.

Six years ago, and until quite recently, it was appropriate, patiently and systematically, to develop the theory of democracy, a theory which may have pre-existed in some of its principles, but which no political philosopher before John Stuart Mill explicitly understood or analytically expounded.[10] But we can-

[9] See "The Theory of Democracy," Part IV, in *The Thomist,* IV, 3, 4; VI, 1, 2 wherein the theory of the forms of government is completely reanalyzed, and the doctrine of the mixed regime is clarified and corrected.

[10] In his *Essay on Representative Government.* See "The Theory of Democracy" Part V, in *The Thomist,* VI, 3, and VII, 1.

not be patient and theoretical any longer. It is necessary now to talk practically about the future of democracy.

The future of democracy is, moreover, inseparable from the future of world peace, which must be brought into existence for the first time by the institution of world federal government. That, in turn, means no future for nationalism, imperialism, or capitalism. Both democracy and world peace require us to attenuate and then eradicate all the exclusionary prejudices of race and locality, and to overthrow all forms of despotism and oligarchy—by education where possible, by revolution where not.

Finally, let me repeat what I have already said: democracy does not exist in practice. It is still an unrealized ideal—yet thoroughly practicable, in no way utopian. Of all the forms of government traditionally recognized, it is the only one which has no past. All the others have pasts which teach us not to wish a future for them, and to wish that democracy would replace them wherever they still exist, precisely because it corrects in principle and will remedy in practice their fundamental injustices and faults. *Democracy belongs entirely to the future; but the future will belong entirely to democracy only if we can completely overcome the various obstacles to its existence, preservation, and growth.*

The nature of these obstacles and the steps to surmount them are the main matters I wish to discuss. But I must begin by summarizing the theory that, absolutely speaking, democracy is the only perfectly just form of government. Have no fear. After-dinner time is for digestion, not demonstration. I shall merely state conclusions, not give arguments. The theoretical position stated, I shall then proceed to deal with the practical problem of what must be done to turn theory into fact, to put the political principles of democracy into action. I shall do this under three heads:

First, the economic obstacles to the realization of democracy;

Second, the human obstacles, which must be met by education; and

Third, the political obstacles—war and international anarchy—which can be solved only by world government.

I turn at once to a summary statement of the theoretical doctrine, and I begin with the basic distinction between two ways of considering the diverse forms of government, i. e., *absolutely* and *relatively.*

Relative justification is by reference to contingent and limited historic conditions. In this manner, a form of government which is not the best absolutely, nor free from essential injustice, may be justified as the best that is practicable for a given people at a given time.

Absolute justification is by reference to the nature of man as a rational, free, and political animal; to the nature of the political community as an indispensable means to the good life on the natural plane and in the temporal order; and to the nature of government as organizing and regulating the community so that it may serve effectively as a means to this end.

The absolute consideration does not neglect the range of individual differences within the human species, any more than it ignores the differences between the normal and the abnormal, the mature and the immature. It does, however, abstract from those defects or inadequacies which are not due to nature, but to nurture—to failures of education, to deficiencies of experience, to economic impediments, to restricted opportunity, to cultural limitations of all sorts.

The *theory* of the forms of government should be stated absolutely. The relative mode of consideration is significant only in relation to judgments about *historic societies.* I shall, therefore, first speak *abstractly* and then *historically.*

Absolutely or abstractly speaking, there are only four forms of government.

A. Tyranny, which is absolutely unjust because it totally perverts government from its natural and due end.

B. Despotism, or absolute as opposed to limited government; personal government by men above all positive law, rather than political government by men holding office under constitutional law. The intrinsic injustice of despotism is that mature, normal men are ruled as children, with no voice in their own government and with no juridical defense against their governor.

C. Oligarchy, or constitutional government with restricted citizenship, in which the restriction is based on wealth, race, color, sex—anything except immaturity, abnormality, and criminality. The intrinsic injustice of oligarchy is simply that no accidents of human nature, other than legal infancy, mental abnormality, and criminal conduct, provide a just criterion for determining who shall and shall not be admitted to citizenship.

D. Democracy, or constitutional government in which only the immature, the abnormal, and the criminal are excluded from citizenship; or, positively, that government under which all normal human adults enjoy political equality as citizens and exercise political freedom through the juridical rights and powers vested in the fundamental political status of citizenship. The injustice intrinsic to despotism is absent because no man rules except he be first a citizen and except as an officeholder with limited powers. The injustice intrinsic to oligarchy is overcome by the abolition of all unjustified exclusions from citzenship.

Let me briefly comment on these four forms of government.

Strictly speaking, tyranny is not a distinct form of government, but a perversion, in different ways, of the other three. Despotism and oligarchy are more susceptible to tyrannical perversion than democracy, though both may avoid tyranny, as when the absolute power of the despot is benevolently exercised. The benevolence of a despotism, however, in no way minimizes the intrinsic injustice of absolute rule. I shall not deal here with the other perversions of government, beyond the simple observation that oligarchies can suffer degradation into despotisms, and democracies into oligarchies. The line of political progress is in the opposition direction, usually by means of revolution: despotism overthrown in favor of republican or constitutional government; or the oligarchical constitution gradually amended in the direction of democratic universalism.

The three distinct forms of government, despotism, oligarchy, and democracy, are not coordinately divided. Because both are constitutional or political government, both oligarchy and democracy are divided against despotism which is nonconstitutional, or personal, absolute government. Then within the generic sphere of constitutional government, oligarchy represents every species of unjust constitution, and democracy the one species of just constitution.

This analysis permits no mixed regime or combination of the distinct forms of government. Absolutely speaking, despotic and constitutional government totally exclude one another; and so do the oligarchical and the democratic constitution. Aristotle's polity or mixed constitution, combining what he called oligarchy and democracy, arises from imperfect conceptions of the meaning of oligarchy and democracy, and could have political reality only under the conditions of injustice intrinsic to the best of Greek political institutions. So, too, in the case of the mediaeval *regimen regale et politicum,* which unstably combined the contradictory opposites of despotism and constitutionalism, and which could have political reality only under the peculiar historic circumstances of feudalism, and in terms of the injustices peculiar thereto.

Anyone who understands the basic terms of this analysis can work out the demonstration for himself by applying, at every step, two principles: (1) that all men are by nature political animals; and (2) that justice consists in treating equals equally. Wherever any normal, mature man is treated as a slave, as a subject of despotic rule, or as a political pariah excluded from citizenship, there, absolutely speaking, injustice is being done.

Now let me briefly apply this analysis historically in order to verify the principle that democracy has never existed at all in the past and does not fully exist today.

In the absolute mode of consideration, I have used dyslogistic names for the unjust forms of government. There is no one in this audience, I hope, for whom the words "despotism" and "oligarchy" do not immediately connote injustice, even as the words "tyranny" and "imperialism" do. No one in this audience would defend these institutions or practices on absolute grounds. That would be as irrational as the recommendation that Ireland again submit to England would be unIrish.

But we are all acquainted with the defense of despotism and oligarchy—never tyranny, of course—on historical grounds, justifying them relative to certain imperfect conditions of man and society. When despotism is relatively justified as the benevolent absolute rule of a people who are as yet incapable of self-government, it is eulogistically called royal government, monarchy or kingship. And when oligarchy is relatively justified as the benevolent constitutional rule of a population some portion of which is, or is supposed to be, as yet incapable of citizenship, it is eulogistically called a republic, or given the generic name of constitutional government.

With these considerations in mind, we can briefly review the political history of the west in order to verify the proposition that until fairly recently democracy did not even begin to exist, either in legal principle or actual practice.

In the ancient world there were two basic political conflicts: first, that between the Greeks and barbarians, in which the principle of constitutional government was opposed to oriental despotism; and, secondly, that among the Greek cities themselves, in which there was opposition between two forms of *oligarchical* constitution. These were called by the Greeks "oligarchy" and "democracy," *but both were oligarchies because both involved slavery and other unjust exclusions from citizenship.*[11]

[11] I am sorry that I must so flatly disagree with Don Sturzo's leniency in being willing to say that democracy *in some sense* existed in the Greek city-states. (See his paper published elsewhere

In a later, the Roman, phase of the ancient world, the first of these two oppositions repeats itself—the conflict between despotism and oligarchy, in terms of the monarchy which preceded the republic, or in terms of the empire which succeeded it.

In the mediaeval world, the major tension was between purely royal government (or absolute kingship) and government both royal and political; but apart from a few free self-governing cities, there were no republics in the mediaeval world, and the few that existed were oligarchical in constitution.

In the modern world, there have been two movements. First, the gradual dissolution of the *regimen regale et politicum*, which turned more and more despotic in the fifteenth and sixteenth centuries, thus causing republican revolutions that began by setting up limited monarchies and then predominantly constitutional governments. Second, beginning no earlier than the nineteenth century, the gradual amendment of republican

---

in these Proceedings.) If we wish to keep our analytical terminology clear and precise, we must say that *in no sense* did Athens or any other ancient city ever live under a democratic constitution. And if, with a clear analysis in mind which we are not willing to compromise, we wish to deal charitably with the historical facts, we ought to say that the Athenian constitution in the Periclean age was, at best, in motion away from oligarchy and toward democracy. (See W. R. Agard, *What Democracy Meant to the Greeks*, Chapel Hill, 1942.) Father Ward who declared himself as agreeing with Don Sturzo, must also admit a difference between motion and being. The fact that the world so far has not seen democracy in being, but only the motion toward it, does not warrant the inaccurate statement that democracy has existed at various times in various degrees. That would be like saying that as a person gradually overcomes a vice, thus moving toward the correlative virtue, he possesses that virtue in increasing degrees; whereas, in principle and in fact, until the vice is completely overcome, the virtue does not begin to exist in any degree.

constitutions by extensions of the suffrage and by correction of various forms of oligarchical injustice, both with respect to citizenship and office-holding.

What is our situation in the present day? For the most part, the people of the world live under despotisms of one sort or another, domestic or colonial. A comparatively small part of the human race enjoys the blessings of constitutional government—the liberty of life under law which is due every being who by nature is rational, free, and political. And where constitutional governments exist, many of them still retain operative vestiges of oligarchy, whether overt or concealed. Few, if any, are by explicit enactment perfectly democratic in constitution; and where these are democratic on paper or in constitutional principle, not even they are even remotely democratic in actual practice.

I shall illustrate my point by taking the United States. Reforms, like charity, ought to begin at home. To become perfectly democratic, the constitution of the United States still needs amendment; specifically, the explicit abolition of all poll taxes or restrictive property qualifications for suffrage. Until that is done, we have first- and second-class citizens in this country, even as women were second-class citizens before the woman suffrage amendment.[12]

Let us suppose that the constitution of the United States is presently amended and becomes in legal principle the charter of perfectly democratic government. Does that mean that democracy will then exist in fact in this country? That the principles will operate in practice? Far from it. If we are concerned with democracy as a practical, political reality, we must

[12] Let me say in passing that I have recently had certain experiences which have taught me how radical the doctrine of democracy is. During the war I lectured on the theory of democracy in Army camps all over the country to assemblages of officers and men. On all occasions, officers arose to say, with some vehemence, that I was not preaching democracy, but communism.

go beyond the acceptance of its principles in theory, and beyond their enactment into the laws of the land.

I turn therefore now to the three basic obstacles which we must overcome to make the practice conform to the theory, and to ensure democracy a future in reality as well as in principle . . . .

[In this section the authors deal with "the economic obstacle" which they define as "oligarchy" and "the economic servitude of the working class in a capitalist economy." They see a solution in "what R. H. Tawney describes as the functional economy, very much like guild socialism" or "the kind of democratic socialism Father George Dunne advocates." Later, they take up "the educational problem" which they consider as "the failure of our educational institutions in the sphere of specifically intellectual training." Finally, they dwell on the "political" obstacle, namely "the anarchy of separate sovereign states," the remedy for which is seen in "the formation of a single world-wide political community through federal union." Their conclusion follows. Ed.]

Permit me a few words in conclusion. We have been considering the future of democracy in terms of the necessity for economic, educational, and political reforms, and in the light of one fact which desperately shortens the time left in which to accomplish these reforms—the fact of the atomic bomb.

That fact may mean no future for democracy at all. The day of judgment may be at hand. It will soon be feasible, the scientists tell us, for man to blow this planet to smithereens by setting up a chain reaction which explodes all terrestrial matter. Should that event occur, terminating the earthly existence of the children of Adam, it will be an act of God, not a human deed.[22] Only the Creator can destroy. Man, exercising his free will, had a choice between Eden and the world, but man playing with atoms cannot choose whether to stay in the world or to commit race suicide.

[22] See *God and the Atom*, by Msgr. Ronald Knox, New York, 1946.

There is another possibility. Through man's discovery of atomic fission, God may be preparing another cataclysm, a second—though perhaps not the last—cleansing of the world, by fire this time instead of water. In that alternative, a few may survive to begin a new cycle of human history, the stages of which are totally unpredictable by us.

On neither of these alternatives can we talk practically about the future of democracy. To think practically at all, we must proceed on the hope that God's plan permits the continuation of human history as we know it, moving toward the realization of a temporal common good in which all men participate without distinction of class or boundary. Corrupt as it may be, our civilization seems to contain the seeds of a better world. The slow motion of history toward economic emancipation, democratic government, and a world community has brought us to the point from which we can at least glimpse the promised land. Whether we shall be permitted to enter it depends on our making the right choices in the short time which remains before there will be no choices left for our civilization to make.

We are still free to choose, but, it seems to me, we are no longer free to think which choices are right and which wrong. Our choices can still spring from our passions, and in that fact our freedom to turn the wrong way still resides; but if our decision is determined by reason, it must be determined for democracy and world government against all other alternatives.

33 John Courtney Murray, S. J.

A NEW LOOK AT CHURCH AND STATE

The dechristianization of society, the totalitarian threat, and the growing conviction that the human person was, of right, the center, source, and end of the social order—these were the three realities which, in the opinion of Jesuit theologian, John Courtney Murray, justified a new approach to the perennial problem of church-state relations. In Father Murray's opinion the dualism of temporal and spiritual was and should be as real and vivid as in times past. He felt that the tension between the two was now the concern primarily of the human person, who was both citizen and Christian, and no longer that of the Church and the State as organized entities. It was the responsibility of the Christian citizen through his participation in the democratic process to maintain just and harmonious relations between things spiritual and temporal.

In this view the State was not obliged in truth to make Catholicism the established religion or to heed the assertion that "error has no rights." Murray's argument collided head-on with the traditional Catholic theory of church-state relations. Understandably, he met with stiff opposition. Few critics, however, failed to pay tribute to the learning and eloquence with which he defended his position.

ON RELIGIOUS FREEDOM

What the foregoing exposés perhaps chiefly reveal is a common realization that the problem of religious liberty and of the relations between Church and state has once more altered in the manner of its position. The concrete problem that confronts us is not precisely that which the Church faced in the nineteenth century. The problem then was relatively simple. Its framework was the Continental nation-state. The enemy

---

John Courtney Murray, "Current Theology on Religious Freedom," *Theological Studies*, X (September 1949), 420–423, 430–432.

was Liberalism—the religious, philosophical and political forms of autonomous rationalism: this enemy was acting as a solvent within nation-states traditionally Catholic. The basic categories of argument were "thesis" and "hypothesis." And the practical question was, whether this or that nation-state was in situation of "thesis" or "hypothesis." If the latter, a constitutional guarantee of religious freedom was the rule; if the former, the constitutional concept, "religion of the state," had to apply. And there you were.

Three factors, and their implications and consequences, have powerfully contributed to alter this problematic: first, the dechristianisation of society (not so much the fact of it, which was far advanced in the nineteenth century, but the realization of the fact); second, the emergence of the threat of the totalitarian state; third, the corresponding struggling effort to validate the right of the human person to be the center, source and end of the social order. The first two factors are of course damnably evil, but their consequences on the thinking of the Church have been good. The consciously accepted fact of the dechristianisation of society has brought a realization of the need of a spiritual effort exerted on society from the bottom up, so to speak, rather than an influence brought to bear on it from the top down, through the state and government. The nineteenth-century problem of *Kirchenpolitik* has now only a secondary importance. Moreover, there is the corresponding realization that the new effort from below, in the direction of spiritual and social change, must be carried on through the processes of freedom.

Secondly, the totalitarian threat is dispelling certain naïve illusions which Catholics are perhaps prone to cherish with regard to the whole fact and concept of "power," especially in its relations to the things of the spirit. More importantly, it has brought new clarity of meaning to the ancient principle of the freedom of the Church, in a twofold sense. There is her freedom from any sort of enclosure in the state or subordination to the purposes of the nation of which the state is the political form; there is also her freedom to enter the state, as it were; that is, her right not to have the state closed against her, either hampering her spiritual mission to men or inhibiting the repercussions that this mission, remaining always solely spiritual, necessarily has on the structure, institutions and processes of society.

Furthermore, the totalitarian threat has made it clear that the freedom of the Church is intimately linked to the freedom of the citizen; where one perishes, so does the other. It is through the freedom of the citizen that the freedom of the Church is actively and effectively defended. In turn, the freedom of the citizen finds its surest warrant in the freedom of the Church; for where the state closes itself against the Church, it likewise closes down on the freedom of the citizen. Finally, the totalitarian threat of its nature is such that it can only be met by the united effort of all men of good will; this fact gives new meaning to the problem of interconfessional relationships. The post-Reformation concept of Catholic-Protestant relations as being solely in terms of rivalry or even enmity cannot longer hold. A common Christian good has appeared, that does not indeed blur or bridge differences in religious faith, but that does make necessary a common striving for a common purpose in the temporal order; this in turn supposes positive relationships.

Thirdly, the twentieth-century experience has resulted in a sense of the significance of human personality more acute and profound than the nineteenth century knew. This is a broad phenomenon—and, if you like, a confused one too. Insofar as it is relevant here, it entails three things: first, a sensitiveness with regard to the rights of conscience; secondly, a concept of a living personal faith as the goal of the apostolate (the nominal Catholic is something of a social menace), to which is allied the notion of "Christian" society as a qualitative, not a quantitative designation; thirdly, a more exact appreciation, and likewise distrust, of the methods of constraint and coercion, in the light of fuller experience of their sociological and psychological effects. Briefly, the principle of the freedom of faith has assumed new sharpness of definition and breadth of implication.

If then the contemporary problematic of religious freedom has been significantly altered—altered, I should repeat, in part by factors that are evil in themselves but that have stimulated reflection on principles, which is very good—an important question arises. It is suggested by Leclercq when he speaks of a "deepening of the meaning of the 'thesis' "; it is more strongly suggested by Pribilla when he distinguishes what is "permanently obligatory doctrine" and what is the "theoretical echo of a passing historical situation." Both authors thus imply that we confront here a problem in the development of doctrine. In other words, we see rising in this area the same problem that is central in all other areas of theological thought today; for I take it that the central problem of today is not "faith and reason" but "faith and history." It is not so much with the essential categories of philosophy as with the existential category of time that theologians are today preoccupied.

I am inclined to think that neither of the two authors cited quite grasps the nettle where the bristles are sharpest. The primarily crucial question is simply put: Does the dogmatic concept, "the freedom of the Church," entail by necessary consequence the constitutional concept, "the religion of the state," in such wise that, where the latter concept does not obtain, an inherent right of the Church is violated and the constitutional situation can therefore be the object only of toleration, on grounds of factual necessity, the lesser evil, etc.? Or on the contrary, is this constitutional concept, as applied in the nation-state, simply a particular and contingent, historically and politically conditioned realization of the dogmatic concept, "the freedom of the Church," in such wise that, even where it does not obtain, all the inherent exigences of the freedom of the

Church may still be adequately realized and the constitutional situation may be the object of approval in principal as good in itself?

. . . .The only proper point of reference is the freedom of the Church, which is the single necessary end that the Church directly seeks in her relations with political society. Consequently, only insofar as the constitutional concept, "religion of the state," is a means to this end can it claim any doctrinal standing. The question then is, what kind of a means is it? Is it a permanently necessary means apart from which the freedom of the Church cannot be properly secure? If so, it becomes a constitutional "ideal" by this relation to a dogmatic "ideal," and can claim to be "thesis," as the freedom of the Church is "thesis." If not, it sinks to the rank occupied by other constitutional institutionalizations of principle—the rank of a relative, not an absolute, a valid and valuable institution that can be defended in a context but that need not and cannot be proclaimed an "ideal."

. . . . The issue is whether the Spanish constitutional concept of "the religion of the state," in all its presently operative consequences, actually is that inherent exigence of Catholic *faith* which Spanish apologists maintain it to be. Does Spain in point of principle represent "the ideal Catholic regime"? Does the Spanish constitutional method of realizing the freedom of the Church so necessarily relate to the tenets of Catholic faith that it would somehow automatically become an obligatory method as soon as a nation is able to assert, in the sense that Spain asserts, "We are morally a Catholic nation"? This is the question that, in the U. S. at least, has become rather urgent. It is a *quaestio de futuro,* and by the same token it demands an answer in principle. Moreover, it should be emphasized that the question is doctrinal. It is not a matter of passing judgment on the merits or demerits of the Spanish regime; the Spaniard is rightly sensitive of such judgments passed by foreigners (as Anglo-Saxon political society is somewhat sensitive of Spanish judgments passed on it). I simply raise the question here, and leave it: Is the Spanish constitutional concept of "religion of the state" permanently and unalterably part of the Catholic thesis, obligatory from the nature of Church and state in any "Catholic society"? (Were I to give an answer, it would, of course, be no.)

The second issue concerns the theory of civil intolerance proposed by Spanish theorists as, in their judgment, the "Catholic" theory. Essentially involved in it is a theory of the state, its competences and functions. The theory is curious by reason of its admixture of abstract and concrete elements. The starting point is the fact on which the Spanish continually insist—that Protestants are an absolutely insignificant minority in Spain. A booklet circulated by the Spanish Embassy states that "the percentage of communicants to the total population is 0.023 percent and that of the Christian Community [the name used for themselves by Protestant Spaniards] 0.08 percent."[78] Moreover, after elaborate calculations the booklet gives the number of foreign Protestants as 44 percent of the whole Christian Community. One would suppose that these figures would conclusively prove that Protestants are not a danger to religious unity in Spain, especially since Spaniards since Balmés have loved to insist that Protestantism makes no appeal in Spain; Spaniards are either Catholic or nothing. One would then expect the further conclusion that no restrictions should be placed on them by government, since they are not a danger to the public welfare. As a matter of fact, however, an opposite conclusion is drawn: precisely because Protestants are such a tiny, unpopular minority, government may and should suppress their public activities. On this showing, therefore, the Spanish state acts on a theory of abstract religious

[78] Manuel Maestro, *Spanish Problems* (Spanish Embassy, Washington, D. C.), p. 19. An English translation of Cavalli's article, mentioned above, was likewise circulated by the Spanish Embassy.

intolerance; that is, it exerts its coercive power even in the absence of any serious danger to religious unity. It coerces simply because it is possible to coerce, not because it is necessary. If one then inquires what manner of political philosophy supports this concept of state function, the answer seems to be another abstraction: "Error has no rights." Therefore, it ought to be suppressed by the state, where possible. On this showing, therefore, the Spanish state further acts on a theory of abstract civil intolerance; that is, it represses religious error simply because it is error, apart from any formality of danger to the state.

However, the question rises, whether this theory of abstract civil and religious intolerance can claim to be a Catholic theory. Certainly it has no support in medieval doctrine or practise. In the Middle Ages heretics were never "exterminated" by the prince formally because they were heretics, men holding erroneous religious beliefs; they were punished because they were a serious danger to public order (so indeed the Albigensians were). Moreover, they were exterminated, not because it was possible to exterminate them, but because it was necessary. For my part, I had supposed that the theory of abstract intolerance was a Protestant intervention, not a Catholic one, and that its first illustration was the burning of Servetus by Calvin. Moreover, I had supposed that in Catholic political philosophy the action of the state was determined by the *exigences* of public order; it is to do what necessarily must be done to preserve civil peace, not what possibly can be done without disturbing civic peace.

This is the abstract part of Spanish theory, as far as I understand it. However, alongside of it there is a concrete part. Side by side with the constant assertion that Protestants are a negliible minority there stands the likewise constant assertion that they are a serious danger to the public welfare—religious and national unity. The two assertions are not reconcilable—save perhaps in the concrete. What perhaps reconciles them is the concrete fact of the weakness in religious and national unity. In this situation religious freedom, as an institution, would be a menace, and very largely a political menace, since it would afford a focus for political protest. The only remedy therefore is recourse to the methods of governmental constraint, in which—as Guerrero's judgment, cited above, readily shows—the Spaniard has great trust. Here the Spaniard seems to embrace the opposite of the Liberal illusion. The Liberal theory maintained that everybody would stop being bad as soon as government stopped trying to make them good. The Spanish theory seems to hold that everybody will begin to be good as soon as government stops being bad (i.e., Liberal).

This is, of course, a way of looking at things. And if a people decides on an experiment in the forging, or restoration, of national and Catholic unity on this view of the relation between government and goodness, the decision is theirs. However, the issue remains, whether this abstract theory of religious and civil intolerance, projected from such a concrete basis, is actually Catholic "thesis."

ON CHURCH AND STATE

Leo XIII solved the clash in principle by his newly clear assertion of the Gelasian thesis; and he surely led the Church far along what Pius XII called "the providential path of history and circumstances" by his definitive establishment of the principle that the Church's action in the temporal order is purely spiritual. However, there remained, as I have said, a further problem, a further step to be taken in obedience to the "vital law of continual adaptation." This question does not concern

---

John Courtney Murray, "Contemporary Orientations of Catholic Thought on Church and State in the Light of History," *Theological Studies*, X (June 1949), 218–227.

the substance of the right of the Church to judge and—in the medieval terms—to direct and correct all human affairs under their religious and moral aspects. The question concerns rather the manner of exercise of this right. More exactly, the question is, who shall be the immediately responsible agent of this direction and correction? Who shall be the executor, so to speak, of the Church's moral judgment? This has always been the ultimately crucial question. It has always been posed in function of the autonomy of the temporal order. And its answer has always given an ultimate nuance of meaning to the concept of the indirect power. The question arose in medieval times in connection with the classic exercise of the Church's power in the temporal order, the deposition of kings. Who deposes the king in actual and political fact—the Pope himself directly (as many canonists said) or the people acting with a conscience informed by the Pope (as another school of thought, including John of Paris, maintained)? The division of opinion rested ultimately on varying judgments with regard to the autonomy of the temporal order.

The problem arises today on a much wider scale, and it is necessarily posited in terms of the democratic development—the more complete institutionalization of the medieval political principles to which I have already referred. If with Pius XII one regards this development as the operation of a rational human dynamism and its term as "a demand of reason itself," as this demand is made manifest through the medium of historical circumstance, one confronts the old problem in a new form. Now the autonomy of the temporal order requires that its spiritual direction and correction be accomplished from within the temporal order itself, through the agency of its own institutions, and not from without—not therefore by the efficiency of the Church as such; for the Church as such stands outside the political order, transcendent to it.

In a sense, this requirement is not new. In olden days the Church directed the processes of the temporal order through her action on the conscience of the king, who was a political institution—in fact, the cardinal political institution, unique and almost single as an influence on the shape of the temporal order. However, in another sense the requirement is new; for in the modern situation, in which democratic government is recognized as a rational postulate, the institutions for the direction of the temporal processes are manifold and many-headed—the people (in Pius XII's sense of "people" as opposed to "the masses," who are simply passive instruments of a governmental clique) and popular institutions of rule. This is the situation to which Cardinal Manning referred in his famous utterance that, as reinforced by Cardinal Gibbons' repetition of it, made such an impression on Leo XIII: "A new task is before us. The Church has no longer to deal with Parliaments and princes, but with the masses and with the people. Whether we will or no, this is our work; we need a new spirit and a new law of life."[117] It is to this situation that the Church's "vital law of continual adaptation" must be applied.

And the application, I should insist, is not properly called expediency, any more than it was expediency when the Pope ceased to consider the kings of Europe as papal vassals. On the other hand, the adaptation is simply adaptation—the Church's conformation of her thought and conduct to the juridical exigences created by a situation of political fact in whose genesis a rational dynamism is at work. There can be no question of the Church identifying herself with democracy—either as an idea or in any of its national realizations. The political thought that has its home in the Church has traditionally, by reason of its Aristotelian roots, recognized as a political ideal the regime in which "all should have some share in rule." However, the transcendence of the Church forbids

[117] Cf. E. Soderini, *The Pontificate of Leo XIII,* transl. by B. B. Carter (London, 1934), p. 174.

her enfeoffment to any political regime, even an ideal one, at the same time that her immanence in the world requires a vital adaptation to any political regime that is rational.

It is a question whether Leo XIII fully realized the modern problematic in regard of the manner of exercise of the indirect power. Nevertheless, I consider that by some manner of genius he put forth the principle of solution. It is contained in the special twist, so to speak, that he gave to the Gelasian doctrine. Consistently he posits as the root of the necessity of an "orderly relation" between the two powers the fact that "utriusque imperium est in eosdem," the rule of both is over the same one man.[118] If therefore there is conflict and not harmony between them, the conflict is felt in the depths of the personal conscience, which knows itself to be obligated to both of the powers which are from God. Their harmony therefore is required by the unity and integrity of the human personality. The whole Gelasian doctrine is thus made to grow, from the standpoint of the finality of the dyarchy, out of the essential datum, "civic idem et christianus,"[119] the same one man who is citizen and also a Christian.

This sets the Gelasian doctrine in genuinely modern perspectives, which are not those of medieval times. In the medieval universe of discourse the root of the matter was not the unity of the human person, citizen and Christian, but rather the unity of the social body which was both Church and state, the *respublica christiana*, whose unity required the subordination of *regnum* to *sacerdotium* because it was an inferior function within the one body, instrumental to the good of the body, which was identically the good of the Church. The medieval starting point was the Church, and it set the doctrine of the

[118] *Immortale Dei, op. cit.*, II, 152; *Libertas, op. cit.*, III, 108. The same phrase occurs in these two cardinal loci; the idea often occurs elsewhere.

[119] *Immortale Dei, op. cit.*, II, 154.

two powers in characteristic social perspectives. Their "union" was a requirement of social unity. These perspectives and their consequences were carried over into the so-called confessional state with its "Union of Throne and Altar." Its predominant finality was likewise social unity, now conceived as national unity. It is obvious, for instance, how in contemporary Spain, where the Union of Throne and Altar still exists in a special form, the problem of Church-state relationships is conceived in function of the problem of national unity.

However, the Leonine starting point is not the Church nor are its perspectives social. Its starting point is the dualism within the human person, who is both child of God, member of the Church, and also member of the human community, citizen of a state—endowed in each capacity with a set of rights, which are of different origin but which must be organized into an organic whole. And the principle of organization is the primacy of the spiritual aspect of his nature, which implies the fundamental right to have the two powers to which he is subject in harmony with each other. The finality of this harmony is not a social unity but a personal unity—the integrity of the human personality. It is only by preservation of this integrity that man is truly "free," empowered to be in fullness what he *is*—citizen and Christian. This freedom is a positive empowerment—the full faculty of obeying the law which he knows to have the primacy (the law of Christ as mediated by the Church), under due obedience to the other law to which he is also subject, the human law of the state. Unless these two obediences are in harmony, there is no freedom.

My point is that this Leonine restatement of the Gelasian doctrine opens in principle the way to the solution of the ancient problem in its modern position—the manner of exercise of the indirect power, the manner of maintaining the primacy of the spiritual under respect for the autonomy of the temporal. Leo XIII was in advance of Pius XII in placing "the whole man in his concrete and historical reality at the center of the whole social order" in its two components, Church and state, whose dualism corresponds to the dualism in man himself and whose orderly relationship is the exigence of the unity of human personality. Between the essence of *Immortale Dei* and the essence of the 1944 Christmas Radio Message there is, to use the famous antithesis of Vincent of Lérins, "profectus fidei, non permutatio."[120] Taken together and in their relationship, the two doctrines—the Leonine concept of Gelasianism and the Pian concept of a juridical democracy—contribute to one effect, which is the establishment in principle of what the effective terms of the contemporary dyarchy really are. In the developed conditions of modern political society they are not the medieval *sacerdotium* and *imperium,* nor yet the Throne and Altar of the confessional state. They are *sacerdotium* and *civis idem et christianus.*

Leo XIII took the first step in thus defining the dyarchy by defining its finality—the unity of human personality. Moreover, in saying that the human person and his integrity as citizen and Christian was the end and object of the harmony between the two powers, Church and state, Leo XIII was implicitly saying that the human person by his action as Christian and citizen ought to be the instrument and agent of establishing this harmony in actual fact.[121] Responsibility for the harmony rests on its beneficiary. Pius XII simply completed the progress by making explicit what had been implicit; he took the Leonine phrase that expresses the root of the matter, and developed the concept of *civis.* The citizen, he says, who is "a human person, the subject of inviolable rights and duties, and the root and end of social life," is therefore not "a passive element" under the processes of society but their active agent,

[120] *Commonitorium,* 23, Rouët de Journel, *Enchiridion Patristicum* (ed. 6a, Freiburg i. Breisgau, 1929), n. 2174.

[121] The whole idea of the *ralliement* had the same implication—in itself, if not in some of the interpretations given of it.

through the exercise of his rights as citizen. Through them he has a share in the public power and therefore a responsibility to see that the processes of government, and of society in general, tend to their proper end, which is the freedom of "the whole man in his concrete and historical realization." This freedom, as I said, supposes the harmony of human obediences, which in turn supposes the harmony of the two powers that require obedience. Of this harmony therefore the human person is the responsible artisan, through the exercise of his civic rights under the guidance of his Christian conscience.

Thus in terms of recognized principle the contemporary dyarchy is constituted. The Church no longer, as in medieval times or in the classic confessional states, directly confronts "the temporal power" in concentrated, centralized form, in the person of the prince, who was "the government" and indeed "the state," in the sense that he wielded or delegated at his discretion the full power of the state (subject, of course, in medieval theory to the limitations of law and private right). Modern political development has operated a dispersion, as it were, of the temporal power by adding the principle of the political responsibility of government, institutionalized in the system of free elections and the other civic freedoms, to the ancient principle of the legal limitations of government, itself newly institutionalized in modern forms of constitutionalism. Consequently, what the Church immediately confronts is not the temporal power in the sense of "the government" or the state in the sense of the constitutional and legal order of society, but rather the citizen, armed with all the institutions of popular rule. To him government is responsible, and he is himself responsible as well for the actions of government as for the order of the state. (It is striking, for instance, to see the recognition of this situation of political right in Pius XII's encyclical on the Holy Land, April 15, 1949.) This citizen, and the institutions through which he shares in rule, are possessed of a genuine autonomy. It is only through him and through them that the Church can reach the temporal order (as indeed the Pope could only reach the empire through the emperor). Standing thus in the middle, so to speak (where Leo XIII put him), the citizen looks two ways. As Christian, he looks, as it were, behind him to the Church as the "general teacher *(informator)* of faith and morals," to use the phrase of John of Paris; as citizen, he looks before him to the state, to the whole order of human life in its temporal aspects. The action of the Church on him terminates at conscience, forming it to a sense of its Christian duties in all their range and implications for temporal life. The Christian then as citizen, in the full panoply of his democratic rights, prolongs, as it were, this action of the Church into the temporal order, in all the matters in which Christian doctrine and law has implications for the life and law and government of society. First of all, it is through the freedom of the citizen (in the modern sense) that the freedom of the Church (in the medieval sense) is effectively assured—her right to exercise her spiritual sovereignty over her subjects and to reach those elements of human affairs which are "quoquo modo sacrum."[122] Secondly, it is through the freedom of the

[122] Moreover, theoretically, and apart from special problems of historic right, it may be said that the fundamental right of the Church—the right to recognition of her unique juridical personality—claims a place in the legal order, which is the state, only through the citizens; that is, the Church is a reality for the State because she is a reality for its citizens—a reality in a higher order, in which the state as such has no competence. The state may not undertake to give a juridical definition of the Church; the Church defines herself, and it is for the state to accept this definition inasmuch as it is the definition accepted by its citizens. So, by analogy, it is not for the state to define what the human person is, in its fundamental rights and freedoms; the human person defines itself, and the state accepts this definition. Here was the core of the quarrel, for instance, between the Church and the Third Republic over the Law of Separation of 1905. This law presumed to define the

citizen that the freedom of the City itself is effectively assured —that freedom which consists in the establishment and dynamic maintenance of an order of justice and charity. In these perspectives, which are set by the full development, through theological reflection and political experience, of the Gelasian doctrine, the whole system pivots on the principle of freedom. There is first the free obedience of the Christian conscience to the magisterial and jurisdictional authority of the Church; there is secondly the free participation of the citizen, as a Christian, in the institutions whereby all the processes of temporal life are directed to their proper ends.

This, I take it, is the Catholic thesis in its application to democratic society. Its essence is a concrete conception of the ancient dyarchy to which the Church has come, following "the providential path of history and circumstances." I have illustrated this conception only as it emerges from the doctrine of Leo XIII and Pius XII. There is however a resounding confirmation of it to be found in the epoch-making doctrinal and pastoral work of Pius XI—I mean his elaboration of the concept of Catholic Action, which has been called "the modern form of relations between Church and state." However, I can only refer to this subject, without pursuing it.[123]

My conclusion at this point should be obvious. In the first part of this essay I sketched the contemporary problematic in the matter of Church-state relationships and illustrated it by

---

Church as a simple *association cultuelle*, a corporation of private right, which the state, by reason of its juridical omnipotence, was entitled to charter, set on a par with other such corporations, and minutely regulate (as it did in the forty-four articles of the Law). The Church cannot admit that any such right to assign her a juridical status within the state lies within the competence of the state.

[123] Cf. H. Carpay, *L'Action Catholique* (Paris, 1948) for a good statement of the function of Catholic Action toward the solution of the ancient problem of the relations between spiritual and temporal.

the example of the American Constitution and the political system it sets up. My point then was the sheer matter of fact that in the native structure of the American system the citizen-of-religious-conscience is placed in the mediating position between Church and state. The Church is free to form the consciences of her members; and they as citizens are free to conform the life of the City to the demands of their consciences. Both freedoms are part of an organic system of freedom. And the system itself, as a system, rests on the collective judgment of the people that this whole system is for the common good, and that no element of it may be tampered with without damage to the whole.

With this point of fact made, I went on to analyze the Church-state problematic as it has emerged in the thinking of the Church under the operation of the "providential law of history and circumstances." For all its length, the analysis was much too brief. However, three things are clear. The first is the clarification of the concept of the indirect power, as being a purely spiritual power that indirectly, by repercussion, is productive of effects in the temporal order; with this has also come a more sharply defined recognition of the autonomy of the temporal order and its processes. Secondly, there has been a new accent put on the finality of the Catholic thesis stated by Gelasius I; the orderly relationship of Church and state has always in view the inner unity and integral freedom of the human personality. Consequently, as the human person is the end of this relationship, so he is the immediate agent responsible for seeing that it is orderly. Thirdly, there has been a somewhat parallel development in political ideas: as the human person is the end of the state, so he is the participating agent in the processes of state, responsible for an order of justice and charity.

The net result of the whole development has been the resolution of the ancient dyarchy into a new, concrete, operative form—on the one hand is the Church, in the fullness of her spiritual liberty; on the other is the citizen-Christian, in the fullness of his civil liberty. It is in terms of this dyarchy that, in Gelasius' words, "this world is authoritatively ruled," now that it has reached conditions of political maturity. No doubt laicism had much to do with this development. As Sturzo says: "It took the experience of laicism to bring out the moral character of the relations between Church and State and to show how sociologically the dyarchy Church-State has its roots set at a deeper level than that of a legal co-partnership in society."[124] I would add that this sociological discovery has resulted in doctrinal formulations, that are not opportunistic concessions to hard circumstance but a form of obedience to the vital law of adaptation to a human progress that for all its aberrations has been fundamentally rational. In a curious sort of way, we have now come back to "the eternal Middle Ages," after the long parenthesis initiated by the fourteenth-century rise of state absolutism and the modern idea of sovereignty. I mean that the relationship of Church and state now assumes more the form of the medieval *union coutumière,* but in a newly institutionalized form, that situates the essential dynamic relationship at a level that permits a fuller achievement of its finality.

My conclusion then is that the Church-state problematic, as it has emerged in the thinking of the Church, presents certain striking similarities to the problematic envisaged in the American Constitution (which I used as a sort of laboratory example of the modern political category—the state that is lay in finality and function, that situates its competence within the sphere of "the natural, terrestrial, temporal," in Pius XI's words, but that is not—at least not in theory—laicized, secularist and secularizing, animated by the doctrine that the natural, terres-

[124] *Op. cit.,* p. 548.

trial and temporal are All That Is; for it recognizes that there is a "spiritual power" in society that must be free, through an ordered system of civil liberties, indirectly to achieve the due temporal incarnation of the spiritual).

This of course does not mean a political canonization of the American state, which, like any political realization, labors under ambiguities and defects. Still less does it mean that the American state receives a sort of religious canonization by the Church. However, it does mean that the statement of the contemporary problem itself, as conceived by modern political society in terms of political principle and fact, is substantially the same statement of the problem that is now accepted by the Church, in terms of an organic development of her ancient Gelasian doctrine. This may seem like a very modest conclusion, of no great import. Actually, however, one will see that it is enormously important, if one simply refers to the controversy between Boniface VIII and Philip the Fair. The trouble then was that neither side had really grasped the full scope of the problematic, as it had altered from its former position under the impact of the new political development—the rise of the nation-state, with a political unity of its own, which raised in a new form the question of the autonomy of the temporal order and its processes, that is, the question of *libertas regalis*. Because neither side had fully grasped the problem, the result of the controversy was an impasse. The contemporary controversy, in which the term *libertas regalis* has dissolved into the term *libertas civilis*, likewise reached an impasse on the Continent in the nineteenth century, again because neither side had fully grasped the problem. However, if it be true, as I think it is, that the problem has now been grasped (at least by the Church—no state that considers itself The One Power ruling All That Is has yet seen the problem), an impasse is no longer necessary. And the avoidance of an impasse, in a world that is full of them, is no mean achievement.

34 Joseph H. Fichter, S. J.

"UTILITY OF SOCIAL SCIENCE FOR RELIGION."

Since World War II the Church itself, especially the urban parish, has become an object of sociological investigation. Studies of this kind in America have been pioneered by the Jesuit sociologist, Joseph H. Fichter, who has strongly urged and amply demonstrated the utility of social science for religion. Father Fichter believes that only through comprehensive surveys of its area at periodic intervals can the parish evaluate the effective quality of its work. In an earlier and simpler age, he points out, the urban Catholic parish could count on and easily measure the religious loyalties of ethnic and working-class groups which in effect constituted more or less homogeneous religio-social communities. This self-evaluating and in some degree self-correcting situation has disappeared; the large parish in the big city is now a complex, secondary and associational structure, and has become an artificial and impersonal institution whose operations can be observed and understood only through the aid of social science.

Like all sociologists of religion, Fichter is on the sharp lookout for failures and shortcomings in parochial and other forms of Catholic work. But he also recognizes that scientific research provides new insights into positive programs of religious and civic improvement.

It appears that the sociologist of religion must concern himself with two questions: *(a)* Is it possible to study religious

---

Joseph H. Fichter, "Utility of Social Science for Religion," Appendix to *Social Relations in the Urban Parish* (Chicago: The University of Chicago Press, 1954), pp. 235–248.

groups with the tools and methods of social science? *(b)* Is a study of this kind useful, not only to social science, but to religion?

The first question need hardly detain us. The work of Pinard de la Boullaye, Max Weber, Émile Durkheim, and others in Europe has demonstrated the answer.[1] Books like Joachim Wach's classic *Sociology of Religion,* Liston Pope's *Millhands and Preachers,* and J. Milton Yinger's *Religion in the Struggle for Power,* as well as numerous monographs which have appeared in American scientific journals, have shown that the sociological approach to religion is respectable, reliable, and valid.

This does not mean that the sociologist turns theologian or that religious mysteries can be reduced to scientific formulas. It does mean that the trained social scientist is competently at home wherever people associate and function co-operatively in the pursuit of known goals. While religious functions are sacred, and religious aims are higher than those of any other social institutions, the fact remains that they are *social* functions and aims. The economic man is also the religious man, and, if social behavior can be successfully studied in the former role, it can also be successfully studied in the latter.

The second question—concerning social science's utility to religion—seems of much more importance to all who are wor-

[1] Weber and Durkheim have been severely criticized by philosophers and ethicians for their positivistic tendencies. Despite these strictures, their pioneer work in the sociology of religion provided insights to the whole problem discussed here (see Simon Deploige, *The Conflict between Ethics and Sociology* [St. Louis: B. Herder Book Co., 1938]; Henri Pinard de la Boullaye, S.J., *L'Étude comparée de religions* [2 vols.; Paris: Beauchesne, 1922, 1929]; Max Weber, *Gesammelte Aufsätze zur Religionssoziologie* [Tübingen: Mohr, 1920–21]; Talcott Parsons, "Theoretical Development of the Sociology of Religion," *Journal of the History of Ideas,* V [1944], 176 ff.).

ried about the balance of the sacred and the secular, the conflict between faith and reason, the assumed incompatibility between religious functions and social science research. This question of *Cui bono?* ("What good is it?") is raised by religious-minded people and must be answered by the social scientist, whether the latter regards himself as a pure scientist merely in the search of knowledge for its own sake or whether he considers himself a kind of applied scientist whose conclusions should be of benefit to society.

In order to focus the question more clearly, and because our own research has been largely in the area of parochial systems, the test of utility will be made here on the sociological study of the Catholic urban parish as a social unit. The arguments to prove this utility of social science for organized religion, and the various empirical evidences provided in this book, imply much wider generalizations and applications. If we substitute Protestant congregations for Catholic parishes and Protestant religious practices for those of the Catholic Church, the same general thesis concerning the utility of scientific research can be demonstrated.

In other words, every religious group, whether Catholic, Protestant, or Jewish, must have a local history and must be composed of people who follow institutionalized patterns of religious behavior. The human experiences which constitute its history, and the human relations which characterize its present existence, are the essential material of sociological research. No religious group, especially in its administrators, is completely unaware that it has both problems and potentialities within its system of social relations. The trained social scientist can help to sharpen and focus this awareness even though the religious and theological differences among the various groups are deep-seated and weighty.

The specific question here is: Why make a scientific social study of the Catholic urban parish? What "good" can come from the sociological approach to an institutionalized system which the Catholic Church has employed for centuries? Elsewhere I have made a tentative answer to this question in the assumption that "a vigorous parochial system not only bespeaks an internally strong Catholic social structure but also promises solidarity for the larger community and nation in which it exists. . . . The sociological roots of Catholicism are in the parish."[2]

This tentative assumption is open to question because the parochial system is a man-made institution and because the Church employs many other institutional mechanisms in carrying out its primary spiritual function. At some time in the distant future the Church may emphasize some other form of social structure as the basic social unit of the Church, but at the present time (and probably for many decades to come) the sociological basis of Catholicism is the parish. Hence it seems important to study things as they are and to analyze and appraise objectively the social unit in which and through which most Catholics strive for eternal salvation.

The remainder of this appendix is a brief exploration of some of the reasons why the sociological study of the urban American parish is a vital enterprise, which has the utmost utility for

[2] See *Dynamics of a City Church,* Vol. I of *Southern Parish* (Chicago: University of Chicago Press, 1951), p. 8. See also T. S. Eliot, *The Idea of a Christian Society* (New York: Harcourt, Brace & Co., 1940), where he remarks that "the traditional unit of the Christian Community in England is the parish. . . . How far the parish must be superseded will depend largely upon our view of the necessity of accepting the causes which tend to destroy it. In any case, the parish will serve my purpose as an example of community unit. For this unit must not be solely religious, and not solely social; nor should the individual be a member of two separate, or even overlapping units, one religious and the other social. The unitary community should be religious-social, and it must be one in which all classes, if you have classes, have their centre of interest" (p. 28).

the Church itself and for the society in which it exists. In general, these reasons evolve from the premise that knowledge of objective facts is a preliminary essential to the proper and intelligent functioning of any social group or community. If this knowledge can be achieved and analyzed through sociological techniques, the Church has at its disposal a potent instrument of internal and external progress.

1. The Catholic Church in America has grown with the nation. At the middle of the twentieth century it has reached a point where it may profitably "take stock of itself." It has successfully passed through the youthful stage of establishing itself in what had been an alien Protestant culture. It has been preoccupied with proving itself an institution which could resist attacks from organized Know-nothingism, Klanism, and other antagonistic ideologies; which could overcome the internal problems of trusteeism and of ethnic disputes among immigrant clergy and laity; and which could build a tremendous physical plant of churches, seminaries, schools, convents, and hospitals, in spite of the relative poverty of most of its membership.

Catholicism in America is an urban religion in the sense that more than 80 per cent of its adherents are city dwellers. It has become a "success" there in the cities, which tend to be the models and forerunners of American cultural change. The brick-and-mortar phase is almost passed; the "build-up" has been phenomenal. If the process of urbanization continues in this country, it is almost inevitable that the largest urban religion must have an influence in its development.

Impatient criticism has been made of the Church's failure to evolve with other social institutions and to develop with contemporary civil society. "She has remained frozen in feudal forms which worked in times past. In our time, instead of being fused with society as she was in the middle ages when the parish and the commune had the same extension and the same life, the Church is 'absent' from the City. She hovers over humanity instead of being incarnate in its flesh and blood. In her message to men she has everything she needs, even more than she needs, to animate the contemporary structures and to draw up plans for the future, but she does not use her resources. She lets strangers, or adversaries, take the decisive initiative on questions of doctrine, culture or action. When she acts or speaks it is often too late. In scientific research, social legislation, or humanism she has few innovators. It is not in this way that she will win the world to Christ."[3]

The Church in America, particularly the urban Catholic parish, is ready for a thorough analysis of the present objective facts of its existence. Its values are eternal, and its doctrines are incorrupt; but these are concretized by human agents in a social system. This concrete day-by-day operation of Catholics in an institutionalized structure is the present foundation upon which the future is to be built. The planning of new directions, of new forms, of greater vitality, must be projected from a thorough knowledge of the present.

2. The Catholic Church is existing in urban America, which is the most fluid and dynamic society the world has ever seen. The members of the Church are members of this society, and there is a tremendous mutual influence between their religious and their secular roles. Even the holiest, most intelligent, industrious, and able priest needs help in understanding and interpreting this society. In their own social organizations high-powered and high-salaried business executives recognize this need and are turning more and more to the social scientists for help. The clergyman is performing a much more valuable function than the business executive, but he is doing it with the same people in the same society. The priest's aloofness from, or disregard of, the scientist indicates a neglect of these natural instruments which can be made to subserve supernatural work.

[3] Emmanuel Cardinal Suhard, *The Church Today* (Chicago: Fides Publishers, 1953), p. 99.

The man who is most involved in the activities of a social group, whether the manager of a factory or the pastor of a parish, is frequently unable to grasp the significance of the social change occurring all around him. Usually he has neither the training nor the objectivity nor the time to make the social analysis which would be most fruitful for the objectives of his group. That is why the trained and careful social researcher is in such great demand today. His services can be of paramount importance to the Church, not merely by gathering facts, but by helping to interpret these facts in relation to the changing society.

This point was made by an experienced parish priest in reviewing a study on parochial sociology: "When a priest offers the holy sacrifice he is tempted at times to assume all is well back of him in the church and throughout the parish. Complacency is his enemy. The priest needs a rear-view mirror. This book picks up some of the reflections that would fall on such a mirror in one parish. The priestly reader will ask what images would fall on such a mirror if a study were made in his parish."[4] Using the same figure of speech, another priest remarked that this research publication "mirrors the three parishes I pastored in my forty-one years as a priest. I dare say that every priest exercising the care of souls in a parish will find the book a revelation of what needs to be done to improve his field for a better harvest."[5]

3. The puzzling inconsistencies of our urban social behavior, oversimplified in the dichotomy of religion and secularism, seem to have resulted from the dynamic shift in our social structures and institutions. This means that the volatile character of our group values and goals, which disturbs the minds of religious people, cannot be interpreted separately from the

[4] Book review by Francis J. Gilligan in *Worship,* XXVI, No. 5 (April, 1952), 271.

[5] Book review by Anthony Rothlauf, in *Integrity,* Vol. VI, No. 3 (December, 1951).

changing patterns of our group living. Sometimes an elderly pastor is naturally bewildered because the large city parish which he administers is so different from the little village parish in which he grew up during the first decades of this century. He may find psychological security in the role of *laudator temporis acti,* or he may be frustrated by present social conditions while he bemoans the "good old days," but neither attitude is profitable in God's service.

The Catholic parish in America, even among the urban immigrants, was once a simple, primary, social community. But it seems now that the sense of community, which once existed even in the "old neighborhoods" of the city, has largely vanished. The large parish in the big city is now a complex, secondary, associational structure. This is not necessarily the fault of the Church or the fault of the people or the priests; it may not necessarily be a "fault" at all. The social relations and structure of a parish cannot exist completely apart, and different, from the social relations and structure of the society within which it exists. The changing customs, patterns of behavior, even the mores, of the one affect those of the other.

How can the Church understand, interpret, and meet these structural and relational changes in modern urban society? None of the great theologians and moralists of the past ever experienced this particular kind of society. Urban America is unique in the history of the world. There is not available, even in the vast storehouse of Catholicism's social experience, a systematic body of knowledge to which the Catholic can go for help. Just as in times past the Church has turned to philosophers and physical scientists for help in philosophical and physical problems, so it must now turn to social scientists for help in social problems.

The oft-repeated mission of the Church to bring all Americans within its fold does not necessarily presage a perfect "City of God" on earth, but it does require at least an elementary recognition of the new and unique in American society.

What Father Murray says in a different context seems to apply here. "In the providence of God and by the intelligent zeal of the Catholic citizen there may be a Christendom again; but it too will be imperfect and not ideal. And no one can foresee in detail its form. What was true and valid in the old will find place in the new, but the new will be new in all its texture."[6]

4. The social scientist's contribution to the work of organized religion was sought by the late Cardinal Suhard, who recognized the "crisis of growth and change" in modern society. He praised the "extensive research of scholars, sociologists, and technicians," and he advised them to "draw up an objective evaluation of our urban civilization of today with its gigantic concentrations and its continual growth: with the strains of its inhuman production, its unjust distribution, and its exhausting forms of entertainment."[7]

His authoritative voice spoke from France, where the religious faith of the man on the street has come upon unhappy days. It is said that in France and other parts of Europe the masses of the people (who in the last analysis are the constituents of the Church on the parish and neighborhood level) have become alienated from the Church. In an almost desperate attempt to reach the people, the Cardinal sponsored the programs of priest-workmen and city missionaries. These measures could have been adopted more successfully a generation ago had there been objective sociological studies of the religious and social conditions of French Catholics.[8]

[6] John Courtney Murray, "Governmental Repression of Heresy," from the Catholic Theological Society of America, *Proceedings of the Third Annual Meeting* (Chcago, 1948), p. 38.

[7] Emmanuel Cardinal Suhard, *Growth or Decline?* (South Bend: Fides Publishers, 1948), p. 83.

[8] The experimental character of the priest-worker movement, as well as its lack of a basic scientific preparation, is perhaps indicated in the crisis which it encountered in the winter of 1953–54.

As far as we can learn from the few research projects so far conducted in American parochial life, the loyalty of the Catholic masses is much stronger here than in France. This is largely a guess and an assumption. There are many differences between the two countries, and it is only through patient and tedious research that we can honestly judge the present condition of American Catholicism. However, if we wait another generation, the Church in America may be suddenly confronted with the need to apply hasty measures of dubious value. The groundwork for planned and sound adaptions to social needs may best be laid at the present time.

5. Whether or not the Church is flourishing in its urban American parishes, no Catholic priest or layman will argue that the Church's social institutions are beyond improvement. The central religious function of the Church is predicated on the perfectibility of the human individual and of human society. The fact that the Holy Spirit will always be with the Church and the fact that the sacramental system provides a tremendous flow of supernatural grace are no guaranties of a steady linear social and spiritual progress.[9] Religious institutions are human institutions,[10] and they too are subject to the fluctuations of human actions and social pressures.

It appears that the movement must now proceed in a modified form and at a more cautious pace. For a balanced account of the problem see Friedrich Heer, "Die Arbeiterpriester in Frankreich: Ursprung und Hintergründe," *Hochland,* XLVI (April, 1954), 326–41.

[9] See above [Fichter, *Utility of Social Science*] chap. 15, pp. 207–9, for the discussion on the social implications of liturgy and sacraments.

[10] This term is used here in its technical sense and does not deny the "divine origin" of religion. As Hertzler says: "Religion is a universal attribute of man at every stage of his culture and in every period of history. In all races and in all times there is a

Some priests contend that the whole parochial system (especially in its rigid territorial aspects) is outmoded, that it has outlived its usefulness, and that new social structures are required to meet the exigencies of our urban, industrial society. Others maintain that the territorial parish is the best social mechanism ever devised by man for the practical day-to-day operation of Catholicism in the lives of the laity. There are numerous intermediary opinions between these two extremes; but all are centered on an issue of vital importance to American Catholicism: Is the parochial system, as it now operates in our urban American society, an adequate instrument for the salvation and sanctification of souls?

This question can not be answered, and these opinions cannot be tested, by an appeal to the Bible, to Thomas Aquinas, or to canon law. The mere fact that there is this diversity of opinion among clergymen and that zealous laymen are also concerned about the problem should make religious people eager for any scientific studies which may help to provide answers. Improvements and changes can best be instituted if we have at our disposal a studied analysis of the objective facts of parish life.

It is the function of the social researcher to discover the facts, to analyze them, and to make tentative generalizations. These in turn must be tested in similar situations with the use of similar methods. Without this conscientious preliminary labor we cannot have valid judgments to offer in the controversy over the parochial system; we can have only questionable opinions limited to some specific area and to some particular experiences.

6. Personal opinion and subjective evaluations are not scientific expressions of actual social conditions any more than they

---

human experience and a congeries of problems which is specifically religious" (J. O. Hertzler, *Social Institutions* [Lincoln: University of Nebraska Press, 1946], pp. 124–25).

are scientific guides to the practical improvement of social structures and institutions. The overworked and harassed priest, like the enthusiastic and energetic layman, tends to judge only from the surface of the parish. He sees the immediately visible and the easily measurable behavior of the parishioners. His natural optimism and loyalty to the Church may provide a state of mind in which it will never occur to him to question the obvious.

The high birth and marriage rates (which are not exclusively Catholic phenomena) and the urbanward migration of the postwar era have not only increased the numbers who receive the sacraments of marriage, baptism, and confirmation. They have also helped to account for the fact that the parish school is crowded, confessions are more numerous, and the Sunday-noon Mass congregation overflows onto the sidewalk. This obvious and bustling activity may obscure the fact that this is a numerical but not necessarily a *proportional* growth. The priest may not even suspect the number of dormant Catholics who are living in his parish. These signs of a flourishing parish may make it seem unnecessary to make a thorough periodical census of the parish, with the result that urban Catholicism continues to "prosper" in blissful ignorance.

Even the most casual survey of the parish by a trained social scientist will bring to light objective facts which will dim this nimbus of optimism. It will open up areas of spiritual activity and suggest procedures through which large numbers of people may receive the benefits of religious ministrations. In other words, scientific social research uncovers not only the negative elements of the parochial system but also gives new insights into positive programs of improvement. Above all, it lifts the veil of illusion and permits the observer to judge critically and objectively.

7. In one sense, the dedicated religious adherent is often guilty of an attitude of presumption. He realizes that religion is above science and feels that the higher level requires no help from the lower. This is shown in the outright dependence on a

few memorized philosophical maxims or theological tenets as an explanation of, or excuse for, certain realistic social situations. An incontinent scoffing at social science and social engineering usually accompanies this attitude. After all, the Catholic Church has been in business for two thousand years, while social science is a newcomer with overextended ambitions.

Father Joseph Fitzpatrick exposes this presumption when he says that "Catholics have a tendency to allow their faith and their philosophy to substitute for knowledge that can be gained only through competent empirical research."[11] In other words, there is a legitimate and necessary area of truth which is not readily discerned by the trained philosopher or understood by the competent theologian. The presumption that social science has nothing to offer for the improvement of religious groups seems to be a misunderstanding of Divine Providence in human relations. God expects us to employ our minds, our talents, and our training in the pursuit of knowledge, in the formulation of plans, in the application of solutions. Any technical sociological study of the parish is an instrument in the hands of alert priests and of zealous laymen for the better understanding and operation of the parish.

8. The emergence of a vocal and educated laity is a relatively recent phenomenon of urban American Catholicism. The change from immigrant status to native status over the last two generations means that American Catholicism is culturally unique. "The intensely sentimental Catholicism of Spain; the fiercely Puritanical Catholicism of Ireland; the relaxed and affectionate Catholicism of Italy; the reasonable and sophisticated Catholicism of France; the deeply devotional Catholicism of Hungary and Poland—all were displayed in American parishes."[12] Most of the ethnic differences are now disappear-

[11] Joseph P. Fitzpatrick, "Catholic Responsibilities in Sociology," *Thought,* XXVI (autumn, 1951), 389.

[12] Thomas Sugrue, *A Catholic Speaks His Mind* (New York: Harper & Bros., 1952), p. 42. This small controversial work was discussed with indignation by some religious reviewers.

ing, and what remains has gradually blended with the distinctively American pattern of social behavior.

Just as the Church, without changing its substantive features, adapts itself in accidental features to the social institutions of China, France, the Philippines, Mexico, and other countries, so also must the Church here adapt itself to American culture. This adaptation seems to have occurred more rapidly in the laity than in the clergy, and some of the spiritually disastrous results appear to have been due to lack of understanding and direction by the clergy. Souls are not saved nor is society Christianized, by ignoring the culture of the people among whom this work is done, or by merely wishing that the culture were different, or by constantly condemning it.

It would be a serious failing in the lay apostle and in the sociologist of religion to forget that *civis idem et Christianus,* that the individual person is both a citizen and a Christian, and specifically that *civis Americanus idem et Christianus.* The "vital law of continual adaption" must be applied to the fact that the Church is of the people in a more pertinent sense now than it ever was. "This is the situation to which Cardinal Manning referred on his famous utterance that, as reinforced by Cardinal Gibbons' repetition of it, made such an impression on Leo XIII: 'A new task is before us. The Church has no longer to deal with Parliaments and princes, but with the masses and with the people. Whether we will or no, this is our work; we need a new spirit and a new law of life.' "[13]

The Catholic laity, in this time and in this place, constitute the overwhelming majority of the members of the Church. The Catholic clergy is, in a true sense, the servant of the laity.[14] It

[13] John Courtney Murray, "Contemporary Orientations of Catholic Thought on Church and State in the Light of History," *Theological Studies,* X (1949), 219.

[14] The popes have termed themselves "servant of the servants of God," and this title is widely understood and accepted by the laity. At the same time Pius XII cautions that "those who exercise

is also the servant of all those non-Catholic Americans whom the Church would like to enfold in its universal embrace. Most of these are in some way "Americanized," and they are not likely to be attracted in large numbers to a transplanted species of German or Irish Catholicism or to parishes which retain the cultural patterns of Spain, Poland, France, or Italy. The student of social relations and structures, the expert in cultural patterns and institutions, can provide interpretations of American society for the practical use of religious administrators.

9. American Catholic social scientists are only beginning to apply their energies and talents to a study of the Church as a social system. These men and women—most of whom are relatively young—have a thorough understanding of the relation between religion and social science. As educated Catholics they have an adult knowledge of religious functions, of the ideals and aspirations of religious society. As parishioners they have had intimate experience of the parochial social system. As trained scientists they are able to make an effective contribution to the urban American Church.

In some ways the European social scientists have done much more work in the sociology of religion than have the Americans. Their findings have sometimes met with clerical suspicion and opposition, but they continue their studies with the frankness and humility which characterize the true scientist. They have even formed an international congress for the study of the sociology of religion. It may be said, however, that American sociologists have enjoyed a type of scientific training which enables them to pursue a more empirical kind of research—and to that extent probably more valuable.

If the young social scientist is not permitted to employ his training in the study of religious groups, he will apply his competency to research in other fields—housing, race relations, delinquency, marriage problems, etc. This is socially valuable

---

sacred power in this Body are its first and chief members" (*Mystici Corporis* [New York: America Press], p. 10).

research, but one need not be a Catholic to do it, nor does the progress of the Catholic Church benefit from it, except indirectly. In a sense, these Catholic sociologists are at the core of the whole problem discussed in this appendix. The esteem or disesteem in which they are held is a matter of vital importance to the Church. Without them the sociological analysis of the urban parish cannot be done.

10. Seminarians who are themselves in preparation for the priesthood are sometimes employed for parish work during the summer vacations. This gives them some small acquaintance with parish routines, they may act as rectory doormen, sacristans, bookkeepers, secretaries, perhaps as catechists in the children's vacation school. Such experience is excellent, but it cannot substitute for the work of trained social scientists, nor can it supply the type of knowledge available through a scientific study. Seminarians are future priests, prospective guides in social relations and social groups, and their training needs scientific implementation.

At some time in their academic career seminarians take a course called "Pastoral Theology," which is intended to teach them the practical aspects of the pastoral function in the parish. This academic procedure suffers the difficulties present in all "vocational training" processes but has an added hindrance in the lack of a scientific literature of socioreligious relations. While the textbooks which supply "ready answers for the busy pastor" are valuable instruments for the parish priest in action, they do not provide a deep analysis of social structures and institutions for the seminarian.

The result is that there is a definite lacuna in the seminary training program, and in the seminary library, which can be filled by up-to-date sociological studies of the parish and the church. At the present time, if he has the interest, energy, and time, the seminarian must scratch his own way through the parochial labyrinth without much practical help either from the older generation or from the books. He sorely needs some dependable studies which can demonstrate the social trends in parish life, give him an insight into organizational problems, and prepare him for the leadership role which he must later assume.

11. Every year hundreds of newly ordained American priests enter eagerly upon their first contact with parochial realities from the vantage point of the parish rectory. They are fledglings, apprentices whose faltering steps are guided by their experienced superior, the pastor. This is a time-consuming and often erratic process. One may speak in high praise of the leisurely apprentice system of yore in which a young man learned his trade under the careful tutelage of a master-craftsman. The modern urban parish is not a leisurely place, and there is no essential logic in allowing the newly ordained priest to "start from scratch" even when the priest in charge of his practical training is a master-pastor. There are also many pastors who have a shrewd insight into the social conditions of their parish but find it extremely difficult to transfer this insight to their assistants.

The young priest in the parish frequently has to learn through the hit-or-miss technique or by circumventing the categorical negatives which are thrown in the path of his zealous efforts. This may be a by-product of the hierarchical structure or of fairly rigidly institutionalized pastoral roles, but it is also undoubtedly the result of his own unpreparedness in social science. In spite of these difficulties it is true that he may in time become an expert parochial assistant and a successfully functioning pastor. But even the assistant who begins his priestly career in an ideally administered parish will be all the more eager to improve himself through the study of reliable parochial research findings.

12. In all human institutions and social structures the roles and statuses have a relative permanency, but the agents, or official incumbents, are relatively short lived. This may appear to be an absurdly superficial observation, but it has implications of deep importance. It is true that the generic pastoral

role is not created by the newly appointed functionary, but it is also true that this role is not left unchanged during the years in which he holds office. The specific pastoral role in a particular parish is forged out of the accumulated wisdom, information and experience of decades of hard work. For practical social purposes almost all this evaporates when the pastor grows old and dies.

This is more than a "dead loss" to the Church. It is the squandering of a social heritage. The Church does not allow theological knowledge to die; it carefully nurtures the development of dogma and preserves over the centuries the institutionalized varieties of liturgical practices. This preservation is due not only to the essential importance of dogma and liturgy but also to the fact that there have been trained and alert thinkers and writers in these fields. Enough has been said to show that social relations are extremely important in our times and that trained social scientists are available to analyze and report on them.

The fact that pastors and other ecclesiastical functionaries have often failed to hand on to their successors the benefit of their experiences is no reflection on their clerical competence. On the contrary, it is probably a proof of their complete dedication to the immediate work on hand, as well as of their professional absorption in their specific pastoral roles, that they were unable to sift and analyze their experience in a scientific way. They have had some brilliant ideas, and have suffered some heartbreaking disappointments, in the direction of personal and group relations of lay Catholics. These events have not been analyzed and systematized into a body of reliable scientific knowledge for the use of successive incumbents of the ecclesiastical roles.

In the last analysis, all the arguments demonstrating the utility of social science research for the improved functioning of organized religion must be focused from a scientific rather than a religious orientation. Science properly seeks truth; religion properly uses truth. Since truth is one and cannot contradict itself, neither the scientific researcher nor the religious adherent need have any fear of truth. The extent to which the social scientist will be encouraged to study religious groups and to publish his findings will largely influence the extent to which objective social truth will be effectively employed for the benefit of the Church.

This is another way of saying that one of the major functions of professional social scientists is to impart their findings not only to colleagues but also to nonspecialists through publication and teaching. The clerical religious functionary and the active lay Catholic are nonspecialists in social science, and they are immediate beneficiaries of this major function of the social scientist. As Parsons says: "This function derives above all from the fact that science contributes to human life in two directions, first in giving men knowledge about the world in which they live so that they may orient themselves more intelligently to it, and second in making it possible, through technological applications of the findings of science, to satisfy human needs and wants more effectively."

35 John F. Cronin, S. S.

THE ROLE OF GOVERNMENT IN A PLURALISTIC ECONOMY

Since before World War II Catholic thinkers in search of social justice have been critical of the role government played in the American economy. Before the New Deal they criticized government for exercising too little power; they now believe it to have too much power or, more accurately, to have misused its power. In commentaries on the social encyclicals, American Catholic thinkers have indicated with no little precision the positive, though limited, function of government in the economic field. It devolved upon the Rev. John F. Cronin, S.S., economist and assistant director of the Social Action Department, National Catholic Welfare Conference, to comment anew on this phase of social action in the context of pluralism, a central concept in recent social philosophy. The primary need, he felt, was to prevent giantism in business, labor, agriculture and government from suppressing vital centers of personal power. He believed the federal government should exercise supreme power only in the monetary and fiscal field and delegate most of its regulatory power, with proper safeguards of the public interest, to the various occupational groups. Government should discourage monopoly and impersonalization within each segment of economic life by fostering and invigorating small groups, close to the individual and the family—small businesses, small labor-unions and farm organizations, and by encouraging freedom of entry into lower levels of government. In fact, it should encourage "any type of grouping that is small enough to allow individual members a really effective voice in the conduct of their organization."

From a semantic viewpoint, pluralism can best be understood by contrasting it with monism and dualism. A monistic society has a high degree of uniformity and homogeneity. It achieves unity by ruthlessly striking down all semblance of diversity. In a complex industrial society this is best accomplished by the use of political power. The ideal model here would be the totalitarian state, which is monistic by its very

---

John F. Cronin, S.S., "Government in a Pluralistic Economy," *Review of Social Economy*, XIV (March 1956), 47–55.

nature. It achieves unity of policy, control, ideology, and achievement by its power to destroy all those who would act outside the framework of the monolithic power center.

One type of dualism, as noted in earlier papers, is based on the classical model of *laissez-faire* capitalism. Here we have a model conceived as the social parallel to the physical universe of Newtonian physics. As the physicists of that day tried to explain everything in terms of matter and energy, so the political economists conceived of society as formed by the impact of buyer and seller of goods and services, interacting with the order and precision of molecular forces as then depicted.

With the Keynsian approach, also noted previously, we have, as it were, an imperfect pluralism. The elements of diversity that have arisen in modern capitalism are retained. But they are relatively unimportant as related to the macroeconomic techniques of the state and central banking authority working to achieve equilibrium at a level of high employment of all resources. Maximized physical production, quantitatively conceived, is the controlling goal of such an economy.

By contrast with all these models, a true pluralistic society starts from qualitative and ethical premises. Its *ethos* is based on certain basic assumptions regarding man and society. It makes man, and the family, central in its universe. Neither the state, nor the impersonal forces of competition, nor even the objective of maximization of physical output are considered primary in economic order. The ultimate test of both economic and political organization is its impact upon the family and family related groups. This must be primary, not a mere by-product of an otherwise oriented system.

Two tests may be used to discover whether or not an industrial society is truly pluralistic. We could examine first the structure of such a society. A truly pluralistic society achieves unity without sacrificing diversity. Such a society has often been described as organic, with emphasis upon harmonious co-ordination of groups performing diverse functions. In the organism the parts minister to the whole without losing their separate natures or identity. The whole in turn provides to the separate parts the means for healthy growth and proper functioning. In the living body there is subordination, co-ordination, and control; but no organ is without its purpose and its ability to contribute to the well-being of the whole.

A second test of a pluralistic order is found in what, to change the metaphor, might be called the direction of flow of power. Under pluralist conditions, the general tendency is for power to flow from the bottom to the top, not the reverse. The reason for this is clear: the closer the centers of power are to the individual and the family, the more society respects the individual personality. Surely one of the attributes of an intelligent being is the power to direct his life, with proper allowances for his obligations toward other members of society. Power cannot effectively be exercised *in distans*. There must be some degree of personal contact for intelligence to be used and will to be asserted.

On the basis of this analysis, one of the first tasks of government should be to move toward pluralism in the *structure* of economic society. Its aim should be to foster and encourage structural diversity so as to maximize the opportunity for individuals, families, and related groups to function freely and effectively. It should stimulate rather than discourage or prevent the utmost variety in economic life. At the same time, it should do all within its power to minimize its own area of detailed control. Government by its very nature has the right and duty to direct and control such phases of economic life as the common welfare demands. But it is an agency of society, not a power superior to it.

When we apply these concepts to economic life, certain conclusions inevitably follow. Certainly it is the duty of government to prevent any tendency toward a monolithic structure of industrial society. The techniques used by our government are well known. The Sherman and Clayton Acts, with other subsidiary legislation including more recent moves directed at controlling mergers, fall within the pattern of a proper exercise of state power. While the ideology motivating these enactments is mixed, including a large element of nostalgia for atomistic competition, nevertheless the end result is not incompatible with the demands of pluralism. The economic trends which provoked these laws were basically monistic both as they affected economic structure, and as they influenced the flow of economic power. Had the American economy become rigidly cartelized, there would have been an unhealthy concentration of economic might in the hands of the few.

At the same time we must remember that such measures are in themselves negative. They are as compatible with *laissez-faire* dualism as they are with pluralism. They do not necessarily lead to the structural diversity which is characteristic of a pluralist economy. Prevention of business monopoly directly affects only the owner group in industrial society. Of itself it gives no guarantee that labor, the farm population, and the professions will have an effective voice in matters which so intimately affect them.

It follows that a second phase of government action, in fostering plurality in the structure of the economy, is the encouraging of organization on the part of groups which unorganized do not have adequate economic power. The Wagner Act for labor and the various forms of farm legislation for the agricultural community did in fact encourage such organization. Once again, the motivation was mixed. Certainly the idea of countervailing power was not absent from these moves. In fact, monopoloid tendencies soon began to manifest themselves in groups conceived as means for countering excessive concentration of power.

Striking confirmation of the thesis that the concept of countervailing power, rather than pluralism, motivated these moves is found in the way that our government exercised its control functions in the economic order. All too often there has been the tendency to concentrate and centralize such controls. The state has absorbed the regulatory function, instead of considering itself as the highest co-ordinating body in a society where substantial control is exercised at lower levels. Subordinate groups competed for influence and control in the federal government, instead of seeking direct power to govern their own operations. The result was a different form of centralism, with government trying to compete with and restrain economic giants. Recently there has been much discussion of this trend and some action to reverse it. But basically our economy is but imperfectly pluralistic both in structure and function.

What more can the government do to encourage the development of a pluralistic economic structure? Realism compels the answer that the function of government, while important, is yet limited. It can often prevent conditions which lead toward monism in the economy. The state can encourage the formation of organizations which permit various economic groups to have effective power. But it cannot, of itself, induce such groups to co-operate in an organic fashion. This is basically a task of education. By education here we do not mean merely the dissemination of ideas or the encouragement of occupational groups. Much more important, in the long run, is education through practice. The more these groups have the opportunity to realize the vital nature of their common interests, the greater the probability that co-operation can be formalized and structuralized.

To cite a concrete example, when government favors sound collective bargaining it can encourage both industry and labor to develop attitudes of mutual understanding and trust. But such efforts can be rendered fruitless by intransigeance on either side. Here the mediating function of government could be helpful, but it is not necessarily decisive. As in other areas, government can set up certain pre-conditions of pluralism, but it cannot supply the elements of good will and social statesmanship to realize these potentialities.

Once a pluralistic economy is realized, the functions of government would be mainly three: (1) to foster and preserve the structure of such an economy; (2) to prevent abuses in its functioning; and (3) to supply the necessary co-ordination and control at the top level, so that the requirements of the common good will be met.

Pluralistic structure is preserved by the preventing of monopoly and the delegation of real powers to subordinate groups, so that they may have a vital interest in functioning. Where today we have state regulation and control, it may be feasible and advisable to delegate such powers to more immediate economic groups, with proper safeguards for the common good. Freedom of entry within trade, business, professions, and unions can be very helpful in keeping flexibility and freedom within such an order. By this approach we can have regulation of the more unsocial forms of competition, without the rigidity and sterility that often accompany monopoly situations. This is what many Europeans term the social market economy.

The aim of government in a pluralistic economy is the securing of maximum power for smaller economic units more subject to control by individuals, families, and manageable groups. At the same time, however, the granting of a high degree of self-regulation to such economic units does pose the possibility and danger of abuse. Hence an important phase of any pluralistic economy will be the prevention of abuses on the part of the self-regulated units. One of the more potent weapons against abuse of power is the fostering of genuine competition within a pluralistic order. To the extent that competition is vital, the classical objections against older pluralistic orders, such as the medieval guilds, will no longer be applicable.

Government techniques for fostering competition are well developed today. Not only do we have a long history of anti-trust regulations, but we also have such devices as the use of tariffs and subsidies, and the direct stimulation of research and small enterprise. With reasonable use of such devices, we have no real ground to fear a pattern of competition within a societal framework of co-operation.

Thus far we have considered what may be called ancillary government functions in regard to a pluralistic order. One important function remains to be discussed. This is the function peculiar to the supreme authority of the state; that of top-level co-ordination and control, so that diverse groups may function together for the good of all. Even granting the salutary effects of the market mechanism in allocating resources of capital and labor in proper proportions, it is widely conceded today that the market cannot be the final directing force in economic life. The obvious case of credit control comes to mind as a function of the central authority of the economy. There are also the situations in which the impact of a freemarket creates conditions which are socially unacceptable. Such is the present status of the agricultural segment of our economy.

Even where government must exercise supreme control, it does not follow that it must do so in an arbitrary fashion, without consulting the parties to be regulated. Just as in the political order we speak of government with the consent of the governed, so in the economic order there should be mechanisms for consulting the economic groups which are affected by federal control. Perhaps an extension of the system of advisory bodies until we have a truly national economic council would be a feasible method for introducing the pluralistic principle into areas in which state control impinges upon the economic order.

Since this is the final paper in the series on pluralism, it might be fitting to conclude with an *apologia* for such an order. Many persons may understandably contend that it is brash to tinker with an economic system that is working so admirably. They may well point out that ideas for social reform are better received in times and places that are characterized by a substantial breakdown of production and gross inequality in distribution. American industry, they may say, has attained levels of production and distribution unparalleled in man's history. Under such circumstances it might be the part of wisdom to leave well enough alone.

The impact of these objections is not easily contested. They might readily be accepted were it not for two facts: (1) there is nothing in a rightly conceived pluralistic economy that would negate the dynamism of our present system; and (2) the trends toward impersonalization within our current economy may, in the long run, destroy the effectiveness of that economy. Dynamism depends to a considerable degree upon freedom and flexibility in an economic society. One of the postulates of pluralism, as presented here, is that its structure and functioning be such as to preserve and enhance dynamic trends in our institutions. By contrast, to the extent that our present economy is characterized by increased impersonalization in industry, labor, and government, it faces the danger of growing rigidities and consequent loss of dynamism.

Moreover, we must always remember that our economy should be oriented toward the individual and the family. What indeed does it profit us if we achieve the utmost of technical excellence in production and in the process lose the souls of the producers? There is no evidence that we face a dichotomy between a highly productive economy and a pluralistic society. But if such were the case, it would seem the part of wisdom to choose a structure that preserves human values rather than one which attains a maximum level of production at the cost of man's freedom and sense of achievement.

Too often the evolution of man's historical development is characterized by pendulum-like swings from one extreme to another. An excessively rigid society is replaced by one which is quasi-anarchic, *laissez faire* gives way to statism. We in the United States have gradually evolved our economy from a preponderance of atomistic individualism into a stage marked by giant concentrations of countervailing power. Labor and capital, farm and government today are gigantic power centers. It is the part of sound statesmanship, of political economy in the older sense of the term, to seek a middle way between these pendulum-like extremes. That is the unfinished task of our day. May we hope that the thoughts expressed in these papers may be a modest contribution toward the accomplishment of this task.

So much of the abstract treatment of the issue. Before concluding this paper, I should like to give a few concrete examples to illustrate the main points of the argument. This may have the added advantage of clarifying concepts which may seem overly abstruse and philosophical.

As we noted before, the best example of a purely monistic economy is found in a totalitarian regime, such as the communist or national-socialist models. If we examine a small manufacturing plant operating under such conditions, we find that it must function according to a centralized plan. The nature of its product, the cost and source of raw materials, the amount of production, prices for labor and for the end product—all of these are virtually controlled. The same power that dictates management policies also directs labor functions. In brief, no important decisions are made from below. No groupings of consequence may exist apart from the state apparatus. Government is not only supreme, it is all absorbing.

Under dualism, there is no centralized control, only the impersonal functioning of the market. There are whole series of competitive, antagonistic relationships. Our small manufacturer is in many ways a law unto himself. But his freedom of action is limited by conflicts with other equally free agents. He is constantly competing with other manufacturers of the same product, with suppliers of raw materials, and his labor force, with distributors, and ultimately with other producers for the consumer dollar. In this model, government is mostly a spectator. The role of the state in such a society is highly limited.

The first extreme made society and the state coterminal, with the result that liberty was destroyed. There can be no freedom when men derive all their rights from the state. The second extreme tended to be equally destructive of society, although from different premises. It denied the unity upon which society must be founded, and reduced all men to a status of antagonists rather than co-operators.

Because these two extremes were so obviously contrary to man's nature, it was to be expected that men should revolt against them and form some type of pluralistic economy. Actual attempts along these lines have not yet achieved the proper balance. Our typical small manufacturer tried to avoid excessive competition by the use of devices to stifle competition. He may have merged with larger firms, or he may have sought price-fixing and market allocation agreements. The resultant protests from labor and the consumer led to increasing government intervention in business. While the growth of countervailing power tended to reduce some of the abuses caused by big business, it created its own dangers of submerging smaller groups and individuals as more and more power was exercised by competing giants from industry, labor, the farm, and government.

Real pluralism would foster and invigorate small groups that are close to the individual and the family. The key point here, it seems, is to preserve and strengthen freedom of entry into all areas wherein individuals can exercise effective power. This means small business, small labor unions and farm organizations, lower levels of government—in short, any type of grouping that is small enough to allow individual members a really effective voice in the conduct of their organization.

This is not a protest against bigness as such, or a nostalgic call for a more primitive, distributist type of society. There are many valid reasons for large groups today in business, labor, agriculture, and government. The critical point is whether such giants tend to foster or to suppress what I may term personal (in contrast to impersonal) centers of power.

Concretely, we need not worry about big business, so long as small business can thrive and find sources for funds, research, markets, and labor. Large labor unions and farm organizations can be most useful, provided they do not stifle smaller constituent units or independents outside their fold. Our federal government must exercise extensive powers today, but it should not leave the states and cities as mere relics of past political customs. Yet diffusion of power is but a first step. By itself it could lead to conditions no different from those prevailing in the eighteenth or nineteenth centuries in France, England, and the United States. For a truly pluralistic economy, these separate groups must work together for the common good of all. There must be co-operation as well as competition.

The small manufacturer cited before would compete vigorously in many areas. He might be a hard bargainer with the union in his plant. But he would also co-operate with other manufacturers in setting and maintaining decent standards of production and sales. They would work jointly for promotion and research. Labor also would be considered a partner in production, even though its interests might clash with the employer's in regard to distribution of the income received from the product.

All these groups would co-operate with government in areas where central control is needed, especially in regard to monetary and fiscal policies directed toward stable, high levels of production and consumption. Here again there should be a partnership mentality, rather than the concept of countervailing power.

It is not going to be easy to achieve such a pattern of society. We shall need to insist constantly upon two types of arguments to win converts to this approach: (1) the dangers inherent in power centralization, anarchic individualism, or mixtures based on elements of these extremes; and (2) the results achieved where co-operation has been tried. Such an educational task should be one of the prime objectives of our small Association.

36 Victor C. Ferkiss

FOR CATHOLIC "SOCIAL ACTION IN THE AFFLUENT SOCIETY"

Discerning Catholics have increasingly realized in the last several years that economic reform, historically the primary concern of the American Catholic social movement, should no longer receive the emphasis it once was thought to deserve. This viewpoint was strongly presented by Victor C. Ferkiss, who was teaching political science at St. Mary's College, Calif.

The "working classes," he alleged, had gained immense material advantage from the economic reforms that were chiefly the result of labor unionism and legislation, but no substantial improvement, in their cultural, intellectual, moral, or spiritual condition. Economic reform was quantitative in character, not qualitative and for this reason had been powerless to affect the socially marginal and unaccepted groups—Negroes, Spanish-speaking immigrants, migrant farm workers, and the physically and mentally handicapped.

Ferkiss stressed the point that it was the structure of social relationships, not the structure of the economy, except incidentally, that needed reconstruction. This meant that Catholic social actionists should give more attention to the study of sociology, local government, and community planning. By so doing they would overcome some of the limitations of the purely economic approach—the indifference to preventive medicine and the problems of mental health, the neglect of adult education; and the handling of family disintegration as simply a moral problem, unrelated to the community environment.

If evidence be needed that American Catholicism is in tune with its environment it is readily available in the current mental state of most of those persons and groups concerned with Catholic "social action." Just as socio-economic reform seems a dead issue in contemporary America generally, so also it currently appears to excite little interest among Catholics. Many persons within and without the Church continue to mouth the traditional war cries, but the old fire, if not conviction itself, is gone.

Since World War II we have been living in an era in which American capitalism, even if not in theory the best of all possible worlds, seems in practice highly preferable to any but the most remote alternatives. A phrase such as "the condition of the working classes" has almost as much of a Victorian ring to it as "temperance" or "the emancipation of women." Our concern is no longer with reconstructing the social order but with preserving it against dangers arising not from within that order itself but from foreign enemies without.

Whether Americans generally have any business being satisfied with contemporary American society is not our problem here. Our concern is whether a person interested in Catholic social action should be satisfied with the state of modern American society, which is quite something else again, and this despite the fact that historically the interests of Catholic social reformers and those outside the Church have often coincided. Although during most of the 19th century American Catholics generally held aloof from popular reform movements, beginning with the Knights of Labor controversy in 1887 leading Catholic social thinkers have frequently made common cause with social reform movements of secular[1] origin. During the

---

Victor C. Ferkiss, "Social Action in the Affluent Society," *Social Order,* VIII (September 1958), 330–335.

[1] The term secular is used throughout as synonymous with the term non-Catholic despite the recognition of the author that many social reform movements in the United States have been motivated directly or indirectly by religious factors.

1920s, 1930s and even the 1940s both Catholic and secular social reformers were primarily concerned with the rights of labor and the amelioration of the condition of the ill-starred "one-third of a nation."[2] Even today concern about the position of the Negro in American society serves to perpetuate old alliances. But if Catholics have been interested in many of the same problems as reformers outside the Church there has always been, in theory at least (if often attenuated in practice) a difference in emphasis and to some extent, in motivation between Catholics and their secular allies. The Church is the expounder of natural law and the protector of the rights of men as men. The Church's mission is essentially a supernatural one and this gives a distinctive character to her concern with human society.

The Catholic social movement of modern times has been motivated not solely by a revulsion against social and economic injustice *per se* nor by a desire to blunt the strength of the Socialist challenge but also by the realization that a man's ability to attain his supernatural destiny is affected by the earthly conditions under which he lives—a motivation unknown to purely secular reformers.

As Catholics our concern with social questions is based in part at least on the belief that a minimum amount of leisure and of material goods is necessary if men are to have an opportunity for normal family or religious life. Gradually we are even coming to realize that a minimum standard of living is ordinarily a prerequisite for the development of an integrated, truly human being, capable of the free acts necessary to a meaningful spiritual life. Behind all the Catholic social actionists' agitation for minimum wages and maximum hours, collective bargaining, family allowances, social security, behind all the hard work of labor schools and all the loose talk about "corpor-

[2] For a summary of authoritative Catholic views on social reform see Wilfrid Parsons, S.J., *Social Thought of the American Hierarchy,* SOCIAL ORDER (June, 1952) p. 259.

ativism" and industry councils, has been the implicit belief that a world in which the so-called "working class" had a higher quantitative material standard of living would not only be a wealthier and more abstractly just world but would result in a substantial improvement in the quality of individual and social existence. Secular social reformers quite frequently held parallel hopes.

Well, we've seen the future and it doesn't seem to work, at least not as we all hoped it would.

The poor are richer but neither they nor the rich seem to be any better off culturally or intellectually, nor any better morally or spiritually. The alleged religious "revival" of the postwar years has a cheap and hollow ring to it. The secular reformers' confidence that the "workers," freed from backbreaking toil, would turn to cultivation of their higher faculties seems to have met its nemesis in the triumph of "mass culture."[3] The secular liberals may denounce the "hidden persuaders"[4] of Madison Avenue or the fact that we have become "organization men"[5]; the religiously motivated may decry a vaguely defined "materialism"; but both seem inclined to throw up their hands when it comes to non-hortatory remedies for our present discontents.

The meliorist approach to building the good society seems to have failed, but if economic reform is not the means to a better life, what is?

One possible reaction to the present state of affairs is to in-

[3] The classic collection of articles on this subject is *Mass Culture,* edited by Bernard Rosenberg and David Manning White, (The Free Press, Glencoe, Ill, 1957). The pessimistic obsession of social scientists with this alleged phenomenon is deplored by Edward Shils in "Daydreams and Nightmares," *The Sewanee Review,* 65 (1957), 587–608, and by Harold Rosenberg in "Pop Culture and Kitsch Criticism," *Dissent,* V (1958), 14–19.

[4] The subject of a sensationalized book of that name by Vance Packard (David McKay, Philadelphia, 1957).

[5] A species analyzed by William H. Whyte, Jr., in *The Organization Man* (Simon & Shuster, New York, 1956).

sist that the primarily economic attack on our social problems has not actually been proven a failure because it has not really had a chance to succeed or to achieve its objectives. For most of the world this argument has some plausibility. In most of the world poverty is still the number one problem, a poverty in some part at least the result of economic injustice. But as far as America is concerned, this argument just won't do. Frugal comfort, indeed! By any standards but their own most Americans are rich, individually as well as collectively. As John Kenneth Galbraith points out in his brilliant new book, *The Affluent Society,*[6] we in this country have already solved the economic problem of producing enough for our material needs. Though gross inequalities persist[7] and some Americans seem to have the ability to dispose of more goods than anyone could ever possibly use, at least virtually everyone has enough. Where there is still want, moreover, the problem is not basically economic but *social.*

Who, after all, are the American poor, the economically underprivileged? Not the wage earners *per se,* though for many their conditions of work are still highly unsatisfying,[8] but rather certain kinds of wage earners[9] and many persons who are not and cannot be wage earners in our modern economy. The poor are the Negroes, the migrant farm workers, the Spanish-speaking immigrants, the aged, the Indians, the Southern mountain-

[6] (Houghton Mifflin, Boston, 1958).

[7] An interesting attack on the widely held belief that inequality of income distribution in America is decreasing is to be found in Gabriel Kolko, "America's Income Revolution," *Dissent,* IV (1957) 35–55; criticism of Kolko's position appears *ibid.*, 315–320.

[8] Especially is this true in mass production industries such as the automotive. See Daniel Bell, *Work and Its Discontents* (Beacon Press, Boston, 1956); Frank Marquart, "The Auto Worker," *Dissent,* IV (1957), 219–233, and Harvey Swado's novel, *On the Line* (Little Brown, Boston, 1957).

[9] See Richard L. Heilbroner, "Who are the American Poor?" *Harpers,* 200 (January, 1950), pp. 27–33.

eers, the physically and mentally handicapped—in short the *socially* marginal and unaccepted.

Since our problems are not primarily economic but social in nature the reforms we need are accordingly not in the structure of our economy but in the structure of our social relationships. They involve not reorganizing the market system or the wage contract but changing our patterns of community life and raising the level of our intellectual, aesthetic and spiritual aspirations. It is with these areas that Catholic social action must concern itself in the future if it is to be a meaningful constructive force in American life.

If America could solve its special problems our remaining quasi-economic problems would solve themselves overnight. Eliminate race prejudice and you have virtually eliminated the slum.[10] Solve the problems of the place of the aged in society and half of our low-income households disappear. Eliminate ignorance and disease where possible and to that extent you destroy poverty. None of these aims will ever be completely realized in a world under the influence of original sin; in any society there will be individuals whose inborn incapacities will require special consideration;[11] but the economic aspects of our present social problems are obviously result not cause.

The more perceptive secular "liberals" are already awakening to the changed nature of our problems. Several years ago Arthur Schlesinger, Jr., called for the replacement of our outdated "liberalism of quantity" by a new "liberalism of quality."[12] John Galbraith suggests that to solve our problems it is

[10] There will, of course, always be areas of sub-average housing in which socially marginal groups will congregate.

[11] The problem of what to do with the near moron in an industrial economy becomes even more difficult as automation advances.

[12] See his "The Future of Liberalism: 1. The Challenge of Abundance," *The Reporter,* February 3, 1956, pp. 8–11. The objections made in subsequent issues to Mr. Schlesinger's argument could also be raised against my basic assumption concerning the essentially non-economic nature of our social problems.

not enough to increase our Gross National Product year after year since the GNP includes not only food, houses, schools, and hospitals but hot rods and switch-blade knives as well.[13] We need to recognize that the issue today is not one of gross production or even of equitable distribution but of what we, as individuals and as a nation, ought to do with our capacity to produce and consume. Socio-economic reforms aimed at increasing our productivity or altering the terms of its distribution are today largely irrelevant save insofar as they affect the kind of non-economic social relationships which prevail in the community.

Economic reforms for their own sake have in the past been the dominant concern of most persons engaged in Catholic social action. This must be the case no longer. In the past the basic problem was one of creating a minimum material standard of living for all our people. Today it is one of providing the conditions requisite to the full development and expression of the human personality and to the effective participation of the individual in the life of his community.

What we have to reconstruct is not the economy but now, at last, the social order itself. In this task Catholics must not be content, as so often in the past, to be followers merely but must assume leadership. As Catholics we should be especially well prepared to spearhead the struggle to create in America a civilization of quality rather than quantity since we have always held that wealth was not—could not be—an end in itself.

What must be done to reconstruct the social order so as to make it a fitting earthly sojourning place for human beings? Space does not permit detailed discussion of particular problems and the means for their solution but it is possible to set forth certain fundamental prerequisites to the needed reorientation of our efforts.

First of all, we as Catholics must broaden our sense of social morality to include the realization that social justice requires

[13] *Op. cit.*, especially Chapter IX.

not only the provision of a living wage but the provision of an appropriate social and physical setting in which to live. What point is there in taking home a wage adequate to buy food, clothes and shelter if one must live in a dirty congested neighborhood, wasting long hours each day commuting to a distant job, denied effective participation in the making of community decisions, lacking intellectual or cultural stimulation, deprived of any access to nature and unable to walk the streets with safety after dark? Yet many if not most Americans despite their high wages, more than adequate diets, abundant TV sets and new automobiles are in just such a situation. Our concept of what rightfully falls within the sphere of judgment of the informed Catholic social conscience must be expanded to include this kind of problem. Until Catholics feel as guilty about their part in polluting beaches and streams as they do about the failure to pay a living wage, until they come to look upon social disorganization in the local community as affording as great an obstacle to the development of the human personality as a depression, for so long will they be incapable of working toward the establishment of a decent, humane social order.

If we broaden the scope of our social conscience to include all of our community life, we will need also to sharpen our ability to make sound prudential judgments in this sphere. At least as much energy as has been spent by Catholics in studying economics in order to discuss intelligently the operations of the just economy must in the future be devoted to studying sociology, local government, and community planning so that Catholics may become aware of the impact of all that we do or fail to do on the shape of the communities in which we live.

Not only do we as Catholics have an obligation to broaden and sharpen our own social consciences but we must also be prepared to join actively—both as individual Catholics and as Catholic groups—with all those working to make our cities and regions better places in which to live. In the past Catholics have done valuable work in some areas of community social action, though for the most part they have conceived their tasks in isolation from any over-all concern with the community as such.

Needless to say, Catholics have been in the forefront of work to strengthen the family as the fundamental unit of society, though too often they have tended to regard family disorganization as a purely moral problem unrelated to the community environment. Catholics traditionally have taken responsibility for the education of youth through the provision of Catholic schools, though we have lagged behind in the field of adult education and in the development of community cultural facilities generally. Catholics have helped provide remedial aid for the physically and mentally ill through homes and hospitals, yet we have shown little interest in preventive medicine or the problems of mental health. The liturgical movement both consciously[14] and otherwise has served as a focus for the renewal of community life at the parish level, yet Catholics as such have usually paid little attention to general problems of community organization and betterment.

In the future Catholics must consciously accept their responsibility for the building of communities fit for the human being to live in. Just as Catholics in the past have been active (though perhaps not to so great an extent as we might have been) in the field of labor-management relations, so now we must become active in the field of community and regional planning in order to check the blights of ugliness, congestion and disorder that stalk so much of our land. We must take an active part in the conservation movement, since we have always regarded man as the steward not the master of created things and because of

[14] The leaders of the liturgical movement in the United States have traditionally been interested in the relationship of the liturgy to social problems. See Paul B. Marx, O.S.B., *Virgil Michel and the Liturgical Movement* (The Liturgical Press, Collegeville, Minn., 1957), and the periodical *Worship*.

our emphasis on the desirability of continued population growth. Finally, American Catholics must also devote more attention than we have so far to the creation of a more humane international order and to the improvement of the quality of life in the rest of the international community.

America has developed an economy which, despite dislocations and stumblings, has made available to us the means for achieving what measure of the good life can be expected here on earth. Now we have the task not of continuing the largely settled argument over the division of the means available in the affluent society but of ordering them toward the end for which they were given us, the creation of the good society.

37 Goetz A. Briefs

AN ATTACK ON "COMPULSORY UNIONISM"

Not a single worker should be compelled against his will to join a labor union as a condition of employment—this was the impassioned conviction, only slightly less vitriolic than scholarly, of Goetz A. Briefs, German-refugee professor at Georgetown University. Without validity, in his view, were the arguments in behalf of compulsory unionism—the union security argument, the free-rider argument, and the majority rule argument. By implication, Briefs did not think that either voluntary or compulsory unionism was necessary inasmuch as, in his opinion, workers could secure just treatment under capitalism without organization. By their very nature unions were self-centered organizations, intent on monopolizing industrial benefits for their own members and only on occasion and incidentally concerned with the welfare of all workers and of society at large.

Briefs directed his fire at the American Catholic leadership which for the most part continued, wrongly as he believed, to see in unionism the only efficient instrument for justice and the common good. When first formed—in pre-New Deal days—this union bias may have seemed plausible and proper, but it was utterly without justification, he claimed, after the passage of the Roosevelt and subsequent labor laws. Rather than insist on the duty of the worker to join a union, the Church should say he was morally bound to keep out of unions. The strongest and most forthright, although not the most widely known, defense of right-to-work laws, Briefs's argument failed to swerve the "labor priests" of the Association of Catholic Trade Unionists from their pro-union course.

I

Many Catholics, both clergy and laymen, subscribe to the union arguments for compulsory membership. Which are these arguments?

1. Unions claim to need the union shop because without it the union would be insecure. This argument is void of any foundation in fact, except perhaps at the fringe of the American economic scene where workers' indifference or resistance to unionization allows employers protected by State right-to-work laws to escape union pressure for compulsory organization. Note, within these fringes voluntary unionism enjoys precisely the same legal protection and administrative backing as do unions in their industrial strongholds. No country has enacted such drastic legislation in favor of unions as has the United States; and no administrative agencies of other countries have fostered and endorsed unionization as has the National Labor Relations

---

Goetz A. Briefs, "Compulsory Unionism," *Review of Social Economy*, XVIII (March 1960), 61–67, 69, 71–72, 76–77.

Board. In the face of these facts to say that unions need the closed or the union shop (between which the difference from the worker's standpoint is more academic than practical) is absurd. This has been recognized by union leaders themselves, e.g., by the president of the Brotherhood of Railway Clerks, Mr. G. M. Harrison:

> No, I do not think it [the union shop] would affect the power of bargaining one way or the other. . . . If I get a majority of the employees to vote for my union as the bargaining agent, I have got as much economic power at that stage of development as I ever will have. . . . (Hearing before the Committee on Interstate and Foreign Commerce of the House, H.R. 7789, 81st Cong., 2d Sess., 20–1, 1950.)

Labor economists of rank agree. We mention Professor John Spielmans who, by the way, favors compulsory unionism. In his article, "The Dilemma of the Closed Shop" (*Journal of Political Economy,* Vol. LI), he stated that in 1941 President Roosevelt declared that his government would never compel employees to join a union. President Roosevelt said: "That would be too much like the Hitler methods of forced labor." The author continues:

> . . . But actually these are the methods which are in substance and effect being employed today when compulsory union membership is authorized by law and put in force by labor leaders in the exercise of the tremendous powers granted them by law. . . . With the clamor of that battle subsiding, the worker's front, as the unions' chief remaining line of fighting, has moved into clearer view. The closed shop in particular, no longer seriously needed to combat employers' antiunion policies, has thus turned more and more into a weapon to coerce the workers into the unions —not against the will of the employers but against their own will.

Professor Selwyn H. Torff summarizes his opinion:

> If the union-survival theory were to be accepted as the motivating basis for the demand for compulsory union membership

today, there would be little support in reality for such a demand. The American labor movement has not been feeble for a long time; it is vigorous, aggressive and effective. It is protected by law and fortified by strength. It is one of the most dominating, economic, political and social institutions in the nation. It is beyond the capacity of employers to destroy it, even if they so desired or attempted. And the day of attempts by employers to destroy unions as such seems long past; "union-busting" exists today largely as a propaganda term. For the great majority of employers, labor unions and the collective bargaining process are established facts of economic life. Whatever the compulsory union membership issue may once have involved, it is no longer an issue that involves the survival of labor unionism in the United States. (Selwyn H. Torff, *Collective Bargaining*, New York, 1953, McGraw-Hill, p. 35.)

Finally, we quote another labor economist of high reputation and certainly a friend of unionism. In his book, *Economics of the Labor Market* (Philadelphia, 1949, J. P. Lippincott Co.), Professor Joseph Shister analyzed the arguments for the union shop as presented by the unions. Here is what he says:

By and large, employers are opposed to union security clauses. . . . It is to be expected, therefore, that employers will strongly resist union demands for security provisions. And from this it follows that where unions have been successful in obtaining union security, notably the closed or union shop, they must have possessed a great deal of bargaining power; otherwise the employer never would have yielded. A union is therefore strong before it obtains a security clause in its contract. . . . We must conclude therefore that a union which succeeds in obtaining a union shop clause, e.g., does not really need this clause to insure the survival and growth of the institution with an eye to the welfare of the membership. (p. 360).

2. We turn to the second argument in favor of the union shop. This is the so-called free rider argument. Its meaning is that nobody should enjoy benefits without having joined the benefit-securing institution. The implications of this principle become clear when it is universally applied. It would mean that

all churches, civic societies, the Red Cross, trade associations, farm associations, in short all voluntary associations working towards some self-defined group good, would be entitled to the identical claim of compulsory membership. There would be no longer an operating field for free and independent men and women. Coercion all around would kill the spontaneous endeavor and desire to band together for some good cause. Drab compulsion would destroy the most valuable impulses of our free society. And the end? Partial collectives claiming primacy over human rights would pave the road for total collectivization.

For pragmatic reasons unions may ignore these considerations. Given the closed or union shop they are exempt from competition and enjoy a more or less monopolistic stature. The last chink in the union armor would be closed. The workers would have to belong, and to submit to union rules, regulations and policies, or quit their jobs. Unions have pressed hard for the statutory right to represent all workers of a plant or industry; once they got it they turned it into an argument for compulsory membership.

But let us look a little more closely into the free-rider argument. At first glance there seems to be some justification for it —provided the free rider was clamoring for a free ride. Now *the very fact that unions demand the right to represent all employees of a firm or industry (after union certification) is proof that there are many workers who do not wish a free ride, but the union forces the free ride on them.* They must give up their individual bargaining rights in favor of the union's right to exclusive representation. This may sound very academic but it is not, as some American, British and Swedish workers and unions have found out. Some highly skilled crafts, most of all in manufacturing industries, have lost bargaining strength through the specific wage policies of industrial unions; their wages would be higher under individual bargaining. Limited as this range may be, it does exist. It is a fact that equalizing tendencies of union wage policies reduce the differential between the top level and the middle and lower wage levels. Swedish and British authors and labor leaders have complained that the recruitment of workers for higher skills has suffered on account of insufficient wage differentials caused by union policies. Indeed, the highly skilled workers in mass industries can certainly not be called "free riders" enjoying union benefits by staying out.

But most important is the following consideration. The free-rider argument implies that collective bargaining is a creative power in economic terms. It carries with it the implication that the union gains better wages, shorter hours and fringe benefits from collective bargaining. But this is a mistake. No improvement of wages and other benefits accrues to the workers from collective bargaining. Collective bargaining is *only a device for tapping the sources from which higher wages and all sorts of benefits finally can be secured.* At this point we face the real issue: Which are the sources of improvements mediated through collective bargaining? There are only three of them, no more. Improvements of wages mediated through collective bargaining can derive, firstly, from shifting increased costs to consumers, secondly, from unions cutting the profit margin, and thirdly, from an increase in the rate of productivity.

a. There were and are firms and industries where competition in the labor market leaves the wage level below equilibrium, although higher rates could be paid. This is the appointed range for union operations. Other industries operate in inelastic markets; there, of course, the firms can shift increased labor union cost to the consumer. The fund from which improvements then are paid is consumer's income. Who is the consumer? Dependent on the particular market, the consumer may be only workers, as, for instance, in the market of working clothes, tools, etc., or the consumer may be mostly workers, or a sizable group of workers, or only a few. To the extent that workers are the consumers (and a great majority of consumers are workers and their families) they pay—whether organized or not—for the union-secured improvements in working conditions; thus, there are no free riders. What if the workers are not consumers of the commodities whose costs have been increased through union pressure? In such rather rare situations the impact of increasing labor costs still may hit workers whether organized or not, in a roundabout way.

b. Has the free-rider argument more basis in fact when collective bargaining cuts into the profit margin? We assume intra-marginal firms and industries, that is, enterprises doing better than breaking even. Firms which, over a period of time, fail to break even offer no chances for union pressure anyway. Now, the intra-marginal firms show a wide variety of net returns; some earn huge profits, some average, some operate close to margin. It is obvious that the latter are least amenable to union pressure; however, unions may raise demands anyway when business otherwise is booming and government backs up full employment. The workers in these firms and industries may feel the consequences of union pressure in lay-offs, in unemployment, in unfavorable job classification, in loss of seniority rights, and pensions. The organized, as well as the unorganized workers, must accept the risk entailed in union activities. Where bargaining is industry-wide, the bargaining agency may disregard, or pay insufficient attention to, the many differentials in conditions among firms. There, workers—whether organized or not—may suffer. The free rider argument again fails to apply.

What about firms earning large profits? They, of course, are a promising target for union demands. Their profits may be due to a monopolistic condition, which is a rare case; or to monopoloid or to oligopolic position. Monopolistic conditions disallow shifting of increased costs to consumers, provided the firms have been maximizing their profits. Whenever that happens, unions are able to secure their cut from the monopoly profits. The same may to a much lesser extent apply in the case of oligopolic firms. Is there, in these cases, justification for the free-rider argument? Even if we would subscribe to the Marxian surplus value theory, no case can be made for the free-rider argument; the profits tapped by union pressure derive either from the exploitation of organized and unorganized workers or from consumer prices. If, on the other hand, we assume that profits are the result of specific entrepreneurial innovations, there is again no chance for the free-rider argument —it rather might be said that the *union* appears to be the free rider.

c. Finally, does the free-rider argument apply in the case of improvements derived from increased rates of productivity? These increases result from the combinations of all factors engaged in production; and the share that goes to labor cannot be imputed to organized labor alone. Hence, there is no room for the free rider argument.

The argument under consideration has indeed no base in economic fact. There is only one, and a very limited justification, for it—if it implies nothing more than that the cost accruing to unions because of collective bargaining benefits unorganized workers although they make no contribution. However, this furnishes no argument for compulsory union membership. Still, it may be an argument for a contribution to union funds to meet bargaining expenses. Since the unions are voluntary associations, a contribution to union expenses incurred on account of collective bargaining is in no way morally binding. Traditionally, unions themselves have rejected the suggestion of contributions from unorganized workers toward their bargaining expenses; they used to insist on no less than the union shop.

A third argument for compulsory unionism is based on the claim of majority rule. It is maintained that if a majority of the workers favors the closed or union shop, it is "unjust" and "undemocratic" of the minority to oppose this demand.

The argument is fallacious. It is the very essence of a genuine democracy to protect minority rights. No democratic rule forces the minority to join the majority. Indeed, it is the hallmark of *totalitarian regimes* to sacrifice minorities to the union of the one party. Moreover, the claim would imply revival of the feudal principle of *nulle terre sans seigneur*—no land without its overlord. The freedom of yeomanry and peasants was submerged when feudal lords applied the principle of compulsory overlordship; no land-holding was to be free from submission and dues payment to the lord. It is a feature of neo-feudalism that the same principle is applied without a second thought being given to the moral and social consequences that are implied. The unions' claim to job-territorial sovereignty has its historic parallel in the *nulle terre sans seigneur*. The consequences may not show in the short run; people may believe—and union leaders may be perfectly sincere in this belief—that the democratic process in union administration would prevent the rise of ruling oligarchies. They will be mistaken. The proper functioning of the democratic process depends on the continuing balance of the democratic forces and the strict observation of the rights of the minority. It is an illusion to believe that unions preserve their character as defenders of worker's rights and dignity when organization is compulsory and exclusive. The reader may consider the reality of the situation when a highly exclusive institution covers jobs and jobholders all around without a rival, without a countervailing force—in short without competition. It is commonplace that institutions, once established, want to prove their necessity; they want to grow, to expand, to entrench themselves behind the fullness of privilege and power. Any institution in such a situation will scan the horizon for ever more fields of action and self-expression; even governments may find themselves forced to connive. If abuses went with the power of the Church and anointed Christian kings—how much more abuse must we expect from institutions of a purely secular nature and designed to "get more"! It is strange indeed that unions, which have ever gloried in protecting the workers against the autocracy of the masters in business and industry, now, being themselves well-entrenched and backed by government, make every effort to enforce yellow-dog contracts in reverse and establish their own rule and discipline over their members. But what is more surprising is that Catholics make urgent and vigorous pleas for the unions' request for monopoly and exclusiveness—and do so with reference to the moral law! ! . . .

II

Because of the Church's millenial experience no less than because of her belief in moral law and its foundation in nature and revelation, Catholics should be the first to realize the tremendous danger implied in the drift of modern society towards collectivism via an unbalanced pluralism. The Christmas message of 1952 of Pope Pius XII expressed the profound concern of the Church about the growing power of organizations and the threat to human rights and dignity. The principle of subsidiarity so strongly proclaimed by the Church and so utterly forgotten by latter-day liberals as well as totalitarians expresses just this—that man as a person needs a field within which to activate reason and free will. If his self-expression, self-determination and responsibilities are whittled away by particular collectiva, man loses exactly those qualities which distinguish him from animals. What actually happens today, under the compulsion of the growing power of such collectiva, is that almost by force of circumstance the individual person's sphere of self-determination and responsibilities is ever more narrowly circumscribed, if not undermined. This process has gone farthest in communistic nations; but, in one form or another, trends point in that direction in all western societies. There is, in the west, evidence of creeping absorption of personal self-determination and self-responsibility; the principle of subsidiarity is increasingly ignored while the dignity and responsibility of the person is more and more absorbed by collectivities. Man is in danger of being reduced to a mere epiphenomenon of, and an instrument for, powerful collectiva.

In western Europe *since the war* there has been a gradual reversal of this trend. But in the United States the trend is still growing as it did in *prewar* Europe.

III

The advocates of compulsory membership in pluralistic organizations of whatever kind should be on their guard. Given favorable circumstances a society may violently turn into a totalitarian structure; historic examples are fresh in our mind. Again, they may, over a period of time and without noting it, just slip into collectivism. Old and well-grounded democracies such as ours may go a long way fostering partial collectiva without giving thought to danger signals; once, however, safely on the road, they will find it hard to stop. Socio-economic and political difficulties inherent in creeping collectivism may be charged to insufficient collectivization; more of the hair of the dog that bit us is cried for. There are always many ideologists and power-conscious leaders who seek salvation in a bigger dose of the disease. In such a situation there is no other remedy but eternal vigilance and recourse to principles. The Catholic Church has known that all along; but there are numbers of Catholics who still have to learn it. . . .

Important as personal and environmental circumstances may be in the explanation of the stand taken by many Catholics with regard to right-to-work laws, yet they do not tell the whole story. It would rather seem that they carry weight because of a prior concept and evaluation of the nature of unions. This assumption can be checked with reference to Catholic attitudes regarding communist-infected unions; no one doubts that a Catholic worker is morally obliged not to join them.

Here none of the environmental circumstances made Catholics waiver in their conviction. What then is it that makes so many Catholics urge on workers a moral obligation to join unions? Are non-communist unions good *per se?* Is their policy strictly in line with the Church's doctrine regarding justice and charity?

We submit the suggestion that a definite ambiguity inherent in unionism gave rise to a misconception of their nature and to a biased opinion concerning their programs and policies.

The ambiguity expresses itself in the fact that unions claim to speak for "labor," to represent "the rights and dignity of the toiling masses," to improve "the lot of the workers" who, presumably as a social group, "cannot find justice in the capitalistic system." In the eyes of many the mere fact that workers must seek their living by way of a wage contract implies their being in a state of servitude and exploitation. The workers' natural right to organize for the purpose of securing justice for their group is one aspect of unionism. The normal agency of this aspect of unionism is overall national federations. Theirs is the particular mission "to represent labor," "the working man" as such. It is commonly agreed that in this regard unions have done a splendid job.

However, this is not their whole job; indeed, not even their foremost job. There exists another union job, one which may or may not tally with the one just mentioned. In its day-to-day operations the individual union's chief concern is in the interest and aggrandisement of its organization and the improvement of the working conditions of its members. Unions do not forego possible benefits for their members just for the welfare of the working class, or because increasing labor unit cost (pursuant to collective agreements) is a burden on other unions, workers and consumers. It is the rule and not the exception that the individual union, jealous of its autonomy in matters of policy looks out for itself. Whenever its interest collides with that of a rival union, it is ready for battle. In short, in their day-to-day activities unions are of the nature and character of actual or would-be monopolies; at the very least, they are cartels—organizations designed to influence the supply and other conditions of sale in their respective markets. Where they attain the stature of the closed union operating under a closed shop rule, they approach the nature of syndicates in the precise meaning of the term—they allocate the jobs to their members.

Except where their respective interests clash, such union cartels or monopolies display a mutuality of institutional interests and a united front against actual and potential dangers and adversaries. This solidarity gives them the semblance of fighting for labor, although in reality they are fighting for the survival and expansion of their respective institutions. Sympathy strikes and similar expressions of union solidarity belong here. The mutuality of interests is not *prima facie* proof of their defense of the workers' rights.

This dual aspect of unionism is obvious; unions do not deny it by their current behavior. It is one thing to defend labor; it is an entirely different thing to pursue particular ends. No need to elaborate; according to their intent and purpose, as well as their structures, unions are cartels. As such, they are concerned about labor's rights if and when pending general labor issues (such as Taft-Hartley or Landrum-Griffin Bills) have a bearing on immediate union interest.

If unionism presents itself as a multiplicity of group-interest pressuring units, it follows that unions cannot be identified as "the labor movement." The claim to represent "labor" as raised by Marxist workers' organizations was ideological; they really meant to speak for wage earners as such. No union ever did that except for *ad hoc* emotional or political considerations reflecting its own interests. The unions' very structure and function (sectional bargaining) point rather to their special interests.

The ambiguity inherent in unions could long remain obscure.

Until the New Deal legislation they could easily be mistaken for "labor's vanguard"; what one union gained today, others, through similar organization, would gain tomorrow. Moreover, since before the New Deal union pressure was held in check by employers' resistance, the law and the courts, monopolistic features could not find expression. In the eyes of Msgr. J. A. Ryan and of many others the workers generally were the underdog; fairness as well as justice demanded that they be given a chance. It was in that pre-New Deal era that the basic union-consciousness of Catholics was formed. It appeared as though unions were fighting for "the rights of the workers"; and didn't *Rerum Novarum* insist on the workers' natural right to organize?

Against such a background there arose the widespread belief among Catholic leaders—first, that labor as a social group cannot find justice in the capitalist system; second, that the workers' natural right to organize for the pursuit of a common good finds expression in unions, supposedly the only efficient instrument for justice and the common good; and thirdly, since the common good has precedence over individual rights, workers on moral grounds, must join the unions.

This interpretation is grounded on the notion of unions being a natural community of men concerned with the achievement of justice. In reality, unionism does not bear out this conception. . . .

Unions can put government and business under duress, but the Catholic Church has no such excuse. However, it may happen, and to our mind it has happened, that some Catholic leaders fail to realize the nature of the institution whose claim to total coverage and exclusivity they back. They did, indeed, reject Communist unions as incompatible with moral principles, but they did not have an adequate concept and notion of the non-Communist union. In spite of warning voices they continue to mix up the group-individualistic union with a natural community of workers pursuing a common good and guided generally by moral principles. Thus, being misled by labor aspect of unions, they fail to penetrate to the unions' essential core: their character as a multiplicity of actual or tentative monopolies guided by group-individualistic principles. They interpret morally objectionable strategems, tactics and policies of unions as mere incidental abuses, and even regarding them they often bend over backwards in pleading extenuating circumstances. The environmental circumstances of earlier periods in the growth of the Catholic Church in this country invited the failure to grasp the essential link between liberal capitalism and the unions. This was excusable up to the advent of the New Deal policy and its consequence of powerfully entrenched unions; it is no longer excusable now.

Catholics must give a second thought to the question as to whether or not workers are morally obliged to join unions. It might well be, that from the standpoint of the Church, insistence on the *right* of workers not to join would be the better advice. We quote from an article by John E. Coogan, S.J., published in the *American Ecclesiastical Review* for December, 1955. The author, having outlined a list of union abuses, continues:

But even so incomplete a list of types of union misconduct should not close without reference to union mistreatment of unionists. Enough to mention the very pro-union *Commonweal's* description of the Taft-Hartley law as not going far enough in the protection of workmen from their unions: "The union still has the power to deprive a man of his rights as a member. It still has the power to make it difficult, if not impossible, for him to find work once he is unemployed. . . . The power over a man's job is the power over his life . . . and so it happens that in one of the freest countries in the world you run into these pockets of tyranny, dictatorship, ruthless and violent absolutism, where men, American men, live and work in a state of fear that can only be compared to life under Communism and Fascism. The paradox is that even decent labor leaders who support every bill designed to protect civil liberties will oppose any attempt to protect the rights of union members, calling it 'an unwarranted interference in the internal affairs of private associations.'" *Commonweal* says, too, that "Men have been deprived of their jobs, of their homes, even of their lives by racketeers and others who look upon a union only as a source of wealth and power to feed their own bellies and their egos." (l.c., p. 375)

In the eyes of the Church unions are institutions designed for the protection of the right of the working men; hence, they should not override a basic right of the worker himself; it bodes ill for union policies as a whole. When prominent labor leaders and experts in the labor field, courts and lawyers raise their voices in defense of the workers' rights to organize or not, and in disapproval of compulsory membership, no Catholic should forget that his place is in the vanguard of the fight for both the workers' rights *and* the unions' moral standards.

To sum up, unions are no different from other human institutions. They are not good per se, neither from a moral nor an economic and social aspect. Their goodness or badness depends on the moral and economic judgment of their leaders and members. Justice is a human virtue, not the function of an institution or a mechanism. Institutions can protect the exercise of this virtue, but they can equally well be conducive to utter abuses. The temptation to abuse union power is deeply rooted in their adoption of the rules of the game of an individualistic society, of the ethos of the more and more, and of the imperialist urge to expand in influence and power. The great success precisely secured by adopting the ethos of more and more as adjusted to group action enhances the temptation to override the rights of non-union workers, of employers and of other unions alike and, indeed, of the common good of the nation as a whole. The present-day pressure-type mass-democracy in conjunction with welfare state policies offers the ideal climate for the establishment of a consolidated and formidable union power bloc. To expect this bloc automatically to adhere to moral principles betrays ignorance doubly confounded by naïvete.

38 Rupert J. Ederer

A PROGRESS REPORT ON INDUSTRY COUNCILS

This selection is a progress report on Industry Councils, the American term for the vocational or occupational groups urged by Pope Pius XI in his encyclical Quadragesimo Anno *of 1931. The author, labor economist Rupert J. Ederer, shows that the idea of group harmony is widely accepted in America and has been gaining in recent years a seemingly secure foothold, especially in the electrical, construction, coal, and steel industries. The Council on Industrial Relations in the electrical industry, successful from its formation in 1921, has consciously aimed not at destroying or replacing unionism and employer organization, but rather at strengthening them and utilizing them to solve the problems which confront the industry as a whole. The more recently formed Industry Councils, no one of them yet a decade old, have recapitulated the experience of the electrical industry, and this fact prompts Ederer to suggest that a pattern may be forming in the evolution of the Industry Council plan.*

But the main thing in the evolution of these Councils, he insists, is growth, not plan—natural and spontaneous growth. They owe little, if anything, to the blueprints of Catholic zealots who failed to realize that Pius XI was concerned less with forms and schemes than with a few directive points based upon a reasonable social philosophy. In the true spirit of Pius XI and his successors, additional Industry Councils will evolve, Ederer predicts, from the countless instances of labor-management cooperation and the thousands of successful profit-sharing arrangements which dot the industrial landscape.

It has been said that if Catholic social scientists finally come face to face with an industry council, they will not recognize it. The fraction of truth in this charge stems from the undue obsession that many of these zealots have had for form, rather than for matter. In hammer and tongs fashion, many Catholic economists and sociologists, after studying the directives regarding industry councils in *Quadragesimo Anno* set about drawing blueprints for such councils. These were varied, and some were interesting, but by and large, in this writer's opinion, they missed the point. Pius XI intended nothing more than to provide certain reference points based upon a reasonable social philosophy. These reference points could be adapted to various national temperaments and institutional frameworks. No one form is correct for all times and all places, nor is the form as important as the spirit! That spirit, based soundly on reason, is one of group harmony flowing from common interests and problems. A social organism which serves to further this harmony—always with respect for the broader common good—could be an industry council.

Basing ourselves on Pius XI's directives we may tentatively define an industry council as *a continuous organization of men working in the same industry, regardless of rank or position, for the purpose of solving the problems and furthering the legitimate aims of their industry.*

Such councils are to be a remedy for what Pius called "this grave disorder which is leading society to ruin." By the disorder he meant the situation in labor relations which *"divides man on the labor market into two classes, as into two camps, and the bargaining between these two parties transforms this labor market into an area where the two armies are engaged in combat."*

The Pope suggested groups which in his words would *"bind*

Rupert J. Ederer, "The Industry Council Arrives in America," *Review of Social Economy,* XIX (September 1961), 155–165.

men together not according to the position they occupy in the labor market, but according to the diverse functions which they exercise in society."

A significant fact is the Pope's reference to these groups as "natural" and "spontaneous." How could something natural be totally absent from a social framework? Simply because the framework is just a *framework* and not an *order*. But if the concept of the industry council is natural, it is also reasonable, and reasonable men, whether or not they belong to the Church of Pius XI, will ultimately work out reasonable solutions to their problems. Perhaps this is why Arthur Goldberg,[1] a Jew, recently suggested that a "labor-management assembly" was needed. Such an assembly could, in Goldberg's words, "discuss and think about the important issues in the labor-management area on a broader basis than is possible in collective bargaining, not to fight and bicker over the words of a contract or a resolution."[2]

Also, the naturalness of the industry council may be the reason why John L. Lewis, a Protestant, launched an era of model labor management cooperation in the mining industry after decades of bitter class conflict.

It is time now for a brief progress report on the industry council in the United States. For, in this writer's opinion the industry council has begun to be a part of the American social fabric—*spontaneously!* Reasonable men, it seems, have begun to sense that the area of common interest between labor and management is broader than the area of conflict!

Possibly as an advanced portent of what was to come, there was this noteworthy development. When the AF of L and the CIO met in Atlantic City to merge their two federations during the December of 1955, the delegates to that convention drafted a preamble to the AFL-CIO Constitution which was

[1] Special Counsel, AFL-CIO.

[2] Sidney Hillman Address, Nov. 5, 1958, Univ. of Wisconsin.

radically different from that of the old AF of L. Note the wording of the AF of L Constitution's preamble that was drawn up in 1881:

"Whereas a struggle is going on in all the nations of the civilized world between the oppressors and the oppressed of all countries, a struggle between the capitalist and the laborer, which grows in intensity from year to year . . ."

This could have been written by Karl Marx. Nevertheless, the class conflict which it describes was quite real at the time. It was only as workingmen won their rights and became free citizens of industry that they could begin to talk about cooperation. Slaves and servants do not cooperate, they merely obey. It is to the credit of American labor that its attitude is as flexible as it is. Against the background of gains that were bitterly contested most of the way, they might have remained far more embittered and class conscious than they actually are. Instead, organized American workers, having won their right to deal with their employers as equal human beings, are now ready in increasing numbers to talk seriously about this vast area which they have in common with management in their industries.

The preamble of the new AFL-CIO Constitution says nothing about a struggle between capital and labor. It replaces the language of Marxian warfare with an appeal to "Divine guidance" and a statement which reads:

"We seek the fulfillment of these hopes and aspirations through democratic processes within the framework of our constitutional government and consistent with our institutions and traditions. . . . At the collective bargaining table, in the community, in the exercise of the rights and responsibilities of citizenship, we shall responsibly serve the interests of all the American people."

This wholesome revision, like Arthur Goldberg's suggestion for a "labor-management assembly" away from the bargaining table is an indication that men are beginning to think correctly. Nor are these isolated instances. Labor-management discussions away from the bargaining table have become almost the stock-in-trade of U.S. Labor Secretary James P. Mitchell whenever he addresses labor and management groups. In a recent speech, Mitchell stated:

"Collective bargaining 'business as usual'—without a real effort to join outside the bargaining table and develop competitive measures could mean no business at all."[3]

Again, before the Railway Operating Brotherhoods' Spring Institute held at the State University of Iowa in April, 1960 the Labor Secretary said:

"The rejection of compulsion, the rejection of forced change, the rejection of the status quo, and the need to face squarely the responsibilities that labor and management bear toward the public, all of these things point the way, in my mind, to the only manner in which labor-management relations can keep pace with progress, and that is by supplementing the bargaining table, prefixing it with a new form of communication disassociated from bargaining and deadlines and demands."

Nor are such thoughts the sole property of "neutral" outsiders. One of the men in Mitchell's audience was Guy L. Brown, then Grand Chief of the Brotherhood of Locomotive Engineers. Brown has played the industrial unity motif for some time. In addressing a conference of Rail employees, Brown said:

"I see absolutely no reason why a man or woman can't be a loyal Cheasapeake & Ohio employee and a loyal member of the Brotherhood of Locomotive Engineers or one of the other rail labor organizations. In fact the two loyalties should complement one another very well."[4]

[3] Speech, May 2, 1950 before Railway Employees Dept. of AFL-CIO.

[4] Speech before C & O Railway Employes' Better Service Conference, September 1957.

In the same address, the Engineer's Chief foresaw an era *"in which intelligent self-respecting men from both sides of the bargaining table can achieve a harmony of interests that previous generations found impossible."*

So much for correct thought, but has there been any action? The answer is decidedly, yes—and significant action! Although it is too early to discuss outcomes, the top level labor-management assembly first suggested by President George Meany of the AFL-CIO in 1955, and more recently recommended by Labor Secretary George Mitchell and Arthur Goldberg are now a reality. The first attempt at such an "assembly" took the form of "peace talks" between Meany and Charles R. Sligh of the National Association of Manufactures back in 1956. These first "summit talks" faltered over the union shop issue, and you might say that the opposing forces took cover in previously prepared positions. It took the paralyzing impact of the 116 day steel strike in 1959 to coax the parties into serious top level talks. The loss from this strike was so great and so obvious that even the most stubborn warriors realized at last what was meant by the *common good.*

Accordingly, on May 19, 1960, a Committee of six, three from the AFL-CIO and three from the NAM met in a Washington, D.C., hotel to lay the groundwork for a more reasonable labor-management pattern. While it is too early to assay the results of such summit talks, they are encouraging because they indicate the coming of the dawn in this matter of a common good which transcends positions in the labor market.

A Council for Steel

Although labor management summit talks do not constitute an industry council in the strict sense of the word, since they cut across industry lines, the arrangement that has been worked out in the steel industry since the steel strike does, in this writer's opinion, represent a real nascent industry council.

It was born amid the gloom, name-calling, and newsprint warfare of the recent steel strike. It first saw the light of day when Edgar Kaiser of Kaiser Steel of Fontana, California, fled from the bristling camp of the steel giants and made peace with "the enemy," if you will. The Kaiser settlement shattered the smug "togetherness" of the steel captains, but it then set the pattern for further settlements. What is more, Kaiser's action provided the type of leadership which Americans have come to expect of their industrial leaders, and especially of the Kaiser brothers!

Briefly, the Kaiser agreement provides for two committees. One is a committee of nine members, three each from the public, labor, and management. It will deal with long range problems affecting the steel industry. This tri-partite group will recommend ways of sharing the company's future economic progress equitably among workers, stockholders and the public. Of its prospects, Steelworkers' President, David McDonald said: *"If we are successful in establishing this idea as the pattern for the American Steel industry, I feel certain in my heart that the International Wage Policy Committee will never again have to call a nationwide strike."*

The Kaiser settlement provides for a second, plant level, committee, three from the union and three from management. This is known as a work-rules committee which will act on problems resulting from automation, technological change and local working conditions generally. Asked what would happen if this committee votes three for and three against a proposal, Kaiser replied:

> "That's what the industry tells us will happen. They say, this is for the birds. Well, if faith that you can work out something with somebody else is for the birds, we had better fold the whole country up."

There may well be a connection between the spirit behind the Kaiser settlement and reports by Kaiser officials that grievances have declined by more than 50% since the strike ended. Also, the council idea has since spread to Kaiser Aluminum where impromptu meetings between labor and management are being held.

Eleven other basic steel giants, while more gingerly than Kaiser, did steal a considerable page from the book. Section 8, paragraph 3 of their settlement calls for the establishment of a joint committee headed by a neutral chairman to study local working condition provisions. The committee has been formed and named the "*Human Relations Research Committee.*" Steelworkers' President McDonald has intimated that this committee may well work out all contract terms before the next negotiations are due in 1962.

We dare say that this nascent industry council in steel is not due to the fact that David McDonald of the Steel workers' is a Catholic who has read *Quadragesimo Anno.* It is more due to the fact that both he and Mr. Kaiser are reasonable men who have grown weary of the periodic strife over a few cents an hour which ties up a major industry and creates widespread unemployment, reduces the national product, and trims the slice of the pie going to workers as well as stockholders!

The Building Trades

Although without the fanfare and pyrotechnics that accompanied the birth of an industry council in steel, a council that is every bit as genuine, and for the time being more clearcut, has arisen in the construction industry. In January 1959, a group of building contractors met in Florida with building trade union leaders and probed the possibility of setting up a permanent joint council at the national level to solve mutual problems and promote their industry by warring on waste and inefficiency. As a result, the *Construction Industry Joint Conference* was born in Washington on April 7. This council, set up on a permanent and continuous basis with offices in Washington, D.C., is made up of the national presidents of building trade unions and of contractors' associations. Professor John T. Dunlop of Harvard University is its impartial chairman. It cites as its objective to promote the welfare of the *building trades and construction industry in the public interest!* Specifically it strives to improve performance and productivity by contractors and workers, and to promote the contract system.

The Construction Industry Joint Conference operating at the national level would have valuable though limited effectiveness. Significantly, it provides for the establishment of local joint conferences which can better come to grips with local industry problems. St. Louis has the distinction of forming the first such local council, and note, this is called a *council*—the *St. Louis Construction Industry Joint Council!* Its establishment occurred on June 9, 1959, and it involves over 35,000 men, including the 19 building trades unions and 10 large contractor associations.

Perhaps the St. Louis Council was sparked by the experience of brother tradesmen across the Mississippi in East St. Louis. In 1958, nine unions and the Southern Illinois Builders' Association signed the ten point "Statement of Policy" that the AFL-CIO Building and Construction Trades Department adopted in February of that year—to cut featherbedding in construction. Almost immediately, the Granite City Steel Company announced that it would build its new main office building in the area. Soon afterward, the Shell Company announced a major expansion of its large Wood-River, Illinois, Refinery. Whether or not this is a formal council in East St. Louis—the fact remains that this is an industry council action with positive and dramatic results.

The Electrical Industry

Older than any of these councils is the one that has been working quietly, but with phenomenal success in the electrical industry. It is known as the *"Council on Industrial Relations"* involving the International Brotherhood of Electrical Workers and the National Association of Electrical Contractors. Harmony in this industry first came to life in 1919 when the Electrical Contractors and the IBEW signed a "Declaration of Principles." The second of these Principles states:

> "Close contact and mutually sympathetic interest between employee and employer will develop a better working system and will tend constantly to stimulate production while improving the relationship between employer and the community."

Principle number seven is also significant:

> "Cooperation between employee and employer acquires constructive power, as both employees and employers become more completely organized."

This almost suggests that unionization and employer organizations must precede effective industrial cooperation.

The Council on Industrial Relations was not actually set up until 1921 and it has functioned ever since. Known as the "supreme court in the electrical industry," the Council is made up of six representatives from the National Electrical Contractors Association, and six from the IBEW. These members meet quarterly in various parts of the country and decide *unanimously* on a wide variety of industry problems.

Cooperation in the electrical industry has spread far beyond the Council on Industrial Relations. Periodic joint conferences between contractors and the IBEW members are held throughout the United States. Also, a National Joint Apprenticeship and Training Committee meets annually to evaluate apprenticeship programs throughout the country.

Finally, where else would one find a union conducting seminars to improve efficiency in the industry. Imaginative Harry Van Arsdale, Business Manager of Local 3, IBEW, in Greater New York, is running such seminars for his men. They are the fulfillment of a promise made to contractors in return for the 1960–61 wage-fringe package.

But such cooperation is not novel to Local 3, IBEW. For seventeen years there has been in New York City a *Joint Industry Board of the Electrical Industry.* This Board was formed in 1943 under the terms of a contract between the union and industry, *"to find ways and means to expand the harmony between management and labor."* It is made up of twelve members from the union and twelve from management. In addition, there is one public member. Besides administering the extensive welfare plans of Local 3, this Board operates a hiring hall, an apprenticeship training program, and a safety program. Finally, it includes a committee working full-time on the development of modern tools and techniques for the industry. In a descriptive brochure entitled "The Team," one finds this opening statement:

> "This is the story of the accomplishments of Local #3 I.B.E.W. AFL, and the electrical contractors who together comprise the great electrical contracting industry in New York City."

Few would deny that here is an industry council in the finest sense of the word.

The Coal Industry

Then there is John L. Lewis the man who probably more than any other has earned the title *The Lion of Organized Labor.* The Lewis career, which ended with his retirement early in 1960, is significant. This man has run the entire course from grim and bitter industrial warfare to a harmonious cooperation between labor and management which can, without exaggeration, be termed exemplary.

Ten years ago any professor of labor relations would have cited Lewis as the example of belligerence and intransigence in a labor leader. Incidentally, ten years ago also, the coal industry was classified as a "sick industry." Today both these facts have changed, at least so far as bituminous is concerned, and the fact that both have changed is no mere coincidence. When two determined people stop pulling in opposite directions and start pulling together, there is bound to be a change. Today, this "sick industry" can deliver American coal on German doorsteps at a price lower than the price for which German mines can offer it. This is because Lewis' sledge hammer tactics have forced the inefficient mine operators to modernize and mechanize or get out of business. A whole maze of unsafe, unhealthful mines had been able to maintain themselves because of substandard wages and primitive working conditions. To this, Lewis put an end. "We decided," he said, "it is better to have half a million men working in the industry at good wages and high standards of living than it is to have a million men working in the industry in poverty and degradation." The miners who work at their craft today enjoy among the highest wage rates, the shortest hours, and the best fringe benefits of any workers here or abroad!

With the mine operators who survived, Lewis cooperated to make American bituminous a most feared competitor in world markets. In June of 1956, John L. Lewis sparked the formation of the American Coal Shipping Company. This unique enterprise was composed of the United Mine Workers, several coal producing companies, and three coal carrying railroads. Together these partners leased and later bought World War II liberty ships to carry coal to Europe under the American flag and at American seamen's wages. There is scant sign of class conflict here.

Moving a step closer to a formal industry council, Lewis suggested, in a speech of May, 1958, that the coal industry should be represented by an organization which could speak for the entire industry including his mine workers. Accordingly, in 1959, the *National Coal Policy Conference* was formed. It is made up of the United Mine Workers, coal operators, coal carrying railroads, and coal using public utilities.

The aim is to promote the good of the coal industry. About this, the UMW journal commented editorially:

"We would not go so far as to say that this conference is a perfect example of a vocational group as envisioned in *Quadragesimo Anno*. Yet we certainly must regard it as being in harmony with the spirit of group cooperation as advocated by all modern Popes." (United Mine Workers Journal, Nov. 15, 1959, p. 9.)

To this we would reply that an industry council by any other name is an industry council still!

The crowning testimonial for Lewis' industrial statesmanship was a scorching article in a Communist weekly, the National Guardian (January 26, 1959), condemning his cooperative tendencies.

Embryo Councils

Aside from John L. Lewis metamorphosis and the councils in steel, construction, and the electrical industries, there are countless examples of sincere cooperation and manifestations of good will between labor and management in other industries. Many of these industries are, we dare say, just a "nudge" away from setting up formal industry councils.

For example, recently the Chicago Waiters' Alliance, Local 25, agreed to postpone wage demands served on Chicago restaurant owners. The Alliance described its position in these words:

"This settlement takes into consideration the competitive situation of the employers who composed the bargaining unit. It is a settlement that should permit and encourage the employers to absorb additional payroll costs without raising menu prices."

In January, 1960, 900 members of the United Furniture Workers Union in Gardner, Massachusetts, voted to take a 10% pay cut to help their employer, the 133 year old Heywood-Wakefield Company, meet the competition of non-union plants in the South. In an even more dramatic action, Carpenters Local #3115 in Herkimer, New York, came to the rescue of their employer. Involved was the 75-year-old Standard Furniture Company, manufacturer of office furniture. The firm notified the mayor of Herkimer that it would have to close its doors unless it could raise $150,000 immediately. The company's plight was made known to the 300 members of Local 3115 at a special meeting, and before the meeting was over, the men had pledged $75,000. The union also provided canvassers for the general appeal, and Standard Furniture was saved for Herkimer.

At its 1957 convention, the International Leather Goods, Plastics and Novelty Workers Union called for a program of Labor-Management cooperation to secure remedial legislation in the area of excise taxes and tariffs. Representatives of labor and management have been meeting regularly since that time on this *common ground.*

In 1958, the Textile Workers Union, AFL-CIO, distributed 25,000 copies of a pamphlet outlining proposals to cure the ills of the textile industry. It was distributed to legislators, governors and other influential persons with the union paying all expenses. The same union had sponsored an essay contest to gather suggestions for solving the industry's problems. To show that it would back words with action, the union decided to drop its demands for a wage increase because, in the words of its International President, *"the industry is and has been in its most serious depression in 20 years."*

In Detroit, the members of Packinghouse Workers Local 190 voluntarily agreed to give financial assistance to their employer to enable him to remain in business. They agreed to loan the employer 10% of their earnings for five years! This would give the ninety-nine year old Hammond-Standish Company some $900,000 in capital with which to modernize its facilities.

Conclusion

We may conclude that industry councils do in fact exist today in the United States. This should blunt the barbs of those cynics who have for years pronounced the industry council idea stillborn. Furthermore, it is noteworthy that councils are emerging typically in situations where there are strong bona fide labor unions. This proves that sycophant unions or non-union conditions are not prerequisite for the virile labor-management cooperation which produces industry councils. Labor unions serve legitimate though narrower interests than industry councils, and it is not likely that they will disappear as councils arrive, any more than cities disappeared when nations arrived in the political order. Parties on both sides of the bargaining table are beginning to realize that they both eat off that table, and that it is possible, in fact advisable, to be a loyal member of the industry as well as of the employer or labor organization. This is, after all, as true in the economic order as in the political order; being a loyal citizen of Chicago, does not imply disloyalty to the United States.

In addition to the councils that have already been established, countless instances of labor-management cooperation and thousands of successful profit sharing arrangements indicate the presence of abundant raw material for more industry councils. Once the good will and common sense which foster a sense of industrial citizenship are present, a modicum of imagination is all that is still needed for setting up industry councils.

Unfortunately, one finds other situations where an industry is desperately in need of a cooperative solution to its problems, but where myopic bickering forestalls constructive action. The railroad industry is an example. This writer is convinced after four years in the industry that nothing but a joint labor-management attack on its many serious problems will save the railroads from eventual nationalization.[5] This may be

[5] The writer was Research Consultant for the Switchmen's Union of North America.

another instance where an industry must be at death's door before its members find inspiration to advance beyond the "cave-man" stage of industrial relations.

In any case, American labor and management men have begun *spontaneously* to set up industry councils. This is because councils are natural to a well-ordered society and because the majority of these men are reasonable men. This is genuine and significant social progress.

39 Daniel Callahan

COMMUNITY v. CATHOLIC INTERESTS IN THE NEW PLURALIST SOCIETY

The old plurality of values and interests functioned within a Protestant-oriented consensus of social direction. Regnant before World War I and still powerful until World War II, this consensus has now definitely disappeared from the American scene. In its place may emerge a new consensus which will be, many people fear, non-religious and secular. Although too weak to impose one of their own, American Catholics are numerous and influential enough to help shape any new consensus that may finally appear. What course of action should Catholics follow? This question Daniel Callahan, the brilliant associate editor of Commonweal, *poses and attempts to answer.*

There is no agreement among American Catholics on the manner or content of their contribution to the formation of the overall consensus, Callahan contends. Catholics continue in fact to be divided into two broad schools of thought: the grievance-conscious Catholics who wish to mobilize the

Catholic body to force public authority to subsidize parochial schools, censor juvenile literature and the movies and to withhold tax support from birth-control programs; and secondly, the community-minded Catholics who would minimize or ignore grievances and seek instead to impart something of Catholic quality and wisdom to debate and decision on all public issues. The community-minded Catholics oppose pressure tactics in serene assurance that all Americans are basically fair-minded and will in due time accord Catholics a full measure of justice.

Catholics and Pluralism

The decisive point of contact between American Catholicism and American Society now lies in the new problems of religious pluralism posed by the disintegration of a traditional American consensus, of Protestant origin, on the relationship of religion and American society. In very rough terms this consensus involved three ingredients: a firm belief that America is a religious nation dependent upon Christian values to sustain its national life; that "Christian" is to be understood in a Protestant sense; that the minority religious rights exist because the right of freedom of conscience and worship are an essential part of the Protestant understanding of man. This consensus no longer exists. At the roots of its disappearance are a number of contemporary social realities. The most basic is the existence of massive non-Protestant minority groups; Protestants no longer have the numerical strength or the social cohesion necessary to sustain a Protestant-American national ethos. Nor, consciously at least, do they appear to have any great desire to do so.

But it is necessary to understand the dynamics of this disintegration; and here the previously hidden social realities are now appearing in the open. For one thing, there now exist a large number of Americans—among them many Jews, unbelievers and Protestants—who believe that the laws, public institutions, perhaps the very signs, seals and symbols of the nation, should be scrupulously neutral concerning religion. In practice, this means a basic challenge to the belief that this is a "religious" nation. For another, Catholics, while supporting a Christian tradition, are now in a position to reject any assumption that "Christian" is to be understood as "Protestant Christian." Finally, both Catholics and those in favor of a purely secular basis for American public life reject any theory of religious freedom which presupposes a Protestant theological understanding of constitutional civil rights. Thus, of the three ingredients of the traditional religious consensus mentioned above, at least two are rejected by Catholics and all three by those favoring a secular society. The very size and power of these two dissenting minorities make these rejections a potent social force.

It is beyond my province here to discuss the general implications of this change in consensus. What is germane, however, is to inquire into the implications for the Catholic community. For what is now apparent is that Catholics, because of their newly-achieved social assimilation and their potential political power, are now in a position to help shape whatever new consensus will emerge from the ruins of the old. At stake is the kind and quality of the contribution which Catholics will make to the heated debate on religion and the aims of American life which has recently erupted. Its main elements are the challenge of Communism; federal aid to parochial schools; recent Supreme Court decisions on Sunday Blue Laws; disagreement over the place of religion in the public schools; and issues of public policy which have arisen out of conflicts over abortion and state-supported birth control programs.

With the exception of Communism, each part of the debate has turned on the meaning of pluralism. Does pluralism, which all ostensibly support, mean a plurality of values only within a religious framework? Does it imply the right of any one group to attempt through legislation and political power to impose its values on other groups or have its institutional needs recognized as long as this is done in a constitutional way? Does it imply the necessity of a rigid understanding of the separation of church and state or an understanding flexible enough to allow some forms of government encouragement of religious values? Along with these pressing questions, however, the problem of Communism has come to have a special importance. Is the best way to strengthen this nation against the threat of Communism a re-affirmation of America's religious heritage? Or would it be better to recognize honestly that such an approach is bound to be offensive to many who prefer to see American values grounded in non-religious beliefs? These are the questions which now exercise the Catholic community—and divide it; though they overlap the older debate on liberalism and conservatism, the ground of discussion has shifted to the more acute problems of pluralism.

Yet it is important to note that they have arisen not only for Catholics as individuals but also, and perhaps more acutely, for Catholics as members of the American sociological community of Catholics. To ask how Catholics as individuals ought to respond to these questions is not the same thing as to ask how they ought to respond as a body—or whether they ought to respond as a body at all. The distinction can be made clear by one prominent example. In the effort to gain federal aid for parochial schools under any broad education bill, different approaches have been employed by different bishops. Some, in arguing the merits of the case for such aid, have urged the laity to study the question personally and, if convinced, to support it as individual citizens. Others have made a conscious appeal to group loyalty; they call upon the laity to join together as a cohesive body to exert massive political pressure. In the one instance, the stress is laid on the layman as a discrete, assimilated citizen; in the other, it is on the layman as an integral member of a minority group which has specific rights and needs precisely as a group.

In my final chapter, I will attempt to suggest some ways in which the layman as an individual should answer these questions. It is necessary now, however, to spell out in greater detail the meaning and implications of the changing relationship between American pluralism and Catholics as a group.

Among the laity, perhaps no question has been raised so frequently or insistently as this: what contribution should Catholics try to make to American life? This question means not only what Catholics as individuals should try to accomplish, but also what the Church, as a community of clergy and laity, should aim for. There is still another sense in which this problem is often understood: how ought the Church seek to preserve, sustain and protect itself from harmful forces? How ought it to seek to strengthen itself internally to ensure faithful and effective service to its members? The first sense of the basic question bears on the positive, apostolic task of the Church; the second on its defensive, preservative task. At first glance, it might appear that these different senses of the question are of only academic interest. Nothing could be further from the truth. The different interpretations of the question account for very different attitudes concerning the Church and American life, and for some of the sharpest arguing among Catholics.

To grasp the significance of these differences, it is helpful to recall the early conflict among American Catholics between the established Anglo-American Catholics and the incoming, insecure immigrants.[12] Each group, in its own way, sought to make a Catholic contribution to America. The Anglo-Ameri-

[12] See [*Mind of Catholic Laymen*] Chapter 1, p. 16.

cans, solidly integrated in the community, on easy terms with the Protestant majority, accepted with little complaint those liabilities which their Catholicism may have imposed on them. They sought to gain acceptance for the Church by the way of intellectual and cultural attainment, social conformity and the influence of good personal character. Sharing the language and social mores of their non-Catholic neighbor, they had little trouble adapting themselves to the life they found about them. The immigrant had few such advantages. Rejected and discriminated against by the established majority, the immigrant could not easily take a confident, positive stance toward the America he found: he had to fight and struggle for anything he got. America, if it meant some relief from the oppressions and privations of the Old Country, also meant new forms of fear, discrimination and Catholic-baiting—and some very great dangers to religion itself.

Although it is very difficult now to find many direct descendants of the Anglo-American families, it is exceedingly easy to find many children of the immigrant tradition.[13] What is important, however, are not the blood lines of descent but rather the permanent existence among American Catholics of the two different attitudes each of these traditions embodied. Thus one can find large numbers of Catholics, particularly among intellectuals, who hold that Catholics ought not to press aggressively for their rights or for public acceptance of their Church's internal needs. Instead, they should, by the quiet force of slow persuasion and good example, by dialogue with non-Catholics, attempt to make its beauty as well as its

[13] It is worth observing that in certain Catholic schools—Portsmouth Priory, Canterbury, St. David's in New York, some of the Sacred Heart Convents—the direct heirs of Anglo-American families are heavily represented. Not surprisingly, they appear to favor Harvard, Yale and Princeton for their college work rather than a Catholic college.

legitimate needs self-evident. Very much like the liberal bishops and clergy during the Americanist period, they assume a natural compatibility of Catholicism and American life and count on the basic good will of non-Catholics eventually to resolve any conflicts. Above all, they urge that Catholics not be tempted to band together to conduct political struggles on matters of public policy affecting religion. In particular, they deplore any manifestations of Catholic separatism and would prefer to see Catholics work as individuals within pluralistic organizations rather than form specifically Catholic movements.

For many other Catholics, a more aggressive approach appears necessary. Far from believing that non-Catholics are necessarily amenable to enlightened dialogue or the quiet force of individual example and persuasion, they would hold that the forces of anti-religion and anti-Catholicism are rife in the land. If Protestantism is no longer looked upon with the old suspicion, then its place as a *bête-noire* has been taken by the powers of secularism and agnosticism. If Catholics are to make their message and their needs known, then they must be willing to enter the political thicket and use the political power potentially in their grasp. There is no suggestion, on this side, of turning America into a Catholic state; but only of making certain that Catholics have every iota of rights due them under our Constitution and every bit as much voice in the shaping of the public consensus as any other group. According to this view, the best way to gain federal aid for parochial schools is through active lay pressure groups, political lobbies, and legal efforts. The best way to combat secularism and unbelief is through public complaint, the power of the law, and an aroused citizenry ready to apply pressure where needed.

The two viewpoints sketched here are abstractions; it would be difficult to find them in a pure form in any given individual. But in their general lines they characterize the two main streams of the present Catholic response to American pluralism. Both assume that Catholics have some contribution to make; but they differ sharply on what that contribution should be or how it should be made. For the adherents of the first-mentioned viewpoint, the overriding consideration is that Catholics make some creative contributions to the problems which face all Americans. The institutional needs of the Church are of secondary importance; the first task of the Church is to bring its wisdom to all men. For the adherents of the second viewpoint, the institutional good of the Church is tantamount to the good of the nation. And the great need of the nation is not for some new, better solutions to national problems, but a return to those old, tried values which for centuries have sustained American and Western life. For the former one, the great failure of American Catholicism is that it has not sufficiently addressed itself to the common good but has remained preoccupied with its own troubles and the faults of its neighbors. For the latter, the great failure is the timidity and obsequiousness of Catholics, their refusal to stand up for their rights and their unwillingness to make their views and values forcefully evident to all.

Yet to put these broad differences in a proper light, it is essential to recognize that every emerging minority has had to face a similar choice. Significantly, the American Negro community has become divided in recent years over the issue of aggressiveness. Many of the older Negro leaders have pressed for a steady reduction in those local laws and customs which discriminate against the Negro; they have, mainly through the N.A.A.C.P., instituted court suits and carried on a program of public education on Negro problems. A younger generation, impatient with the pace of Negro emancipation, has resorted to the more direct means of the sit-in and the Freedom Ride. Similarly, the Jewish community has experienced important internal conflicts over how to get those laws and local practices changed that place the Jew in an unfavorable light or emphasize his non-Christian, minority status. For a great number of Jews, the question whether they should attempt to resort to vigorous political and legal efforts to have Sunday Blue Laws changed, crèches removed from public parks, or prayers banned in the public schools, is as tortured as the one Catholics face in seeking federal aid to parochial schools.

Each minority, of course, has to fashion its own group solution to such problems; each, especially the Negro minority, has particular difficulties not shared by the others. For the Catholic community—even if there was one voice to speak for it—no easy solution is possible; and this precisely because, unlike the Jews and Negroes, there is very little overt discrimination against Catholics. What remains for Catholics are mainly those problems arising from successful assimilation; for a variety of reasons, the Jew and the Negro have still to overcome many of the hurdles which Catholics have now surmounted.

Yet in speaking of "successful assimilation" this cannot be taken to mean that Catholics, in general, are necessarily happy with the quality of their social acceptance. For those of a more aggressive mentality, it still leaves much to be desired. For them, an issue like that of federal aid to parochial schools shows all too well that many non-Catholics are still insensitive to the problems and difficulties felt by Catholics. For them, the measure of true pluralism would be a sympathetic hearing and a creative solution to the Catholic desire to provide a religious education for their children, to protect their children from harmful literature and movies, and to save them from being forced to pay taxes to support such things as public birth-control programs. Among others, however, genuine assimilation would mean that Catholics were making a visible contribution to the problems facing all. For them, the quality of the Catholic contribution to public education, to the rights of Negroes and Jews, and to the correction of massive social welfare ills would be a better index of assimilation.

It should be clear that the way the Catholic community eventually resolves these new dilemmas will have serious implications for the future of American pluralism. It will have no less a bearing on the kind of contribution the Catholic layman will be able to make to American life. If a broad Catholic consensus should emerge equating the good of the nation with the solution of internal Catholic problems—whether these problems are seen in such narrow contexts as the preservation of parochial schools or such broad ones as the danger of secularism for Catholic faith—then one could expect religious battles to erupt at regular intervals. What Catholics gained for themselves by such a course could easily be offset by the hostility it would generate among non-Catholics. Should the consensus turn in the other direction, however, there could well be some important gains for religious peace. At the same time, Catholics might also have to accept some losses in the strength of their own institutions—or find ways of solving internal problems without non-Catholic assistance.

A good example of these different implications can be seen in the 1961 decision (still in force) of the bishops to oppose any federal aid to education bill which does not make provision for aid to parochial schools. Though well aware that their stand could mean that no bill of any kind would be passed—thus hurting the public schools—they chose to wage a full-scale political campaign. Nor, in the face of Protestant opposition to such aid, could they have been unaware of the religious tensions their stand would produce. At the basis of this decision was a belief that the "rights" of Catholics would be jeopardized by a bill providing aid for public schools alone—and that they are worth whatever danger a vigorous political campaign would entail. In addition, they believed that unless Catholic rights, needs and desires were recognized at the outset of any massive federal aid program, they would possibly not be met at all; the time for pressure was before a program got under way, not after. The result has been, of course, to exacerbate religious differences, to help stymie a federal aid to education program and, so far, to gain nothing for the parochial schools of any great importance. Yet, given their intentness on the strengthening of Catholic education and the hostility felt by many non-Catholics toward it, there was doubtless some practical wisdom in the Bishops' stand; in American politics, it has many precedents (some successful) among other minority groups.[14]

Pluralism and Catholic Solidarity

But the implication in the potential responses to pluralism are hardly confined only to the place of the Catholic Church in American life. They are just as important for the internal peace of the Church and for an effective and meaningful lay loyalty. To grasp the meaning for the Church of these new pluralistic dilemmas, one primary social fact must be kept well in mind: the Catholic layman has now almost decisively broken his old ethnic ties. In the past, for a variety of reasons already described in earlier chapters, the Catholic was forced by circumstance to look to his fellow Catholics for mutual support and protection. It was both natural and unavoidable for him to foster community solidarity; it was his best protection against a sometimes hostile and dangerous society. Now all that has changed. Not only a change in his circumstances brought about the break; but it was also brought about by his own distaste for the old state of affairs. Ghettoism, at first an asset, was soon seen to be a social liability. Catholicism itself creates enough problems; why complicate them with ethnic Catholicism? Even more, why complicate them by a species of Catholicism which is narrow, parochial and insular, ever wary of the non-Catholic world, ever ready to take offense at real or imaginary slights?

[14] The results of a Gallup Poll taken early in 1963, moreover, indicated a shift of non-Catholic sentiment toward federal aid for private schools. This may well reflect the success of the bishops in publicizing their case.

Given this changing Catholic temper, it is hardly coincidental that Catholic writing and preaching in recent years have turned on the ways in which the Church and the layman can make a positive contribution to American life. In part, of course, this emphasis has reflected a theological response to the recognition that Christianity, including Catholicism, is failing to make a vital impact on society. But it also reflects the need of Catholics to find a spirituality which will take account of their desire to escape from a narrow, socially defensive Catholicism to a confident, positive, creative Catholicism. In sum, the great demand has been for a renewal of Catholicism which would reflect the altered social status of American Catholics. The need of the day is not for better defenses of the Church, better arguments in her favor, better justifications for Catholic belief—it is for a Catholicism which seeks the good of all, which has something to say to all (and not just to embattled Catholics), and which is a source of wisdom and unity for all.

Yet if this has been a main trend in recent Catholic thinking, it has co-existed with a more deeply-rooted belief that the American Catholic community has never received its just portion of recognition. Until the election of John F. Kennedy, however, this latter belief was all but obscured by the work of those pressing for an emphasis on Catholic responsibilities for the common good. The surge away from the ghetto was a far stronger force than that which animated many to hold firmly to their old grievances. It now appears that the election has served to strengthen both tendencies. On the one hand, it has encouraged many to seek to remove whatever lingering traces there are of an outmoded ghetto mentality. But, on the other, it has encouraged many others to press more forcefully for the recognition of Catholic needs.

It is the strengthened re-emergence of this latter tendency which is bound to be a source of friction among Catholics. For the essential condition of a reassertion of Catholic rights and needs is that the Catholic community be shaped into a cohesive, unified political body. The only way that Catholics can gain their "rights" is by political unity. But such unity can be attained only by invoking once again the spirit of communal loyalty which marked the days of immigration. For what clearly stands in the way of Catholic group solidarity is precisely their assimilation—and the power of this assimilation to dim a sense of communal solidarity can only be overcome by re-animating a sense of grievance, external threat and thwarted needs. Here is the rub: for a great number of Catholics, the one temptation they have most sought to overcome is *exactly* that of allowing these old grievances and needs to dominate their mind. The main thing they do not want, after struggling for years to overcome it, is a return to a Catholic spirit of grievance and complaint, a Catholic spirit of aggressive unity.

Now for many Americans it is taken for granted that a strong measure of aggressive Catholic unity already exists. This is hardly correct. Catholics have been for a number of years sharply divided on many major issues, ranging from domestic politics to the meaning of papal teachings. It is hard to think of a single major national issue within the past decade that did not see Catholics opposed to one another; and the same can be said of a great variety of theological issues. Moreover, since Catholics now occupy all steps on the social ladder, there are important class and educational distinctions among Catholics, differences which in practice lead to many conflicts. As far as Catholics are concerned there are good reasons to doubt the validity of Will Herberg's and Gerhard Lenski's thesis that "The successor of the ethnic subcommunity is the socio-religious community."[15] What these observers fail to recognize is that many Catholics resist strenuously any

[15] Gerhard Lenski, *The Religious Factor* (New York, 1961), p. 326. Cf. Will Herberg, "Religious Group Conflict in America," *College of New Rochelle Alumnae News* (Fall, 1962), pp. 7-8, and *Catholic-Protestant-Jew* (rev. ed.; New York, 1960), p. 39.

tendency to see their loyalty to the Church as equivalent to an identity with the Catholic "socio-religious community."[16] More precisely, it could be said that Catholics are now faced with a choice between trying to erase any suggestion that such a cohesive social community exists (or should exist) and trying to form such a community and making it a strong social and political reality.

Inevitably, the conflict between supporters of these two options means conflict within the Church. To those who would minimize the socio-communal aspects of American Catholicism, their more solidarity-minded Catholic brothers are like throwbacks to an era which should be buried and forgotten. In the eyes of the aggressive, the minimizers are bound to appear disloyal to the Church, or at least grossly deficient in their sensitivities to the needs of the Church. The prime instance of such conflicts—the one that overshadows all others —is, again, the one over federal aid to parochial schools.

By now it has become clear that the major tactic within the Church of the ardent supporters of such aid is the invocation of communal loyalty. Just as vigorously as various bishops, priests and lay publicists have urged the so-called "Catholic case" on federal aid to parochial schools on the nation, as vigorously have they tried to persuade Catholics themselves that their rights are being infringed. They have learned that they can by no means expect a unanimous Catholic acceptance of their case. The reason for this is surely that many Catholics, accepted and secure in their communities, have no sense of deprivation or grievance. More importantly, a large number of Catholics appear to resent any effort to induce such a sense; and they strongly resist being drawn back into an orbit

[16] Cf. Joseph H. Fichter, S.J., *Social Relations in the Urban Parish,* Chap. IV, "Social Solidarity and Model Parishioners," pp. 40ff., for some evidence on an absence of social solidarity among Catholics.

of aggressive Catholic communal solidarity. This does not mean that they are uninterested in aid to parochial schools; but it does mean that they are not interested in jeopardizing inter-religious understanding to gain it. Nor, as citizens, are they interested in fighting for a Catholic cause if this fight will entail some potential harm to the community at large.

The fruits of assimilation are thus many. They pose dilemmas on the personal level which are sharper than those faced by earlier generations. But, above all, they raise in a direct way the question of how the layman ought to relate himself to American life. And that question in turn can only be answered by determining at the same time how the layman ought to relate himself to American Catholicism as a social community. In the end, the problem of the layman's place within the Church is inextricably related to the problem of his role as a citizen. We may now turn to this relationship.

INDEX